Daily Learning Drills

Grade 3

Thinking Kids®
An imprint of Carson-Dellosa Publishing LLC
Greensboro, North Carolina

Thinking Kids®
An imprint of Carson-Dellosa Publishing LLC
P.O. Box 35665
Greensboro, NC 27425 USA

Printed in the USA • All rights reserved.   ISBN 978-1-4838-0086-8

14-085187784

Table of Contents

Name _____

A World of Its Own

Connect the words in alphabetical order.

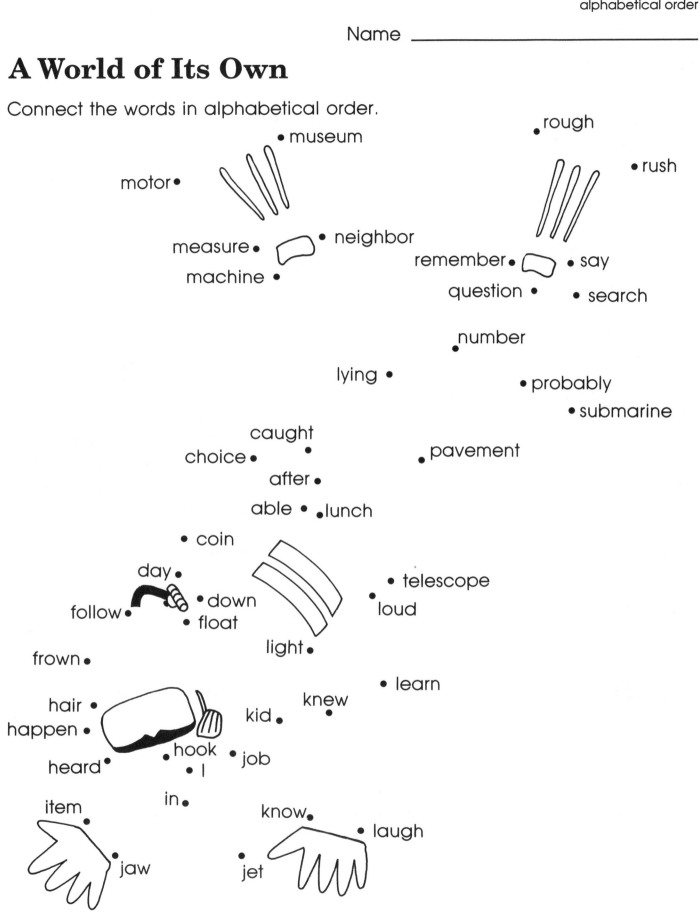

Name _____

What's Your Name?

Column A lists general insect names while **Column B** gives more specific names for the same insects. Number the two columns in ABC order and then answer the questions below.

Column A

____ grasshopper

____ butterfly

____ wasp

____ flea

____ moth

____ fly

____ cricket

____ bee

____ ant

____ beetle

Column B

____ long-horned grasshopper

____ monarch butterfly

____ paper wasp

____ snow flea

____ silk moth

____ housefly

____ tree cricket

____ bumblebee

____ army ant

____ whirligig beetle

1. Does the ABC order change when a more specific insect name is used? _____

2. The insects whose order remained the same in both lists were _____ and _____ .

3. I find _____ insect names more interesting
   (Column A, Column B)

   because _____

   _____ .

Name _____

The Bus Route

This map shows all the stops this bus makes on its route.

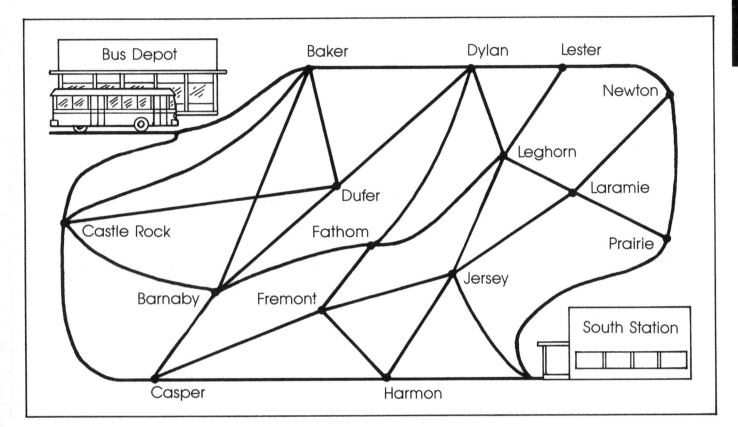

Write the names of the stops in alphabetical order to show the bus route.

1. _____
2. _____
3. _____
4. _____
5. _____
6. _____
7. _____
8. _____

9. _____
10. _____
11. _____
12. _____
13. _____
14. _____
15. _____

- Use a crayon to connect the stops in the order of the bus route.

Name _____

Ouch!

Color the space **orange** if the word has one syllable.
Color the space **blue** if the word has two syllables.
Color the space **black** if the word has three syllables.

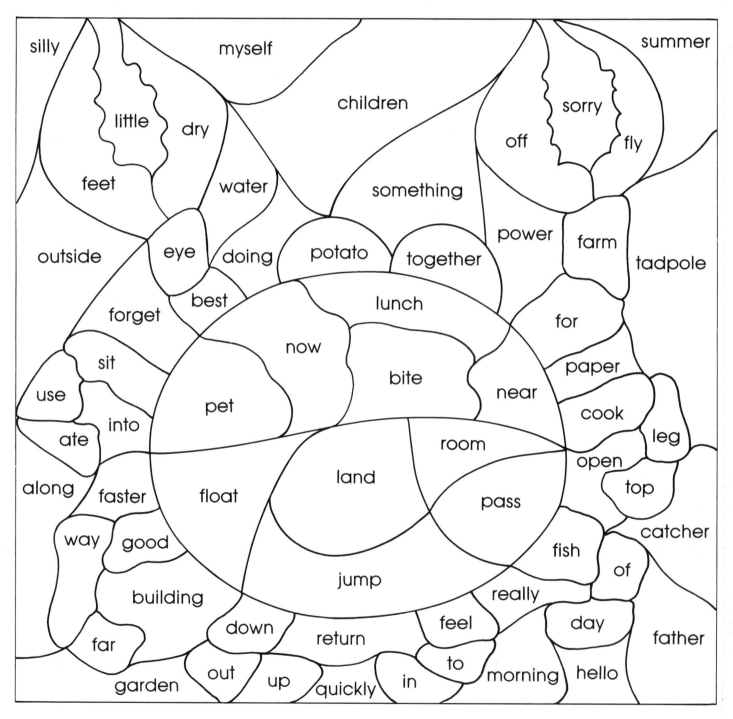

What can make you say ouch? _____

Name _____

Quilting Bee

Ruth and Naomi threaded the needles for the quilters. Follow the code to color the quilt squares.

1-syllable words = blue	3-syllable words = green
2-syllable words = red	4-syllable words = yellow

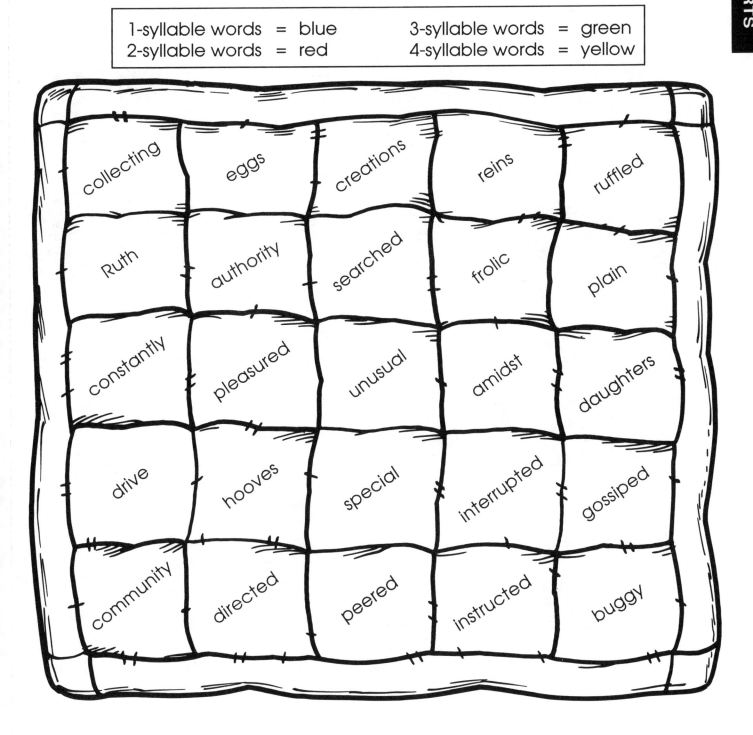

collecting   eggs   creations   reins   ruffled

Ruth   authority   searched   frolic   plain

constantly   pleasured   unusual   amidst   daughters

drive   hooves   special   interrupted   gossiped

community   directed   peered   instructed   buggy

Name _____

Together We Stand

Some insect names are compound words which are made up of two smaller words. Look at each picture and write each insect name. Some words in the Word Bank will be used more than once.

1. _____

2. _____

3. _____

4. _____

5. _____

6. _____

7. _____

8. _____

9. _____

10. _____

Word Bank

bug	worm	butter	honey
fly	bee	hopper	bed
grass	fish	fire	silver
house	lady	glow	dragon

Name _____

Beautiful Butterflies

After the baku devoured Yukio's nightmares, his dreams were pleasant ones of yellow butterflies fanning him on a hot day. If the two words on a butterfly's pair of wings make a compound word, color the butterfly **yellow**. If they do not, put an **X** on the butterfly.

Name _____

Lead or Follow?

Write a word that can be placed in front of the bold-faced word to form a compound word. Then write a word that can follow the bold-faced word to form a second compound word.

Example: __back__   **door**   __knob__

_____ **to** _____

_____ **tree** _____

_____ **path** _____

_____ **line** _____

_____ **noon** _____

_____ **button** _____

_____ **room** _____

_____ **body** _____

_____ **side** _____

_____ **house** _____

Word Bank				
up	tow	out	hole	way
swingle	after	on	every	time
clothes	mate	lunch	top	belly
night	boat	doll	walk	guard

Name _____

Brother Eagle, Sister Sky

Eagle has a long **e** sound. **Sky** has a long **i** sound. Cut out and glue the words below the picture with the matching vowel sound.

Brother Eagle

Sister Sky

brief	buy	delay	dessert	drive	style
dye	easy	eye	fright	giant	stream
cry	knees	leaf	lion	private	regal

Name _____

The Money Box

When Xiao Sheng put the pearl in the money box with its one remaining coin, the coin multiplied and the box brimmed over with gold coins.
Cut out and glue the coins that have the same vowel sound as **coin** in and around the money box.

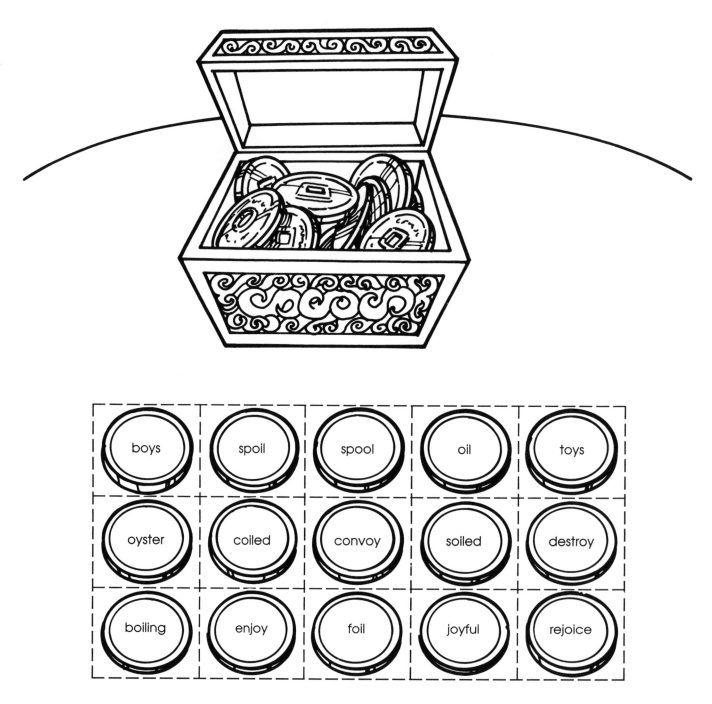

boys	spoil	spool	oil	toys
oyster	coiled	convoy	soiled	destroy
boiling	enjoy	foil	joyful	rejoice

Name _____

Phonics Fun

Help Richard with his phonics by following these directions.

Circle the short a words in black.
Underline the short i words in pink.
Put a red box around the short e words.
Draw an olive green X over the short o words.
Draw a green line over the long e words.
Draw a wavy gray line over the long a words.
Put a white X over the long i words.
Draw a gold circle around the long o words.

Beast	Drake	plane
Holly	Hansel	kids
Kettle	teacher	Noah
Matthew	banner	Mancina
stage	best	
Richard	wished	liar
smell	smile	top
Gretel	fig	piece
Polk	class	stop

Name _____

The Puzzling Printout

Professor Gizmo built his own computer. But sometimes the professor was a little absent-minded, and he would push the wrong buttons. Today he printed some "Funny Food Facts."

Read each silly sentence. Cross out the noun that doesn't make sense. Find a noun in another sentence that fits but still makes a silly sentence. Write it over the crossed-off word. The first one is done for you.

Funny Food Facts

1. Lazy people eat ~~chili~~. meatloaf. (from sentence #7)

2. The Easter Bunny's favorite vegetables are chicken.

3. The best fruit to drink is strawberries.

4. If you're scared, don't eat dough.

5. Jellybeans must be a cold food.

6. Dancing cows make blueberries.

7. Cavemen ate meatloaf.

8. Bread is rich because it has watermelon.

9. Milkshakes are an unhappy fruit.

10. Club sandwiches grow on the floor of a barn.

Name _____

Nouns in the Clouds

Look at the list of words. If a word is a **common noun**, copy it in the cloud titled common nouns. If it is a **proper noun**, change its first letters to capital letters and copy it in the cloud titled proper nouns.

Common Nouns   Proper Nouns

common nouns

1. ohio
2. dr simon
3. ocean
4. president lincoln
5. dog
6. jane
7. new york
8. ice cream
9. mount everest
10. columbus

11. teacher
12. second avenue
13. circus
14. sheriff

proper nouns

Name _____

Pencil in the Plural

Write the plural for each of the nouns below.

wish *Example* <u>wishes</u> ____	hobby _____	sheep _____	day _____
deer _____	bluff _____	child _____	boss _____
rash _____	cookie _____	match _____	knife _____
car _____	success _____	pony _____	foot _____
kiss _____	city _____	couch _____	mouse _____
woman _____	half _____	mirror _____	trout _____
person _____	tooth _____	dress _____	girl _____

Name _____

Bright and Beautiful

Color the space **yellow** if you have to only add an **s** to make the word plural.

Color the space **orange** if you have to add **es** to make the word plural.

Color the space **blue** if you have to change the last letter and then add **es** to make the word plural.

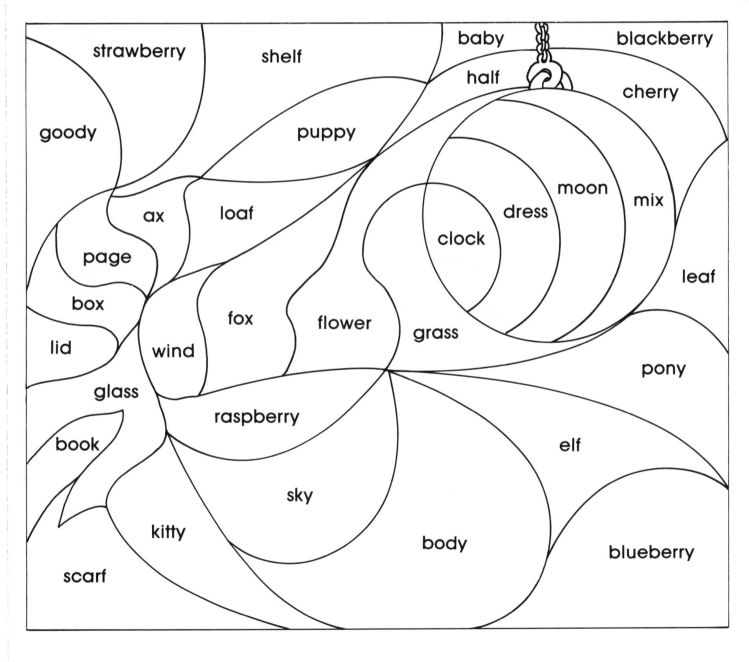

What is this ocean creature? _____

P.J.'s Cup

Name _____

Change the underlined word to show possession by adding an apostrophe or apostrophe and s. Write the possessive form on the line.

	possessive
Example > The <u>balloon</u> string is long.	balloon's

1. The three <u>cats</u> paws were wet.

2. <u>Mary</u> pencil was broken.

3. Both <u>boys</u> grades were good.

4. This house is <u>Cliff</u> house.

5. <u>Tony</u> aunt came to visit.

6. Some <u>flowers</u> leaves were large.

7. We saw two <u>bears</u> tracks.

8. The <u>children</u> room was messy.

9. My <u>sister</u> birthday is today.

10. The <u>clowns</u> acts made us laugh.

11. Charlie Brown filled <u>Snoopy</u> dish.

12. Mark joined the game with the <u>boys.</u>

13. The baseball <u>players</u> uniforms are clean.

14. The <u>dog</u> dish was empty.

1. _____
2. _____
3. _____
4. _____
5. _____
6. _____
7. _____
8. _____
9. _____
10. _____
11. _____
12. _____
13. _____
14. _____

Name _____

Be a Star!

Follow the rules to color each design.

Rule 1: Add **ed** to most verbs to show the past tense. Color these words **blue**.

Rule 2: If the verb ends in **e**, drop the **e** and add **ed**. Color these words **green**.

Rule 3: If the verb has a short vowel followed by a single consonant, double the final consonant and add **ed**. Color these words **white**.

Rule 4: If the verb ends in **y**, change the **y** to **i** and add **ed**. Color these words **yellow**.

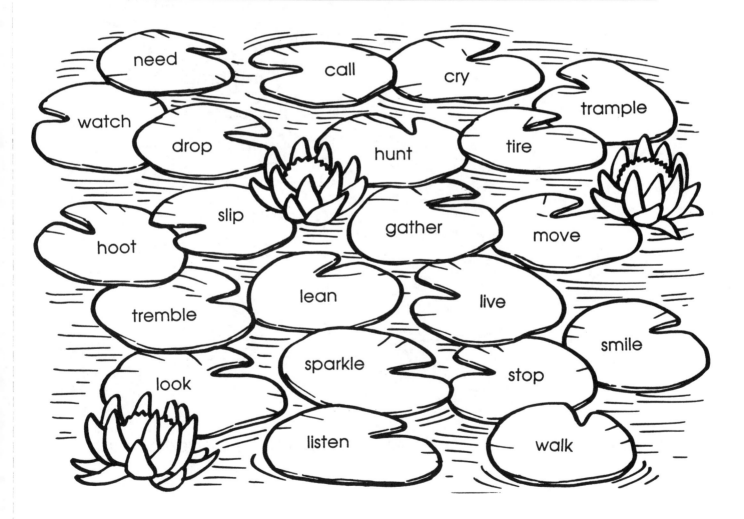

Name _____

Hop – Hopped – Hopping!

Help bouncy Bong hop to his special piece of liver. If you can add an "**ed**" or "**ing**" to a word, color that piece of liver brown. Do not color the other pieces.

Bong is certainly a frog of action. All of the words he hopped on are . . .

_____ .

Name _____

Little Words Mean a Lot

A pronoun is a word that takes the place of a noun. Above each underlined word below, write a pronoun from the Word Box that could replace it.

Word Box										
she	it	her	we	he	his	I	him	they	your

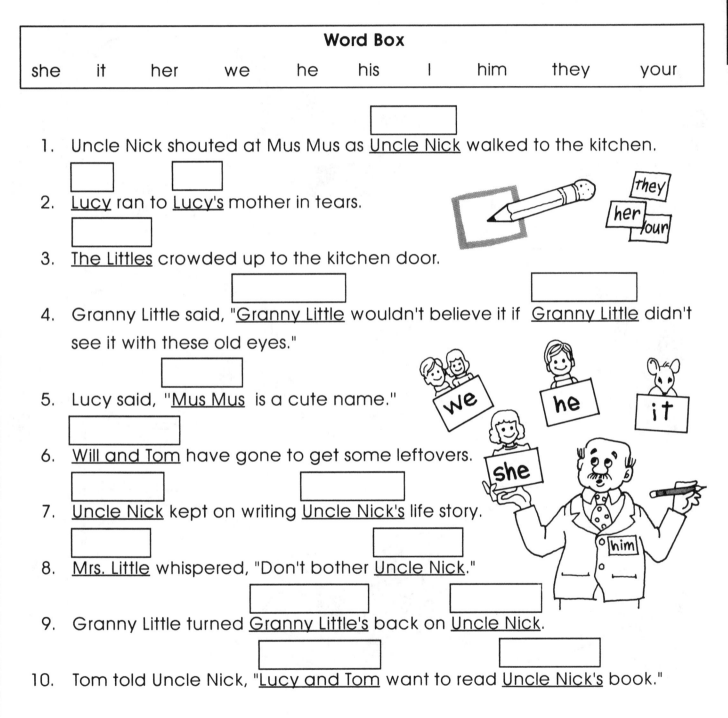

1. Uncle Nick shouted at Mus Mus as <u>Uncle Nick</u> walked to the kitchen.

2. <u>Lucy</u> ran to <u>Lucy's</u> mother in tears.

3. <u>The Littles</u> crowded up to the kitchen door.

4. Granny Little said, "<u>Granny Little</u> wouldn't believe it if <u>Granny Little</u> didn't see it with these old eyes."

5. Lucy said, "<u>Mus Mus</u> is a cute name."

6. <u>Will and Tom</u> have gone to get some leftovers.

7. <u>Uncle Nick</u> kept on writing <u>Uncle Nick's</u> life story.

8. <u>Mrs. Little</u> whispered, "Don't bother <u>Uncle Nick</u>."

9. Granny Little turned <u>Granny Little's</u> back on <u>Uncle Nick</u>.

10. Tom told Uncle Nick, "<u>Lucy and Tom</u> want to read <u>Uncle Nick's</u> book."

Name _____

Words of Worth

The words below are adjectives. They describe nouns (persons, places or things). Write a noun to go with each adjective. Then draw its picture in each Indian shield.

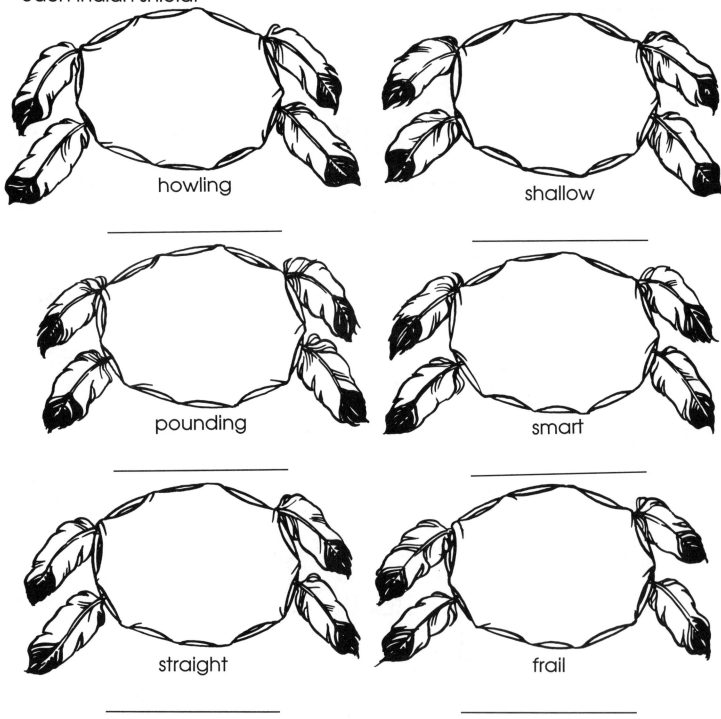

howling

shallow

_____

_____

pounding

smart

_____

_____

straight

frail

_____

_____

Name _____

Marvelous Modifiers

Words that describe are called adjectives.
Circle the adjectives in the sentences below.

1. Lucas stared at the cool white paint in the can.
2. The green grass was marked with bits of white paint.
3. The naughty twins needed a warm soapy bath.
4. The painters worked with large rollers.
5. Lucas thought it was a great joke.

For each noun below, write **two** descriptive adjectives. Then write a sentence using all three words.

1. marshmallows _____ _____

_____

_____

2. airplane _____ _____

_____

_____

3. beach _____ _____

_____

_____

4. summer _____ _____

_____

_____

5. teacher _____ _____

_____

**A
NOW . . .
D** Some adjectives like *good* and *bad, big* and *little, happy* and *sad* are overused. Make a list of more descriptive adjectives that could be used in place of these words. Compare your list with the lists of other classmates.

Name _____

Where's That Monkey?

In the sentences below, write an adverb on the line to complete each sentence. The word in parentheses tells the kind of adverb to write. Do not use an adverb more than once. Answers will vary.

Example > The car is ____here____ .   (where)

1. Our team played _____ .   (when)

2. Brian writes _____ .   (how)

3. The cows move _____ .   (how)

4. Melissa will dance _____ .   (when)

5. My dog went _____ .   (where)

6. We ran _____ .   (how)

7. The choir sang _____ .   (how)

8. The cat purred _____ .   (how)

9. Hilary spoke _____ .   (how)

10. We'll go on our vacation _____ .   (when)

11. The sign goes _____ .   (where)

12. Mother brought the groceries _____ .   (where)

13. David read the directions _____ .   (how)

14. We'll be leaving _____ .   (when)

15. We have three bedrooms _____ .   (where)

16. Our family goes on a vacation _____ .   (when)

17. Jim ran _____ down the street.   (how)

18. They_____ laid the baby in the crib.   (how)

19. The man went _____ with his paper.   (where)

Name _____

Speech Puzzle

Unscramble each word to name the parts of speech. Write each word in the correct puzzle spaces.

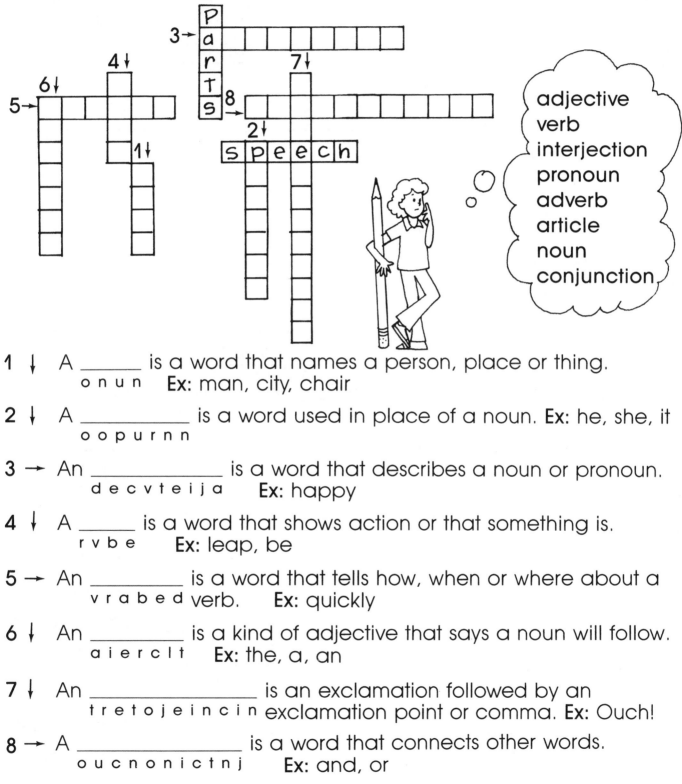

adjective
verb
interjection
pronoun
adverb
article
noun
conjunction

1 ↓   A _____ is a word that names a person, place or thing.
      o n u n   **Ex:** man, city, chair

2 ↓   A _____ is a word used in place of a noun. **Ex:** he, she, it
      o o p u r n n

3 →   An _____ is a word that describes a noun or pronoun.
      d e c v t e i j a   **Ex:** happy

4 ↓   A _____ is a word that shows action or that something is.
      r v b e   **Ex:** leap, be

5 →   An _____ is a word that tells how, when or where about a
      v r a b e d verb.   **Ex:** quickly

6 ↓   An _____ is a kind of adjective that says a noun will follow.
      a i e r c l t   **Ex:** the, a, an

7 ↓   An _____ is an exclamation followed by an
      t r e t o j e i n c i n exclamation point or comma. **Ex:** Ouch!

8 →   A _____ is a word that connects other words.
      o u c n o n i c t n j   **Ex:** and, or

Name _____

Abracadabra

Write a complete sentence using each of the following subjects.

Example > The magician <u>performs difficult tricks</u> _____ .

1. The truck _____ .
2. Mr. and Mrs. Turner _____ .
3. The clowns _____ .
4. Fresh strawberries _____ .
5. Our team _____ .
6. A large crowd _____ .
7. Pancakes _____ .
8. All of the joggers _____ .
9. The skeleton _____ .

Write a complete sentence using each of the following predicates.

Example > _____ The busy street _____ was noisy.

1. _____ was funny.
2. _____ will be ready.
3. _____ went too quickly.
4. _____ is on the corner.
5. _____ were ruined.
6. _____ still exists.
7. _____ was fun.
8. _____ were on my desk.
9. _____ turned to gold.

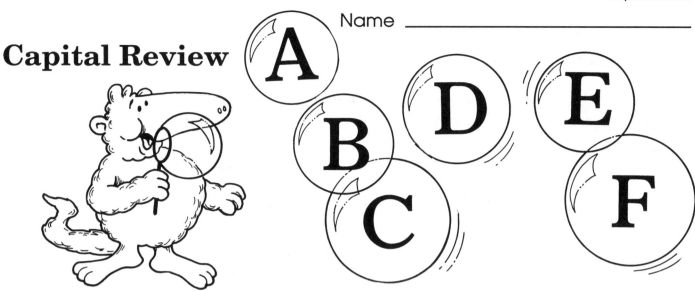

Capital Review

Name _____

In the sentences below, circle the words that should begin with a capital letter.

Example > (is) ("i love lucy") still on television?

1. "after lunch," said sue, "let's go shopping."

2. i learned a lot from the book, *inside the personal computer.*

3. my class from hudson school went to forest park.

4. carlos speaks spanish, french and english.

5. the carter family lives on terrace drive.

6. "the new kid on the block" is a great story.

7. we saw the movie "ghostbusters" last saturday.

8. christopher columbus discovered america in 1492.

9. i was born june 12, 1965, in denver, colorado.

10. next thursday, mr. and mrs. evans have an anniversary.

11. my brother will attend harvard college in boston.

12. the letter to montie ended, "love from aunt rose."

13. in hawaii, kamehameka day is celebrated each june.

14. mrs. hardy said, "don't be late for the party."

15. stone brothers hardware is on elm street.

Name _____

Patriotic Punctuation

Decide which punctuation mark should follow each sentence. Add it. Then draw its design in the matching numbered area on the flag.

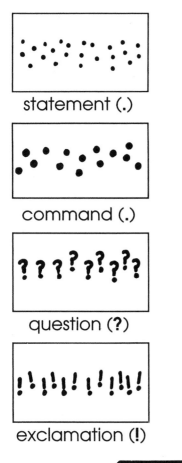

statement (.)

command (.)

question (?)

exclamation (!)

1. Phoebe was thirteen years old
2. Finally, everyone would be free
3. Trust no one
4. Where was Mr. Hickey
5. Should she go back to Queen's Head
6. You must find out who it is
7. Run, get my father
8. Phoebe packed and headed for Mortier House
9. Mr. Green never spoke to Phoebe at all
10. Thomas was "T"
11. Should Phoebe tell Mr. Hickey the secret
12. Go feed the seed to the chickens
13. Did you air and turn Mrs. Washington's quilt
14. Mr. Hickey has put poison in your dinner
15. She placed the peas on the general's plate
16. What jest is this
17. My very favorite, June peas

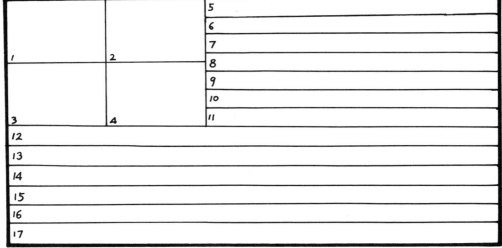

Name _____

Sealed with a Kiss

Read the letter Ut sent to Vietnam.

---

january 20 1993

dearest mother

    i find america to be a beautiful country i even saw many flakes of snow fall on the ground

    father my brother my sisters and i miss you greatly i look at your picture often but sometimes i am so lonely i will try to be your angel child

              love
              ut

Rewrite the letter correctly with capital letters and punctuation.

_____

_____

_____

_____

_____

_____

_____

_____

_____

Name _____

More Than Two, Do!

Commas are used to separate the items in a series when there are more than two items joined by the word *and*. **Example:** Little Abraham was a happy, calm, and intelligent child.

Add commas, where needed, to the sentences below.

1. Abe's parents paid the teacher with firewood venison and potatoes.

2. Abraham could read and write when he was only six years old.

3. A book Abe had borrowed was rained on and became water-stained.

4. Abe liked to tell jokes stories and tales.

5. Abe's mother got sick and died.

Copy the following sentences, adding capitals and punctuation as needed.

6. abraham lincoln lived in kentucky and indiana as a child

_____

_____

7. he loved to read write and talk with people

_____

_____

8. mr lincoln guided his country through a period of frustration hardship and war

_____

_____

_____

Name _____

Rabbit Remarks

For each of the quotes below, add a set of quotation marks around exactly what was said.

Examples: "That's a good sign," said Rahm.
He called, "You can come out now."

Is it Spring yet?

1. I think it is time for us to build the nursery, Silla said.
2. When do you think it will happen? asked Rahm.
3. Silla said, When the moon is round again.
4. How many children do you think we'll have? asked Rahm.

Copy these quotes, adding a set of quotation marks, a capital letter at the beginning and a period or question mark at the end.

5. there is no way of telling, she answered

_____

_____

6. let's just wait and see, said Silla

_____

_____

7. well, then, asked Rahm, where do you want your nursery to be

_____

_____

A NOW ... D   Predict what Rahm and Silla will say about the new kits when they are born. Write a line of dialogue for each of them. Remember to use quotation marks, capitals and other punctuation as needed.

Name _____

The Root of the Problem

Yukio, his family, and the villagers had a problem. No one was able to sleep well because they kept having nightmares. The baku got to the root of the problem—he gobbled up all the nightmares! Everyone was able to sleep peacefully again.

Help the baku gobble up root words by underlining the root of each word in the list. Then circle the root words in the wordsearch. Words may go →, ←, ↓, ↑, ↗, and ↙

1. planting
2. mending
3. fishing
4. golden
5. swimming
6. certainly
7. suddenly
8. arrows
9. foolish
10. sounds
11. sighing
12. rushing
13. safely
14. asleep
15. longer
16. arms
17. stones
18. bandits

A	P	L	A	N	T	H	S	I	F
R	O	C	E	R	T	A	I	N	O
M	E	N	D	D	N	U	O	S	O
I	A	E	L	P	R	E	K	I	L
W	R	D	O	G	N	O	L	G	E
S	R	D	G	O	R	U	S	H	F
N	O	U	T	S	L	E	E	P	A
V	W	S	T	I	D	N	A	B	S

Name _____

Syncopated Synonyms

Choose a word from the Word Bank that means nearly the same as the clue word. Write it in the crossword puzzle.

Word Bank

crate	section	laugh	nation	academy
distant	plank	rickety	stomp	bandana
pretend	fiddle	fancy	lurch	rhythm

Across
1. country
4. elaborate
5. imagine
7. violin
9. stamp
11. unstable
12. scarf
13. beat
14. box

Down
2. school
3. area
5. board
6. far
8. wobble
10. chuckle

Name _____

Serpent's Synonyms

In some dragon stories the dragon has the tail of a serpent. A synonym for serpent is snake. Choose a word from the Word Bank that means nearly the same as the clue word. Write it in the crossword puzzle.

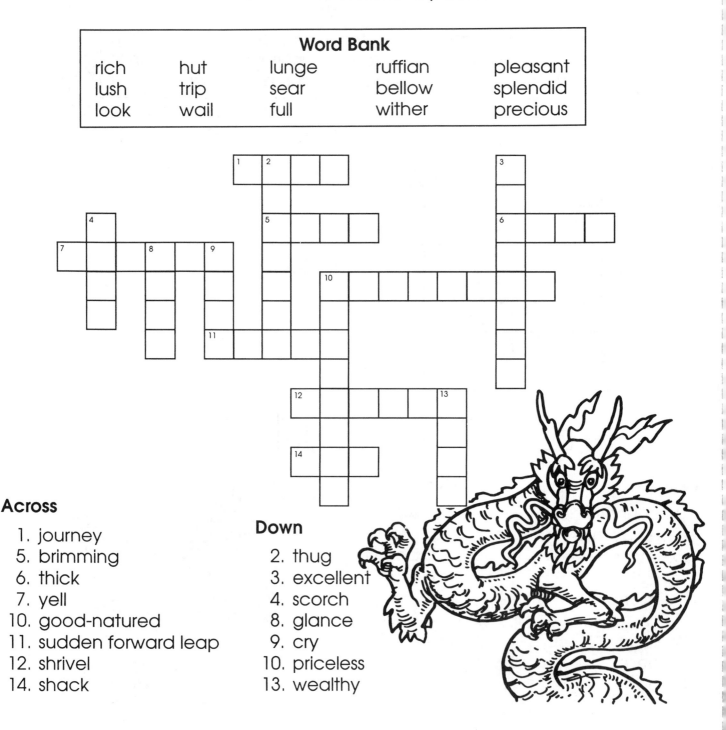

Word Bank				
rich	hut	lunge	ruffian	pleasant
lush	trip	sear	bellow	splendid
look	wail	full	wither	precious

Across

1. journey
5. brimming
6. thick
7. yell
10. good-natured
11. sudden forward leap
12. shrivel
14. shack

Down

2. thug
3. excellent
4. scorch
8. glance
9. cry
10. priceless
13. wealthy

Name _____

Searching for Opposites

Select an antonym for the underlined words in the sentences below from the words in the Word Bank. Write the antonym on the line following each sentence.

Word Bank			
unbolt	strong	purchase	cooked
sharp	evil	ancient	assemble
minor	present	praised	learned
disarray	increase	day	

Example > The salesperson was <u>courteous.</u>   __rude__

1. The old man was <u>feeble.</u>   _____

2. The castle was <u>modern</u> inside.   _____

3. Caroline likes <u>raw</u> carrots.   _____

4. The character in the book was <u>good.</u>   _____

5. She <u>taught</u> Spanish every day.   _____

6. Doug was <u>absent</u> yesterday.   _____

7. The knife was <u>dull</u> and rusty.   _____

8. The teacher <u>criticized</u> the student.   _____

9. <u>Lock</u> the door, please.   _____

10. The meeting will <u>adjourn</u> soon.   _____

11. It was a <u>major</u> decision.   _____

12. I am going to <u>sell</u> shoes.   _____

13. You should <u>decrease</u> your sugar intake.   _____

14. We went fishing in the middle of the <u>night</u>.   _____

15. The room was in great <u>order.</u>   _____

Name _____

Alike or Not Alike?

Choose a word from the Word Box that means just the same or almost the same as each given word. Write your answers on the rungs of the ladder.

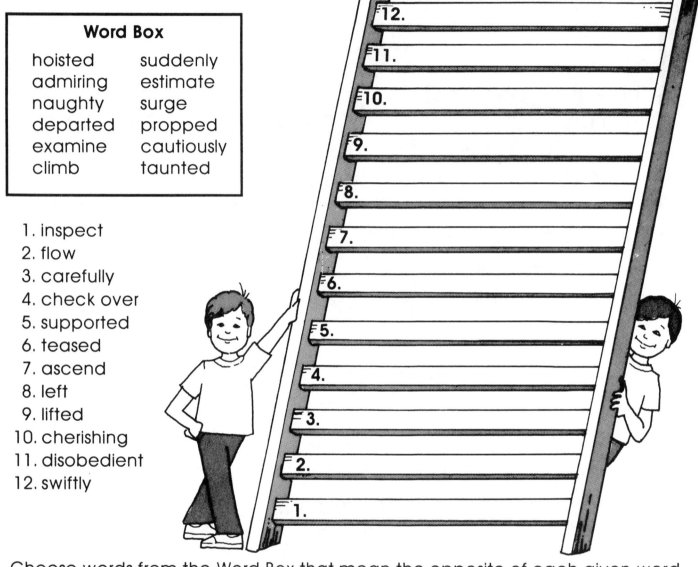

Word Box

hoisted	suddenly
admiring	estimate
naughty	surge
departed	propped
examine	cautiously
climb	taunted

1. inspect
2. flow
3. carefully
4. check over
5. supported
6. teased
7. ascend
8. left
9. lifted
10. cherishing
11. disobedient
12. swiftly

Choose words from the Word Box that mean the opposite of each given word.

1. slowly _____
2. arrived _____
3. recklessly _____
4. hating _____
5. descend _____

Name _____

In Other Words

Amelia Bedelia often mixed up her homonyms, such as when she "pared" the vegetables by laying them in "pairs."

Amelia has used the wrong homonyms in these sentences. Can you help her by underlining the wrong homonyms and writing the correct homonyms on the lines below?

1. How much do you think I way?
2. Amelia Bedelia blue the car's horn loudly.
3. She needed to so Mr. Rogers's torn shirt.
4. The son shone through the curtains.
5. Amelia Bedelia baked the cake with flower.
6. Mrs. Rogers went on a plain to visit her aunt.
7. Amelia Bedelia swept the stares.
8. Mr. Rogers's shirt was bright read.
9. Amelia Bedelia was stung by a be.
10. Amelia Bedelia rode a Ferris wheel at the fare.

1. _____
2. _____
3. _____
4. _____
5. _____
6. _____
7. _____
8. _____
9. _____
10. _____

Hairs on Hares

Name _____

"We weren't born with hair."

Words that sound alike but are spelled differently and have different meanings are called homonyms. On the line before each homonym, write the letter of the phrase that best defines its meaning.

_____ 1. hare

_____ 2. hair

_____ 3. peer

_____ 4. pier

_____ 5. doe

_____ 6. dough

_____ 7. bare

_____ 8. bear

_____ 9. dew

_____ 10. due

_____ 11. nose

_____ 12. knows

_____ 13. prey

_____ 14. pray

_____ 15. tail

_____ 16. tale

A. any creature hunted for food

B. a mass of unbaked bread

C. a body part used to smell

D. something that is owed

E. the end of an animal's body

F. an animal related to the rabbit

G. a large, furry animal with a short tail

H. to look closely; to gaze

I. to beg for or ask for by prayer

J. a female deer, hare or rabbit

K. a platform built out over water

L. a story

M. naked; without any covering

N. growth that covers the scalp of a person or the body of a mammal

O. understands; to be certain of something

P. water droplets

Name _____

Pairs About Hares . . . and Rabbits

Some words have two or more very different meanings even though the spelling remains the same. For each sentence below, write the correct definition of the underlined word.

| **blow** | a. | hit |
| | b. | breathe hard |

| **peer** | a. | one of the same age |
| | b. | look at closely |

| **nurse** | a. | give milk |
| | b. | care for |

| **pelt** | a. | strike; attack |
| | b. | skin with fur |

| **sage** | a. | plant |
| | b. | wise |

| **box** | a. | fight |
| | b. | container |

| **cuff** | a. | end part of a sleeve |
| | b. | slap |

| **buck** | a. | dollar (slang) |
| | b. | male |

| **drum** | a. | beat; pound |
| | b. | musical instrument |

| **sharp** | a. | pointed |
| | b. | alert; observant |

1. Most <u>bucks</u> leave the digging to the does. _____male_____

2. Shortly after the babies were born, Silla <u>nursed</u> them. _____

3. Hares are born with a warm <u>pelt</u>. _____

4. The hawk's <u>sharp</u> eyes searched the ground. _____

5. When he sensed danger, the Old One <u>drummed</u> the ground. _____

6. When the buck tried to come close, the doe gave him a <u>blow</u>.

_____

7. The bucks balanced on their hind legs to <u>box</u>. _____

8. The young hares continued to <u>peer</u> over the tall grass. _____

9. The doe nibbled on a piece of <u>sage</u>. _____

10. The buck gave his opponent one last <u>cuff</u> then ran away. _____

A
NOW . . .   Write a sentence for each word using the other definition.
D

Name _____

Zoo Loos

Zucchini is a ferret who lives in a zoo. Finish each rhyme to identify the other animals in the zoo. Draw the animals.

1. I'm tiny, not chunky,
   A little brown _____.

2. I'm mostly hair,
   I'm a grizzly _____.

3. My name is Ryan,
   I'm a proud _____.

4. So very teeny,
   I'm Billy's _____.

5. See you later,
   A green _____.

6. My tail can shake,
   I'm a rattle _____.

7. My home is no villa,
   I'm a huge, hairy
   _____.

8. You won't have to hunt,
   for this gray _____.

9. You'll love to laugh,
   At the tall _____.

10. Sharp-toothed and dark,
    A man-eating _____.

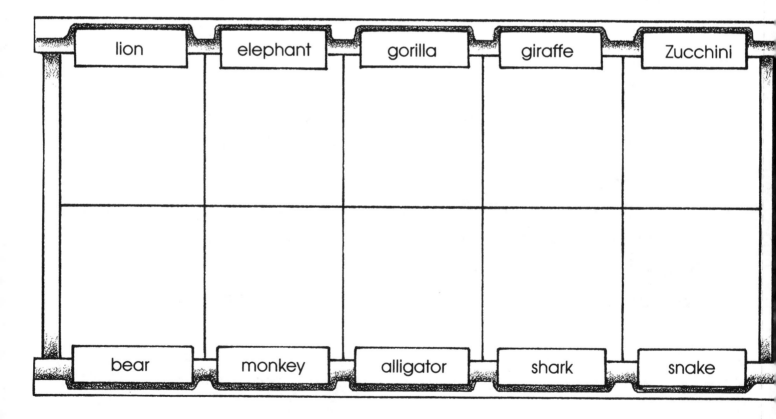

lion	elephant	gorilla	giraffe	Zucchini
bear	monkey	alligator	shark	snake

Name _____

What a Recipe!

Read the clues. Write the words that mean the
same. Find and circle your answers in the puzzle.

Hint: All words start with the prefixes "un," "dis" or "re."

u	n	a	r	e	b	u	i	l	d	i	s	l	i	k	e
u	n	f	a	i	r	n	n	o	i	n	o	r	e	d	o
n	o	e	r	l	u	n	u	n	s	a	f	e	r	f	u
s	d	i	s	a	g	r	e	e	o	b	z	f	e	o	n
e	u	n	t	i	e	d	r	r	b	a	u	i	d	x	f
e	n	r	o	u	t	r	y	s	e	b	n	l	o	m	r
n	e	e	u	n	h	a	p	p	y	d	i	l	s	u	i
r	e	u	s	t	e	d	r	e	w	r	i	t	e	s	e
u	n	h	u	r	t	s	o	r	e	w	a	s	h	l	n
v	e	s	u	u	s	d	i	s	a	p	p	e	a	r	d
p	i	c	r	e	w	r	a	p	i	o	n	s	i	k	l
r	e	o	p	e	n	a	u	n	f	o	l	d	e	d	y

Clues

1. Not happy _____
2. Not true _____
3. To not obey _____
4. Not hurt _____
5. To not like _____
6. Not safe _____
7. To fill again _____
8. Not fair _____
9. To wrap again _____
10. Not seen _____
11. To stop appearing _____
12. To write again _____
13. Wash again _____
14. Not tied _____
15. Not folded _____
16. To not agree _____
17. To do again _____
18. To open again _____
19. Not friendly _____
20. To build again _____

Name _____

Just Buzzing Around

Find the answers to the clues in the maze.
Write them on the lines.

| Prefixes |
| re = again |
| un = not |

Clues

1. make again _____

2. not opened _____

3. not kind _____

4. fill again _____

5. not used _____

6. write again _____

7. not told _____

8. do again _____

9. build again _____

10. not known _____

11. wrap again _____

Follow a path through the maze in the same order
as your answers to get the bee to the honey pot.

Name _____

Tasty Morsels

The baku munched away on everyone's nightmares. In this exercise, the baku will only devour words that have the suffix **ed**. Color those cookies brown. Put an **X** on the cookies the baku will not eat.

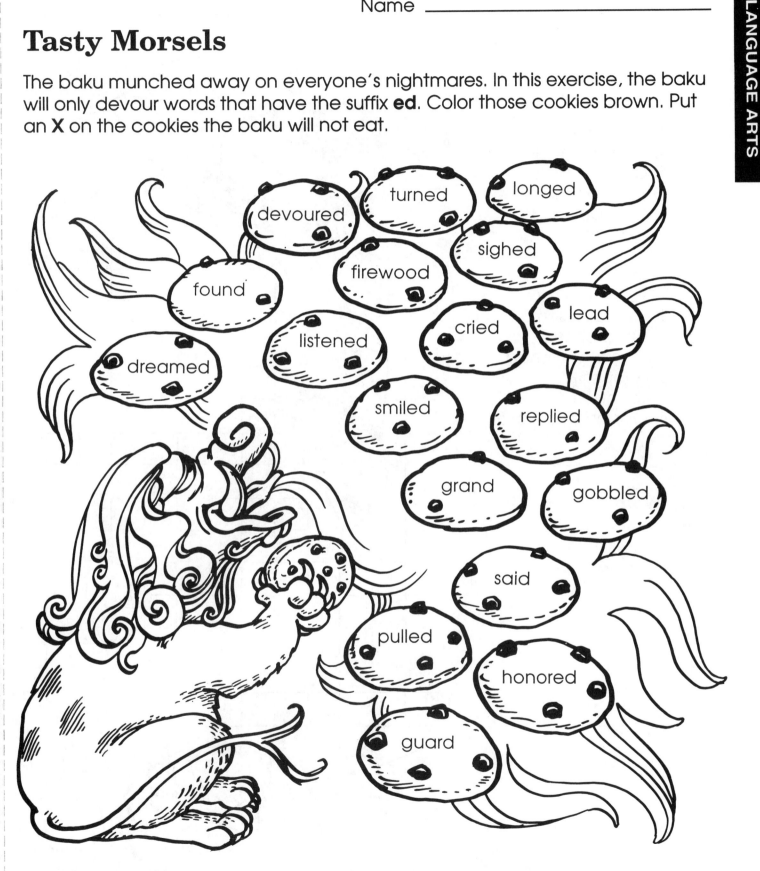

devoured · turned · longed · sighed · found · firewood · longed · dreamed · listened · cried · lead · smiled · replied · grand · gobbled · said · pulled · honored · guard

Daily Learning Drills Grade 3

Name _____

Laughable Fellow

Use the Word Bank to work the puzzle.

Across
2. Opposite of darken
4. To make wider
5. Can be sunk
7. To make hard
8. Can be read
11. Can be broken

Down
1. Put in writing
3. To make something not crooked
4. Can be washed
6. A lot of fun
9. To make darker
10. Opposite of harden

Word Bank

breakable
widen
readable
sinkable
harden
lighten
soften
washable
darken
enjoyable
written
straighten

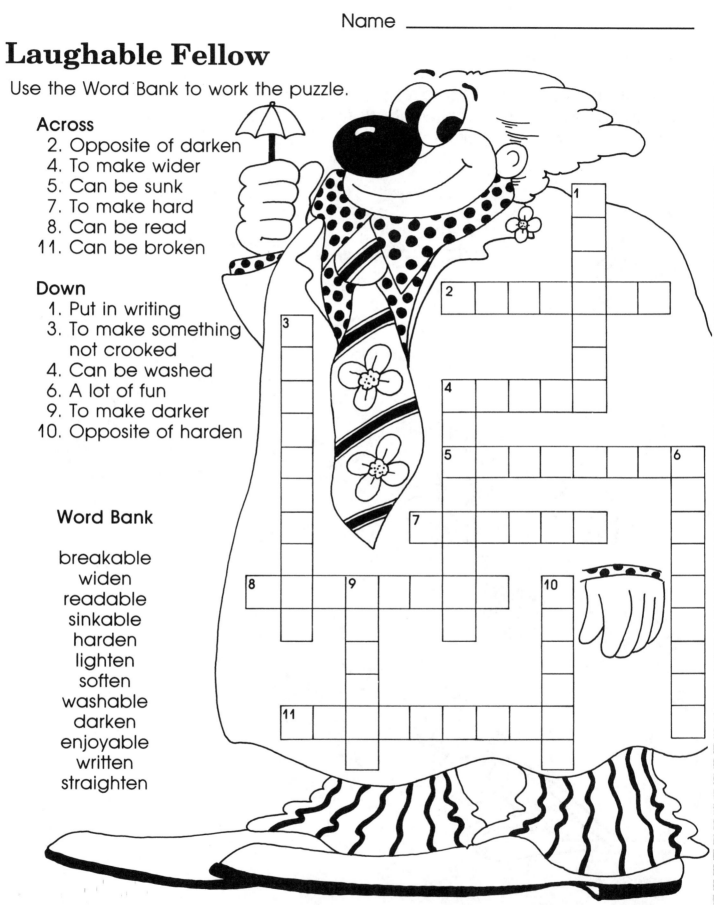

Name _____

Can You Unlock It?

Find the contractions in the puzzle to match
the numbered words. Write them.

1. I am _____

2. we are _____

3. they have _____

4. we will _____

5. she is _____

6. can not _____

7. I have _____

8. he is _____

9. is not _____

10. it is _____

11. you are _____

12. have not _____

13. do not _____

14. that is _____

15. she will _____

16. what is _____

17. did not _____

18. they will _____

Connect the dots. Begin with the answer to
number 1. Draw a line to the answer of
number 2 and keep going until you come
to the last word.

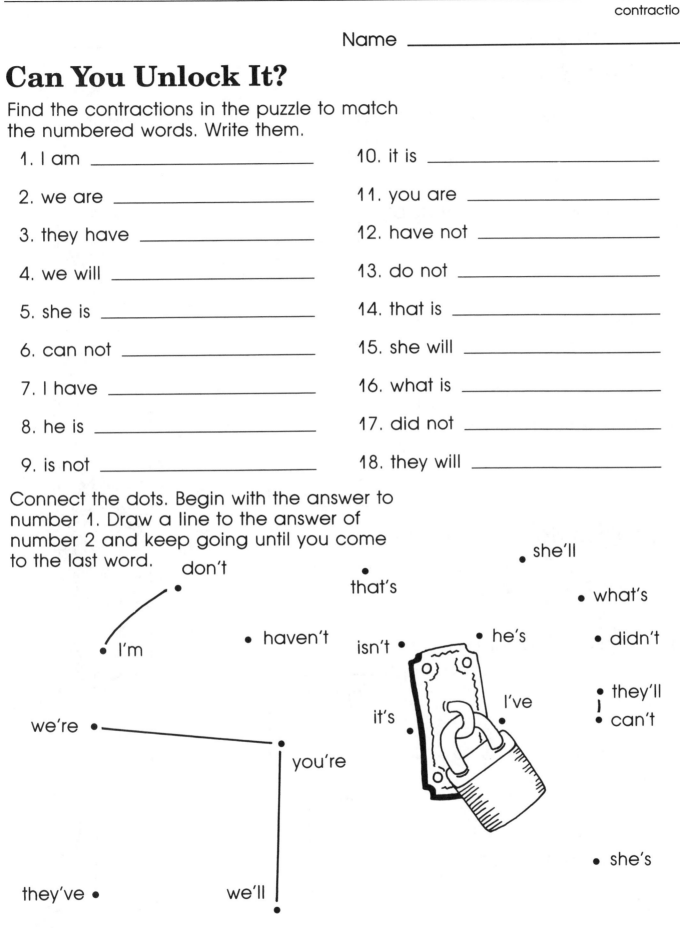

• she'll

don't

that's

• what's

• I'm

• haven't   isn't •   • he's   • didn't

it's •   • I've   • they'll
          • can't

we're •   you're

          • she's

they've •   we'll

Name _____

As Easy As Pie

Cut out and paste a picture to correctly complete each simile.

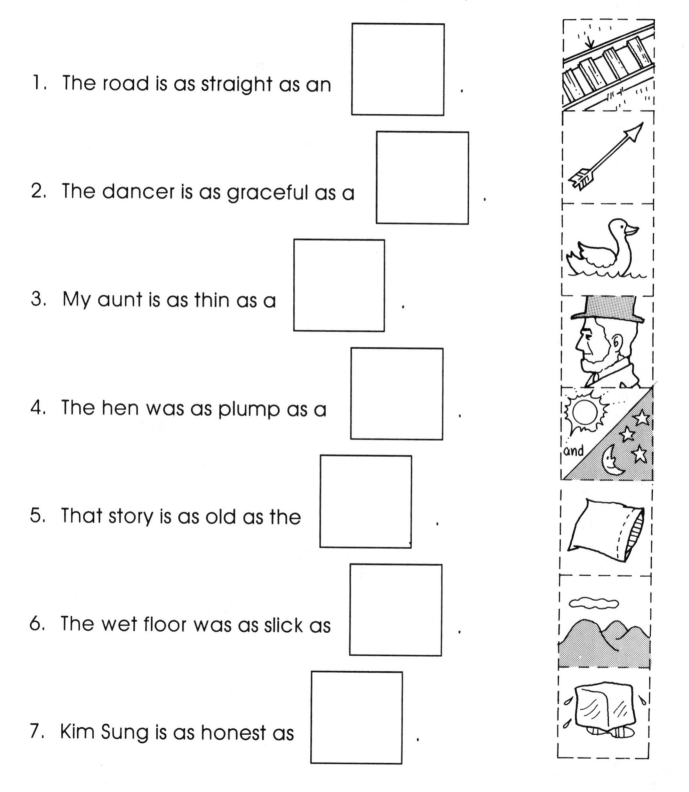

1. The road is as straight as an [ ] .

2. The dancer is as graceful as a [ ] .

3. My aunt is as thin as a [ ] .

4. The hen was as plump as a [ ] .

5. That story is as old as the [ ] .

6. The wet floor was as slick as [ ] .

7. Kim Sung is as honest as [ ] .

Name _____

Animal Analogies

Animals have distinguishing features and inherited characteristics. These traits can be related in quite interesting and unusual ways by the use of analogies.

Use the Word Box to complete these analogies. You may need to use an encyclopedia. Be prepared to explain your answer.

1. An awning is to a window as eyebrows are to the eyes of a _____ .

2. A hand fan is to a human as ears are to an _____ .

3. Four quarters are to a dollar as four stomachs are to a _____ .

4. Flypaper is to flies as an anteater's tongue is to _____ .

5. A needle is to a seamstress as a beak is to a _____ .

6. Glass is to a window as skin is to a _____ .

7. A mouth is to a crocodile as a pouch is to a _____ .

8. A chest beat is to a gorilla as a shaking rattle is to a _____ .

Word Box			
kangaroo	cow	glass catfish	camel
tailorbird	ants	rattlesnake	elephant

Name _____

What's the Connection?

Complete each analogy with a word from the Word Bank.

1. A **tepee** is to some **Indians** as a **cave** is to some _____ .

2. **Hair** is to a **person** as a **mane** is to a _____ .

3. A **bow** is to a **ribbon** as a **knot** is to a _____ .

4. **Galloping** is to a **horse** as **flying** is to an _____ .

5. **Blindness** is to **eyes** as **deafness** is to _____ .

6. **Softness** is to a **feather** as **colorful** is to a _____ .

7. **Shallow** is to **deep** as **beginning** is to _____ .

8. **Mountains** are to **rocks** as **lakes** are to _____ .

9. **Strong** is to **frail** as **brave** is to _____ .

10. **Trot** is to **gallop** as **fly** is to _____ .

11. **Sweet** is to **sweat** as **breed** is to _____ .

12. **Counting** is to **numbers** as **reading** is to _____ .

Word Bank			
ears	afraid	water	horse
end	eagle	bread	soar
rope	bears	words	rainbow

Name _____

Cool As a Cucumber

Sometimes people use funny expressions to say what they mean. Complete each sentence by writing the letter of the word that would best explain what is meant.

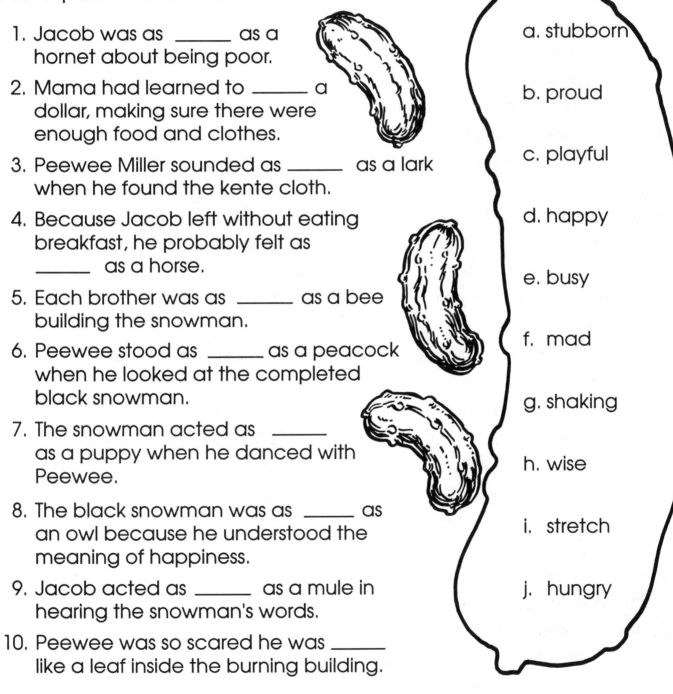

1. Jacob was as _____ as a hornet about being poor.

2. Mama had learned to _____ a dollar, making sure there were enough food and clothes.

3. Peewee Miller sounded as _____ as a lark when he found the kente cloth.

4. Because Jacob left without eating breakfast, he probably felt as _____ as a horse.

5. Each brother was as _____ as a bee building the snowman.

6. Peewee stood as _____ as a peacock when he looked at the completed black snowman.

7. The snowman acted as _____ as a puppy when he danced with Peewee.

8. The black snowman was as _____ as an owl because he understood the meaning of happiness.

9. Jacob acted as _____ as a mule in hearing the snowman's words.

10. Peewee was so scared he was _____ like a leaf inside the burning building.

a. stubborn

b. proud

c. playful

d. happy

e. busy

f. mad

g. shaking

h. wise

i. stretch

j. hungry

Cool Heads

Name _____

Circle sentence "a" or "b" to show which one means the same as the numbered sentence.

1. Eddie Whitestone always had something up his sleeve.
   a. He keeps things up his sleeve.
   b. He liked to plan surprises.

2. His room was a pigsty.
   a. It was very messy.
   b. He lived with pigs.

3. She would be late if she didn't step on it.
   a. She needs to hurry.
   b. She needs to step on something.

4. Sometimes David could be hardheaded.
   a. His head was very hard.
   b. He could be stubborn.

5. Roger always tried to keep a cool head.
   a. He tried to be calm.
   b. He kept ice on his head.

6. Horseplay was not allowed in the hall.
   a. No horses were allowed in the hall.
   b. No playing was allowed in the hall.

7. Ali Baba wrapped up another mystery.
   a. He solved the mystery.
   b. He wrapped the mystery in paper.

8. Ali Baba kept an eye on Eddie Whitestone.
   a. He drew an eye on Eddie's shirt.
   b. He watched him.

9. His neighbors skipped town.
   a. They skipped all over town.
   b. They left town.

10. The criminal was in hot water.
    a. He was standing in hot water.
    b. He was in trouble.

Name _____

What's the Point?

Harry and Sidney giggled as they started painting the winter mural. Instead of painting a snow picture, they painted themselves in a cemetery "burying the hatchet." This meant that they would forget about their past fighting and be friends.

Read each sentence below. Then write the letter of the phrase that tells what the speaker really means.

He says . . .

_____ 1. It's "raining cats and dogs."

_____ 2. I remember when you were "knee-high to a grasshopper."

_____ 3. You "eat like a bird."

_____ 4. He "held up the bank."

_____ 5. You "light up my life!"

_____ 6. Which way should I turn "at the fork in the road?"

_____ 7. The speaker "had a frog in her throat."

What he means is . . .

a.　don't eat very much

b.　make me very happy

c.　robbed the bank

d.　very small

e.　pouring hard

f.　was hoarse

g.　where the road splits

Name _____

Which Is Which?

Like twins, words are sometimes hard to tell apart. Can you tell these word pairs apart? Answer each question by writing the correct word in the box.

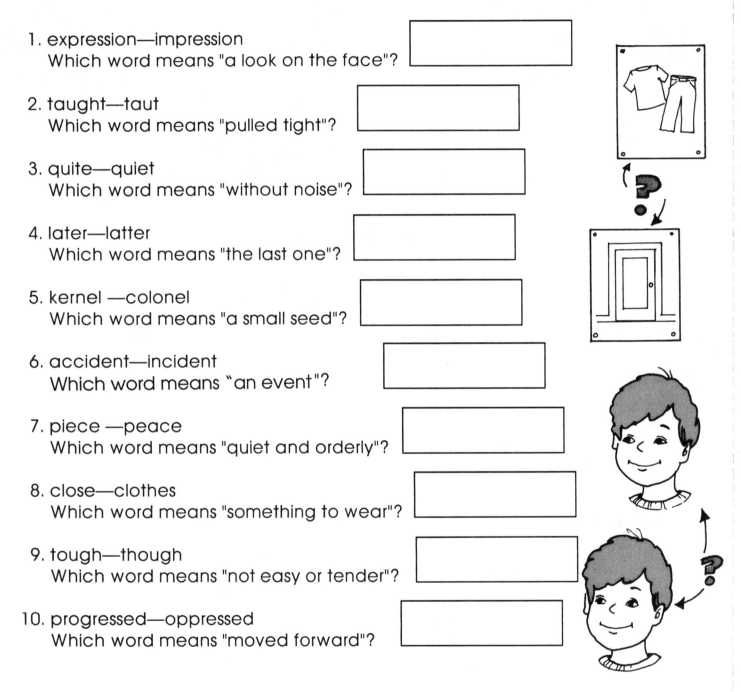

1. expression—impression
   Which word means "a look on the face"?

2. taught—taut
   Which word means "pulled tight"?

3. quite—quiet
   Which word means "without noise"?

4. later—latter
   Which word means "the last one"?

5. kernel —colonel
   Which word means "a small seed"?

6. accident—incident
   Which word means "an event"?

7. piece —peace
   Which word means "quiet and orderly"?

8. close—clothes
   Which word means "something to wear"?

9. tough—though
   Which word means "not easy or tender"?

10. progressed—oppressed
    Which word means "moved forward"?

A NOW . . . D Imagine that you had a twin. What would your names be? Would you dress alike? Would you do and like the same things?

Name _____

Candy Store Dilemma

Read the label on each candy jar. Write the words from the Word Bank on the candy jar where they belong.

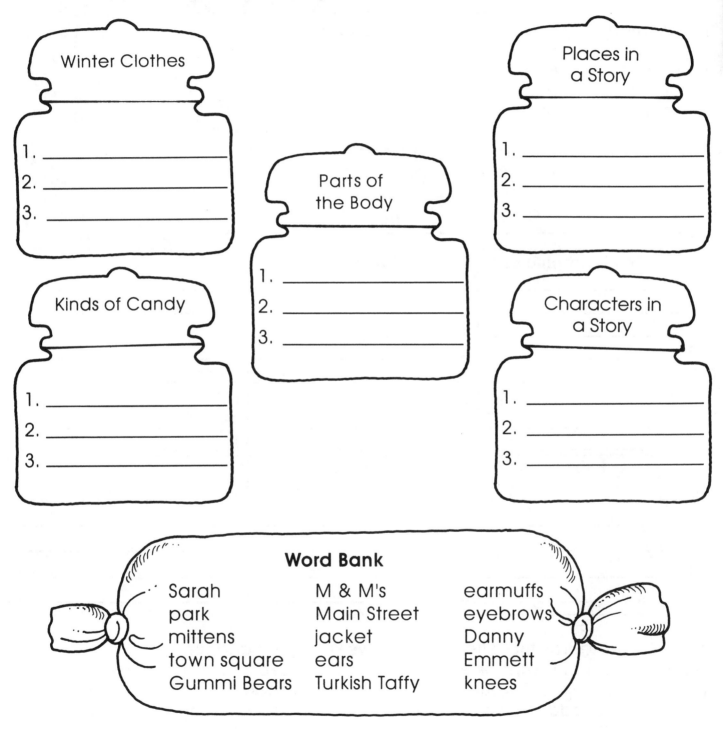

Winter Clothes

1. _____
2. _____
3. _____

Parts of the Body

1. _____
2. _____
3. _____

Places in a Story

1. _____
2. _____
3. _____

Kinds of Candy

1. _____
2. _____
3. _____

Characters in a Story

1. _____
2. _____
3. _____

Word Bank

Sarah	M & M's	earmuffs
park	Main Street	eyebrows
mittens	jacket	Danny
town square	ears	Emmett
Gummi Bears	Turkish Taffy	knees

At the Pet Store

Name _____

Use a dictionary to help you determine in which category each of these words belongs.

malamute	chameleon	mud puppy	mouse
guppy	newt	skink	Pekingese
angelfish	macaw	sheepdog	canary
cockatoo	pointer	rat	tomcat
spaniel	guinea pig	Siamese	goldfish
platy	finch	mutt	hamster
Manx	parrot	Persian	swift
gerbil	swordfish	salamander	setter
parakeet	iguana	mastiff	myna
frog	tabby	cockatiel	

Reptiles & Amphibians	Birds	Dogs
1. _____	1. _____	1. _____
2. _____	2. _____	2. _____
3. _____	3. _____	3. _____
4. _____	4. _____	4. _____
5. _____	5. _____	5. _____
6. _____	6. _____	6. _____
7. _____	7. _____	7. _____
8. _____	8. _____	8. _____

Fish	Rodents	Cats
1. _____	1. _____	1. _____
2. _____	2. _____	2. _____
3. _____	3. _____	3. _____
4. _____	4. _____	4. _____
5. _____	5. _____	5. _____

A NOW ... D   Research the differences between reptiles and amphibians. Separate the "Reptiles & Amphibians" list above into two separate lists. To which list would you add the word *tadpole*? To which list would you add the word *anole*? Find other words to add to these lists.

Name _____

Do We or Don't We?

If the word is a **compound** word, color the space **blue**.
If the word is a **contraction**, color the space **gray**.
If the word is a **verb**, color the space **yellow**.
If the word is an **adjective**, color the space **black**.

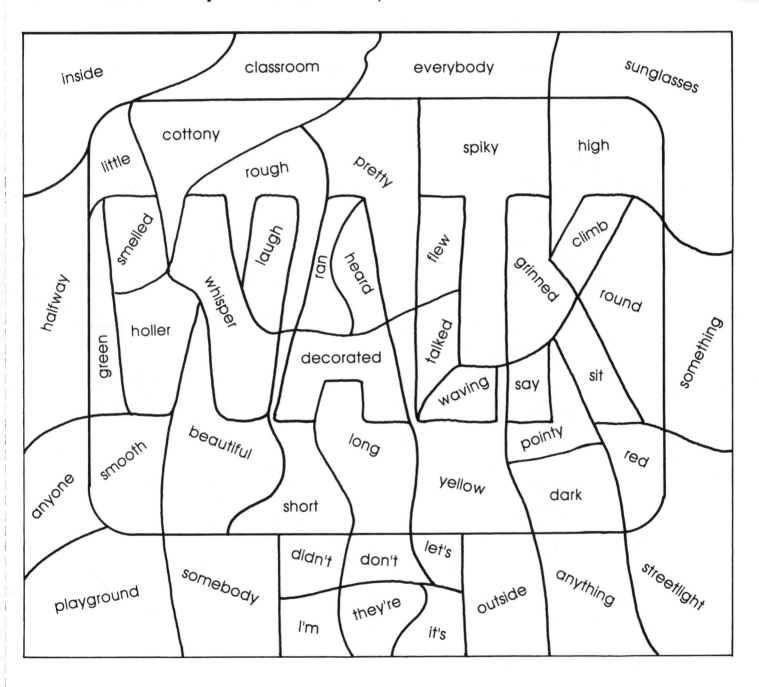

inside classroom everybody sunglasses

cottony spiky high

little rough pretty

smelled laugh ran heard flew grinned climb round

halfway whisper green holler decorated talked say sit something

waving

beautiful long pointy red

anyone smooth yellow dark

short

didn't don't let's

somebody anything streetlight

playground I'm they're it's outside

Daily Learning Drills Grade 3

Name _____

What a View!

On a separate paper, rewrite the story below, substituting the correct word from the Word Box for each underlined word or phrase.

Space shuttle astronauts <u>view</u> our <u>earth</u> from an <u>altitude</u> of 160 miles. Because the shuttle <u>orbits</u> the earth so <u>rapidly</u>, the astronauts see several sunrises and sunsets in one <u>24-hour period</u>.

They pass over the place where the Mediterranean Sea <u>separates</u> Europe from Africa. It is very <u>easy</u> to <u>locate</u> the Nile River and the Red Sea from that altitude.

The shuttle travels across Asia, the largest <u>landmass</u>. The astronauts <u>film</u> the <u>peaks</u> of the Himalaya Mountains before crossing over the Pacific Ocean. Their <u>journey</u> is <u>incredible</u>.

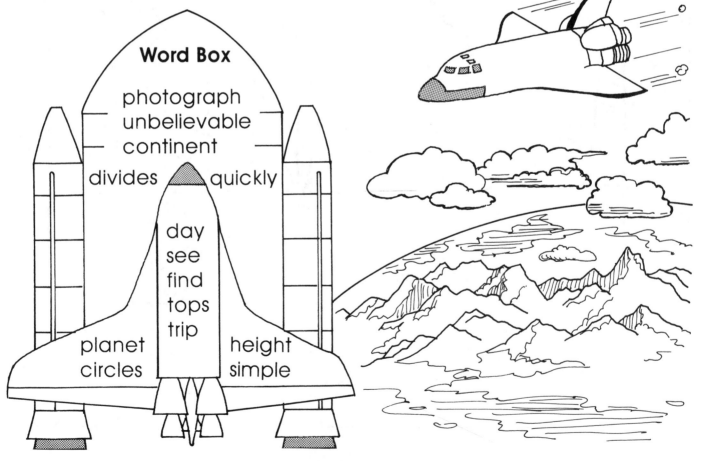

Word Box

photograph
unbelievable
continent
divides   quickly

day
see
find
tops
trip

planet   height
circles   simple

Name _____

I'll Be Switched

A silly sheriff always switched his word parts around when he got excited. Use the Answer Box to write what the sheriff meant to say.

Answer Box

let 'em go
decided to be a hermit
barber shop
haul 'em away
shy as a mouse
one with the beard
burning leaves
swell job of smelling
radio robbers

1. my as a shouse

2. sarber bhop

3. smell job of swelling

4. robbio raiders

5. waul 'em ahay

6. lurning beaves

7. get 'em lo

8. hecided to be a dermit

9. one bith the weard

Name _____

The Prince and the Dragon

The prince had come to save the princess who was trapped in a cave by a huge, ferocious, fire-breathing dragon. The prince brought only a rope, a rock, and a bucket of sand, but he could also do excellent voice imitations.

Help the prince think of ways to save the princess from the dragon.

1. _____

2. _____

3. _____

4. _____

5. _____

6. _____

7. _____

8. _____

9. _____

10. _____

Name _____

Painting with Words

Ut was from Vietnam and didn't express herself in the same way the other children in her new American school did. However, her expressions were colorful and explained what she meant.

Read each sentence. Then use the Word Bank to rewrite each sentence by changing the underlined words to more common English words. Don't forget capitals and final punctuation!

1. The round-eyed children twittered when Ut answered.

_____

2. A snowrock stung her chin.

_____

3. The children screeched like bluejays.

_____

4. She sat down and hid her angry Dragon face.

_____

5. The clock needles ticked slowly.

_____

6. His eyes gleamed like watermelon seeds.

_____

7. Small feathers floated past the frosty windows.

_____

8. Her fingers danced on the desk top.

_____

Word Bank

American children laughed	sparkled	time went slowly	laughed
snow fell	snowball	tapped	scowling

Name _____

What Am I?

Solve each riddle by writing a word from the Word Bank.

1. People usually think I am imaginary, but there is an example of me in the reptile family. I am a _____ .

2. I contain small sticks that can become very hot. I am a _____ .

3. I am very light and cold, although when I am packed in a group, together we become very hard. I am a _____

4. Sometimes I'm fuzzy, and sometimes I'm not. Often I change shape to become something very beautiful. I am a _____

5. I'm the beautiful result of sun and rain. I am a _____ .

6. Although we do not weigh very much, we do a terrific job at keeping certain animals warm. We are _____ .

7. I'm what's left after your piece of cornbread has been eaten. I am _____ .

8. Although I am clothing, you wouldn't wear me out of the house. I am _____ .

Word Bank				
bluejays	dumpster	matchbox	angel	feathers
caterpillar	dragon	oceans	snowflake	crayons
pajamas	crumbs	rainbow	lessons	noodles

Name _____

The Gourmet Grubber

The Grubber Sweet Shop was being rebuilt thanks to the Duke of Hampshire. In the candy box below are some of the sweets now sold there. Help organize the candies by numbering them in alphabetical order.

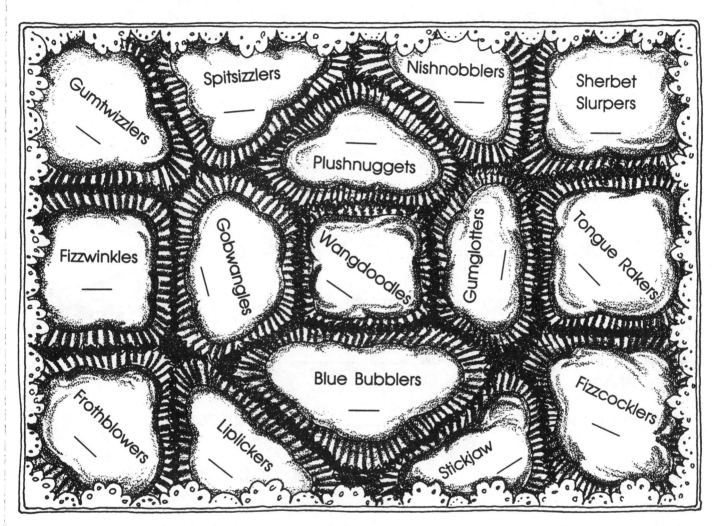

1. Underline all 3-syllable candies in red.
2. Circle all 4-syllable candies in green.
3. Draw a yellow box around the candies that start with the letter "g."
4. Put an orange X above the candy that does not end with the letter "s."
5. Draw a purple line above the words that have more than one "s."
6. Circle in blue the candy that has this color in its name.
7. Draw a pink X after the candy name that you like best.

Name _____

What's Missing?

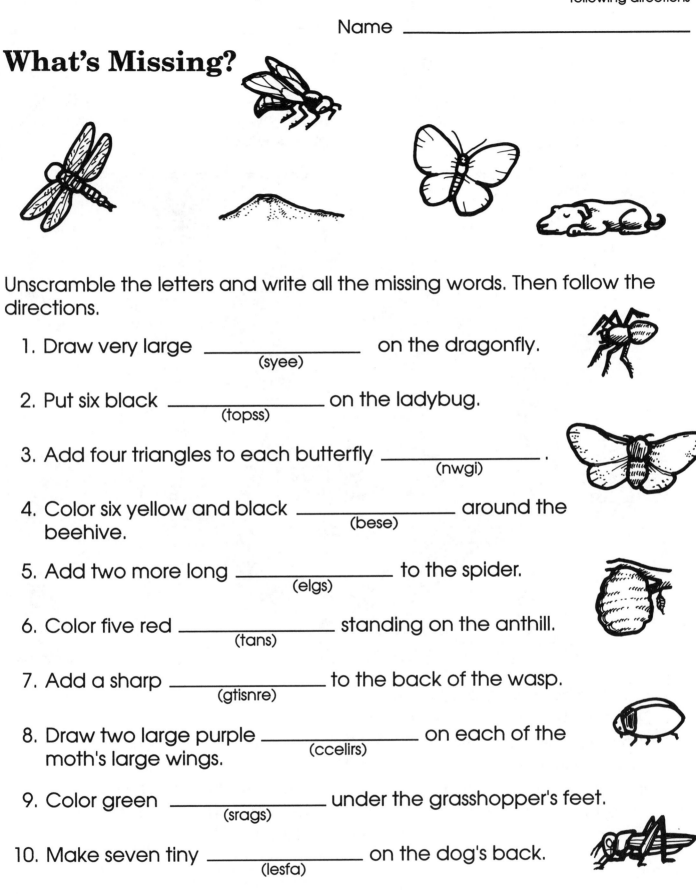

Unscramble the letters and write all the missing words. Then follow the directions.

1. Draw very large _____ on the dragonfly.
   (syee)

2. Put six black _____ on the ladybug.
   (topss)

3. Add four triangles to each butterfly _____ .
   (nwgi)

4. Color six yellow and black _____ around the beehive.
   (bese)

5. Add two more long _____ to the spider.
   (elgs)

6. Color five red _____ standing on the anthill.
   (tans)

7. Add a sharp _____ to the back of the wasp.
   (gtisnre)

8. Draw two large purple _____ on each of the moth's large wings.
   (ccelirs)

9. Color green _____ under the grasshopper's feet.
   (srags)

10. Make seven tiny _____ on the dog's back.
    (lesfa)

Name _____

Step-by-Step

Because Ut had just moved to America, she didn't know how to do some of the things we do. Write complete sentences telling Ut how to do these things.

How to Roller Skate

_____

_____

_____

_____

_____

 **How to Make a Banana Split**

_____

_____

_____

_____

_____

How to Play Tic-Tac-Toe

_____

_____

_____

_____

_____

Name _____

What a Day!

Read the story that goes with each picture. Write the word which best describes each day on the line.

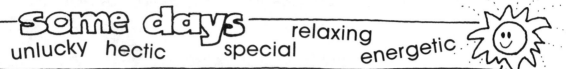

some days

unlucky   hectic   special   relaxing   energetic

At 9:00 Bob played tennis with his brother. At 11:00 he went swimming with friends. At 1:00 he mowed the yard and trimmed the shrubs.

Bob had an _____ day.

At 8:00 Sally dropped her books in the mud on the way to school. At 11:00 she spilled her milk on her clothes. At 4:00 she knocked a lamp off a table.

Sally had an _____ day.

At 10:00 Kirk got out of bed. At 12:00 he ate lunch while watching TV. At 2:00 he read a book while lying in a hammock. At 5:00 he rode his bike to a friend's house.

Kirk had a _____ day.

At 9:00 Kim went shopping with her mom. At 12:00 they ate lunch at her favorite restaurant. At 2:00 they saw a movie. At 5:00 Kim had a birthday party.

Kim had a _____ day.

At 8:00 Tom went to the store for his mom. At 10:00 he took his little brother to the dentist. At 1:00 he cleaned his room. At 2:00 he took his books to the library.

Tom had a _____ day.

Name _____

Brand News

Read the information on each label. Underline the correct sentence to tell the main idea of each package.

This cake will taste good because it is iced at the factory.

This is a quick and easy cake to eat because it has already been prepared and frozen.

This gum tastes great and makes bubbles even though it doesn't have sugar.

The more sugar a gum contains, the larger the bubbles it will make.

This baby food will look white because the color of the food has been removed.

This baby food is nutritional and is the natural color of the food.

This spaghetti is speedy because it just must be heated to serve.

This spaghetti is speedy because it came in an easy-open can.

This aspirin is not to be taken by children.

Adults take this aspirin once every six hours, but children take only one a day.

Name _____

Next ...

Read each sentence. Write two sentences which tell two different things that could happen.

1. The smoke from the oven rose in the air toward the smoke detector.

next: 1. _____
2. _____

2. The crowd cheered wildly as the football player ran toward the goal line.

1. _____

2. _____

next:

3. Bob and Kelly were on their way to the movie when Kelly realized she had left her money at home.

1. _____

next: 2. _____

4. The diver was looking for the old sunken ship when he spotted a huge grey mass ahead.

1. _____

next: 2. _____

5. When Rob arrived for the museum tour, he found that the tour had started ten minutes earlier.

1. _____

next: 2. _____

6. Just as Sam was to go on stage for the class play, he realized he had forgotten his lines.

next: 1. _____
2. _____

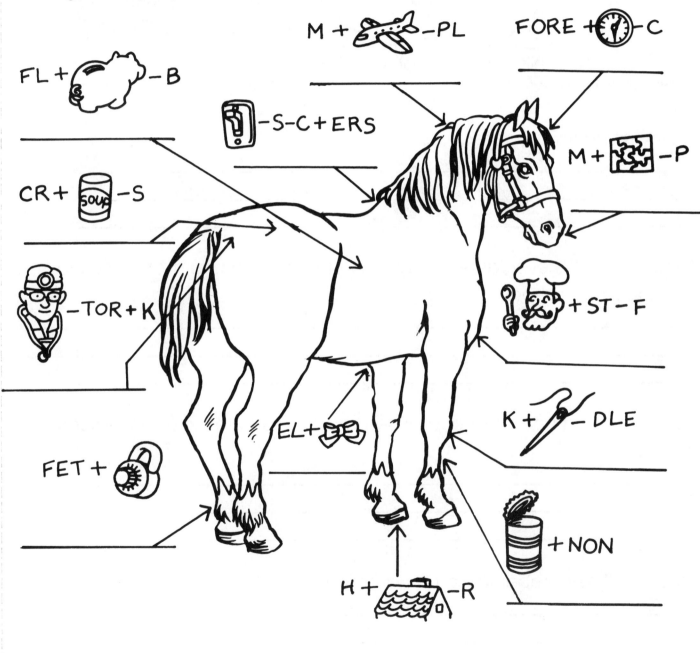

Name _____

Horsing Around

Horses are beautiful and are very smart animals. They have excellent senses of smell, sight, and hearing.

Study this diagram of a horse. Write the names of its body parts shown by solving each puzzle.

Name _____

Forgetful Fred

Each sentence tells about a problem. Think of a way to solve each one. Then write it on the lines.

Cathy is always late for school.

_____

_____

_____

Brian forgets his eyeglasses every morning, and then his mother has to bring them to school.

_____

_____

_____

Sara can't find her library book when she needs to return it to the school library.

_____

_____

_____

Fred can't remember to do his homework.

_____

_____

_____

Name _____

Think About It!

Arthur, the director of a play, had to handle many problems. Think about each problem and then write what you would have done to help each character solve it.

Sue Ellen didn't talk loudly enough.

_____

_____

_____

_____

_____

Buster could not remember what to say.

_____

_____

_____

_____

Muffy kept dropping the basket filled with cranberries.

_____

_____

_____

_____

Daily Learning Drills Grade 3

Is That a Fact!

Name _____

Read each sentence. If it states a fact, write the word **fact** on the line. If it states an opinion, write the word **opinion** on the line.

1. Eighth graders are too old to be rolling snowballs.

_____

2. A town square is part of a town.

_____

3. Enough snow can fall in one night to become a foot deep.

_____

4. Mr. Wetzel sells the best candy in the world.

_____

5. A fence is usually strong enough to stop a snowball.

_____

6. Winter is the season after fall and before spring.

_____

7. Everyone likes to play in the snow.

_____

8. Warm weather will make snow melt.

_____

9. Emmett always makes the biggest and best snowballs.

_____

10. It is hard for wild animals to find food in the snow.

_____

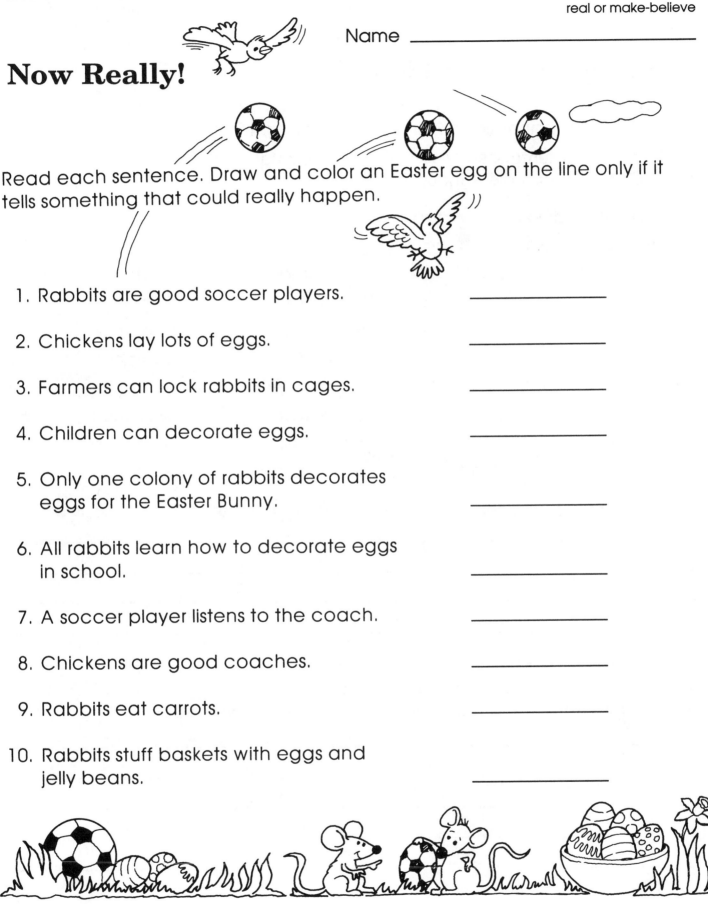

Now Really!

Name _____

Read each sentence. Draw and color an Easter egg on the line only if it tells something that could really happen.

1. Rabbits are good soccer players. _____

2. Chickens lay lots of eggs. _____

3. Farmers can lock rabbits in cages. _____

4. Children can decorate eggs. _____

5. Only one colony of rabbits decorates eggs for the Easter Bunny. _____

6. All rabbits learn how to decorate eggs in school. _____

7. A soccer player listens to the coach. _____

8. Chickens are good coaches. _____

9. Rabbits eat carrots. _____

10. Rabbits stuff baskets with eggs and jelly beans. _____

Daily Learning Drills Grade 3

Name _____

A Penny for Your Thoughts

A **phrase** is an *incomplete* thought—it doesn't make sense all by itself. A **sentence**, on the other hand, is a *complete* thought.

Circle **phrase** or **sentence** to show whether each group of words below is an incomplete or a complete thought.

1. day of feasting in the village   phrase   sentence
2. it was a string of blue beads   phrase   sentence
3. the chief was pleased   phrase   sentence
4. played drums and danced   phrase   sentence
5. he looked at the ship   phrase   sentence
6. pointed to the north   phrase   sentence
7. rowed toward the ship   phrase   sentence
8. we will tell the chief   phrase   sentence
9. she is sad   phrase   sentence
10. going back to England   phrase   sentence

Copy each of the five sentences above using capital letters and periods.

_____

_____

_____

_____

Add words to the phrases above to make complete thoughts. Don't forget to begin each sentence with a capital letter and end it with a period!

_____

_____

_____

_____

Name _____

First Things First . . . But Not Always!

Below each sentence fill in the circle to show which event happened first. Remember that **sometimes** what happened first might be at the end of the sentence!

1. Henry walked straight to the diorama, then leaned over the counter.
   - ○ Henry walked straight to the diorama.
   - ○ Henry leaned over the counter.

2. Henry opened one of the cabinets and took out a jar of peanut butter.
   - ○ Henry opened one of the cabinets.
   - ○ Henry took out a jar of peanut butter.

3. Before eating his sandwich, Henry poured himself a glass of milk.
   - ○ Henry ate his sandwich.
   - ○ Henry poured himself a glass of milk.

4. Tom and Lucy climbed into the jack-o'-lantern as soon as Henry closed the bathroom door.
   - ○ Tom and Lucy climbed into the jack-o'-lantern.
   - ○ Henry closed the bathroom door.

5. After they had climbed to the top of the roof, Tom watched the yard, and Lucy watched the sky.
   - ○ They climbed to the top of the roof.
   - ○ Tom watched the yard, and Lucy watched the sky.

6. Finally, the Littles gave up and went back to their apartment.
   - ○ The Littles gave up.
   - ○ The Littles went back to their apartment.

7. Everyone noticed that things looked different because Uncle Nick had tidied up the living room.
   - ○ Everyone noticed that things looked different.
   - ○ Uncle Nick tidied up the living room.

Name _____

Super Cookies!

Super Cookies

First mix
  1 cup sugar
  1 cup brown sugar
  1 cup butter
  2 teaspoons vanilla
Next add
  4 eggs
Mix in
  4 cups of flour
  3 teaspoons baking powder
  1 teaspoon salt
Stir in
  1½ cups milk
Then stir in
  1 cup chocolate pieces
  1 cup shredded coconut
  1 cup chopped cherries
  1 cup chopped nuts
Bake at 350° for 10 minutes.
Sprinkle on powdered sugar.

Number the directions in the correct order. Use the recipe to help you.

_____ Bake the cookies for 10 minutes. Remove the pan from the oven.

_____ Roll the dough into small balls.

_____ When the cookies are cool, enjoy eating them.

_____ Read the recipe first.

_____ Put the pan in 350° oven and set the timer.

_____ Mix the sugar, brown sugar, butter and vanilla until smooth.

_____ Pour in the milk and stir carefully.

_____ Take out all the ingredients and put them next to the utensils.

_____ Place the balls of dough on a greased pan. Be sure there is a space between each ball.

_____ Stir in the chocolate pieces, coconut, cherries and nuts. Mix well.

_____ Then stir in the flour, baking powder and salt.

_____ Get the measuring cups, spoons, bowls, mixer and pans ready.

_____ Remove the cookies from the pan and sprinkle powdered sugar on top of them.

_____ Add the eggs and mix well.

• Try the recipe!

Name _____

Waterworks

Use the diagram to help you number the sentences in the correct order to tell how water is purified.

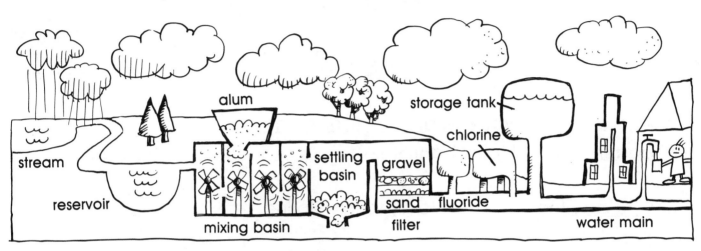

_____ Smaller pipes carry the water to the faucets in our homes.

_____ As the water flows through the filter, the alum and dirt sink to the bottom of the settling basin.

_____ The water in the reservoir goes through a large pipe into a mixing basin.

_____ Now that the water is as clean as possible it is stored in a huge storage tank.

_____ First raindrops fall into streams, lakes and rivers.

_____ Water leaves the storage tank through water mains.

_____ A chemical called alum is added to take the dirt out of the water.

_____ Turn the faucet handle and you have water.

_____ The clear, filtered water passes through a pipe where fluoride and chlorine are added.

_____ Then the streams and rivers flow into a reservoir.

_____ Smaller pipes carry the water from the water main to our homes.

This Is Where It's At!

Name _____

Read each sentence. Write the word **who, what, when, where** or **why** to show what the underlined words tell you.

1. <u>King Shabazz</u> didn't believe in Spring. _____

2. King and Tony would sit <u>on the steps of the apartment</u> and talk about Spring. _____

3. <u>One day</u> they decided to try to find Spring. _____

4. They stopped <u>at the streetlight.</u> _____

5. King <u>cleaned his shades.</u> _____

6. The streetlight changed <u>so they</u> ran across the street. _____

7. <u>The bar-b-q</u> smelled good. _____

8. <u>After they passed the apartments,</u> they saw a red car in a vacant lot. _____

9. The boys ran to look inside the car <u>because they wanted to see where the birds had been.</u> _____

10. King and Tony were happy <u>because they had found Spring.</u> _____

Name _____

In a Class by Himself!

Read each phrase.

If it tells **who**, color the space **brown**.

If it tells **what**, color the space **yellow**.

If it tells **when**, color the space **green**.

If it tells **where**, color the space **blue**.

If it tells **why**, color the space **purple**.

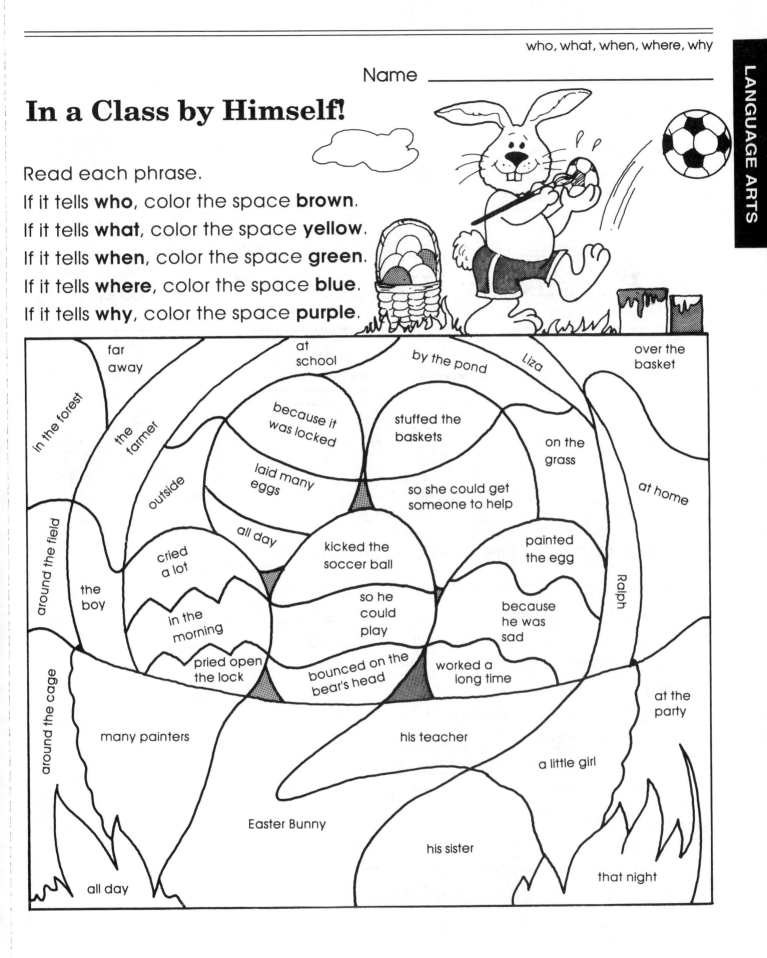

Read All About It!

Name _____

On the lines to the right of the story write the correct category— **who, what, when, where, why** — for each underlined word or phrase.

Huckleberry Heights Daily Herald

SPECIAL WEATHER REPORT

Volume MMI • No. 2   Editor: I.N. Thenews

Snowstorm Turns Streets into Skating Rink

(1) <u>Late last night</u> a (2) <u>major blizzard</u> closed most of (3) <u>the roads</u> here (4) <u>in Huckleberry Heights</u>. (5) <u>Early this morning</u>, (6) <u>the superintendent</u> announced that all schools (7) <u>in the area</u> would be closed (8) <u>due to the bad weather</u>. (9) <u>By noon</u>, the snowplows had cleared most of (10) <u>the snow</u>, but (11) <u>people</u> were warned not to drive (12) <u>because of the dangerously icy streets</u>. This, however, didn't keep (13) <u>the children</u> of Huckleberry Heights from getting around. Almost all of them put on their (14) <u>ice skates</u> and were seen sailing (15) <u>down the streets</u> during (16) <u>most of the afternoon</u>.

1. _____
2. _____
3. _____
4. _____
5. _____
6. _____
7. _____
8. _____
9. _____
10. _____
11. _____
12. _____
13. _____
14. _____
15. _____
16. _____

Name _____

What's It All About?

Underline the **topic sentence** – the sentence that most completely tells what the paragraph is all about – in each paragraph. Then write two phrases that are **supporting details** – they explain or tell about the topic sentence.

1. It happened exactly as Silla said it would. She gave birth to seven beautiful, healthy rabbits at the next full moon. The kits had small, mouse-like ears and were completely deaf. Their eyes were closed tight, and they couldn't see a thing. Their bodies were bare and they needed the warmth provided by the nest their mother had prepared.

   Supporting detail – _____

   Supporting detail – _____

2. Rabbits like to live together in a group. They dig their burrows like underground apartments where they will always have lots of neighbors. They help each other take care of the young. When the weather turns cold, they snuggle up together to keep each other warm.

   Supporting detail – _____

   Supporting detail – _____

3. Rahm and Silla scratched a hole in the sandy wall of the burrow with their front feet. Then they used their back feet to push the loose ground back into the tunnel. Silla smoothed down the walls and then pulled wool out of her fur to line the floor. They both worked hard to prepare a nursery for the babies who were soon to be born.

   Supporting detail – _____

   Supporting detail – _____

AND NOW . . . On the back write a paragraph about yourself when you were young. Be sure to include a topic sentence and several complete sentences that offer supporting details. You might also draw a picture to go with your paragraph.

Name _____

Soaring A-"Cross" Words

Read the clue. Find the word in the Word Bank. Write it in the puzzle.

Across

1. An exciting time
3. The child of your aunt and uncle
5. Your mother's mother
9. Place where boats sail near land
10. A very large town
11. Feel
12. Your mother or father's brother

Down

1. Your mother or father's sister
2. To help you remember
4. Another language
6. To answer
7. Places where things are made
8. A machine for lifting

Word Bank

city	aunt	crane
factories	touch	harbor
Spanish	uncle	remind
cousin	reply	grandma
adventure		

Name _____

Say What You Mean!

Write the vocabulary word from the Word Bank that means the same as each group of words.

1. changes, alters, varies _____

2. frail, tender, fragile _____

3. eliminate, scrap, reject _____

4. anger, fury, temper _____

5. withdraw, depart, retire _____

6. protect, guard, defend _____

7. worn, ripped, torn _____

8. unbelieving, doubtful, skeptical _____

9. common, usual, general _____

10. pause, delay, stall _____

11. bravery, boldness, fearlessness _____

12. transfer, move, disturb _____

13. great, immense, enormous _____

14. rude, ill-behaved, disrespectful _____

15. swallow, gobble, eat _____

16. deserted, vacant, unoccupied _____

17. explode, pop, blast _____

18. fighters, soldiers, combatants _____

19. tear, rip, shred _____

20. trash, junk, rubbish _____

Word Bank			
suspicious	courage	discard	hesitate
retreat	transforms	shield	impolite
devour	delicate	rage	abandoned
ordinary	tattered	fray	dislodge
vast	debris	warriors	burst

Daily Learning Drills Grade 3

Name _____

An A-"Mazing" Rabbit!

Help Ralph find his soccer ball. Read the clues. Find the definition in the maze and write the word on the line. Then draw a line through the maze in the same order as your answers.

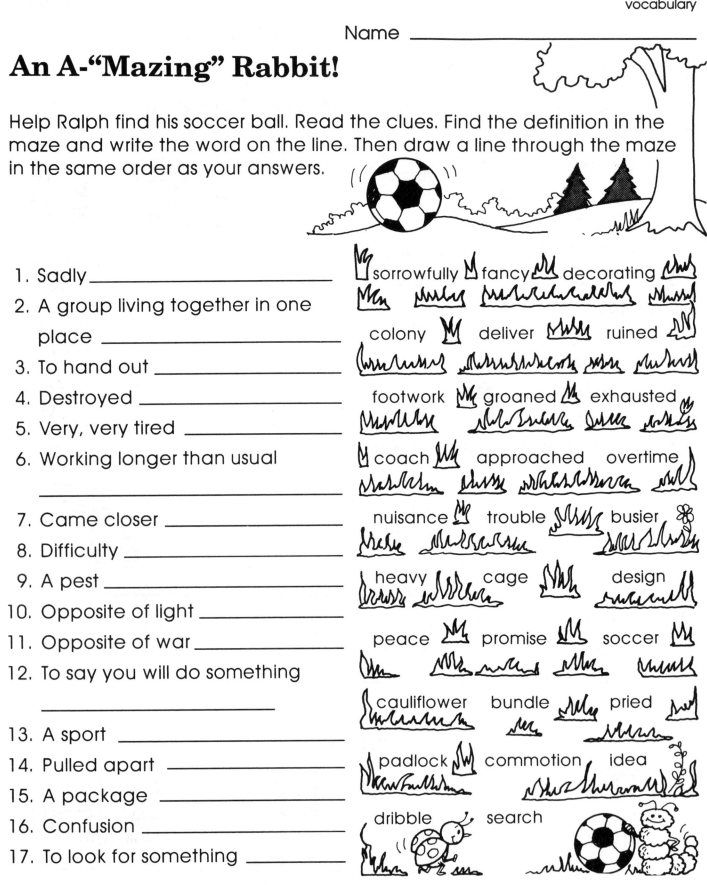

1. Sadly _____

2. A group living together in one place _____

3. To hand out _____

4. Destroyed _____

5. Very, very tired _____

6. Working longer than usual _____

7. Came closer _____

8. Difficulty _____

9. A pest _____

10. Opposite of light _____

11. Opposite of war _____

12. To say you will do something _____

13. A sport _____

14. Pulled apart _____

15. A package _____

16. Confusion _____

17. To look for something _____

sorrowfully fancy decorating

colony deliver ruined

footwork groaned exhausted

coach approached overtime

nuisance trouble busier

heavy cage design

peace promise soccer

cauliflower bundle pried

padlock commotion idea

dribble search

Good-by, Jennie!

Name _____

Many foreign words have worked their way into our American language.
Match each word or phrase below with its meaning. You may use a dictionary
for help.

1. au revoir (French)   _____
2. Gesundheit (German)   _____
3. crepe (French)   _____
4. tortilla (Spanish)   _____
5. pita (Greek)   _____
6. chopsticks (Asian)   _____
7. oui (French)   _____
8. sarong (Malaysian)   _____
9. amigo (Spanish)   _____
10. rendezvous (French)   _____
11. babushka (Russian)   _____
12. lasagna (Italian)   _____
13. madam (French)   _____
14. guacamole (Spanish)   _____
15. torte (German)   _____
16. foyer (French)   _____
17. beret (French)   _____

a. a lobby or entryway
b. a flat bread made from corn or flour
c. thin sticks used for eating
d. a married woman
e. a dip made with avocado
f. a scarf worn on the head
g. fabric wrapped to wear as a skirt
h. friend
i. yes
j. a rich layer cake
k. a meeting place
l. a flat hat
m. good-by
n. a dish made with long, flat noodles
o. thin cloth or pancake
p. round bread with pocket
q. "Good health!" to someone who
   sneezed

**A
NOW . . .
D** You may have noticed that a few of these words have to do with
food. Which ethnic foods do you enjoy most?

Name _____

Fable-ology

Create your own fable about how an animal acquired a particular physical feature. Remember to have the animal learn a lesson. Illustrate your fable.

How the _____ Got Its _____

Long, long ago there lived a _____

_____

_____

_____

_____

_____

_____

_____

_____

_____

_____

Moral: _____

_____

Name _____

Mouse on the Moon

Stories are always more exciting when you can picture them happening in your mind. Descriptive words such as adverbs and adjectives help make the story more exciting. Imagine that the moon is really made of cheese, and that you are a mouse exploring it for the first time. With a partner, write two descriptive words for each category below. Then, use all of them in a story.

What I smell:

1. _____
2. _____

What I see:

1. _____
2. _____

What I hear:

1. _____
2. _____

What I feel:

1. _____
2. _____

What I taste:

1. _____
2. _____

_____
title

_____

_____

_____

_____

_____

_____

_____

_____

_____

_____

_____

_____

_____

_____

_____

_____

Name _____

Star Gazing

The Indians loved to watch the moon and the stars. Following the example, write a poem about the sun, moon, or stars.

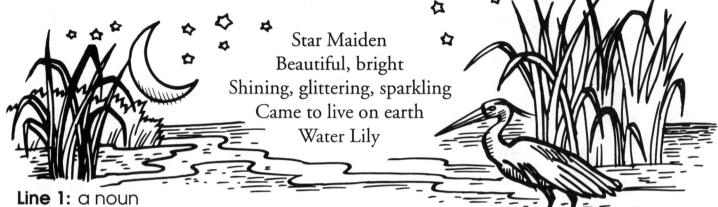

Star Maiden
Beautiful, bright
Shining, glittering, sparkling
Came to live on earth
Water Lily

Line 1: a noun
Line 2: two adjectives that describe the noun
Line 3: three verbs with **ing** endings that tell what the noun does
Line 4: a phrase or sentence that tells something special about the noun
Line 5: a synonym for the noun. Repeat the noun if there is no synonym.

_____

_____

_____

_____

_____

Name _____

Your Turn in the Poets Gallery

Fill in the blanks to make your own silly poems. The number at the end of each line tells the total number of syllables the line should have. Then draw a picture in each frame for the Poets Gallery.

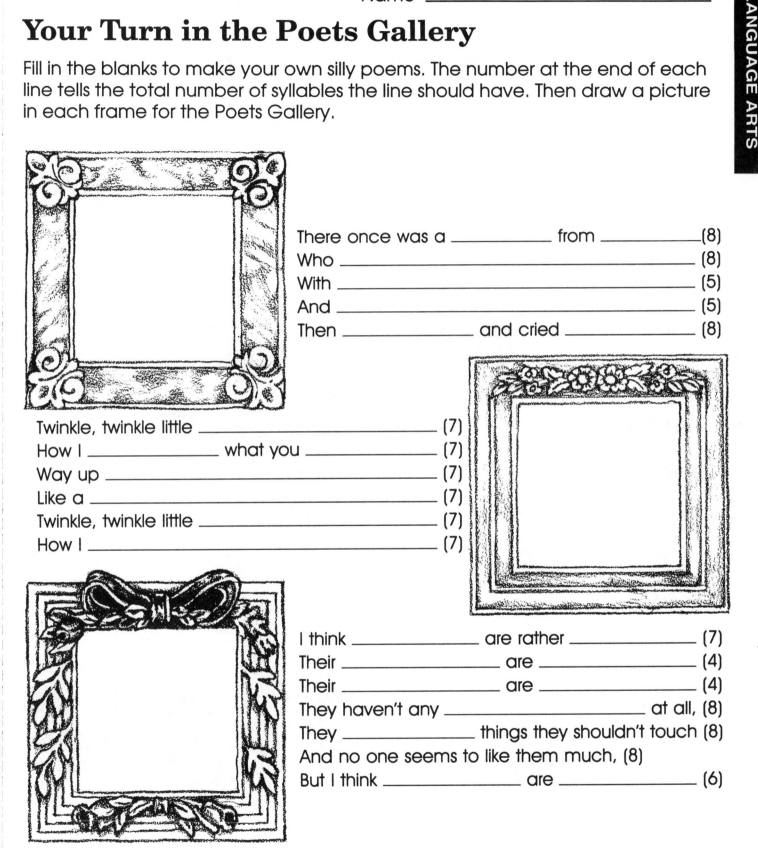

There once was a _____ from _____ (8)
Who _____ (8)
With _____ (5)
And _____ (5)
Then _____ and cried _____ (8)

Twinkle, twinkle little _____ (7)
How I _____ what you _____ (7)
Way up _____ (7)
Like a _____ (7)
Twinkle, twinkle little _____ (7)
How I _____ (7)

I think _____ are rather _____ (7)
Their _____ are _____ (4)
Their _____ are _____ (4)
They haven't any _____ at all, (8)
They _____ things they shouldn't touch (8)
And no one seems to like them much, (8)
But I think _____ are _____ (6)

Name _____

Now Hiring

This is a job application to become a maid.
Please print neatly!

Name _____   _____   _____
          Last   First   Middle

Address _____

City, State, Zip Code _____

Previous experience that would make you a good maid:

_____

_____

_____

Services you perform:_____

Hours you could work:_____

Vacation dates you prefer:_____

Salary required: _____

References (People who could tell us about you):

_____

_____

_____

_____

Signature

_____

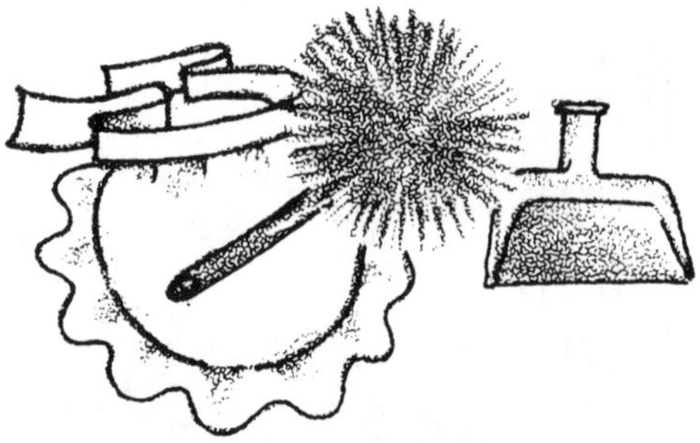

Name _____

Dewey Decimal System

The Dewey Decimal System is used in most libraries to put books in order. This makes it easier for you to find the book you need.

Someone copied the system on a piece of scratch paper with the numbers in the wrong order. Number the system in order starting with 000-099.

Dewey Decimal	Types of Books
_____ 600-699	farming, medicine, building and cooking
_____ 300-399	jobs, education and customs
_____ 000-099	encyclopedias, almanacs and books of facts
_____ 900-999	people, places and events in history
_____ 400-499	dictionaries and languages
_____ 700-799	painting, music, dancing, sports and games
_____ 500-599	animals, math, stars and chemistry
_____ 200-299	religions
_____ 800-899	stories, poems and plays
_____ 100-199	great ideas and logical thinking

Read the titles. Write the Dewey Decimal numbers for each book.

_____ *Tap Dancing*

_____ *Star Gazer*

_____ *Poems about Animals*

_____ *Cookie Cookbook Just for Kids*

_____ *The Spanish Language Made Easy*

Name _____

Skipping Through the Tens

Skip count by tens. Begin with the number on the first line. Write each number that follows.

0, ___ , ___ , ___ , ___ , ___ , ___ , ___ , ___ , ___ , 100

3, ___ , ___ , ___ , ___ , 53 , ___ , ___ , ___ , ___ , 103

1, ___ , ___ , ___ , ___ , ___ , ___ , ___ , 81 , ___ , ___

8, ___ , ___ , ___ , ___ , 68 , ___ , ___ , ___ , ___

6, ___ , ___ , ___ , ___ , ___ , ___ , ___ , ___ , ___

4, ___ , ___ , ___ , ___ , ___ , ___ , ___ , ___ , 104

2, ___ , ___ , ___ , ___ , ___ , ___ , ___ , 92 , ___

5, ___ , ___ , ___ , 45 , ___ , ___ , ___ , ___ , ___

7, ___ , ___ , ___ , ___ , ___ , 77 , ___ , ___ , ___

9, ___ , ___ , ___ , ___ , ___ , ___ , ___ , ___ , ___

What is ten more than ...

26 _____   29 _____

44 _____   77 _____

53 _____   91 _____

24 _____   49 _____

66 _____   35 _____

54 _____   82 _____

Name _____

Counting to 100

By twos:

		6	8				16			22			
30							44						56
				66						78			
							100						

By threes:

3	6					21						39	
					57						75		
	90				102								

By fours:

4	8								40				
60							88			100			

On the back, count by fives to 100. Can you count by sixes? Try it.

Name _____

Outstanding Elephant Math

Connect the dots in order.

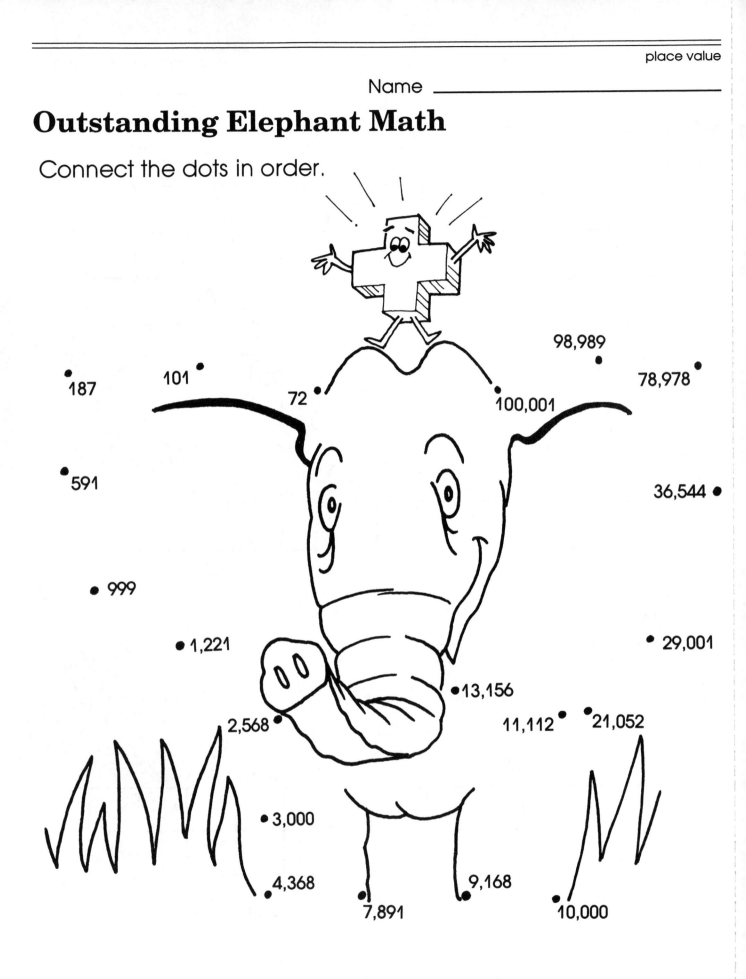

Name _____

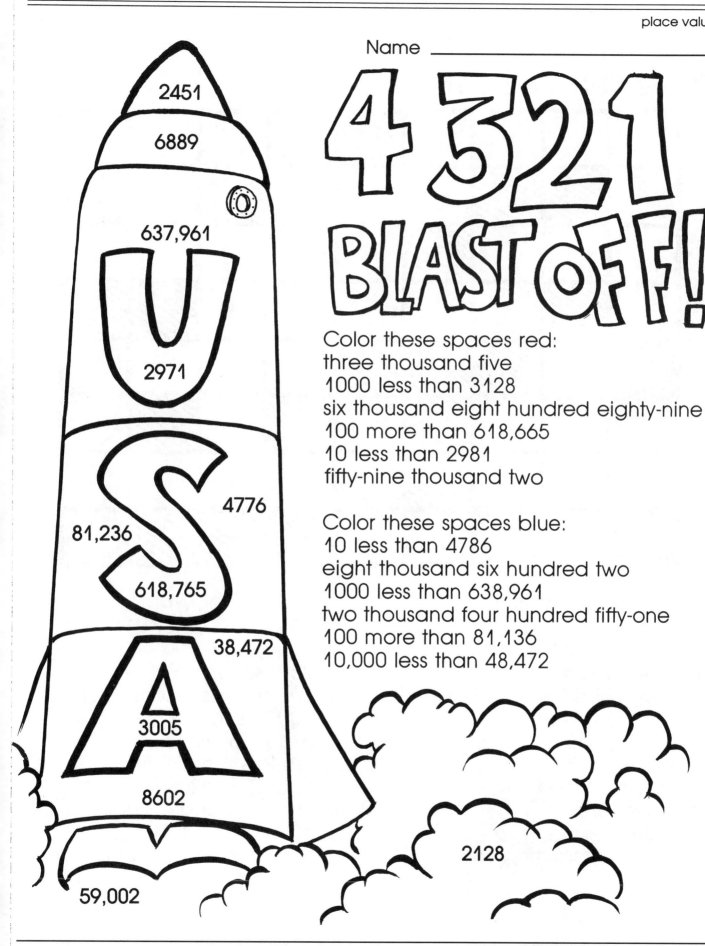

4 3 2 1 BLAST OFF!

Color these spaces red:
three thousand five
1000 less than 3128
six thousand eight hundred eighty-nine
100 more than 618,665
10 less than 2981
fifty-nine thousand two

Color these spaces blue:
10 less than 4786
eight thousand six hundred two
1000 less than 638,961
two thousand four hundred fifty-one
100 more than 81,136
10,000 less than 48,472

MATH

Numbers on rocket:
2451
6889
637,961
2971
81,236
4776
618,765
38,472
3005
8602
59,002
2128

Name _____

Place Value Puzzle

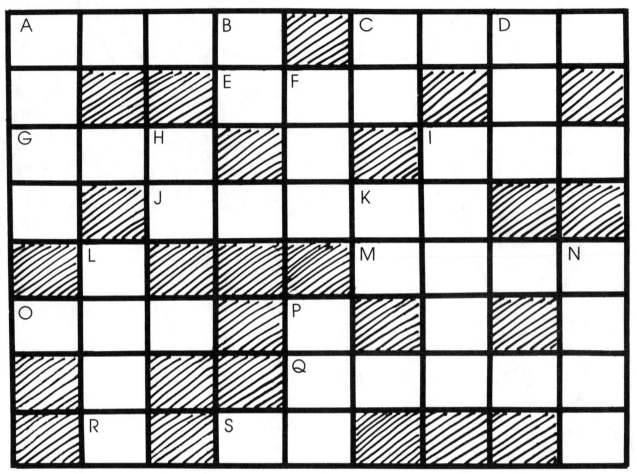

ACROSS

A. 3 thousand 5 hundred 9
C. 100 less than 8754
E. one hundred sixty-two
G. seven hundred eighty-two
I. 100, 150, 200, ___
J. 1, 2, 3, 4, 5 mixed up
L. two
M. 100 less than 9704
O. three zeros
P. eight
Q. 10,000 more than 56,480
R. one
S. 1 ten, 1 one

DOWN

A. 10 more than 3769
B. ninety-one
C. 28 backwards
D. 5 hundreds, 8 tens, 5 ones
F. 100 less than 773
H. 5, 10, 15, 20, ___
I. ten less than 24,684
K. 2 tens, 9 ones
L. two thousand one
N. 1000, 2000, 3000, ___
P. eight hundreds, 6 tens, 1 one

Name _____

Write That Number

Write the following numbers using digits.

1. six hundred fifty thousand, two hundred twenty-five _____

2. nine hundred ninety-nine thousand, nine hundred ninety-nine _____

3. one hundred six thousand, four hundred thirty-seven _____

4. three hundred fifty-six thousand, two hundred two _____

5. Write the smallest number you can using the digits 6, 9, 3, 5, 1, 9.

   The smallest number is _____ .

6. Write the largest number you can using the digits 6, 9, 3, 5, 1, 9.

   The largest number is _____ .

7. Write the number that is two more than 356,909. _____

8. Write the number that is five less than 448,394. _____

9. Write the number that is ten more than 285,634. _____

10. Write the number that is ten less than 395,025. _____

Write the following numbers in word form.

11. 3,208 _____

12. 13,656 _____

13. 451,867 _____

Name _____

Mushrooming Addition

Add 52 + 28 = 80
     28 + 91 = 119
     119 + 80 = ?

Follow arrows.

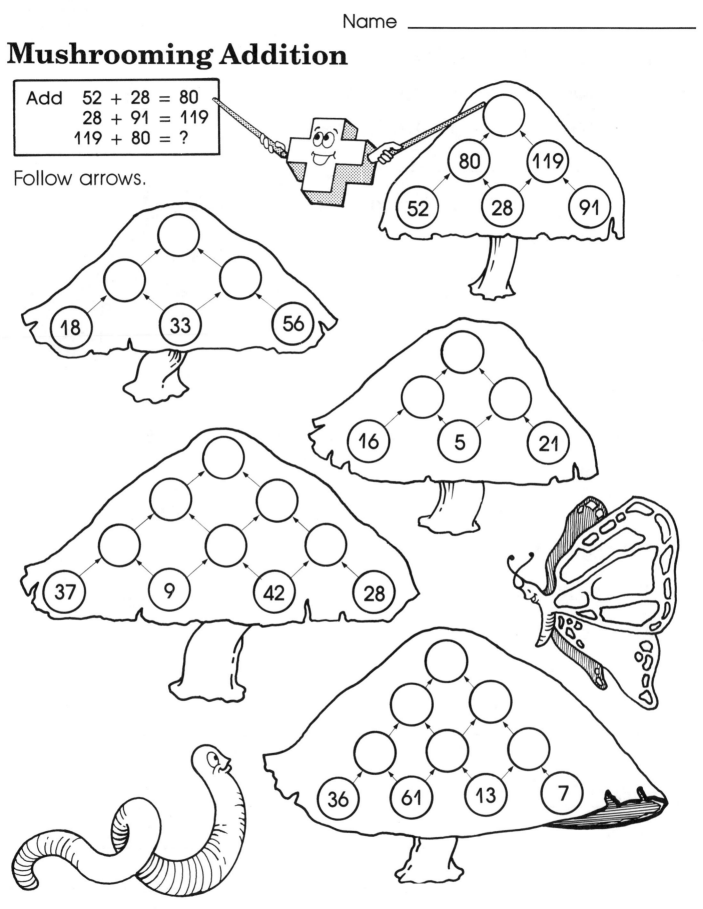

Name _____

Fishy Addition

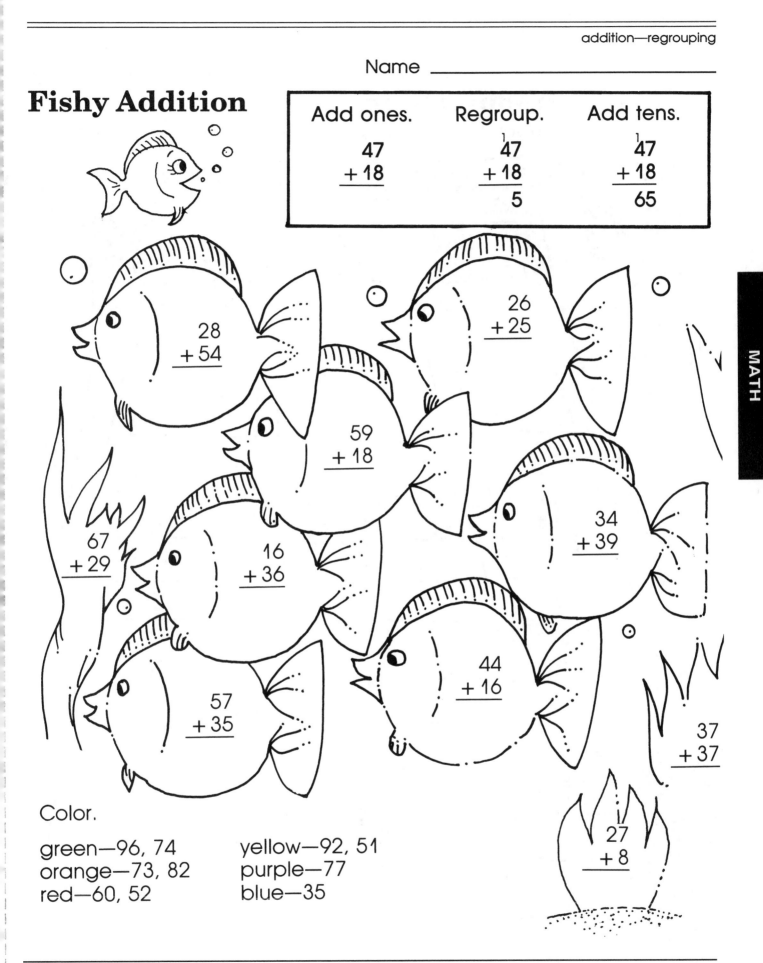

Add ones.	Regroup.	Add tens.
47 + 18	47 + 18 ——— 5	47 + 18 ——— 65

28
+ 54

26
+ 25

59
+ 18

67
+ 29

34
+ 39

16
+ 36

44
+ 16

57
+ 35

37
+ 37

27
+ 8

Color.

green—96, 74   yellow—92, 51
orange—73, 82   purple—77
red—60, 52   blue—35

Name _____

Make the Windows Shine!

Add. Each problem you complete makes the window "squeaky" clean.

$$476 + 319$$

$$248 + 629$$

$$327 + 544$$

$$572 + 318$$

$$815 + 177$$

$$527 + 144$$

$$429 + 343$$

$$462 + 319$$

$$462 + 529$$

$$648 + 238$$

$$756 + 127$$

$$563 + 208$$

$$646 + 248$$

$$924 + 66$$

$$628 + 259$$

$$526 + 347$$

$$927 + 46$$

$$765 + 218$$

Name _____

Addition Ace

Add. The pilot will remain in the air for as long as it takes to complete these problems.

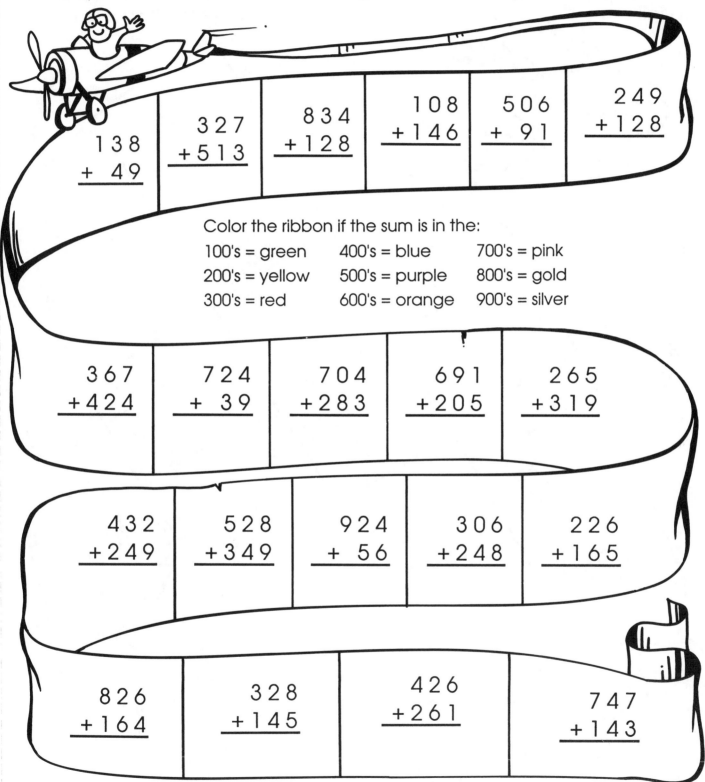

$$138 + 49$$

$$327 + 513$$

$$834 + 128$$

$$108 + 146$$

$$506 + 91$$

$$249 + 128$$

Color the ribbon if the sum is in the:

100's = green	400's = blue	700's = pink
200's = yellow	500's = purple	800's = gold
300's = red	600's = orange	900's = silver

$$367 + 424$$

$$724 + 39$$

$$704 + 283$$

$$691 + 205$$

$$265 + 319$$

$$432 + 249$$

$$528 + 349$$

$$924 + 56$$

$$306 + 248$$

$$226 + 165$$

$$826 + 164$$

$$328 + 145$$

$$426 + 261$$

$$747 + 143$$

MATH

Name _____

Space Shuttle Addition

Experience addition in space as the payload specialist under zero gravity conditions.

$$\begin{array}{r} 371 \\ +439 \\ \hline \end{array}$$

$$\begin{array}{r} 629 \\ +184 \\ \hline \end{array}$$

$$\begin{array}{r} 264 \\ +483 \\ \hline \end{array}$$

$$\begin{array}{r} 146 \\ +587 \\ \hline \end{array}$$

$$\begin{array}{r} 438 \\ +290 \\ \hline \end{array}$$

$$\begin{array}{r} 362 \\ +459 \\ \hline \end{array}$$

$$\begin{array}{r} 347 \\ +328 \\ \hline \end{array}$$

$$\begin{array}{r} 528 \\ +391 \\ \hline \end{array}$$

$$\begin{array}{r} 327 \\ +649 \\ \hline \end{array}$$

$$\begin{array}{r} 382 \\ +249 \\ \hline \end{array}$$

$$\begin{array}{r} 283 \\ +346 \\ \hline \end{array}$$

$$\begin{array}{r} 465 \\ +193 \\ \hline \end{array}$$

$$\begin{array}{r} 409 \\ +292 \\ \hline \end{array}$$

$$\begin{array}{r} 566 \\ +283 \\ \hline \end{array}$$

$$\begin{array}{r} 423 \\ +392 \\ \hline \end{array}$$

$$\begin{array}{r} 283 \\ +519 \\ \hline \end{array}$$

$$\begin{array}{r} 625 \\ +246 \\ \hline \end{array}$$

$$\begin{array}{r} 498 \\ +123 \\ \hline \end{array}$$

Name _____

Let's Climb to the Top!

328
+449

409
+736

921
+ 87

562
+614

824
+597

246
+492

982
+220

207
+913

621
+489

547
+782

462
+781

826
+ 95

284
+493

429
+636

506
+214

200
+489

684
+519

623
+192

536
+184

425
+594

Picnic Problems

Name _____

Help the ant find a path to the picnic. Work the problems. Shade the box if an answer has a 9 in it.

836 + 90	536 +248	952 + 8	362 + 47	486 +293	368 +529
789 526 +214	2846 +6478	932 +365	374 +299	835 +552	956 874 + 65
4768 +2894	38 456 +3894	4507 +2743	404 +289	1843 +6752	4367 +3571
639 + 77	587 342 +679	5379 1865 +2348	450 +145	594 +278	459 +367
29 875 +2341	387 29 +5614	462 379 +248			

Name _____

Bubble Math

Add the problems inside these bubbles.

```
  5642        4629        2647        3426        3690
 +1819       +1258       +3281       +2841       +2434
 -----       -----       -----       -----       -----
```

```
  4625                    6241        5942        5642
 +1817        6843       +2363       +1829       +2919
 -----       +2391       -----       -----       -----
             -----
```

```
                                                      2643
  2648        4826        2641        8465       7205 +7427
 +1923       +2098       +6259       +1386      +1839 -----
 -----       -----       -----       -----      -----
```

```
  5246        4265
 +3187       +3827
 -----       -----
```

```
  9124        3142
 +1348       +2639
 -----       -----
```

These bubbles all popped in order
from least to greatest. Number from
1 to 20 the order in which they
popped starting with the smallest sum.

Name _____

Yummy Additions

Add ones. Regroup.	Add tens. Regroup.	Add hundreds. Regroup.	Add thousands. Regroup.
7465 + 4978 3	7465 + 4978 43	7465 + 4978 443	7465 + 4978 12443

Do the problems. Color an answer containing a **3**–brown, **4**–red, **5**–yellow.

6591
+ 5569

6843
+ 7568

9224
+ 7878

2549
+ 9577

9853
+ 8798

2698
+ 8499

3849
+ 7261

6456
+ 4948

7767
+ 9899

8796
+ 8975

9764
+ 7459

5678
+ 6984

9653
+ 1568

Name _____

Mountaintop Getaway

Work all problems. Find a path to the cabin by
shading in all answers that have a 3 in them.

		98 − 52	46 − 12	68 − 17
	79 − 53	65 − 23	63 − 31	86 − 32
59 − 45	75 − 64	67 − 24	97 − 54	55 − 43
87 − 65	44 − 32	57 − 24	88 − 25	75 − 61	48 − 26
69 − 25	95 − 24	48 − 13	58 − 16	35 − 13	39 − 17

SECRET PATHS

MATH

Daily Learning Drills Grade 3

Name _____

Hats, Hats, Hats

Calculate the difference in each hat below.

736
−629

466
−327

837
−529

742
−428

784
−565

673
−458

648
−426

982
−665

947
−729

543
−426

928
−619

847
−628

427
−318

524
−318

245
−126

852
−328

545
−221

Name _____

Soaring to the Stars

Connect the dots to form two stars. Begin one star with the subtraction problem whose difference is 100 and end with the problem whose difference is 109. Begin the other with 110 and end with 120. Color the pictures.

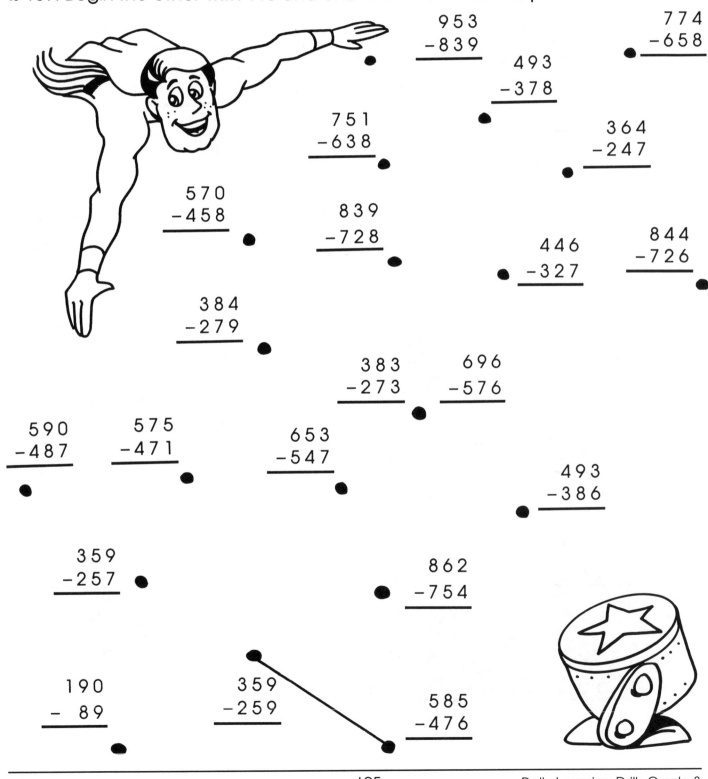

$$953 - 839$$

$$774 - 658$$

$$493 - 378$$

$$364 - 247$$

$$751 - 638$$

$$570 - 458$$

$$839 - 728$$

$$446 - 327$$

$$844 - 726$$

$$384 - 279$$

$$383 - 273$$

$$696 - 576$$

$$590 - 487$$

$$575 - 471$$

$$653 - 547$$

$$493 - 386$$

$$359 - 257$$

$$862 - 754$$

$$190 - 89$$

$$359 - 259$$

$$585 - 476$$

Daily Learning Drills Grade 3

Name _____

Dino-Might

Whenever you're using "kid transportation," what is the best thing to do? To find out, work the problems. Then write the letters on the matching blanks.

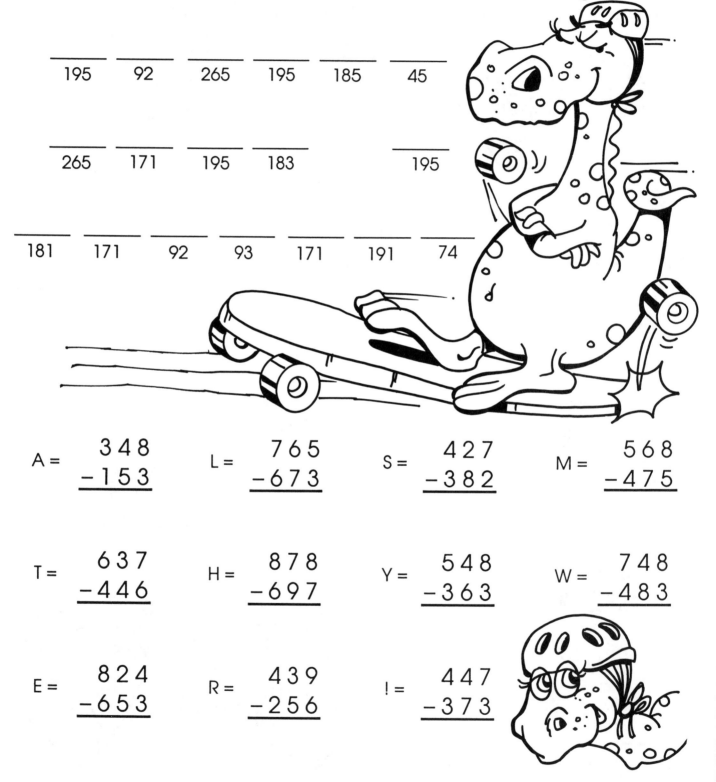

195	92	265	195	185	45

265	171	195	183	195

181	171	92	93	171	191	74

A = 348 − 153

L = 765 − 673

S = 427 − 382

M = 568 − 475

T = 637 − 446

H = 878 − 697

Y = 548 − 363

W = 748 − 483

E = 824 − 653

R = 439 − 256

! = 447 − 373

Name _____

Find the Hidden Instrument

Solve each problem. Color each shape according to the key below.

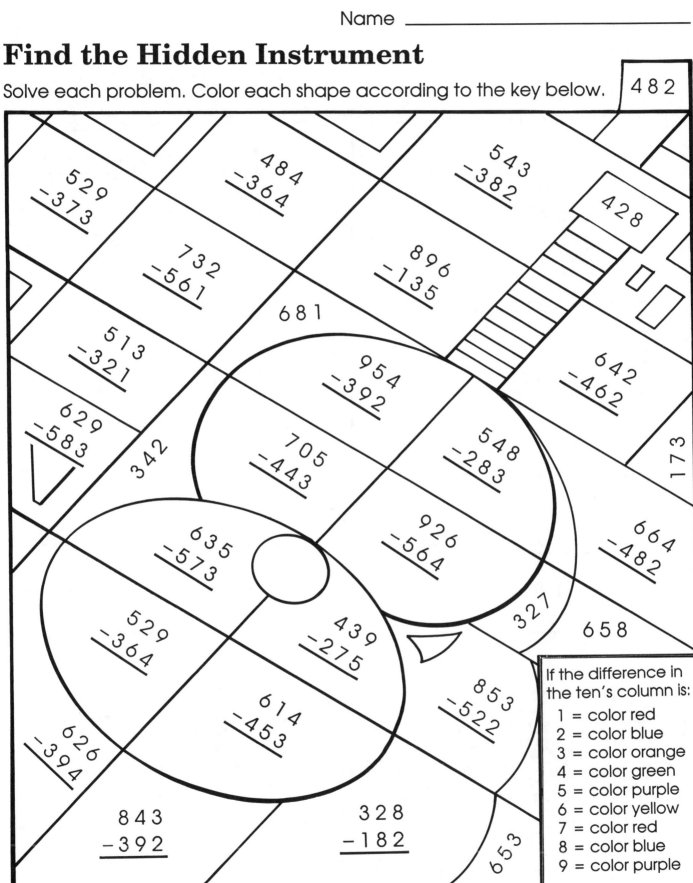

482

$$529 - 373$$

$$484 - 364$$

$$543 - 382$$

428

$$732 - 561$$

$$896 - 135$$

681

$$513 - 321$$

$$642 - 462$$

$$629 - 583$$

342

$$954 - 392$$

173

$$705 - 443$$

$$548 - 283$$

$$635 - 573$$

$$926 - 564$$

$$529 - 364$$

$$439 - 275$$

327

658

$$626 - 394$$

$$614 - 453$$

$$853 - 522$$

$$843 - 392$$

$$328 - 182$$

653

If the difference in the ten's column is:

1 = color red
2 = color blue
3 = color orange
4 = color green
5 = color purple
6 = color yellow
7 = color red
8 = color blue
9 = color purple

Name _____

Sailing Through Subtraction

Start at the bottom and work your way up the sails.

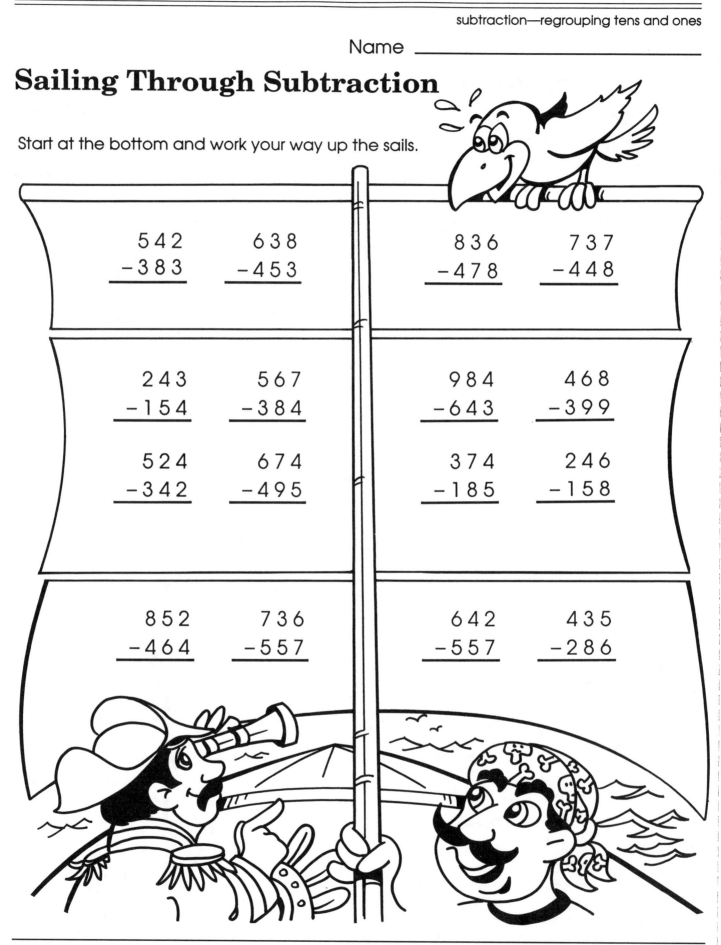

$$542 - 383$$
$$638 - 453$$
$$836 - 478$$
$$737 - 448$$

$$243 - 154$$
$$567 - 384$$
$$984 - 643$$
$$468 - 399$$

$$524 - 342$$
$$674 - 495$$
$$374 - 185$$
$$246 - 158$$

$$852 - 464$$
$$736 - 557$$
$$642 - 557$$
$$435 - 286$$

Name _____

Gobble, Gobble

If answer has a **3** in it, color it orange, **4**–red, **5**–purple, **6**–brown,
7–yellow, **8**–blue and **9**–green.

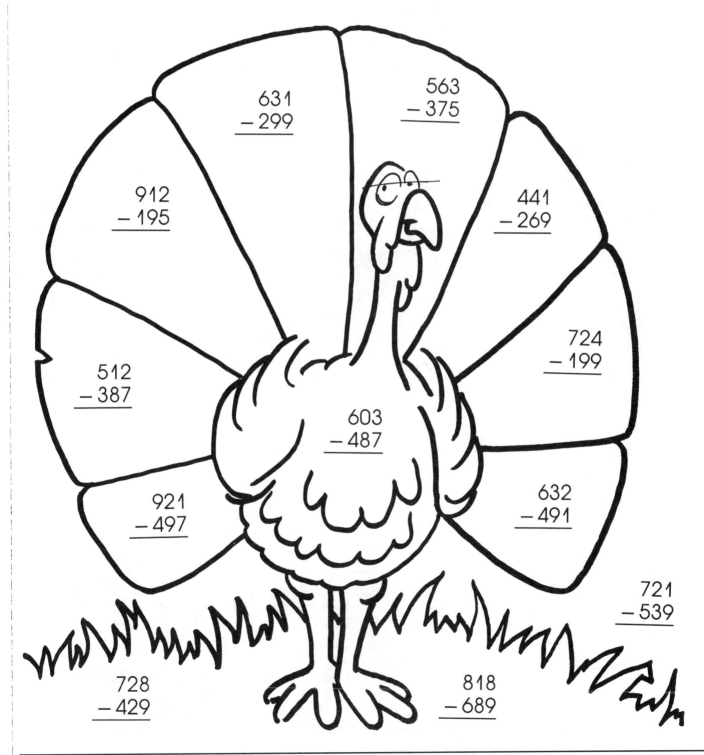

Name _____

Round and Round She Goes . . .

Take a ride around this Ferris wheel.

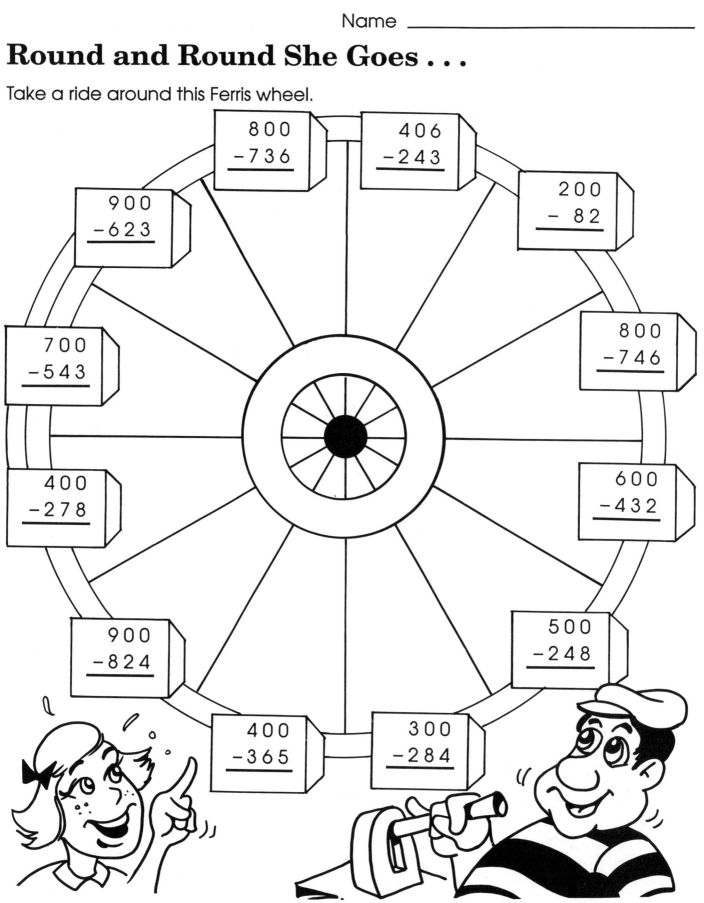

Name _____

Kite Craze!

These subtraction problems are flying high.

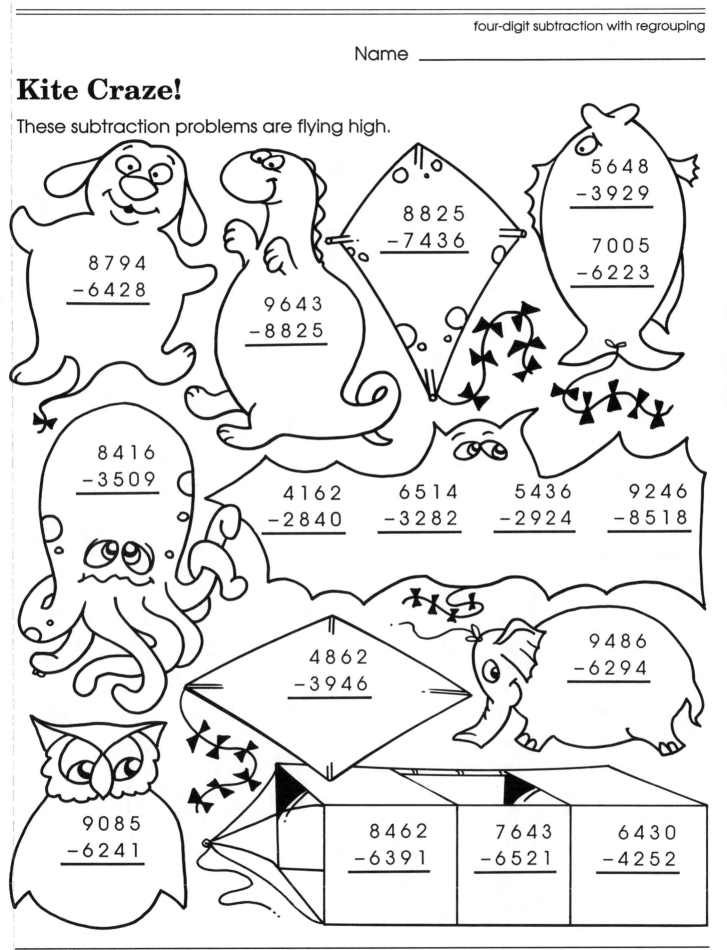

$$8794 - 6428$$

$$9643 - 8825$$

$$8825 - 7436$$

$$5648 - 3929$$

$$7005 - 6223$$

$$8416 - 3509$$

$$4162 - 2840$$

$$6514 - 3282$$

$$5436 - 2924$$

$$9246 - 8518$$

$$4862 - 3946$$

$$9486 - 6294$$

$$9085 - 6241$$

$$8462 - 6391$$

$$7643 - 6521$$

$$6430 - 4252$$

MATH

Name _____

Subtraction on Stage!

These subtraction problems are heading west. Solve 'em. It'll be a bouncy ride.
Just hold on!

$$5648 - 2425$$

$$2148 - 825$$

$$7641 - 5246$$

$$7648 - 3289$$

$$5408 - 1291$$

$$8209 - 4182$$

$$8419 - 2182$$

$$6249 - 1526$$

$$6428 - 4159$$

$$4287 - 2492$$

$$7645 - 2826$$

$$2016 - 1021$$

$$8247 - 6459$$

$$9047 - 6152$$

$$5231 - 1642$$

$$7689 - 2845$$

Name _____

Subtraction Search

Work each problem. Find the answer in the chart and circle it. Answers are in a straight line, but may go in any direction.

2	1	6	3	2	7	5
6	3	3	2	1	0	8
2	2	1	6	3	3	4
0	2	2	6	5	0	6
8	5	4	2	0	8	7
8	9	0	6	1	5	6
3	2	8	4	4	2	1
8	3	4	8	8	5	0
8	1	9	8	7	2	9
3	4	5	8	5	6	7
8	1	3	7	0	4	2
9	3	2	1	7	0	2

$$6003 - 2737$$ $$5040 - 3338$$ $$9000 - 5725$$

$$7200 - 4356$$ $$3406 - 1298$$ $$5602 - 3138$$

$$7006 - 5429$$ $$3006 - 2798$$ $$3605 - 2718$$

$$5904 - 3917$$ $$5039 - 1954$$ $$8704 - 2496$$ $$4081 - 3594$$ $$6508 - 399$$ $$5039 - 2467$$

$$9006 - 575$$ $$5001 - 2351$$ $$8002 - 5686$$ $$6058 - 2175$$ $$9504 - 7368$$ $$7290 - 1801$$

Name _____

Dial Carefully

Add or subtract. Write each answer in the puzzle.

Across

1. 413 + 312 = _____
3. 102 + 415 = _____
4. 223 + 103 = _____
6. 131 + 253 = _____
8. 324 + 321 = _____
10. 207 + 222 = _____
12. 105 + 214 = _____
14. 315 + 400 = _____
16. 121 + 503 = _____
18. 451 + 421 = _____
20. 312 + 281 = _____

Down

1. 859 – 112 = _____
2. 985 – 402 = _____
3. 887 – 344 = _____
5. 789 – 583 = _____
7. 699 – 240 = _____
9. 589 – 100 = _____
11. 767 – 512 = _____
13. 497 – 321 = _____
15. 259 – 151 = _____
17. 974 – 511 = _____
19. 689 – 450 = _____
20. 797 – 236 = _____

Name _____

Wormy Apples

$2 \times 0 = 0$ $4 \times 1 = 4$

$1 \times 0 =$ _____ $6 \times 1 =$ _____

$5 \times 0 =$ _____ $7 \times 1 =$ _____

$3 \times 0 =$ _____ $5 \times 1 =$ _____

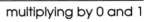

$$\begin{array}{r} 2 \\ \times 1 \\ \hline \end{array} \qquad \begin{array}{r} 0 \\ \times 3 \\ \hline \end{array} \qquad \begin{array}{r} 1 \\ \times 9 \\ \hline \end{array} \qquad \begin{array}{r} 0 \\ \times 4 \\ \hline \end{array} \qquad \begin{array}{r} 5 \\ \times 0 \\ \hline \end{array}$$

$$\begin{array}{r} 0 \\ \times 9 \\ \hline \end{array} \qquad \begin{array}{r} 1 \\ \times 1 \\ \hline \end{array} \qquad \begin{array}{r} 8 \\ \times 1 \\ \hline \end{array} \qquad \begin{array}{r} 6 \\ \times 0 \\ \hline \end{array} \qquad \begin{array}{r} 8 \\ \times 0 \\ \hline \end{array}$$

$$\begin{array}{r} 7 \\ \times 1 \\ \hline \end{array} \qquad \begin{array}{r} 2 \\ \times 0 \\ \hline \end{array} \qquad \begin{array}{r} 1 \\ \times 6 \\ \hline \end{array} \qquad \begin{array}{r} 0 \\ \times 5 \\ \hline \end{array} \qquad \begin{array}{r} 1 \\ \times 5 \\ \hline \end{array}$$

$$\begin{array}{r} 3 \\ \times 1 \\ \hline \end{array} \qquad \begin{array}{r} 0 \\ \times 9 \\ \hline \end{array} \qquad \begin{array}{r} 1 \\ \times 2 \\ \hline \end{array} \qquad \begin{array}{r} 7 \\ \times 0 \\ \hline \end{array} \qquad \begin{array}{r} 3 \\ \times 0 \\ \hline \end{array}$$

Name _____

Factor Fun

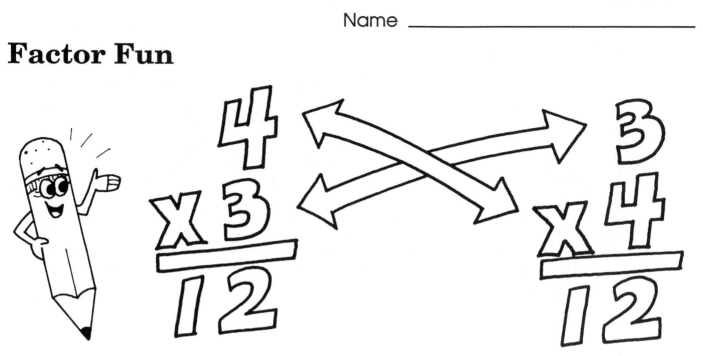

If you change the order of the factors, you have the same product.

7 ×3	3 ×7	6 ×5	5 ×6	2 ×3	3 ×2

4×6= _____   2×9= _____   8×4= _____

6×4= _____   9×2= _____   4×8= _____

7 ×2	2 ×7	3 ×6	6 ×3	9 ×4	4 ×9

8×3= _____   5×2= _____   9×3= _____

3×8= _____   2×5= _____   3×9= _____

Name _____

The Aliens Are Coming!

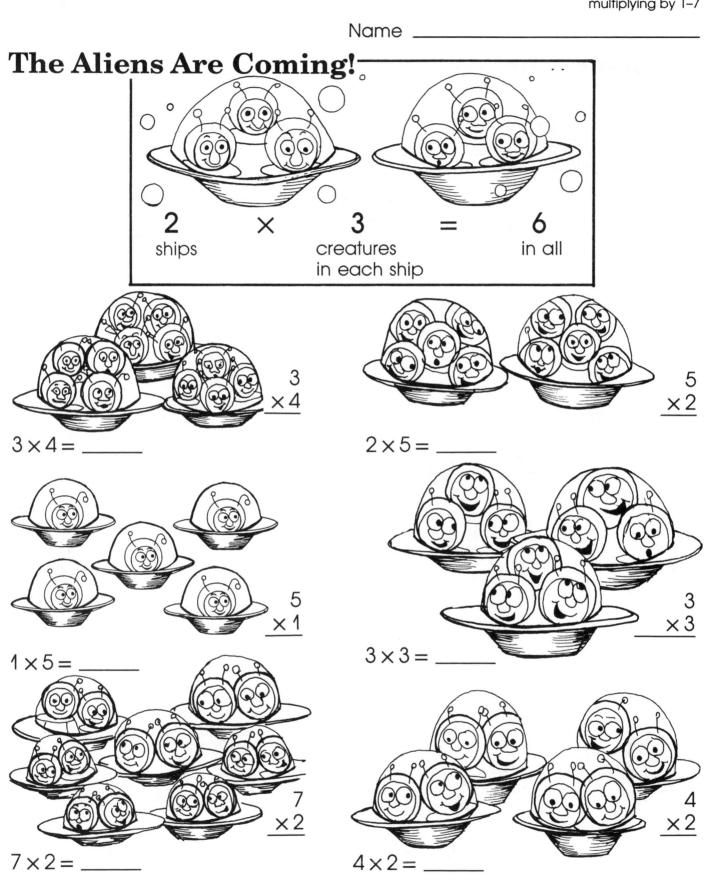

2	×	3	=	6
ships		creatures in each ship		in all

$3 \times 4 =$ _____

$\begin{array}{r} 3 \\ \times\, 4 \\ \hline \end{array}$

$2 \times 5 =$ _____

$\begin{array}{r} 5 \\ \times\, 2 \\ \hline \end{array}$

$1 \times 5 =$ _____

$\begin{array}{r} 5 \\ \times\, 1 \\ \hline \end{array}$

$3 \times 3 =$ _____

$\begin{array}{r} 3 \\ \times\, 3 \\ \hline \end{array}$

$7 \times 2 =$ _____

$\begin{array}{r} 7 \\ \times\, 2 \\ \hline \end{array}$

$4 \times 2 =$ _____

$\begin{array}{r} 4 \\ \times\, 2 \\ \hline \end{array}$

MATH

Name _____

Racing to the Finish

WINNER

3×5

$\begin{array}{r} 5 \\ \times 3 \\ \hline \end{array}$
$\begin{array}{r} 2 \\ \times 8 \\ \hline \end{array}$
$\begin{array}{r} 4 \\ \times 6 \\ \hline \end{array}$
$\begin{array}{r} 9 \\ \times 3 \\ \hline \end{array}$

$\begin{array}{r} 7 \\ \times 5 \\ \hline \end{array}$
$\begin{array}{r} 3 \\ \times 9 \\ \hline \end{array}$
$\begin{array}{r} 4 \\ \times 2 \\ \hline \end{array}$
$\begin{array}{r} 6 \\ \times 2 \\ \hline \end{array}$
$\begin{array}{r} 4 \\ \times 4 \\ \hline \end{array}$
$\begin{array}{r} 0 \\ \times 6 \\ \hline \end{array}$

$\begin{array}{r} 3 \\ \times 2 \\ \hline \end{array}$
$\begin{array}{r} 7 \\ \times 2 \\ \hline \end{array}$
$\begin{array}{r} 6 \\ \times 5 \\ \hline \end{array}$
$\begin{array}{r} 3 \\ \times 4 \\ \hline \end{array}$
$\begin{array}{r} 8 \\ \times 3 \\ \hline \end{array}$
$\begin{array}{r} 4 \\ \times 5 \\ \hline \end{array}$

$\begin{array}{r} 5 \\ \times 2 \\ \hline \end{array}$
$\begin{array}{r} 7 \\ \times 4 \\ \hline \end{array}$
$\begin{array}{r} 6 \\ \times 3 \\ \hline \end{array}$
$\begin{array}{r} 4 \\ \times 8 \\ \hline \end{array}$
$\begin{array}{r} 2 \\ \times 2 \\ \hline \end{array}$
$\begin{array}{r} 8 \\ \times 5 \\ \hline \end{array}$

$\begin{array}{r} 3 \\ \times 7 \\ \hline \end{array}$
$\begin{array}{r} 5 \\ \times 5 \\ \hline \end{array}$
$\begin{array}{r} 5 \\ \times 9 \\ \hline \end{array}$
$\begin{array}{r} 9 \\ \times 2 \\ \hline \end{array}$
$\begin{array}{r} 4 \\ \times 6 \\ \hline \end{array}$
$\begin{array}{r} 9 \\ \times 4 \\ \hline \end{array}$

Name _____

Climbing Granite Boulders!

Start at the bottom of each boulder and work the problems up to the top!

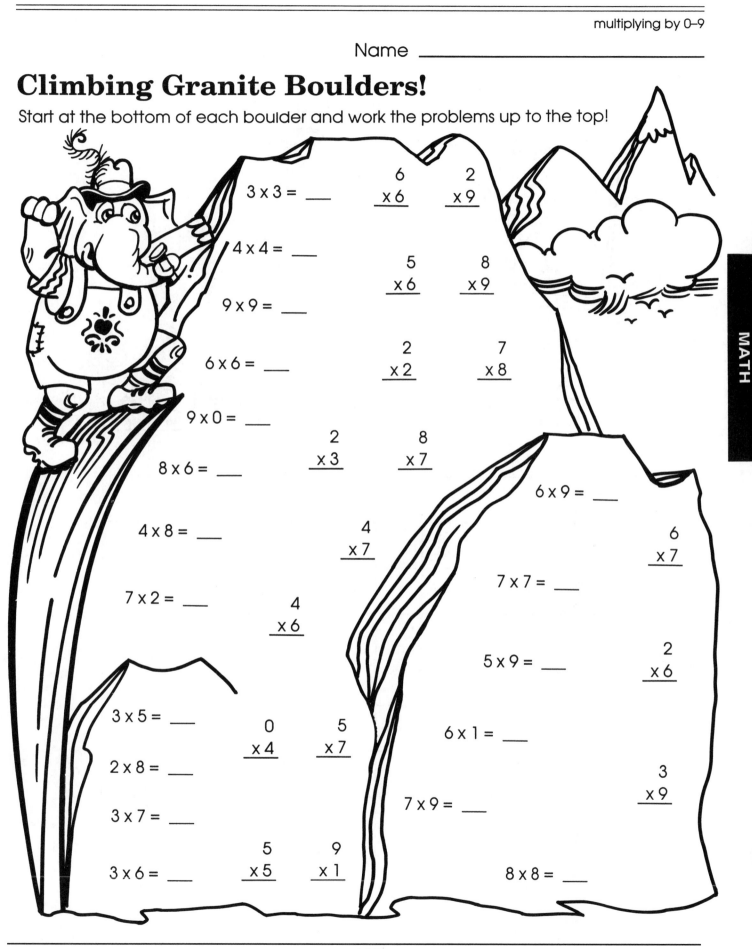

3 x 3 = ___

$\begin{array}{r} 6 \\ \times 6 \\ \hline \end{array}$ $\begin{array}{r} 2 \\ \times 9 \\ \hline \end{array}$

4 x 4 = ___

$\begin{array}{r} 5 \\ \times 6 \\ \hline \end{array}$ $\begin{array}{r} 8 \\ \times 9 \\ \hline \end{array}$

9 x 9 = ___

$\begin{array}{r} 2 \\ \times 2 \\ \hline \end{array}$ $\begin{array}{r} 7 \\ \times 8 \\ \hline \end{array}$

6 x 6 = ___

9 x 0 = ___

$\begin{array}{r} 2 \\ \times 3 \\ \hline \end{array}$ $\begin{array}{r} 8 \\ \times 7 \\ \hline \end{array}$

8 x 6 = ___

6 x 9 = ___

4 x 8 = ___

$\begin{array}{r} 4 \\ \times 7 \\ \hline \end{array}$

$\begin{array}{r} 6 \\ \times 7 \\ \hline \end{array}$

7 x 7 = ___

7 x 2 = ___

$\begin{array}{r} 4 \\ \times 6 \\ \hline \end{array}$

5 x 9 = ___

$\begin{array}{r} 2 \\ \times 6 \\ \hline \end{array}$

3 x 5 = ___

$\begin{array}{r} 0 \\ \times 4 \\ \hline \end{array}$ $\begin{array}{r} 5 \\ \times 7 \\ \hline \end{array}$

6 x 1 = ___

2 x 8 = ___

3 x 9 (written as $\begin{array}{r} 3 \\ \times 9 \\ \hline \end{array}$)

3 x 7 = ___

7 x 9 = ___

$\begin{array}{r} 5 \\ \times 5 \\ \hline \end{array}$ $\begin{array}{r} 9 \\ \times 1 \\ \hline \end{array}$

3 x 6 = ___

8 x 8 = ___

Daily Learning Drills Grade 3

MATH

Name _____

Time to Multiply

Finish table. Can you do it in less than 3 minutes?

X	0	1	2	3	4	5	6	7	8	9
0	0									
1										
2			4							
3										
4										
5						25				
6										
7										
8										
9										

Name _____

Double Trouble

Solve each multiplication problem. Below each answer, write the letter from the code that matches. Read the coded question and write the answer in the space provided.

1	4	9	16	25	36	49	64	81	100	121	144
e	g	h	i	n	o	s	t	u	w	x	y

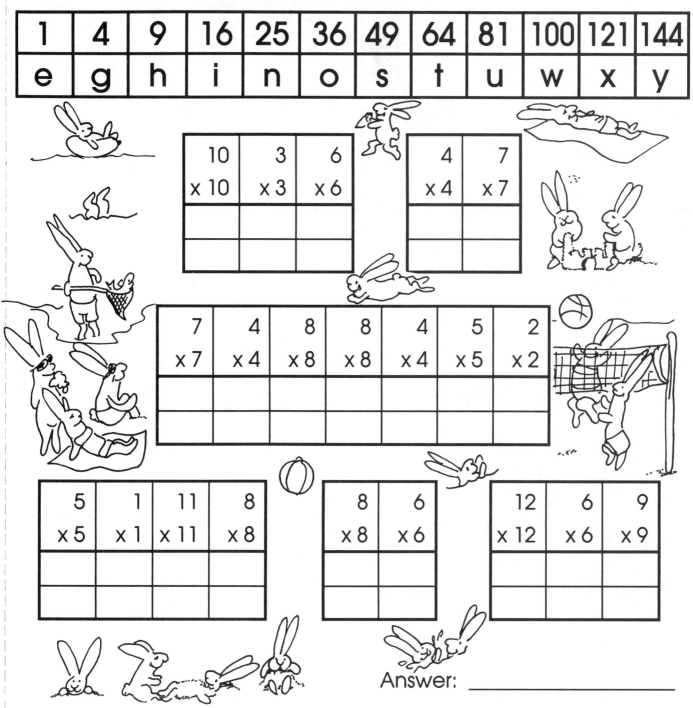

10	3	6
x 10	x 3	x 6

4	7
x 4	x 7

7	4	8	8	4	5	2
x 7	x 4	x 8	x 8	x 4	x 5	x 2

5	1	11	8
x 5	x 1	x 11	x 8

8	6
x 8	x 6

12	6	9
x 12	x 6	x 9

Answer: _____

Name _____

Count the Legs!

Multiply to find the number of legs. Write the problem twice.

1.

_____ horses x _____ legs = _____

_____ x _____ = _____

2.

_____ flamingos x _____ legs = _____

_____ x _____ = _____

3.

_____ insects x _____ legs = _____

_____ x _____ = _____

4.

_____ stools x _____ legs = _____

_____ x _____ = _____

5.

_____ cows x _____ legs = _____

_____ x _____ = _____

6.

_____ birds x _____ legs = _____

_____ x _____ = _____

Name _____

Beam Me Up!

Complete the products before the beam hits Earth!

11
x 4

92
x 1

22
x 3

23
x 3

43
x 2

58
x 1

34
x 2

31
x 3

21
x 4

10
x 5

44
x 2

11
x 6

22
x 4

89
x 1

11
x 8

32
x 3

42
x 2

57
x 1

11
x 5

78
x 1

11
x 9

22
x 4

64
x 1

10
x 7

23
x 2

33
x 2

33
x 3

10
x 4

11
x 5

21
x 3

22
x 3

24
x 2

41
x 2

49
x 1

10
x 9

12
x 4

87
x 1

MATH

Name _____

The Caped Cow

Multiply.

12 x 9	22 x 8	32 x 5	19 x 9	22 x 7	33 x 4	27 x 2
14 x 6	38 x 2	25 x 3	15 x 4	16 x 5	28 x 3	18 x 5
14 x 7	13 x 5	24 x 4	13 x 6	29 x 2	17 x 4	36 x 2
29 x 3	14 x 5	18 x 4	19 x 3	28 x 2	17 x 5	19 x 4
37 x 2	27 x 3	12 x 8	26 x 3	35 x 5	48 x 2	27 x 4

Name _____

Bows, Bows, Bows

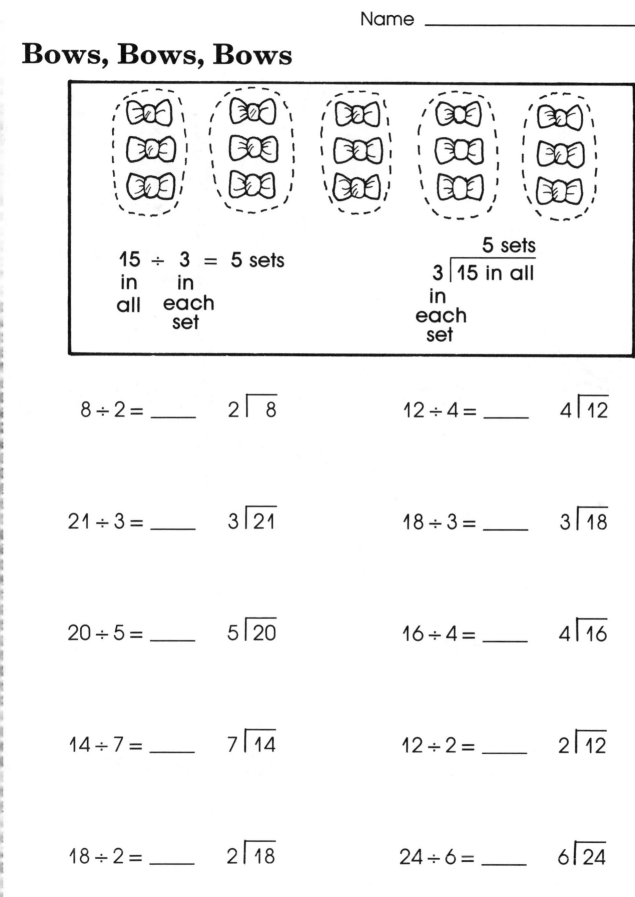

$15 \div 3 = 5$ sets
in   in
all each
     set

$$\begin{array}{r} 5 \text{ sets} \\ 3\overline{\smash{\big)}\,15 \text{ in all}} \end{array}$$
in
each
set

$8 \div 2 =$ _____ $2\overline{\smash{\big)}\,8}$ $12 \div 4 =$ _____ $4\overline{\smash{\big)}\,12}$

$21 \div 3 =$ _____ $3\overline{\smash{\big)}\,21}$ $18 \div 3 =$ _____ $3\overline{\smash{\big)}\,18}$

$20 \div 5 =$ _____ $5\overline{\smash{\big)}\,20}$ $16 \div 4 =$ _____ $4\overline{\smash{\big)}\,16}$

$14 \div 7 =$ _____ $7\overline{\smash{\big)}\,14}$ $12 \div 2 =$ _____ $2\overline{\smash{\big)}\,12}$

$18 \div 2 =$ _____ $2\overline{\smash{\big)}\,18}$ $24 \div 6 =$ _____ $6\overline{\smash{\big)}\,24}$

MATH

Name _____

Blastoff!

$1\overline{)6}$

$20\overline{)0}$

$2\overline{)12}$ $2\overline{)14}$ $2\overline{)16}$ $9\overline{)0}$

$8\overline{)0}$ $2\overline{)8}$ $15\overline{)0}$ $1\overline{)19}$

$2\overline{)18}$ $7\overline{)0}$ $2\overline{)10}$ $1\overline{)35}$

$1\overline{)23}$ $1\overline{)17}$ $1\overline{)7}$ $2\overline{)4}$

$12\overline{)0}$ $2\overline{)6}$ $1\overline{)11}$ $1\overline{)5}$

Name _____

Bubble Math!

The order in which you solve each problem is the same order in which the bubbles will pop!

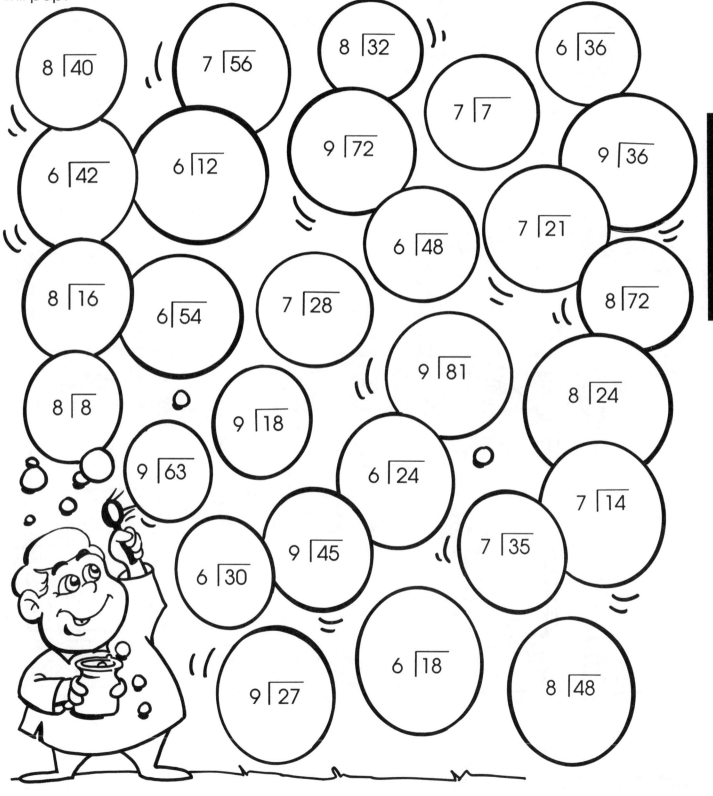

Name _____

Carrier Math Messengers

$3\overline{)12}$ $8\overline{)48}$

$5\overline{)25}$ $9\overline{)72}$ $6\overline{)42}$ $8\overline{)40}$ $2\overline{)4}$

$7\overline{)56}$ $9\overline{)63}$ $9\overline{)45}$ $7\overline{)7}$ $3\overline{)15}$

$2\overline{)8}$ $7\overline{)63}$ $2\overline{)18}$ $4\overline{)24}$ $3\overline{)24}$

$6\overline{)30}$ $9\overline{)54}$ $9\overline{)81}$ $7\overline{)28}$ $4\overline{)32}$

Name _____

Jersey Division

Arrange jersey digits in the balls to get correct answer.

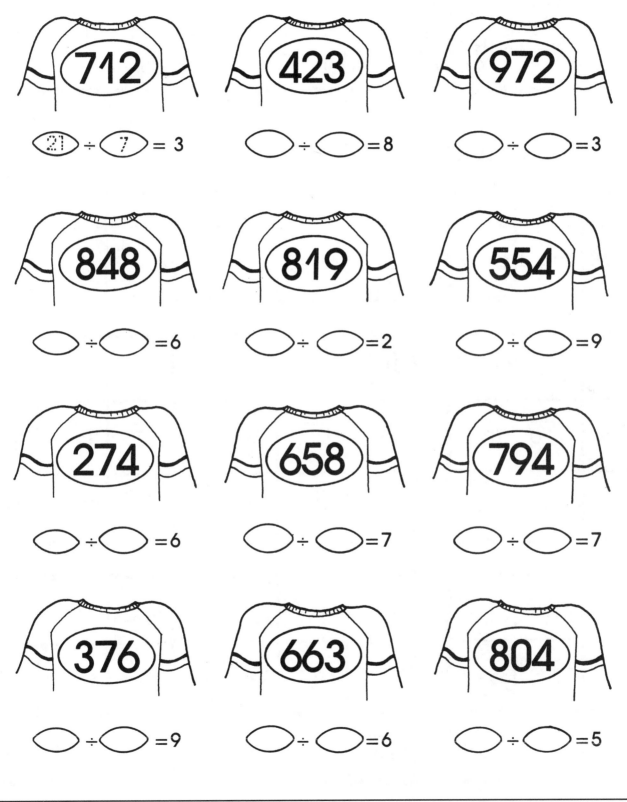

Daily Learning Drills Grade 3

Name _____

Division Tic-Tac-Toe

9, 7, 5, 3 = X

8, 6, 4, 2 = O

X on odd answers   O on even answers

$4\overline{)36}$	$4\overline{)24}$	$10 \div 5$
$5\overline{)40}$	$32 \div 4$	$25 \div 5$
$35 \div 5$	$20 \div 4$	$12 \div 4$

$4\overline{)32}$	$12 \div 4$	$5\overline{)30}$
$4\overline{)28}$	$4\overline{)20}$	$20 \div 4$
$20 \div 5$	$10 \div 5$	$15 \div 5$

$24 \div 4$	$5\overline{)45}$	$28 \div 4$
$5\overline{)45}$	$5\overline{)20}$	$8 \div 4$
$4\overline{)16}$	$5\overline{)15}$	$30 \div 5$

$25 \div 5$	$4\overline{)8}$	$16 \div 4$
$32 \div 4$	$5\overline{)20}$	$5\overline{)35}$
$40 \div 5$	$4\overline{)12}$	$15 \div 5$

$5\overline{)10}$	$4\overline{)8}$	$24 \div 4$
$4\overline{)36}$	$5\overline{)35}$	$4\overline{)32}$
$45 \div 5$	$5\overline{)30}$	$4\overline{)12}$

$8 \div 4$	$45 \div 5$	$4\overline{)16}$
$5\overline{)25}$	$36 \div 4$	$4\overline{)24}$
$5\overline{)10}$	$25 \div 5$	$4\overline{)36}$

$4\overline{)12}$	$5\overline{)10}$	$5\overline{)45}$
$30 \div 5$	$5\overline{)25}$	$35 \div 5$
$4\overline{)32}$	$8 \div 4$	$5\overline{)20}$

$36 \div 4$	$4\overline{)28}$	$16 \div 4$
$24 \div 4$	$5\overline{)35}$	$5\overline{)40}$
$5\overline{)25}$	$8 \div 4$	$36 \div 4$

$28 \div 4$	$5\overline{)30}$	$45 \div 5$
$16 \div 4$	$32 \div 4$	$15 \div 5$
$4\overline{)20}$	$4\overline{)12}$	$4\overline{)8}$

Name _____

Mr. R Means Business

Use me when a problem doesn't come out even.

$$
\begin{array}{r}
6 \text{ NO REMAINDER} \\
4\overline{)22}
\end{array}
$$

$$
\begin{array}{r}
5\,R\,2 \\
4\overline{)22} \\
-20 \\
\hline
2 \text{ REMAINDER}
\end{array}
$$

MATH

$5\overline{)28}$ 5 R

$4\overline{)19}$ 4 R

$8\overline{)26}$ 3 R

$7\overline{)45}$ 6 R

$3\overline{)26}$ R

$2\overline{)19}$ R

$6\overline{)51}$ R

$9\overline{)65}$ R

$8\overline{)43}$ R

$9\overline{)59}$ R

$7\overline{)33}$ R

$4\overline{)27}$ R

Name _____

Make It Fair

Circle the items and then write two division problems to go with each picture.

There are six children. Circle the number of cookies each child will get if the cookies are divided equally.

_____   _____

There are eight dogs. Circle the dog biscuits each dog will get if the dog biscuits are divided equally.

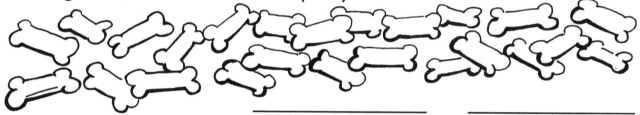

_____   _____

Divide the pepperoni so that five pizzas will have the same amount.

_____   _____

Separate the books so that there will be the same number of books on three shelves.

_____   _____

On the back of this page, draw pictures of your own and write division sentences to go with them.

Name _____

Hmm, What Should I Do?

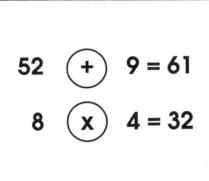

$$52 \; \bigoplus \; 9 = 61$$

$$8 \; \bigotimes \; 4 = 32$$

Write the correct symbols in the circles.

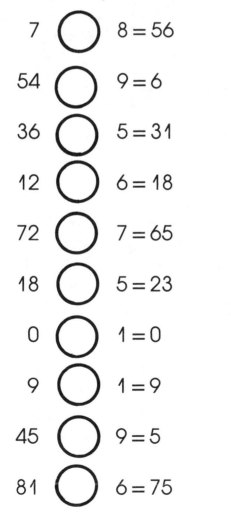

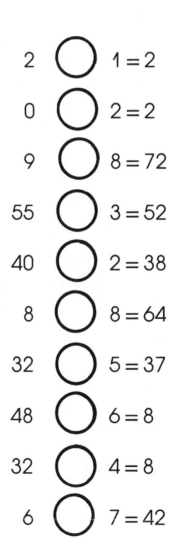

7 ◯ 8 = 56

54 ◯ 9 = 6

36 ◯ 5 = 31

12 ◯ 6 = 18

72 ◯ 7 = 65

18 ◯ 5 = 23

0 ◯ 1 = 0

9 ◯ 1 = 9

45 ◯ 9 = 5

81 ◯ 6 = 75

2 ◯ 1 = 2

0 ◯ 2 = 2

9 ◯ 8 = 72

55 ◯ 3 = 52

40 ◯ 2 = 38

8 ◯ 8 = 64

32 ◯ 5 = 37

48 ◯ 6 = 8

32 ◯ 4 = 8

6 ◯ 7 = 42

Daily Learning Drills Grade 3

Name _____

Easy Street

Easy does it! What is each house worth?
Count the money in each house on Easy
Street. Write the amount on the line.

Example

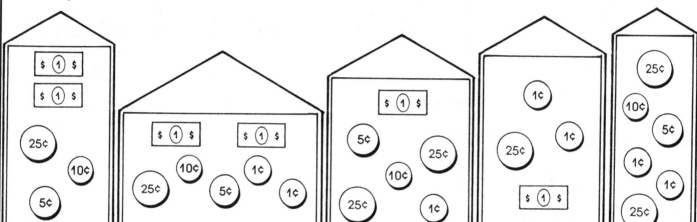

$2.40   _____   _____   _____   _____

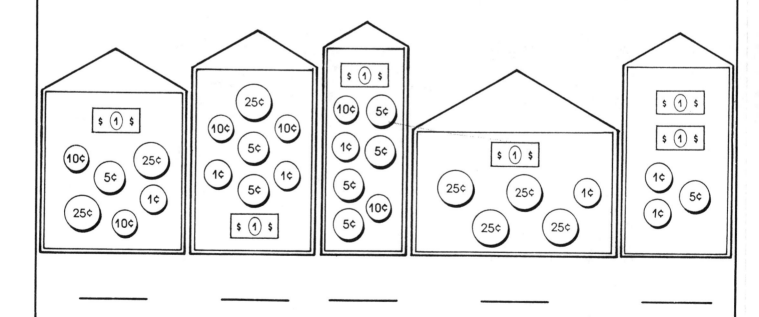

_____   _____   _____   _____   _____

Name _____

Your Answer's Safe with Me

Find the right "combination" to open each safe. Draw the bills and coins needed to make each amount.

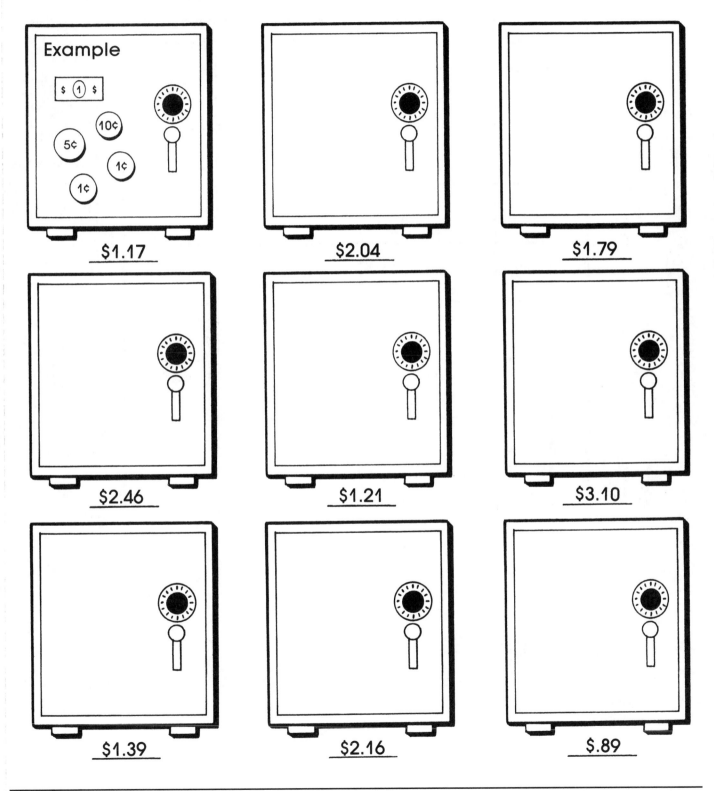

Example		
$1.17	$2.04	$1.79
$2.46	$1.21	$3.10
$1.39	$2.16	$.89

Name _____

A Collection of Coins

Figure out which coins are needed to make the given amount.

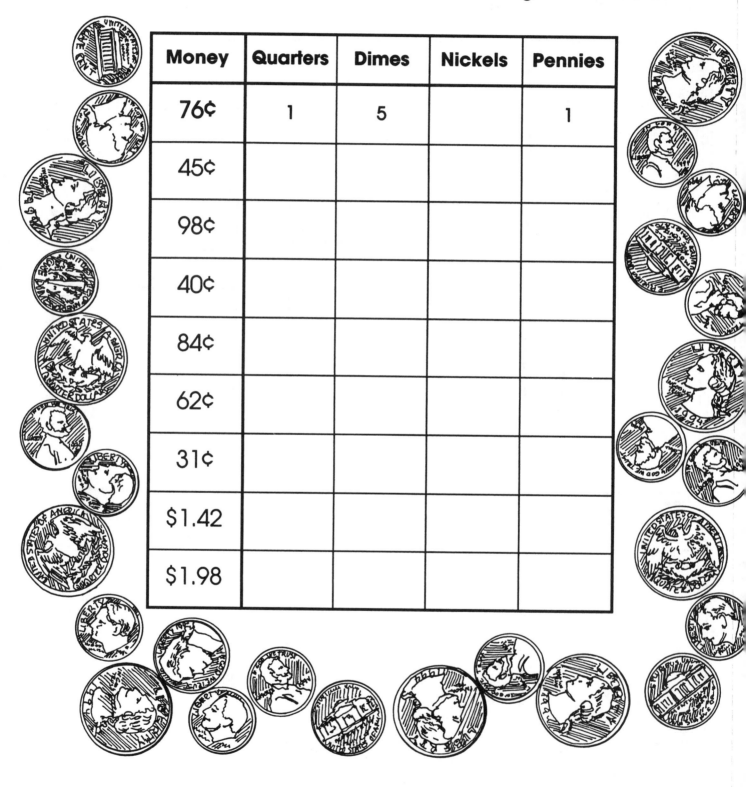

Money	Quarters	Dimes	Nickels	Pennies
76¢	1	5		1
45¢				
98¢				
40¢				
84¢				
62¢				
31¢				
$1.42				
$1.98				

Name _____

Pizza "Dough" Business

The number of pieces tells you how many coins to use. Write in the amounts to equal the total price of these pizzas.

Example

$.25
$.25
$.25
$.10
total price **$.85**

total price **$1.81**

total price **$2.00**

total price **$.74**

total price **$.90**

total price **$.85**

total price **$.87**

total price **$1.26**

total price **$1.51**

MATH

Name _____

How Many Coins?

Take the fewest coins possible to equal the amount shown in each box. Put the coins in the box. Record the coins.

17¢

coins:

98¢

coins:

24¢

coins:

63¢
coins:

58¢

coins:

35¢

coins:

Making Change

When you do not have the exact change to buy something at a store, the clerk must give you change. The first amount of money is what you give the clerk. The second amount is what the item costs. In the box, list the least amount of coins and bills you will receive in change. Write your own problems in boxes 9 and 10.

	Amount I Have	Cost of Item	Change
1	$3.75	$3.54	
2	$10.00	$5.63	
3	$7.00	$6.05	
4	$6.50	$7.25	
5	$7.50	$6.13	
6	$0.75	$0.37	
7	$7.00	$6.99	
8	$15.00	$12.75	
9			
10			

Name _____

Monetary Message

What's the smartest thing to do with your money? To find out, use the key at the bottom of the page to match the letters with the sums in the blanks provided.

___	___	___	___		___	___	___
$42.71	$33.94	$50.42	$100.73		$45.70	$2.39	$1.55

___	___	___		___	___		___	___	___	___
$33.94	$26.13	$88.02		$45.70	$2.39		$51.12	$45.70	$11.01	$11.01

___	___	___		___	___	___
$33.94	$88.02	$88.02		$55.76	$42.79	$6.84

V =
$42.13
+ 8.29

A =
$ 4.56
+ 29.38

N =
$ 4.65
+ 21.48

, =
$ .09
1.25
+   .21

P =
$ 9.31
+ 33.48

L =
$ 6.73
+ 4.28

E =
$ 81.49
+ 19.24

U =
$ 50.84
+ 4.92

I =
$ 7.49
+ 38.21

S =
$ 23.46
+ 19.25

T =
$ .42
1.94
+   .03

D =
$ 3.04
+ 84.98

W =
$ 1.89
+ 49.23

! =
$ 4.35
+ 2.49

Name _____

Add 'Em Up!

Write in the prices and then add. Regroup when needed. Choose the items to be added together in problems 13-18.

Prices shown: $29.32, $4.37, $.69, $4.84, $8.43, $34.99, $43.09, $3.84, $2.41, $84.36, $.84, $3.09

1. skateboard
 + hat

2. dictionary
 + radio

3. purse
 + goldfish

4. hot dog
 + watch

5. dictionary
 + kite

6. rollerblades
 + guitar

7. hot dog
 + rocket

8. skateboard
 + goldfish

9. hat
 + kite

10. radio
 + guitar

11. rocket
 + goldfish

12. skateboard
 + rollerblades

13. _____
 + _____

14. _____
 + _____

15. _____
 + _____

16. _____
 + _____

17. _____
 + _____

18. _____
 + _____

MATH

Name _____

Spending Spree

Use the clues to figure out what each child bought. Then, subtract to find out how much change each had left.

Clue:

1. Katelyn started with: $23.45   She likes to keep warm!

    $-$ _____

2. David began with: $40.25   He loves to see things zoom into the sky!

    $-$ _____

3. Mark started with: $50.37   He likes to travel places with his hands free and a breeze in his face!

    $-$ _____

4. Eva started with: $14.84   She loves to practice her jumping and exercise at the same time!

    $-$ _____

5. Earl arrived with: $26.42   He loves to learn about interesting things!

    $-$ _____

6. Bill brought: $61.49   He wants to see the heavens for himself!

    $-$ _____

7. Michelle brought: $40.29   Fuzzy companions make such great friends!

    $-$ _____

8. Cheryl started with: $16.80   She loves to hear music that is soft and beautiful!

    $-$ _____

9. Heather arrived with: $20.48   She loves to put it down on paper for everyone to see!

    $-$ _____

$9.31
$12.49
$52.28
$15.29
$2.43
$13.45
$21.52
$32.51
$3.95
$47.29

Name _____

Dessert Included

Brenda and Doug really like chocolate — chocolate-covered raisins, chocolate candy, chocolate cake, hot chocolate! Most of all, they are very fond of chocolate sundaes with chocolate chip ice cream. When they find out that the Eats and Sweets Restaurant is offering a free chocolate dessert with any meal costing exactly $5.00, they decide to go there for dinner.

MATH

Menu

Meat

Chicken	$1.95
Roast Beef	$3.05
Shrimp	$3.50
Roast Pork	$2.75

Salads

Cole Slaw	$.60
Potato Salad	$.95
Dinner Salad	$.75
Macaroni Salad	$1.10

Potatoes/Vegetables

Mashed Potatoes	$1.00
French Fries	$.85
Sweet Corn	$.65
Green Beans	$.50

Drinks

White Milk	$.40
Chocolate Milk	$.45
Orange Juice	$.95
Soda Pop	$.55

Choosing one item from each of the four categories, list four different meals they could eat for exactly $5.00, and then receive the free dessert.

Meal # 1 _____ , _____ , _____ , _____

Meal # 2 _____ , _____ , _____ , _____

Meal # 3 _____ , _____ , _____ , _____

Meal # 4 _____ , _____ , _____ , _____

Big Discount

Name _____

The Terrific Toy Company is celebrating its 50th anniversary. All of the toys are discounted.

Original Cost of Toy	Discount
$3.00 – $5.00	$1.00
$6.00 – $10.00	$2.00
$11.00 – $15.00	$3.00
$16.00 – $20.00	$4.00
$21.00 – $25.00	$5.00

As a special bonus, if your bill **after** the discount is exactly $50.00, you also get a free movie video called "Toyland."

Look carefully at the toys and their original prices listed below.

Puzzle – $3.00

Action Figure – $6.00

Board Game – $8.00

Basketball – $10.00

Football – $12.00

Talking Doll – $15.00

Deluxe Blocks – $20.00

Teddy Bear – $22.00

Video Game – $24.00

Remote-Controlled Car – $25.00

Will you play with me?

Using the discount prices, decide which four toys you might buy in order to get the free movie video. Figure out two solutions. Do not choose any toy more than once.

Solution number 1: _____ , _____ , _____ , _____

Solution number 2: _____ , _____ , _____ , _____

Name _____

Mind-Bogglers

These problems will boggle your mind. Don't give up. Try different problem-solving strategies to help you find the answers.

1. Marta receives an allowance of $2.25 a week. This week her mom pays her in nickels, dimes and quarters. She received more dimes than quarters.

   What coins did her mom use to pay her? _____

   Strategy I used: _____

2. You are asked to draw a picture of a dinosaur. You make the head 1/3 as long as the body. You draw the tail as long as the head and the body combined. The total length of the dinosaur is 56 inches. How long did you make each part of the dinosaur?

   head _____   tail _____   body _____

   Strategy I used: _____

3. Mr. Whitman takes his family on a trip to the amusement park. He brings $75 with him to buy the entrance tickets, food and souvenirs for the family. The tickets to get into the amusement park are $12.75 for adults and $8.45 for children. How much money will Mr. Whitman have for food and souvenirs after he buys entrance tickets for himself, Mrs. Whitman and their two children? _____

   Strategy I used: _____

4. There are eight tables in the classroom. Normally, the teacher has two students sitting on each side. Today, she is going to do a special project so she pushes all eight tables together in a long row. How many students can sit at the long table? _____

   Strategy I used: _____

5. Mr. Jonyou gives his three children a weekly allowance. He pays them in dollar bills. Tony is the first to get paid. He receives half the number of dollar bills his dad has. Joe gets his allowance second. He receives half of the remaining dollar bills plus one. Mr. Jonyou now has $2 left, which is Carmen's allowance. How much allowance do Tony and Joe receive?

   Tony _____   Joe _____

   Strategy I used: _____

Vote for Me!

Name _____

Middletown School had an election to choose the new members of the Student Council. Grace, Bernie, Laurie, Sherry, and Sam all ran for the office of president.

On the chart below are the five students' names with three numbers after each name. The numbers represent the votes each might have received.

Grace	21	36	39
Bernie	47	32	26
Laurie	25	44	38
Sherry	34	37	40
Sam	48	33	29

Use the information and the clues below to see who became president, and how many votes he or she received.

- The winning number of votes was an even number.
- The winning number of votes was between 30 and 40.
- The two digits added together are greater than 10.

_____ became the president of the Student Council with _____ votes.

Who would have become president
if the winning number was **odd** and
the other clues remained the same? _____

Name _____

How Many Outfits?

Suppose you had two pairs of jeans (one blue and the other gray) and three shirts (blue, red and green). How many different outfits could you wear? Use the pictures to help you with the answer.

Your friend has six sweaters and five shirts. How many different combinations of shirts and sweaters does she have? Draw your own pictures to help you figure out the answer.

Your dad has five shirts and six ties. How many different ways can he wear his shirts and ties? Draw pictures if you need to do so.

On the back of this paper, make up your own story problems.

Name _____

Emery Prepares for His Party

Read each story problem carefully. What is the question? What information is given that will help with the answer? Will drawing a picture help? Remember that solving story problems takes time.

1. If Emery needed 329 knives, 329 forks and 329 spoons, how many pieces of silverware did Emery need altogether? _____

2. Emery cooked 329 eggs for his guests. How many dozen eggs did he need to buy? _____

3. Emery baked tarts for dessert. The recipe he followed yielded eight tarts. How many batches of tarts would he have to make to get 329 tarts?

   _____

4. If each recipe called for two eggs, how many eggs would Emery need to make the tarts? To solve this problem, you will need the information from problem 3. _____

5. Before Emery peeled his potatoes, he weighed them. He discovered that there were five potatoes in each pound. He planned on preparing enough potatoes to feed 330 people one each. How many pounds of potatoes would he need? _____

6. The guests sat at 54 tables. Each table had two vases. Emery put five flowers in each vase. How many flowers did he have to pick? _____

7. Write you own story problem about Emery Raccoon and his party.

Solving Math Problems

Solving a mystery is like solving a math problem. Jenny Archer had a mystery that she wasn't certain how to solve. Just as she tried several methods in order to solve her mystery, solving math problems may take many tries. Solve the problems below.

1. Your dad wants to deposit money in his bank account. The bank is a very busy place. He has to stand in line. There are 6 people in front of him and 8 people behind him. How many people are standing in line? _____

2. A jogger can jog 1.5 miles in 12 minutes. He jogged for 30 minutes. How far did he jog? _____

3. Your parents are trying to save money to buy something very special. If they save $2 in January, $4 in February, $8 in March, and so on, how much money will they save in a year? _____

4. When you go to a fancy restaurant, it is customary to leave a 15% tip for the server. This means that you pay the bill for your food plus you leave 15% of that bill. If your meal cost $6.00, how much should you leave for a tip?

_____

Name _____

Racing Chimps

One chimpanzee in the forest always liked to brag that it could get more fruit than any other animal in the forest. So an older and wiser chimpanzee decided to challenge him to a race.

"Let us see who can bring back more bananas in one hour," said the older chimp. The race began.

Quickly, the younger chimp picked a bunch of five bananas and carried it back. He continued doing this every five minutes.

The older chimp was not quite as fast. Every ten minutes he carried back eight bananas.

After 45 minutes the young chimp decided to stop and eat one of his bananas before continuing. By the time he finished, the hour was over and the older chimp called out, "The race is over. My pile of bananas is bigger. I have won the race!"

Using the information above, figure out how many bananas were in each pile, and which chimp won the race.

The younger chimp had _____ bananas in his pile.

The older chimp had _____ bananas in his pile.

The winner was the _____ chimp!

The Lion Dance

The Lion Dance, which started in China, became a Japanese folk dance. In this dance many people line up under a long piece of colorful cloth. The person in front wears a mask of a lion's head. As a group, the line of people dance in the streets around the town.

In this Lion Dance the children lined up in this order: 2 boys, 2 girls, 2 boys, 2 girls. The order remained the same through the entire line.

- Masato, a Japanese boy, stood behind the fifth boy. Find and circle his left foot.

- Koko, a Japanese girl, stood in front of the seventh boy. Put a box around her left foot.

- If every two children needed a 4-foot section of the cloth, and the lion's head was 4 feet long, how many feet long is the entire costume?

_____ feet

Challenge!

- How many yards long is the entire lion costume?

_____ yards

MATH

Name _____

How Far Is It?

Drawing pictures can be a good problem-solving strategy. If you wish, use another sheet of paper to draw pictures to help you solve the problems below. Each problem requires three answers.

1. Jimmy has to walk 12 blocks to get to the park where he likes to play ball. It takes him 3 minutes to walk one block. How many minutes will it take him to walk to the park?

   Distance_____ Speed_____ Time_____

2. An airplane leaves the airport at 9:00 a.m. It flies at 200 miles per hour. When it lands at 11:00 a.m., how far will it have gone?

   Distance_____ Speed_____ Time_____

3. Tad rides his bike to his grandmother's house. It takes him 45 minutes to ride there. She lives 5 miles from his house. How many minutes does it take him to ride one mile?

   Distance_____ Speed_____ Time_____

4. Rachael loves to visit her grandparents who live 150 miles from her house. When they make the trip, her dad drives. He averages 50 miles an hour. How many hours will the trip take?

   Distance_____

   Speed_____

   Time_____

5. It is 50 miles between Dakota City and Blue Falls. It takes Mr. Oliver one hour to make the drive. How fast does he drive?

   Distance_____ Speed_____ Time_____

Name _____

Fraction Fun

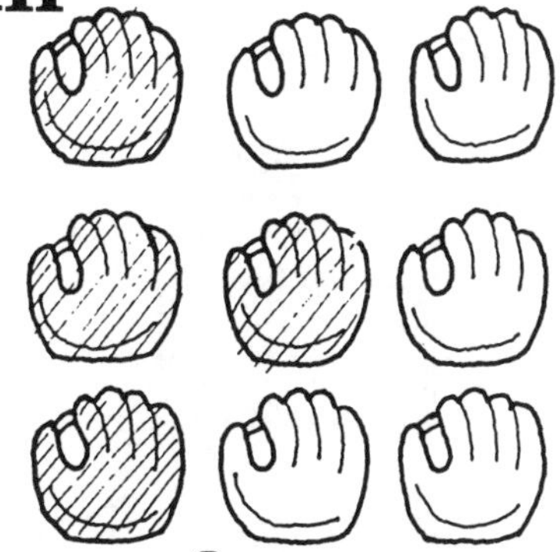

4 gloves are shaded.
9 gloves in all.

$\frac{4}{9}$ of the gloves are shaded.

TOYS

What fraction of the balls are shaded? _____

cars?_____   teddy bears?_____

trains?_____   rabbits?_____

dolls?_____   hats?_____

airplanes?_____   boats?_____

Name _____

More Fractions

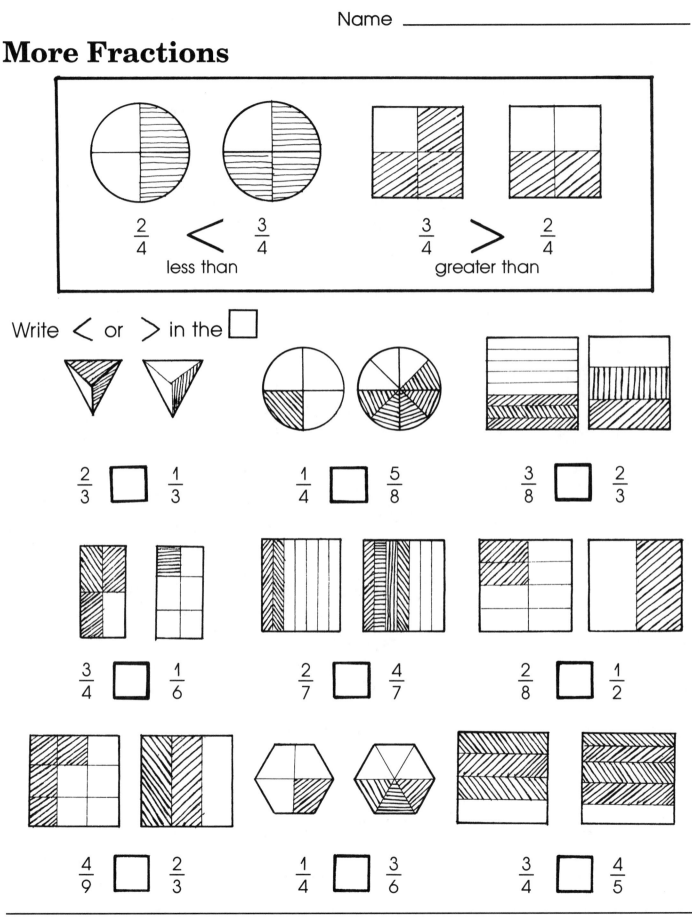

$\dfrac{2}{4}$ < $\dfrac{3}{4}$

less than

$\dfrac{3}{4}$ > $\dfrac{2}{4}$

greater than

Write < or > in the ☐

$\dfrac{2}{3}$ ☐ $\dfrac{1}{3}$

$\dfrac{1}{4}$ ☐ $\dfrac{5}{8}$

$\dfrac{3}{8}$ ☐ $\dfrac{2}{3}$

$\dfrac{3}{4}$ ☐ $\dfrac{1}{6}$

$\dfrac{2}{7}$ ☐ $\dfrac{4}{7}$

$\dfrac{2}{8}$ ☐ $\dfrac{1}{2}$

$\dfrac{4}{9}$ ☐ $\dfrac{2}{3}$

$\dfrac{1}{4}$ ☐ $\dfrac{3}{6}$

$\dfrac{3}{4}$ ☐ $\dfrac{4}{5}$

Name _____

Star Gazing

To find ½ of the stars, divide by 2.

$\frac{1}{2}$ of 10 = 5

$\frac{1}{2}$ of 6 = ____

$\frac{1}{2}$ of 8 = ____

$\frac{1}{3}$ of 9 = ____

$\frac{1}{5}$ of 10 = ____

$\frac{1}{3}$ of 15 = ____

$\frac{1}{6}$ of 18 = ____

$\frac{1}{5}$ of 20 = ____

$\frac{1}{4}$ of 8 = ____

$\frac{1}{2}$ of 16 = ____

$\frac{1}{4}$ of 12 = ____

$\frac{1}{6}$ of 18 = ____

$\frac{1}{6}$ of 12 = ____

$\frac{1}{3}$ of 24 = ____

$\frac{1}{3}$ of 27 = ____

$\frac{1}{4}$ of 24 = ____

MATH

Daily Learning Drills Grade 3

Name _____

Oh, Those Worms!

Color the worms to show the fractions.

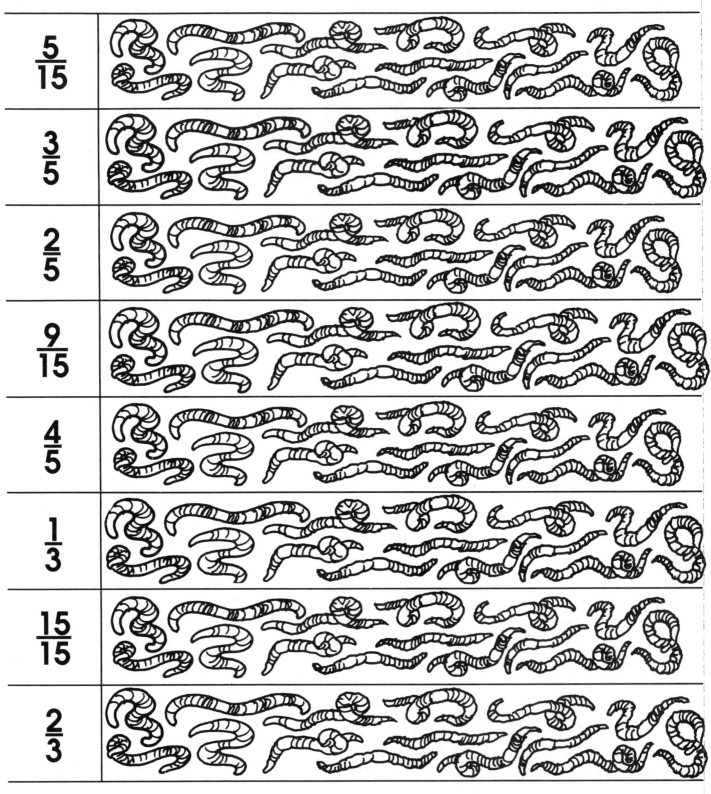

$\frac{5}{15}$	
$\frac{3}{5}$	
$\frac{2}{5}$	
$\frac{9}{15}$	
$\frac{4}{5}$	
$\frac{1}{3}$	
$\frac{15}{15}$	
$\frac{2}{3}$	

Name _____

The Mystery of the Missing Sweets

Some mysterious person is sneaking away with pieces of desserts from Sam Sillicook's Diner. Help him figure out how much is missing.

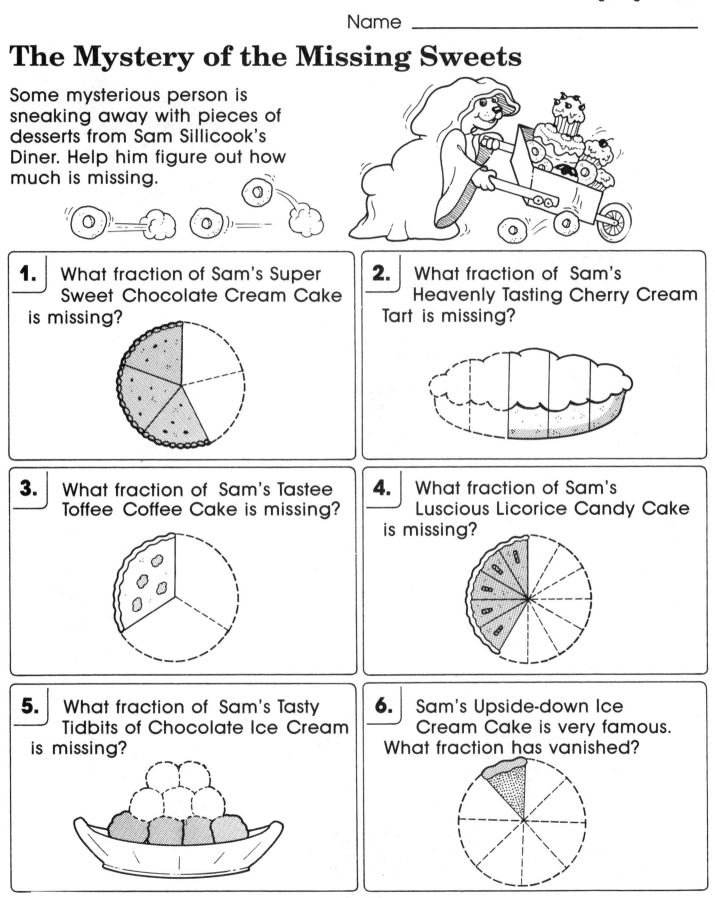

1. What fraction of Sam's Super Sweet Chocolate Cream Cake is missing?

2. What fraction of Sam's Heavenly Tasting Cherry Cream Tart is missing?

3. What fraction of Sam's Tastee Toffee Coffee Cake is missing?

4. What fraction of Sam's Luscious Licorice Candy Cake is missing?

5. What fraction of Sam's Tasty Tidbits of Chocolate Ice Cream is missing?

6. Sam's Upside-down Ice Cream Cake is very famous. What fraction has vanished?

MATH

Name _____

Solar Scholars

Keep your sunny side up! Write the time.

8:20

Name _____

Time on My Hands

Draw the hour and minute hands.

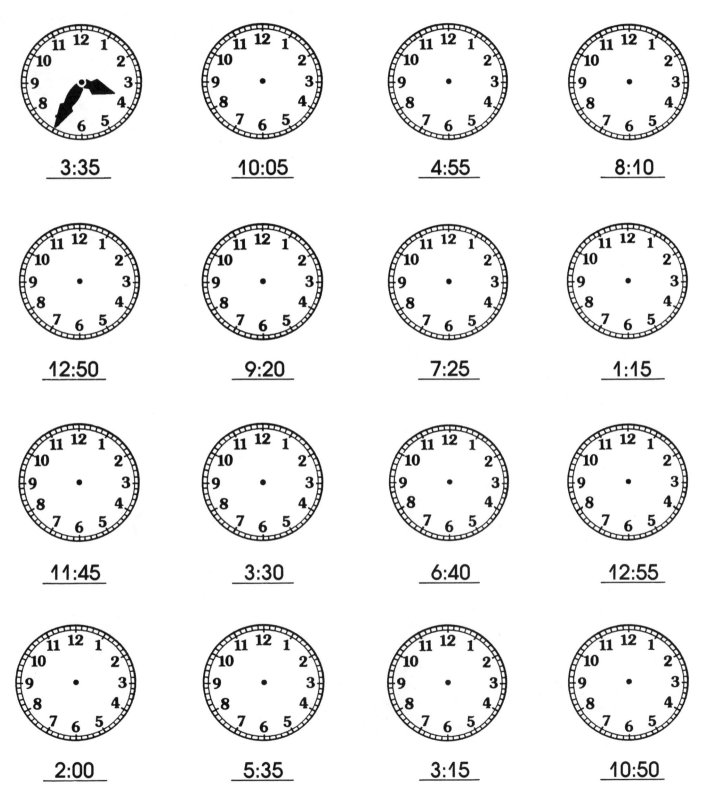

3:35   10:05   4:55   8:10

12:50   9:20   7:25   1:15

11:45   3:30   6:40   12:55

2:00   5:35   3:15   10:50

MATH

Minute Men

Name _____

Add the clock hands to these "Minute Men" clocks.

Example

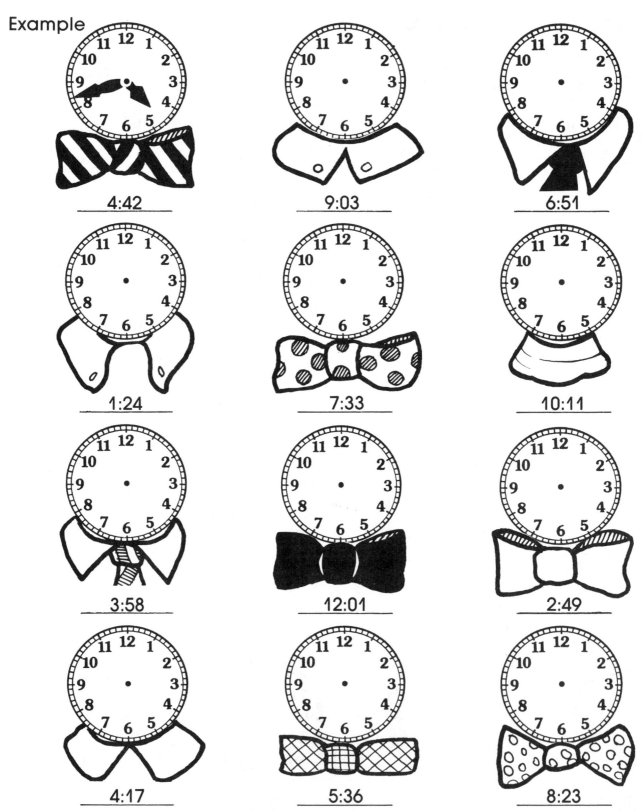

4:42

9:03

6:51

1:24

7:33

10:11

3:58

12:01

2:49

4:17

5:36

8:23

Name _____

Take Time for These

Be right on time! Write the exact time shown on these clocks.

_____6:47_____

MATH

Name _____

Monkeying Around

Nat can't tell time. He thinks that a
minute is some kind of insect and
that a clock is a new kind of soccer
ball. He needs your help to solve
these problems.

1. Nat is supposed to be at
school in 10 minutes. What
time should he get there?

_____

2. Nat started breakfast at
7:10 a.m. It took him
15 minutes to eat. Mark the time
he finished.

3. Nat will leave school in
5 minutes. What time will it be
then?

_____

4. Nat and his brother Not Nit
Wit will eat dinner in
15 minutes. When will that be?

_____

5. It is now 6:45 p.m. Nat must
start his homework in 5 minutes.
Mark the starting time on the clock.

6. Nat will go to the park in 15
minutes. It is now 1:25 p.m.
Mark the time he will go to the
park.

Name _____

Daily Schedule

Fill in your own grade, teacher and room number. Next write the times and subjects that are listed in the order they would take place during a school day.

Subjects/Activity	Times
Art	2:30 p.m.
Reading	8:30 a.m.
Spelling	8:15 a.m.
Science	11:15 a.m.
Health	11:45 a.m.
Social Studies	1:40 p.m.
English	10:00 a.m.
Handwriting	9:30 a.m.
Physical Education	1:15 p.m.
Music	2:00 p.m.
Library	12:45 p.m.
Lunch	12:00 p.m.
Recess	9:45 a.m.
Attendance/Flag Salute	8:00 a.m.
Math	10:30 a.m.
Dismissal	3:00 p.m.

Daily Schedule

Grade ____   Teacher _____

Room _____

Time	Subject/Activity

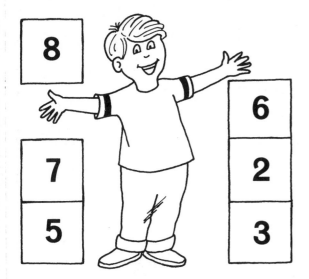

How long is the listed lunch period? _____

How long is the listed recess? _____

What subject do you like the best? _____

What subject do you like the least? _____

MATH

Name _____

Timely Fun

Make an estimate of how many times you can do each activity in one minute. Then, time yourself and see how close you came.

Say the alphabet.

ABCDEFGHIJKL MNOPQRSTUVWXYZ

Estimate: _____

Actual: _____

Clap your hands.

Estimate: _____

Actual: _____

Do jumping jacks.

Estimate: _____

Actual: _____

Count to 20.

6 5 4 3 2 1
7
8
9 10 11 12 13 14 15 16 17 18 19 20

Estimate: _____

Actual: _____

Hop on one foot.

Estimate: _____

Actual: _____

Count backward from 20 to 1.

16 15 14 13
17
18 12 11
19
20

Estimate: _____

Actual: _____

Feeding Time

Name _____

Ken and Angie enjoyed watching the animals being fed at the zoo. However, when they arrived, they were a little confused by the signs.

Help them figure out the feeding time for each kind of animal. Be sure to include if it's A.M. or P.M.

Seals: Feeding time is two hours after the monkeys.

_____ : _____

Tigers: Feeding time is two hours after 9:00 A.M.

_____ : _____

Lions: Feeding time is 1:00 P.M.

Giraffes: Feeding time is one hour before the elephants.

_____ : _____

Monkeys: Feeding time is three hours before the giraffes.

_____ : _____

Elephants: Feeding time is three hours after the lions.

_____ : _____

Now trace the path in the zoo that Ken and Angie would take so that they could see all the animals being fed.

Daily Learning Drills Grade 3

Name _____

Perfect Symmetry

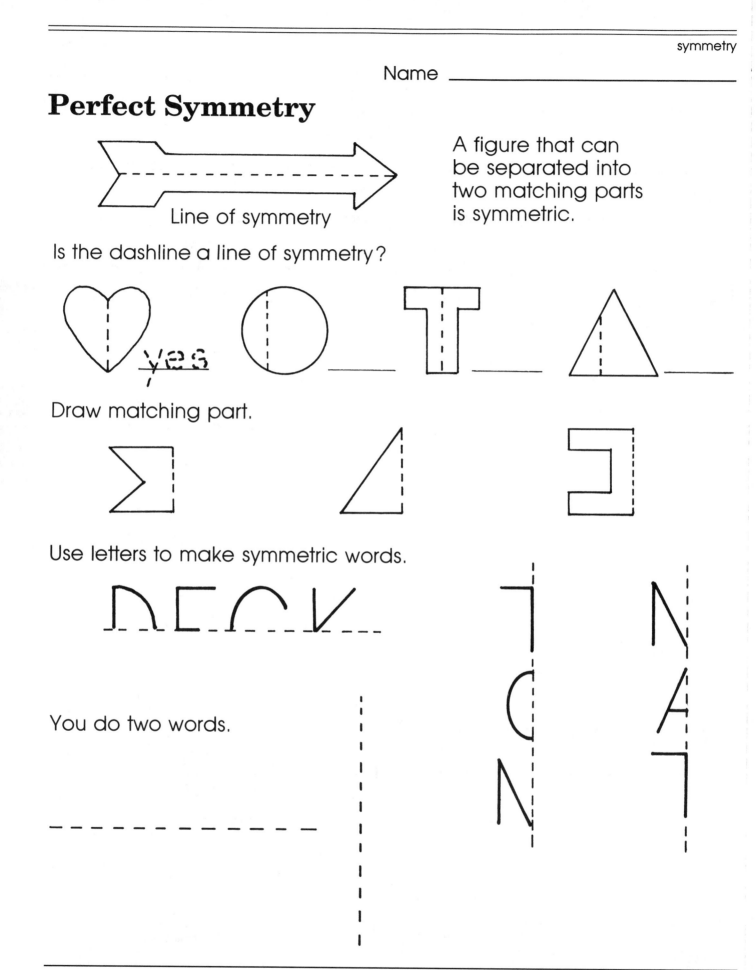

Line of symmetry

A figure that can be separated into two matching parts is symmetric.

Is the dashline a line of symmetry?

yes

Draw matching part.

Use letters to make symmetric words.

DECK

You do two words.

Name _____

A Square Activity

The **area** is the number of square units contained in a surface. Find the area by counting the square units.

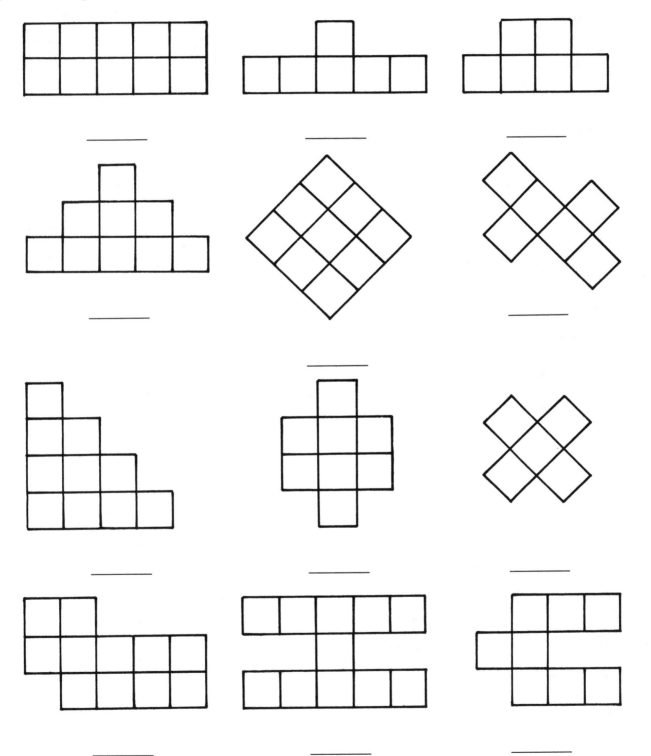

Daily Learning Drills Grade 3

Name _____

Perimeter Problems

The **perimeter** is the distance around a figure. Find the perimeters for the figures below.

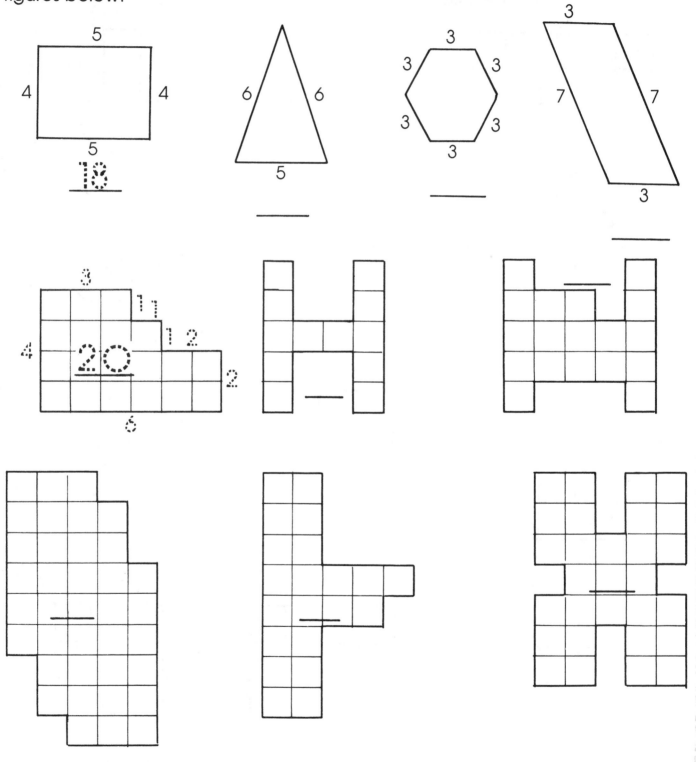

Name _____

Sawing Logs

Measure the logs to the nearest centimeter.

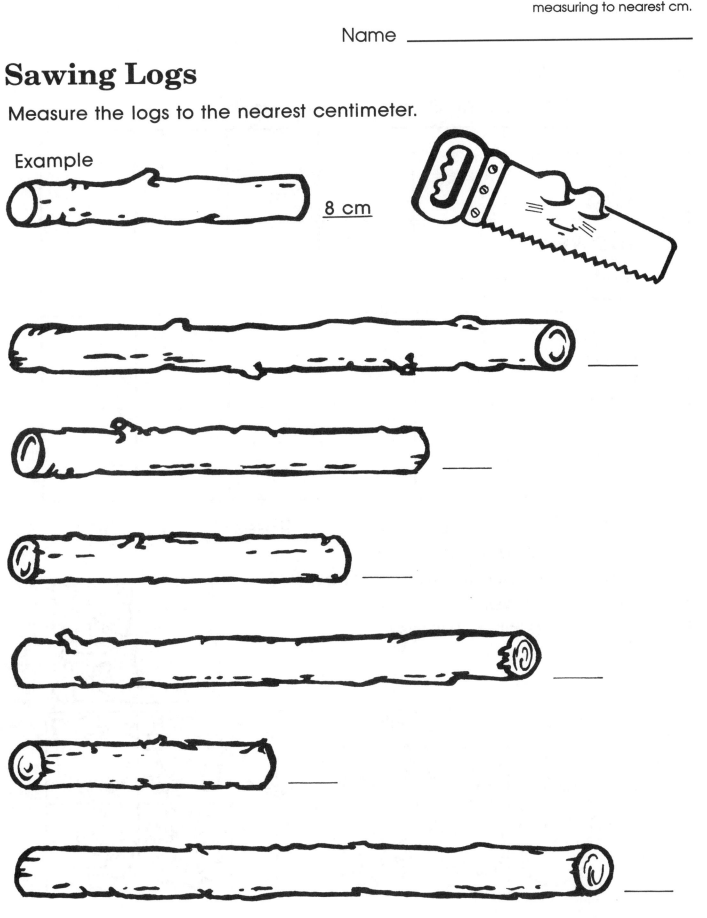

Example

_8 cm_

     Daily Learning Drills Grade 3

Name _____

Flower Graph

Cut out and match the flowers to the graph.

Daisies					
Sunflowers					
Tulips					
Roses					

How many tulips? ___ Sunflowers? ___ Roses? ___ Daisies? ___

How many more tulips than roses? ___

How many more daisies than sunflowers? ___

How many sunflowers and tulips? ___

How many roses and daisies? ___

Name _____

Potato Face

Read the line graphs to draw the potato faces.

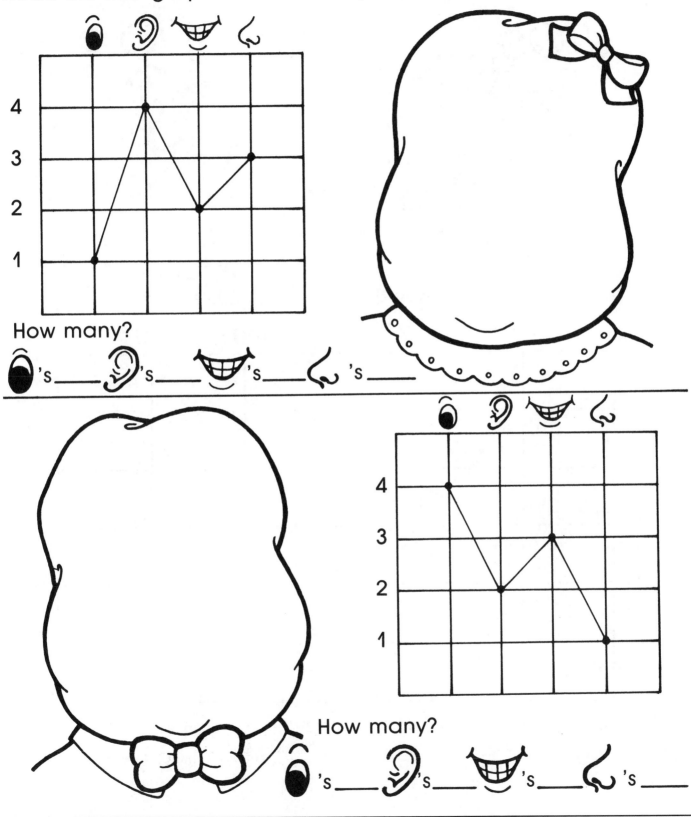

How many?

👁's____ 👂's____ 😁's____ 👃's____

How many?

👁's____ 👂's____ 😁's____ 👃's____

Name _____

Frog Bubbles

Color the picture.

Finish the line graph to show how many bubbles.

	Frog 1	Frog 2	Frog 3	Frog 4	Frog 5

How many bubbles? Frog 1? ____ 2? ____ 3? ____ 4? ____ 5? ____
Which frog blew the most bubbles? ____ Which frog blew the least? ____

Name _____

Candy Sales

Every year the students sell candy as a fund-raising project. These are the
results of the sales for this year.

Grade Level	Number of Sales
Kindergarten	40
First	70
Second	50
Third	80
Fourth	85
Fifth	75

Make a bar graph to show the number of sales made at each grade level.

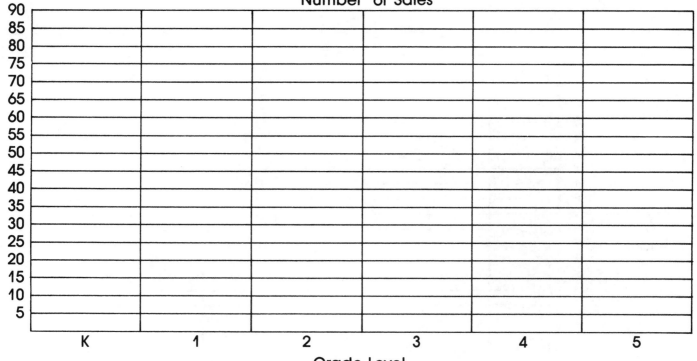

Number of Sales

Grade Level

Write the grade levels in order starting with the one that sold the most.

1. _____

2. _____

3. _____

4. _____

5. _____

6. _____

Name _____

Hot Lunch Favorites

The cooks in the cafeteria asked each third and fourth grade class to rate the hot lunches. They wanted to know which food the children liked the best.

The table shows how the students rated the lunches.
Hint: Each ☆ equals 2 students

Food	Number of Students Who Liked It Best
hamburgers	☆ ☆ ☆ ☆ ☆ ☆
hot dogs	☆ ☆ ☆ ☆ ☆ ☆ ☆
tacos	☆ ☆ ☆ ☆ ☆
chili	
soup and sandwiches	☆
spaghetti	☆ ☆
fried chicken	☆ ☆ ☆ ☆
fish sticks	☆ ☆ ☆

Make a bar graph to show the information on the table. Remember - each ☆ equals 2 people. The first one is done for you.

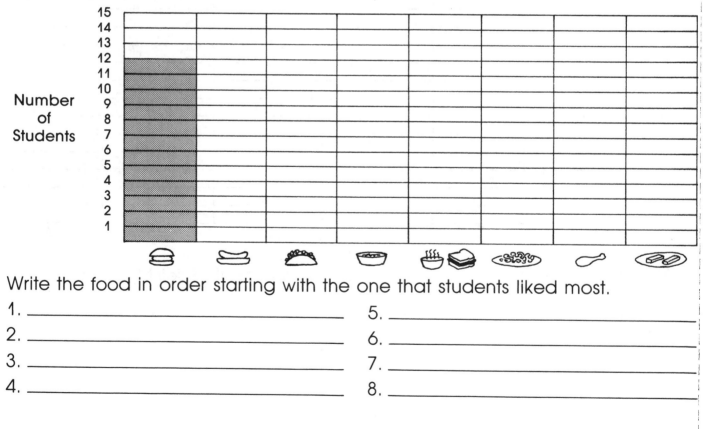

Write the food in order starting with the one that students liked most.

1. _____   5. _____

2. _____   6. _____

3. _____   7. _____

4. _____   8. _____

Name _____

Tooth Talk

Study the drawing of the tooth to help you fill in the blanks.

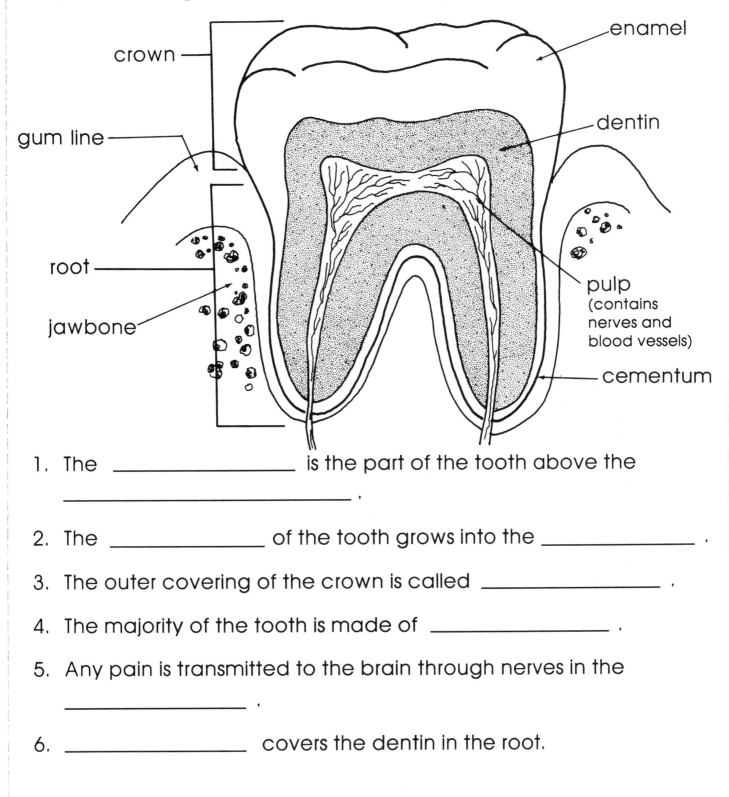

1. The _____ is the part of the tooth above the

   _____ .

2. The _____ of the tooth grows into the _____ .

3. The outer covering of the crown is called _____ .

4. The majority of the tooth is made of _____ .

5. Any pain is transmitted to the brain through nerves in the

   _____ .

6. _____ covers the dentin in the root.

Name _____

Quiet, Please!

A large jet plane rumbles as it takes off down the runway. You can feel the ground vibrate. The plane is also filling the air with vibrations. When the vibrations reach your ear, you hear them as sound.

Your **outer ear** collects the vibrations just like a funnel. The vibrations strike your **eardrum,** making it vibrate too. These vibrations are passed through a series of three small bones. The last bone vibrates against a snail-shaped tube. This tube is called the **cochlea.** It is filled with liquid. Small hair-like sensors in the cochlea pick up the vibrations and send it to the **auditory nerve.** The auditory nerve sends the sound message to your brain.

Label the parts of the ear using the words in bold.

Sounds Around Us

1. What is the loudest sound you have ever heard? _____

2. What is the softest sound you have ever heard? _____

3. What sound wakes you up in the morning? _____

4. What sound relaxes you? _____

5. What sound frightens you? _____

Something Special

Try some of these sound experiments with your classmates. Keep your eyes closed for all of the experiments!

1. Cover one ear and listen for the sounds around you. Then uncover your ear and listen again. What is the difference?

2. Choose one student to make several sounds with objects found in the classroom. Can the rest of you identify the sounds?

3. We usually hear the loudest sounds around us. Listen for the soft, "far away" sounds. List the sounds. Try this experiment outside.

Name _____

Strong Bones

The skeleton is a framework of 206 bones that has three main jobs: to hold your body up, to protect your inner organs, and to produce new blood cells inside the bones. That means our bones must be healthy. The outer part of our bones contains calcium, which keeps our bones strong. What would happen if our bones lacked calcium? Try the experiment below with a partner to find out.

Materials Needed

a chicken bone
a glass jar with a lid
1 cup vinegar

Procedure

1. Clean the chicken bone.
2. Place the bone in the jar and cover it with vinegar.
3. Cover tightly.
4. Let it sit for two weeks.

After two weeks:
How has the chicken bone changed? _____

_____

What would happen to your body without calcium? _____

_____

Rickets is a disease caused by too little calcium in your body. Calcium is found in many of the foods we eat. Check the labels of several foods. List at least ten that contain calcium.

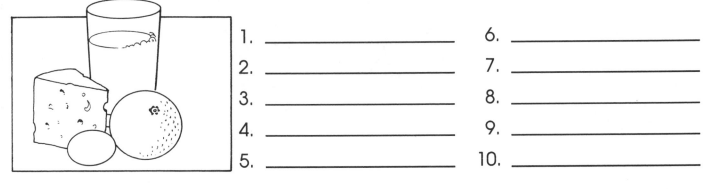

1. _____   6. _____
2. _____   7. _____
3. _____   8. _____
4. _____   9. _____
5. _____   10. _____

SCIENCE

Name _____

Build a Blood Cell!

We cannot live without blood. Our blood is made of millions of cells. There are red blood cells, white blood cells, and cells called platelets. They are so tiny that you cannot see them without a microscope.

Red blood cells carry oxygen from the lungs to the body's tissues and remove carbon dioxide. White blood cells protect the body from disease. Platelets help damaged blood vessels to stop bleeding. Each blood cell has its own parts. Look at the picture below and study the parts of the red blood cells. Remember, this is much bigger than a real cell.

Follow these directions to make a red blood cell.

Materials Needed
1 plastic bag that seals
1 dark button
½ cup prepared red Jell-O™

Directions
1. Put the Jell-O™ in the bag.
2. Place the button in the bag.
3. Squeeze the button to the center of the bag.

Draw your red blood cell and label its parts.

hemoglobin
membrane
Red blood cell (erythrocytes)

nucleus
membrane
White blood cell (lymphocyte)

Platelets

Name _____

Ingenious Genes

Your body is made up of cells. Each cell holds threadlike structures called chromosomes that contain genes. Genes are inherited from your parents and determine how you will look. This is why we often look like our parents. Some genes are stronger, or dominant, and some are carried down through generations. Below is a table listing the characteristics of a mother and a father. See if you can find all of the possible combinations for their children. There are 16 possibilities!

	hair	eyes	skin color	height
Mom	blonde	green	dark	short
Dad	red	blue	fair	tall

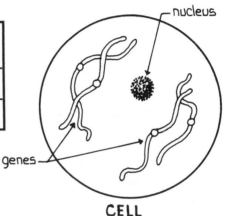

CELL

Examples:

blonde hair   blonde hair
green eyes   blue eyes
dark skin   dark skin
short   tall

_____

_____

_____

Complete the chart below for your mother and father. Then, find all of the combinations that determine how you could have looked! (You may have fewer than 16 if any traits are the same.)

	hair	eyes	skin color	height
Mom				
Dad				

_____

_____

Name _____

Just Swallow It!

Use this diagram to help you number the sentences in the correct order to show what happens when you swallow a bite of food.

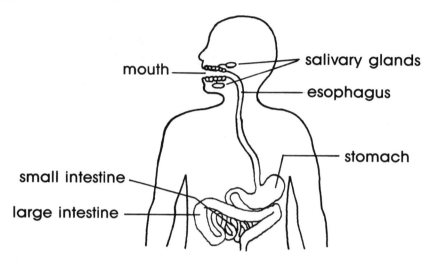

_____ While your teeth are breaking the food into tiny pieces, saliva is making the food softer.

_____ Whatever the body cannot use goes into the large intestine.

_____ While the food is in your stomach, more juices help to dissolve it.

_____ First you must pick up your sandwich in your hand.

_____ When the food in your mouth is soft enough, you swallow it.

_____ Move your hand to your mouth.

_____ When the food has dissolved in your stomach, it goes to your small intestine.

_____ Put a corner of the sandwich in your mouth.

_____ As you swallow your food, it moves down the esophagus to your stomach.

_____ Use your teeth to take a bite of the sandwich.

_____ While the food is in your small intestine, the body absorbs whatever it needs.

What happens when you try to swallow too big of a bite?

_____

Write a sentence about a kind of food that is good for your body.

_____

_____

Name _____

Going Around in Circles!

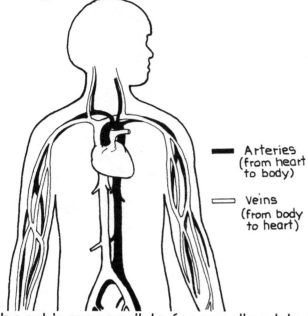

Arteries
(from heart
to body)

Veins
(from body
to heart)

The circulatory system is responsible for moving blood throughout your body. It is blood that carries food and oxygen to your body's cells and carries away carbon dioxide and other wastes. This system also carries disease-fighting substances that help prevent you from getting sick.

The main components of your body's circulatory system are: the heart, blood vessels, blood, and the lymphatic system. Your heart controls this system.

The heart is responsible for sending blood mixed with oxygen to the rest of your body through blood vessels called arteries. Blood vessels called veins return blood to your heart. Your veins look blue because the blood in them has no oxygen. Back toward the heart, the blood gathers more oxygen as it passes through your lungs and becomes red. This cycle occurs about one time every minute. It is your heart's constant pumping that keeps your blood circulating.

Use the information above to solve the puzzle.

Across

2. The _____ controls the circulatory system.
4. Blood without oxygen is _____ .
6. Arteries carry blood mixed with _____ from the heart to the rest of your body.
7. _____ carry blood to the heart.

Down

1. _____ carry blood away from the heart.
3. Blood is _____ when it contains oxygen.
5. Blood gets oxygen from your _____.

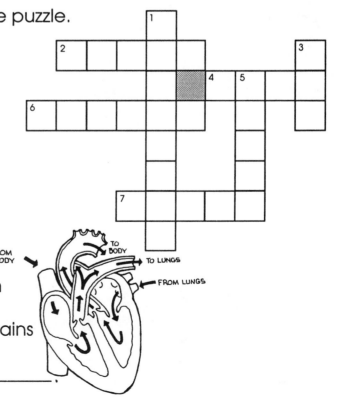

Name _____

Backbone or No Backbone?

Which part of your body helps you stand tall or sit up straight? It is your backbone. You are a member of a large group of animals that all have backbones. Animals with backbones are called **vertebrates.** Birds, fish, reptiles, amphibians, and mammals are all vertebrates.

Some animals do not have backbones. These animals are called **invertebrates.** Worms, centipedes, and insects are all invertebrates.

Classifying

Find the five vertebrates and five invertebrates hidden in the wordsearch. Then write them in the correct group.

Invertebrates

1. _____

2. _____

3. _____

4. _____

5. _____

```
B R A B B I T B U D
E A G I R A F F E L
E W O F H E P R U W
T O G K L C M O T H
L R N F R Y S G I A
E M L I O N O J E L
R S P I D E R M R E
```

Vertebrates

1. _____

2. _____

3. _____

4. _____

5. _____

Your neighborhood has many animals in or near it. Add their names to the lists.

Invertebrates

6. _____

7. _____

8. _____

9. _____

10. _____

Vertebrates

6. _____

7. _____

8. _____

9. _____

10. _____

Find Out

There are many more invertebrates than vertebrates. Nine out of ten animals is an invertebrate. Which group has the largest animals? Which group has the smallest animals?

Insects in Winter

In the summertime, insects can be seen buzzing and fluttering around us. But as winter's cold weather begins, suddenly the insects seem to disappear. Do you know where they go?

Many insects, such as flies and mosquitoes, find a warm place to spend the winter. They live in cellars, barns, attics, caves and tree holes.

Beetles and ants try to dig deep into the ground. Some beetles stack up in piles under rocks or dead leaves.

In the fall, female grasshoppers and crickets lay their eggs and die. The eggs hatch in the spring.

Bees also try to protect themselves from the winter cold. Honeybees gather in a ball in the middle of their hive. The bees stay in this tight ball trying to stay warm.

Winter is very hard for insects, but each spring the survivors come out and the buzzing and fluttering begins again.

Write.

When cold weather begins, _____ seem to disappear.

Unscramble and check.

_____ and_____ find a warm place in:
q u t M s o e o s i   s f i l e

☐ beds ☐ barns ☐ caves ☐ cellars ☐ attics ☐ sweaters

Circle Yes or No.

I n the winter, insects look for a warm place to live. Yes No

n oise, such as buzzing, can be heard all winter long. Yes No

S ome beetles and ants dig deep into the ground. Yes No

e very insect finds a warm home for the winter. Yes No

C rickets and grasshoppers lay their eggs and die. Yes No

T he honeybees gather in a ball in their hive. Yes No

S urvivors of the cold weather come out each spring. Yes No

Name _____

Six-Legged Friends

The largest group of animals belongs to the group called invertebrates–or animals without backbones. This large group is the **insect** group.

Insects are easy to tell apart from other animals. Adult insects have three body parts and six legs. The first body part is the **head.** On the head are the mouth, eyes, and antennae. The second body part is the **thorax.** On it are the legs and wings. The third part is the **abdomen.** On it are small openings for breathing.

Color the body parts of the insect above. head–red, thorax–yellow, abdomen–blue

Draw an insect below. Make your insect a one-of-a-kind. Be sure it has the correct number of body parts, legs, wings, and antennae. Fill in the information.

Insect's name_____

Length_____

Where found _____

Food_____

Warning: _____

_____

_____

_____

Find Out

Many people think that spiders are insects. Spiders and insects are alike in many ways, but spiders are not insects. Find out how the two are different.

Name _____

Go Bats for Bats

Bats live all over the world. The bats found in the rainforest play an important role because they control insects and pollinate and disperse seeds for avocados, bananas, cashews, figs, peaches and other fruits. However, the bats that live in the rainforest are in danger due to the increasing destruction of their habitat. This could mean that our supply of fruits, nuts and spices could decrease and possibly vanish if the destruction continues. Read the description of each bat below. Notice how each one is different and has special features to help it survive. Put the letter of each description next to the bat it describes and the bat's food.

A. Notice the long nose and tongue this bat uses to dip into the durian blossom.

B. This bat's large ears and nose flap enable it to locate insects at night.

C. With its long feet and claws, this bat captures certain small prey.

D. The long snout on this bat helps it eat fruit like figs.

Food

Bats

Once you have matched up the bats and their food, cut all the pictures apart. Glue each bat to a piece of construction paper. Glue the food it eats to the back. Punch a hole in each piece of construction paper. Put a piece of string through each piece of paper and tie the bats to a hanger. Now, you have a bat mobile to hang from the ceiling.

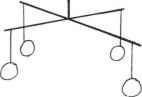

Name _____

A Sampling of Snakes

The Snake House is a very popular place to visit at the zoo. There are many different types and sizes of snakes. Some snakes are poisonous while others are not. Some snakes are harmless to most creatures, and some are very dangerous.

The five snakes described here are held in the cages below.

Decide which snake belongs in each cage by using the clues given here and beneath the boxes. Then write each name in the correct cage.

The King Cobra is the longest poisonous snake in the world. One of these snakes measured almost 19 feet long. It comes from southeast Asia and the Philippines.

The Gaboon Viper, a very poisonous snake, has the longest fangs of all snakes (nearly 2 inches). It comes from tropical Africa.

The Reticulated Python is the longest snake of all. One specimen measured 32 feet 9½ inches. It comes from southeast Asia, Indonesia, and the Philippines. It crushes its prey to death.

The Black Mamba, the fastest-moving land snake, can move at speeds of 10–12 m.p.h. It lives in the eastern part of tropical Africa.

The Anaconda is almost twice as heavy as a reticulated python of the same length. One anaconda that was almost 28 feet long weighed nearly 500 pounds.

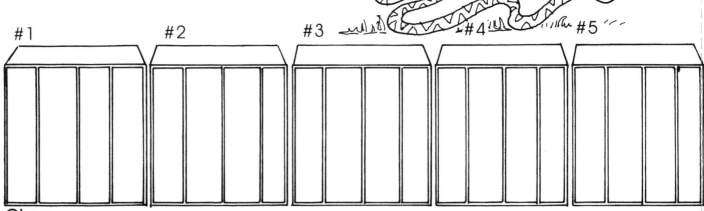

#1   #2   #3   #4   #5

Clues:

- The snake in cage #5 moves the fastest on land.
- The longest snake of all is between the snake that comes from tropical Africa and the longest poisonous snake.
- The very heavy snake is to the left of the longest poisonous snake.

Name _____

From Egg to Tadpole to Frog

The poem below tells about the changes that occur in frogs during their life cycles. In every line, there is one word that doesn't make sense. Find the correct word in the Word Bank and write it in the puzzle. **Hint:** The correct word rhymes with it.

The Life Cycle of a Frog

There is jelly on the legs (13)
  To protect the entire match. (11)
It takes tree to twenty-five days (7 ↓)
  Until they're ready to catch. (5)

Out comes a pollihog (18)
  When the time is just bright. (8)
It breathes using hills (14)
  And its size is very light. (4)

It loses its long scale (9)
  After pegs begin to grow. (1)
Digestion and breathing strange (12)
  In a process fast and glow. (2)

What helps a frog to seethe (3)
  Is its thin and moist chin. (6 ↓)
It also uses rungs (15)
  To let the hair in. (10)

Some frogs can skim like a duck. (6 →)
  And some can mop like a rabbit. (16)
Others climb bees like a squirrel (7 →)
  Which may seem a bunny habit. (17)

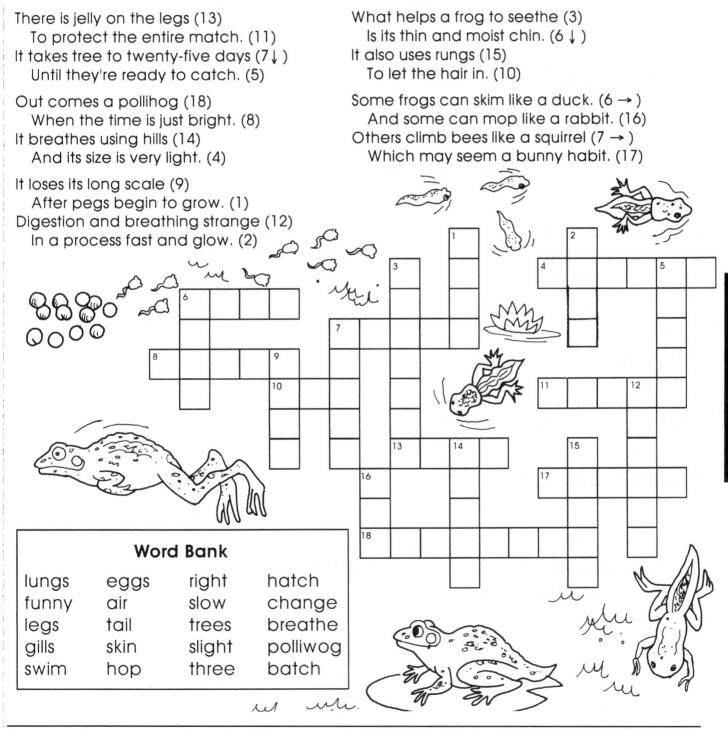

Word Bank

lungs	eggs	right	hatch
funny	air	slow	change
legs	tail	trees	breathe
gills	skin	slight	polliwog
swim	hop	three	batch

Name _____

The Mighty Bear

Bears are large and powerful animals. Depending on the type of bear, they can weigh from 60 to 2,000 pounds.

Listed below are four different kinds of bears. The lengths of these bears are 3 feet, 5 feet, 8 feet, and 9 feet. Use the clues to match each bear to its length. Write the answers in the blanks.

Clues:

Alaskan brown bear + American black bear = 14 feet

Polar bear + Alaskan brown bear = 17 feet

American black bear + Sun bear = 8 feet

The Alaskan brown bear is _____ feet in length.

The American black bear is _____ feet in length.

The polar bear is _____ feet in length.

The sun bear is _____ feet in length.

Name _____

Toadly Froggin' Around

Harry and Song Lee loved frogs and similar creatures. Read the information about frogs and toads. Then write **true** or **false** in front of each statement.

Frogs and Toads

Both frogs and toads are amphibians. Amphibians spend part of their lives as water animals and part as land animals. In the early stages of their lives, amphibians breathe through gills, while as adults they develop lungs. Most amphibians lay eggs near water. Newly hatched frogs and toads both have tails that they later lose. Both often have poison glands in their skin to protect them from their enemies.

Frogs and toads are different in several ways. Most toads are broader, darker, and flatter. Their skin is drier. Toads are usually covered with warts while frogs have smooth skin. Most toads live on land while most frogs prefer being in or near the water.

_____ 1. Both frogs and toads usually lay eggs near water.

_____ 2. Most frogs have drier skin than toads.

_____ 3. Very young amphibians breathe with lungs.

_____ 4. Frogs tend to be lighter in color.

_____ 5. An adult frog's tail helps support him while sitting.

_____ 6. Poison glands often protect frogs from an enemy.

_____ 7. A toad's skin is often bumpy.

_____ 8. Frogs and toads are both amphibians.

SCIENCE

Name _____

A Re-Appearing Act

The starfish is a very interesting sea animal. Most starfish have five "arms" on their bodies. When a starfish is in danger, it can drop off its arms to escape. It then grows new arms to replace the missing ones. Also, if a starfish is cut in two, each of the pieces may grow into a new starfish.

Use the information above to solve these puzzles.

Puzzle #1 – This starfish originally had five arms. If two of these arms were broken off and grew back twice and the other three were dropped off and grew back five times each, how many arms did this starfish have during its lifetime? _____

Puzzle #2 – At first, this starfish had ten arms. It was then cut in half. Each of the halves grew new arms again so that they had the same number as the original starfish. Eventually, the same thing happened again to both new starfish. How many arms were involved in all? _____

Puzzle #3 – This starfish had 24 arms when it was born. If ½ of these arms broke off and grew back 4 times and ¼ of the original arms dropped off and grew back 3 times, how many arms did this starfish have during its lifetime? _____

Name _____

Butterflies and Moths

People sometimes confuse butterflies with moths, but there are some important differences.

Butterflies . . .
- fly by day.
- antennae have knobs.
- have thin, hairless bodies.
- rest with their wings held upright.

Moths . . .
- fly at night.
- antennae have no knobs.
- have plump, furry bodies.
- rest with their wings spread out flat.

Suppose you decided to start a butterfly and/or moth collection. Each mounting page would be divided into 16 sections. Large butterflies or moths would require two sections to mount. Small butterflies or moths would require only one.

If you had three large butterflies for this page and the rest were small, how many small butterflies could you mount? _____

Draw and color these butterflies on the page.

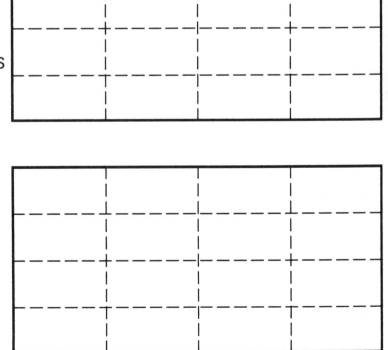

If you had four large moths, and you didn't want any of them to be next to each other, how would you mount them with smaller moths so that all of the sections would be used? Draw and color them on this page.

SCIENCE

Name _____

Secret Code for Worm Lovers

To decode the secret words, use the code below.

A	B	C	D	E	F	G	H	I	J	K	L	M
1	2	3	4	5	6	7	8	9	10	11	12	13

N	O	P	Q	R	S	T	U	V	W	X	Y	Z
14	15	16	17	18	19	20	21	22	23	24	25	26

1. Earthworms can also be called __ __ __ __ __
   14 9 7 8 20

   __ __ __ __ __ __ __ __ .
   3 18 1 23 12 5 18 19

2. Earthworms have no __ __ __ __ or __ __ __ __ .
   5 1 18 19   5 25 5 19

3. Sections of an earthworm are called __ __ __ __ __ __ __ __ .
   19 5 7 13 5 14 20 19

4. Earthworms __ __ __ __ __ __ __ through their __ __ __ __ .
   2 18 5 1 20 8 5   19 11 9 14

5. Earthworms eat __ __ __ __ .
   19 15 9 12

6. As they __ __ __ __ __ __ through the soil, they give plants the __ __ __
   2 21 18 18 15 23   1 9 18
   that they need.

Name _____

Man's Best Friend

Dogs have been called "Man's Best Friend," and there are many good reasons for this. Dogs have been friendly with humans for over 10,000 years. Dogs have helped with hunting and herding. They have helped guide blind people and have also helped the police do detective work. Most often, they are kept as pets to provide both friendship and protection.

There are over 130 breeds of dogs in the United States. Certain breeds are more popular than others. According to the 1990 registrations, the following were the most popular breeds:

Golden Retriever
Cocker Spaniel
Rottweiler
Poodle
Labrador Retriever

Use the clues below to discover the order of the dogs' popularity. Then write each dog's name in the correct ribbon.

- "I'm the third most popular dog. My name is similar to something that forms during a rainstorm."

- "My name includes one of man's most precious metals, and I rank fourth."

- "I have the most vowels in my name, and I rank second."

- "I don't consider it a rotten deal to follow gold."

- "I rank first, which makes me proud as a peacock."

First Place   Second Place   Third Place   Fourth Place   Fifth Place

193   Daily Learning Drills Grade 3

Name _____

A Shark's Fringe Benefit

The largest carnivorous (flesh-eating) fish that can be dangerous to man is the great white shark. Although it doesn't have a very large brain, it has excellent senses.

Great white sharks have several rows of jagged-edged teeth. New teeth replace worn or broken teeth. The replacement teeth move from inside the mouth to the outer edge.

Imagine this. A shark had three rows containing two dozen teeth each on the bottom jaw and three rows containing two dozen teeth each on the top jaw.

First, the shark broke off 8 top teeth and wore down 10 bottom teeth, and these were replaced by new teeth.

Next, it wore down 6 top teeth and 4 bottom teeth and these were replaced by new teeth.

Finally, the shark broke off 9 top teeth and 9 bottom teeth and these were replaced.

How many total teeth had the shark had in its mouth at one time or another?

_____

Pretend the "Good Fairy" put 25¢ under the shark's pillow for each tooth that

was broken off. How much money would she leave? $ _____

Name _____

Endangered Animal Acrostic

Using the animal names below, write the answers to the following definitions in the spaces provided. The circled letters are used as clues for your answers.

blue whale	jaguar	pronghorn
cheetah	okapi	polar bear
vicuna	yak	giant panda

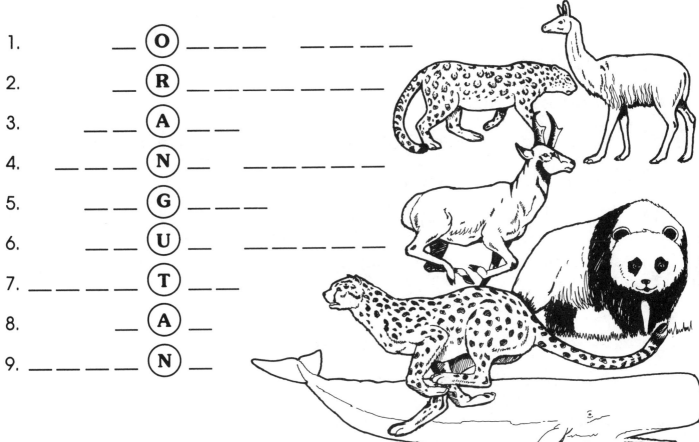

1. __ (O) __ __ __ __ __ __ __
2. __ (R) __ __ __ __ __ __
3. __ __ (A) __ __ __
4. __ __ __ (N) __ __ __ __ __
5. __ __ (G) __ __ __
6. __ __ (U) __ __ __ __ __ __ __
7. __ __ __ __ __ (T) __ __
8. __ (A) __
9. __ __ __ __ (N) __

1. large animal with white coat
2. upright horns and sheeplike feet
3. only living relative of the giraffe
4. lives in bamboo forests in southwestern China
5. largest wild cat in the Western Hemisphere

6. largest animal on Earth
7. cat that can run over 60 miles per hour
8. species of wild cattle in Tibet
9. member of the camel family in South America

SCIENCE

Name _____

Puzzling Problems

Which dinosaur's name means "iguana tooth?" To find out the answer, read each statement about dinosaurs below. If the statement is false, darken the letter in the circle to the left of that statement. The remaining letters will spell out the answer.

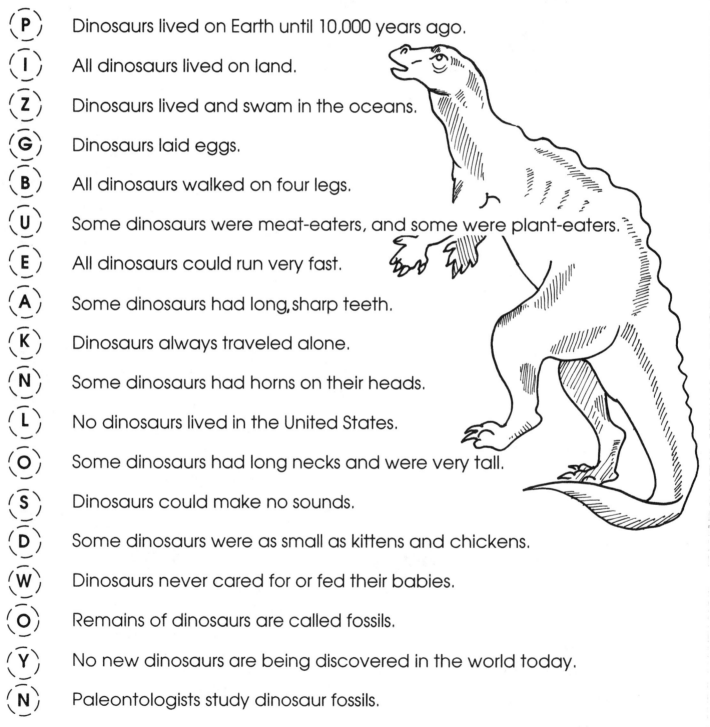

(P) Dinosaurs lived on Earth until 10,000 years ago.

(I) All dinosaurs lived on land.

(Z) Dinosaurs lived and swam in the oceans.

(G) Dinosaurs laid eggs.

(B) All dinosaurs walked on four legs.

(U) Some dinosaurs were meat-eaters, and some were plant-eaters.

(E) All dinosaurs could run very fast.

(A) Some dinosaurs had long, sharp teeth.

(K) Dinosaurs always traveled alone.

(N) Some dinosaurs had horns on their heads.

(L) No dinosaurs lived in the United States.

(O) Some dinosaurs had long necks and were very tall.

(S) Dinosaurs could make no sounds.

(D) Some dinosaurs were as small as kittens and chickens.

(W) Dinosaurs never cared for or fed their babies.

(O) Remains of dinosaurs are called fossils.

(Y) No new dinosaurs are being discovered in the world today.

(N) Paleontologists study dinosaur fossils.

Name _____

A Hidden Dinosaur

I have a big skull with a beak like a parrot's. What am I? To answer this question, circle the correct answer under each question below. Then, follow the directions.

1. A dinosaur that has three horns on its head would be the:
   a. Triceratops - Mark out all letter B's below.
   b. Diplodocus - Mark out all letter P's below.
   c. Brachiosaurus - Mark out all letter R's below.

2. A large plant-eating dinosaur is the:
   a. Tyrannosaurus - Mark out all letter T's below.
   b. Deinonychus - Mark out all letter O's below.
   c. Apatosaurus - Mark out all letter N's below.

3. A dinosaur with large bony plates on its back is the:
   a. Iguanodon - Mark out all letter C's below.
   b. Stegosaurus - Mark out all letter D's below.
   c. Galapagos tortoise - Mark out all letter A's below.

4. A dinosaur with tiny front arms and a huge skull is the:
   a. Tyrannosaurus - Mark out all letter L's below.
   b. Ankylosaurus - Mark out all letter S's below.
   c. Triceratops - Mark out all letter E's below.

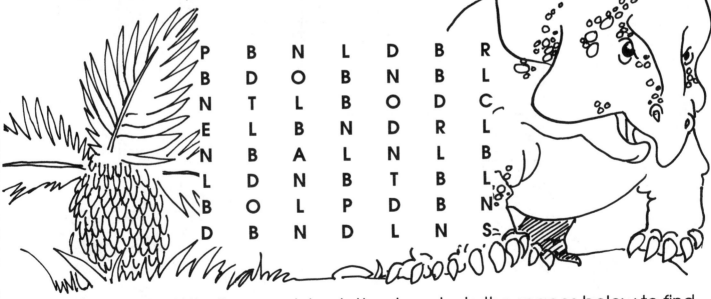

P	B	N	L	D	B	R
B	D	O	B	N	B	L
N	T	L	B	O	D	C
E	L	B	N	D	R	L
N	B	A	L	N	L	B
L	D	N	B	T	B	L
B	O	L	P	D	B	N
D	B	N	D	L	N	S

Start at the top. Write the remaining letters in order in the spaces below to find out the name of the hidden dinosaur.

___ ___ ___ ___ ___ ___ ___ ___ ___ ___ ___ ___

Name _____

How Long Were the Dinosaurs?

Dinosaurs varied greatly in size. Some were up to 90 feet long! Use a dinosaur encyclopedia or other reference materials to find the lengths of some dinosaurs. Write the names of the dinosaurs along the bottom of the line graph. Color in the lengths (in feet) with different colored pens or crayons.

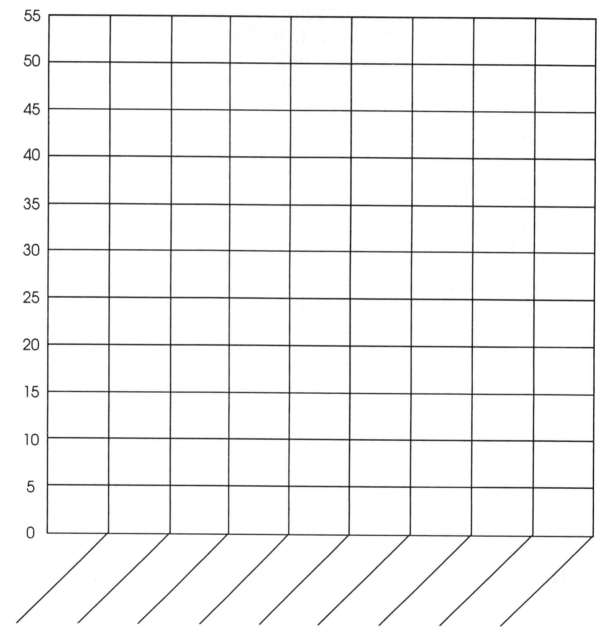

Dinosaur Names

Name _____

Dinosaur Diagram

A Venn diagram is a great tool to use to compare things. Use the one below to compare two dinosaurs. Fill in the Iguanodon with characteristics common only to it. Fill in the Triceratops with characteristics common only to the Triceratops. Above **Same**, write characteristics that both dinosaurs share. Write a story about your findings on the lines below.

Different   **Same**   **Different**

_____

_____

_____

_____

_____

_____

_____

_____

Name _____

A Dinosaur Tale

Study the dinosaurs illustrated below. Then complete each category with words that you associate with these animals. A few examples are already written under each heading. Use the words to compose a poem or short story about these dinosaurs. You can write your own composition or poem or you can share your ideas with other students and write a group composition or poem. Read your work aloud.

Nouns	Verbs	Adjectives
tail	walk	huge
teeth	run	spiked
head	eat	sharp

Title: _____

Name _____

Get a Clue!

Get a Clue! is a fun way to gain information about dinosaurs. To play, read the 16 clues below about a certain dinosaur. Use your science book or other resource materials and your own logical thinking to guess the name of the dinosaur. When you are finished, write your own clues about another dinosaur. Give it to another student to see if he/she can guess the answer.

I am a dinosaur.

1. My name means "three-horned face."
2. My skull is 7 or 8 feet long.
3. I have a beaked mouth like a parrot.
4. I eat plants.
5. I walk on all four legs.
6. I am 30 feet long.
7. I weigh up to 10 tons.
8. I am one of the last dinosaurs to live.
9. I have 3 claws on my front feet.
10. I live in Canada and the U.S.
11. I have a thick neck frill.
12. I have 3 horns on my skull.
13. I am the best-known horned dinosaur.
14. I use my horns for protection.
15. I have a small hoof on each toe.
16. I was named by O. C. Marsh in 1889.

I am a _____ .

I am a dinosaur.

1. _____
   _____
2. _____
   _____
3. _____
   _____
4. _____
   _____
5. _____
   _____
6. _____
   _____
7. _____
   _____
8. _____
   _____
9. _____
   _____
10. _____
    _____

I am a _____ .

Name _____

The End of the Dinosaurs

What could have killed all the dinosaurs? Scientists are not really sure. They have many different **theories,** or explanations, for why the dinosaurs died out.

Several theories are listed below. Each theory has a **cause** and an **effect.** A cause is "a change that happened on earth" and an effect is "what resulted from the change on earth." Draw a line from each cause to its effect.

Cause

A huge meteor hit the earth, starting fires and making a thick cloud of dust and smoke that covered the earth.

Small, fast mammals that liked to eat eggs quickly spread around the world.

New kinds of flowering plants started to grow on the earth. These plants had poison in them that the dinosaurs could not taste.

When dinosaurs were living, the earth was warm all year long. Suddenly the earth became cooler with cold winter months.

Effect

Dinosaurs were cold-blooded and they couldn't find places to hibernate. They had no fur or feathers to keep them warm. They froze to death.

The sunlight was blocked and plants couldn't grow. The dinosaurs starved to death.

Fewer and fewer baby dinosaurs were born.

The dinosaurs ate poison without even knowing it and they died.

Name _____

Animal Mysteries

As long as people have studied animals, there have been mysteries about why animals act in certain ways.

One mystery has to do with some animals' strange behavior **before** earthquakes. Horse and cattle stampedes, screeching seabirds, howling dogs, even animals coming out of hibernation early, are examples of this mysterious behavior.

Another mystery involves birds and ants. No one can explain why a bird will pick up an ant in its beak and rub the ant over its feathers again and again. This is called "anting," and birds have been known to do this for an hour without stopping.

One animal mystery is very sad. For hundreds of years, some whales have mysteriously swam from the ocean onto a beach where they would die. Reports of "beached whales" occur about five times a year somewhere in the world.

There are hundreds of other animal mysteries—such as how and why animals hibernate— that scientists have not solved. Can you think of another animal mystery?

3 Animal Mysteries

Write.

1. Some animals act strangely before an_____.

Check.

This strange behavior includes: ☐ laughing birds ☐ howling dogs

☐ horse and cattle stampedes   ☐ barking whales

☐ leaving hibernation early   ☐ screeching seabirds

Write.

2. This mystery is about _____ rubbing _____ over their feathers.

Write.

3. A sad mystery is about _____ swimming onto

a _____ and dying.

• Write a solution to one of the animal mysteries.

SCIENCE

Name _____

Hibernation

Have you ever wondered why some animals hibernate? Hibernation is a long sleep that some animals go into for the winter.

Animals get their warmth and energy from food. Some animals cannot find enough food in the winter. They must eat large amounts of food in the fall. Their bodies store this food as fat. Then in winter, they sleep in hibernation. Their bodies live on the stored fat. Since their bodies need much less food during hibernation, they can stay alive without eating new food during the winter.

Some animals that hibernate are: bats, chipmunks, bears, snakes and turtles.

Underline.

Hibernation   is a sleep that some animals go into for the winter.
                    is the time of year to gather food for the winter.

Yes or No.

Animals get their warmth and energy from food.	Yes	No
Some animals cannot find enough food in the winter.	Yes	No
Animals hibernate because they are lazy.	Yes	No
Animals need less food while they are hibernating.	Yes	No

Match.

Animals that hibernate. . .

    eat and store food   in the winter.
    go to sleep   in the fall.

Color the animals that hibernate.

Rain in the Rainforest

At least 80 inches of rain falls and thundershowers may occur for 200 or more days each year in a rainforest. Rainforests need a lot of rain so that the plants native to them do not dry out. Fill in the precipitation graph below with the average rainfall of a typical tropical rainforest. The amounts are listed beneath the graph.

```
        0  2  4  6  8  10 12 14 16 18 20 22 24 26 28 30
```

JANUARY	
FEBRUARY	
MARCH	
APRIL	
MAY	
JUNE	
JULY	
AUGUST	
SEPTEMBER	
OCTOBER	
NOVEMBER	
DECEMBER	

J	F	M	A	M	J	J	A	S	O	N	D
24"	20"	13"	11"	10"	7"	8"	9"	9"	11"	14"	18"

What was the total rainfall for the year in this rainforest? _____

What is the total rainfall for a year in your area? _____

Name _____

Lightning

Lightning is a flash of light caused by electricity in the sky. Clouds are made of many water droplets. All of these droplets together contain a large electrical charge. Sometimes these clouds set off a huge spark of electricity called lightning. Lightning travels very fast. As it cuts through the air, it can cause thunder.

Lightning takes various forms. Some lightning looks like a zigzag in the sky. Sheet lightning spreads and lights the sky. Ball lightning looks like a ball of fire.

Underline.

Lightning is a flash of light   caused by sunshine.
caused by electricity in the sky.

Yes or No

Sometimes clouds set off a huge spark of electricity.   Yes   No
Lightning is caused by dry weather.   Yes   No
Lightning travels very fast.   Yes   No
Lightning can cause thunder.   Yes   No

Unscramble and write in the puzzle above.

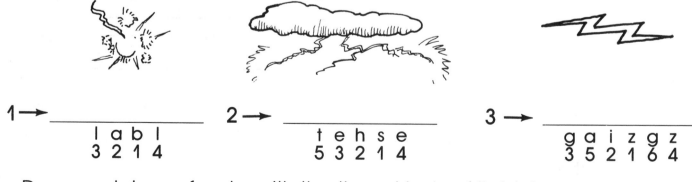

1 → _____
l a b l
3 2 1 4

2 → _____
t e h s e
5 3 2 1 4

3 → _____
g a i z g z
3 5 2 1 6 4

• Draw a picture of a sky with the three kinds of lightning.

Name _____

A Funnel Cloud—Danger!

Did you know that a tornado is the most violent windstorm on Earth? A tornado is a whirling, twisting storm that is shaped like a funnel .

A tornado usually occurs in the spring on a hot day. It begins with thunderclouds and thunder. A cloud becomes very dark. The bottom of the cloud begins to twist and form a funnel. Rain and lightning begin. The funnel cloud drops from the dark storm clouds. It moves down toward the ground.

A tornado is very dangerous. It can destroy almost everything in its path.

Circle.

A thunder
    tornado   is the most violent windstorm on Earth.

Check.

Which words describe a tornado?

☐ whirling ☐ twisting ☐ icy ☐ funnel-shaped ☐ dangerous

Underline.

A funnel shape is: ○ □ ⬭ ▽ ⌇

Write and Circle.

A tornado usually occurs in the _____ on a   cool day.
                                autumn   spring   hot

Write 1-2-3 below and in the picture above.

◯ The funnel cloud drops down to the ground.

◯ A tornado begins with dark thunderclouds.

◯ The dark clouds begin to twist and form a funnel.

SCIENCE

Name _____

The Eye of the Storm

A hurricane is a powerful storm that forms over some parts of an ocean. A hurricane can be several hundred miles wide.

A hurricane has two main parts: the eye and the wall cloud. The eye is the center of the storm. In the eye, the weather is calm. The storm around the eye is called the wall cloud. It has strong winds and heavy rain. In some hurricanes, the wind can blow 150 miles an hour!

As the storm moves across the water, it causes giant waves in the ocean. As the storm moves over land it can cause floods, destroy buildings and kill people who have not taken shelter.

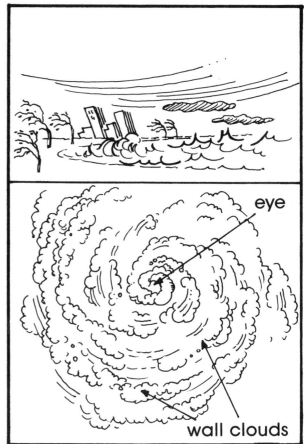

Circle.

A hurricane has two main parts:
tornado
wall cloud
eye

Write.

| wall cloud |
| eye |

_____ The calm center of the hurricane

_____ The wind and rainstorm around the eye

Check:

A hurricane ☐ can be several hundred miles wide.
☐ can have winds that move 150 miles an hour.
☐ is a small storm.
☐ can cause giant waves in the ocean.
☐ can cause floods and hurt people.

Name _____

Soil Study

Soil basically falls into three groups: sand, clay, and loam. Yet soils look much the same on the surface.

Soil is made of small pieces of broken rock. Wind, water, heat, cold, plants, and animals help to break up the rocks in the soil. Sometimes soil contains pieces of decayed plants and animals.

Take two tall, thin jars outside and look at soil in two different places. In each place, use the jar to dig up a soil plug. To do this, twist the jar as you push it in the soil. Then carefully pull the jar up. Tap out one plug of soil on a large piece of paper. Someone may have

to help you by running a knife around the mouth of the jar. Look at your soil with a magnifying glass. Feel it with your fingers. Record what you see and feel in the chart below. Repeat these steps with the other plug of soil.

Use another jar to collect one more plug of soil. Take it to school to share with the class. It will be interesting to look at each other's soil. Repeat the same steps as you did with the first two plugs of soil. Then record these findings on the chart.

Rank the three soil samples below according to their color, texture, and the amounts of moisture and decayed plants present in them. Write about any other interesting characteristics the soil samples contain.

Where I Found the Soil	Color	Texture	Dry or Wet?	Decayed Plants Present?	Other Interesting Characteristics

Name _____

Tidal Waves

Tidal waves are large, destructive waves that can crash onto land like a bomb. They are so strong that they can travel into a town and tear large buildings down. These waves happen only 2 or 3 times a year and are caused by underwater landslides, earthquakes, or hurricanes. Use this information to complete the line graph.

Location	Height	Location	Height
Portugal	50 feet	Japan (1896)	100 feet
Hawaii	20 feet	Chile	35 feet
Alaska	60 feet	Northern Chile	70 feet
Japan (1933)	96 feet		

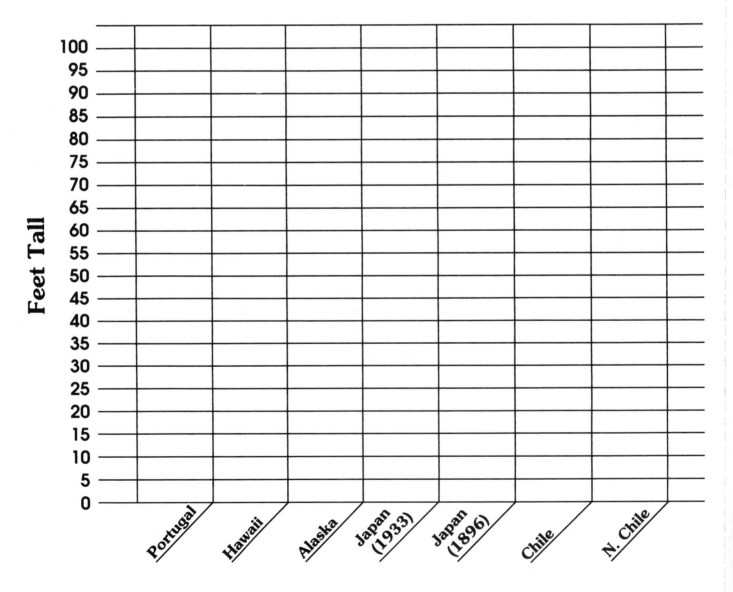

Name _____

Volcanic Activity

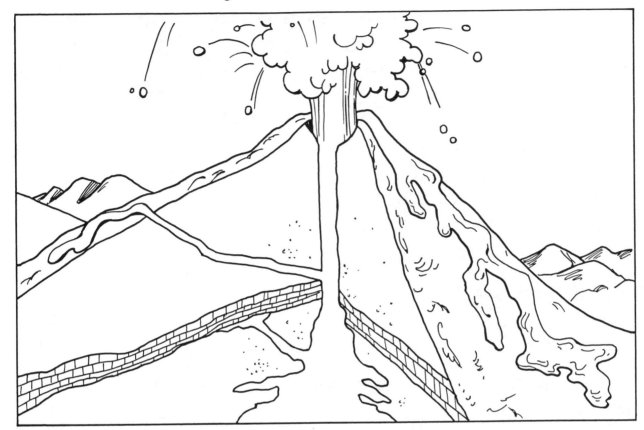

Indonesia is comprised of the world's largest group of islands. These islands are located on the equator in the Indian Ocean between Asia and Australia.

Children living in Indonesia study about the land around them. This includes volcanoes because there are about 60 active volcanoes on the islands.

Use the clues below to label the parts of the volcano.

1. The magma is the hot liquid in the center of the earth. Color it red.

2. The conduit is the passage that leads up the mountain. Color it red also.

3. Rock makes up the outer part of the mountain. Color the rock brown.

4. The vent is the opening. Circle it.

5. The lava is the liquid that runs down the side of the mountain. Color the lava orange and draw more lava at the vent.

SCIENCE

Name _____

Weight Is Not Mass!

Another word for the pull of gravity is weight. Weight changes according to how far away an object is from its source of gravity. The mass of an object does not change regardless of where in the universe that object is located. This is because mass is the amount of matter in the object. To understand weight and mass better, answer the questions below. Pretend you are on a spaceship to the moon.

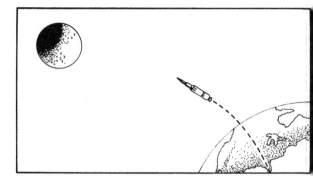

ON EARTH (Earth's pull of gravity)

Your mass: _____ lb X 2.2 = _____ kg

Your weight: _____ kg X 9.8 m/s^2 = _____ N

1/4 OF THE WAY TO THE MOON (Earth's lessening pull of gravity)

Your mass: _____ lb X 2.2 = _____ kg

Your weight: _____ kg X 7.7 m/s^2 = _____ N

1/2 OF THE WAY TO THE MOON (Earth's lessening pull of gravity)

Your mass: _____ lb X 2.2 = _____ kg

Your weight: _____ kg X 5.6 m/s^2 = _____ N

3/4 OF THE WAY TO THE MOON (Earth's lessening pull of gravity)

Your mass: _____ lb X 2.2 = _____ kg

Your weight: _____ kg X 3.5 m/s^2 = _____ N

ON THE MOON (Moon's pull of gravity)

Your mass: _____ lb X 2.2 = _____ kg

Your weight: _____ kg X 1.6 m/s^2 = _____ N

What value is changing in each of these sets of numbers? _____

Name _____

Sun – sational Puzzle

Use words from the Word Box to complete the crossword puzzle about the sun.

Word Box

| sun | flares | sunspots | chromosphere |
| core | corona | photosphere | prominences |

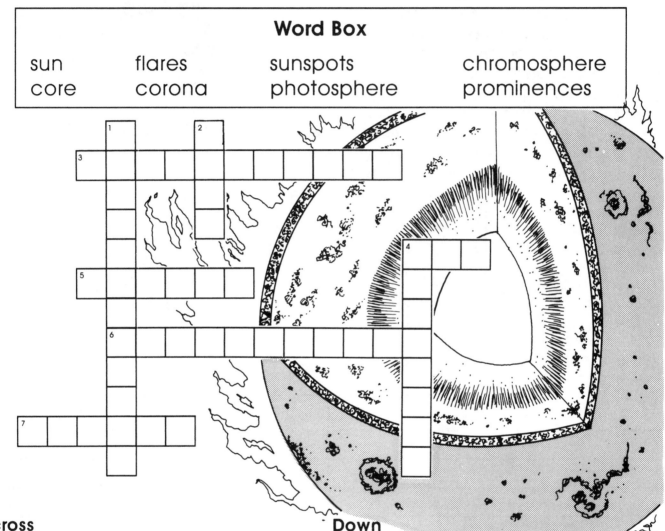

Across

3. the part of the sun you can see
4. huge glowing ball of gases at the center of our solar system
5. the region of the sun's atmosphere above the chromosphere
6. big, bright arches of gas
7. flashes of light on the sun's surface

Down

1. the middle part of the sun's atmosphere
2. the center of the sun
4. dark patches that sometimes appear on the sun

SCIENCE

Name _____

A Time Capsule on the Moon

Scientists have studied the rocky surface of the moon from samples that astronauts brought back to Earth. They found out that the moon is probably 4 1/2 billion years old! Because the moon has no rain or wind, everything stays the same on the surface. The U.S. flags placed on the moon should stay for millions of years. That means future visitors will see them long after we're gone. What do you think would be important to show people millions of years from now? Design a space time capsule to be sealed and left on the moon. What will you put in it? Why?

_____

_____

_____

_____

_____

_____

_____

_____

Bring some of these items to share with the class and make a class time capsule. Seal it until the end of the year.

Name _____

Man on the Moon

Earth's closest neighbor in space is the moon. The moon is very different from the earth. It has no wind, no air, and no water. The sky around the moon always looks black, and stars can always be seen. Because there is a lot less gravity on the moon, astronauts can jump much farther there than on Earth. There are large holes, called **craters**, on the moon.

Pretend you are an astronaut and you have just landed on the moon. You see many craters all around you.

Suppose you begin to travel in the order of the numbered craters on the moon. With your first step you jump from crater #1, over crater #2 and land on crater #3. You continue skipping over one crater with every step, until you come back to where you started. With a red crayon color the craters you landed on.

Now imagine that you started on crater #1, jumped over two craters at a time, and landed on #4. Continue following this pattern until you reach #16 and mark each of the craters you landed on with an X.

Which two craters would you have landed on both times?

Craters # _____ and # _____

SCIENCE

Name _____

Where Will It Lead?

Read the list of famous events in American space exploration. Number them in the correct order.

Year	Event	Spacecraft
_____ 1981	first space shuttle	Columbia
_____ 1961	first American in space	Freedom 7
_____ 1971	first drive on the moon	Apollo 15
_____ 1962	orbit earth three times	Friendship 7
_____ 1973	astronauts live in space station	Skylab
_____ 1965	first walk in space	Gemini 4
_____ 1975	Americans and Russians meet in space	Apollo-Soyuz
_____ 1969	first walk on the moon	Apollo 11
_____ 1983	first American woman in space	Discovery

Make a time line to show the order of these events in American space exploration. Write each year in the top box, each event in the square and each spacecraft name in the bottom box. The first one is done for you.

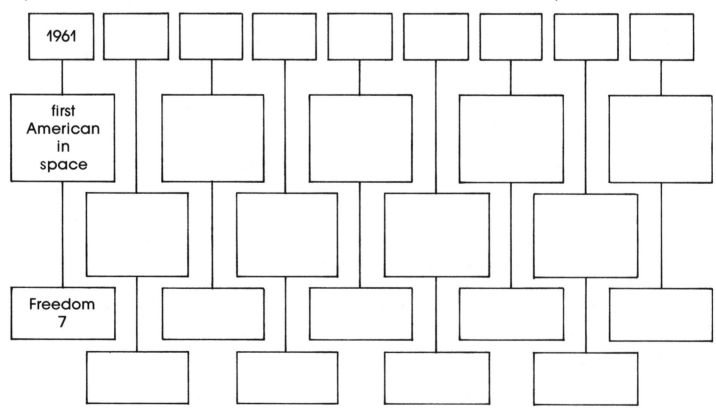

Name _____

A Black Hole

Have you ever heard of a mysterious black hole? Some scientists believe that a black hole is an invisible object somewhere in space. The scientists believe that it has such a strong pull toward it, called gravity, that nothing can escape from it!

These scientists believe that a black hole is a star that collapsed. The collapse made its pull even stronger. It seems invisible because even its own starlight cannot escape! It is believed that anything in space that comes near the black hole will be pulled into it forever. Some scientists believe there are many black holes in our galaxy.

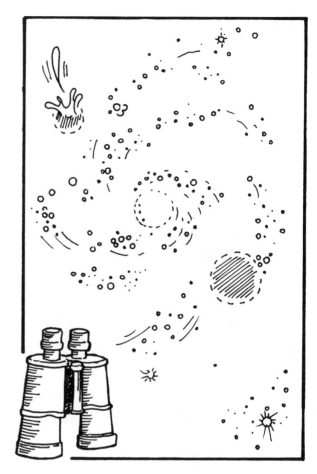

Check.

Some scientists believe that:

☐ a black hole is an invisible object in space.

☐ a black hole is a collapsed star.

☐ a black hole is a path to the other side of the Earth.

☐ a black hole has a very strong pull toward it.

☐ a black hole will not let its own light escape.

Write.

| A - gravity |
| B - collapse |

_____ To fall or cave in

_____ A strong pull from an object in space

Draw a spaceship being pulled into the black hole.

• Draw what you think the inside of a black hole would be like.

SCIENCE

Name _____

The Milky Way Galaxy

The Milky Way galaxy is made up of the Earth, its solar system and all the stars you can see at night. There are over 100 billion stars in the Milky Way!

The Milky Way is shaped much like a record. It has a center which the outer part goes around.

The Milky Way is always spinning slowly through space. It is so large that it would take 200 million years for the galaxy to turn one complete time.

Many stars in the Milky Way are in clusters. Some star clusters contain up to one million stars!

Our solar system

Put a red circle around our solar system.

Check.
The Milky Way galaxy is made up of

☐ Earth.
☐ no sun.
☐ our solar system.
☐ 100 billion stars.

Yes or No

The Milky Way is shaped like a pencil.	Yes	No
The Milky Way is always slowly moving in space.	Yes	No
Many stars in the Milky Way are in clusters.	Yes	No
Some star clusters have one million stars.	Yes	No

Circle.

It would take
200
90
600
million years for the galaxy to spin once.

Underline.
Which object is the Milky Way shaped much like?

 CD   ruler

Name _____

How Big?

Planets vary greatly in size. Look at the list of planets and their diameters.

Planet	Diameter
Mercury	3,000 miles
Venus	7,500 miles
Earth	7,900 miles
Mars	4,200 miles
Jupiter	88,700 miles
Saturn	74,600 miles
Uranus	31,600 miles
Neptune	30,200 miles

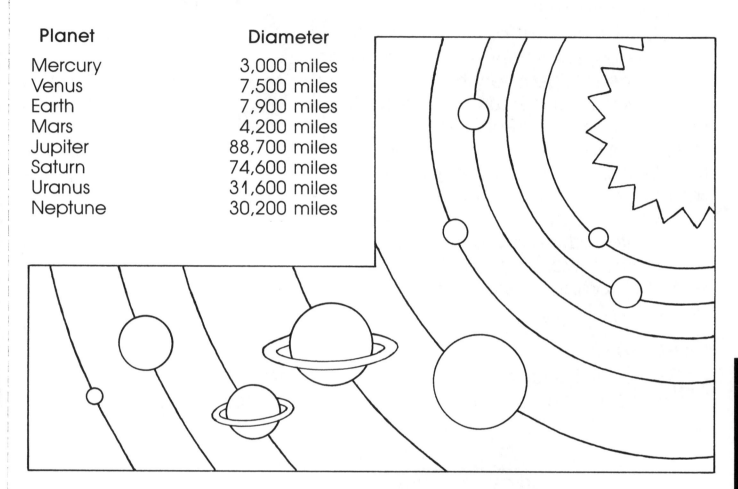

SCIENCE

Write the names of the planets in order by size starting with the planet that has the largest diameter.

1. _____
2. _____
3. _____
4. _____
5. _____
6. _____
7. _____
8. _____

Name _____

Mercury

Mercury is one of the smallest of the nine planets in our solar system. It is also the nearest planet to the sun.

Mercury spins very slowly. The side next to the sun gets very hot before it turns away from the sun. The other side freezes while away from the sun. As the planet slowly spins, the frozen side then becomes burning hot and the hot side becomes freezing cold.

Even though Mercury spins slowly, it moves around the sun very quickly. That is why it was named Mercury— after the Roman messenger for the gods.

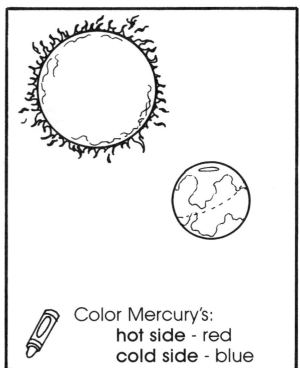

Color Mercury's:
hot side - red
cold side - blue

Underline.

Mercury
is the largest planet in our solar system.
is one of the smallest planets in our solar system.

Write.

Mercury is the _____ planet to the sun.

darkest   nearest

Match.

How does spinning slowly affect the temperature on Mercury?

The side next to the sun   is freezing cold.

The side away from the sun   is burning hot.

Circle.

Mercury moves   quickly   around the sun. Mercury spins very   lightly.
                quietly   slowly.

Check.

Mercury was named for the ☐ famous Roman speaker.
                           ☐ Roman messenger for the gods.

Name _____

Venus

Venus is the nearest planet to Earth. Because it is the easiest planet to see in the sky, it has been called the Morning Star and Evening Star. The Romans named Venus after their goddess of love and beauty.

Venus is covered with thick clouds. The sun's heat is trapped by the clouds. The temperature on Venus is nearly 900 degrees!

Space probes have been sent to study Venus. They have reported information to scientists. But they can only last a few hours on Venus because of the high temperature.

Venus turns in the opposite direction from Earth. So, on Venus, the sun rises in the west and sets in the east!

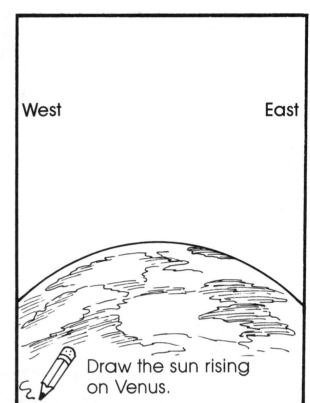

West   East

Draw the sun rising on Venus.

Unscramble and Circle.

_____ is the   friendliest
                              nearest   planet to Earth.

  e s V u n
  2 5 1 4 3

Check.

It is called the   ☐ Evening Sun
                   ☐ Morning Star   because it is so easy to see.
                   ☐ Evening Star

Circle.

The Romans named Venus for their:

goddess of love and beauty   god of light   goddess of truth

Yes or No

Half of Venus is frozen with ice and snow.   Yes   No
Space probes have reported information from Venus.   Yes   No
On Venus, the sun rises in the east and sets in the west.   Yes   No

Name _____

The Red Planet

Mars is the fourth planet from the sun at 141,600,000 miles away. The diameter of Mars is 4,200 miles. Mars is often called the Red Planet because rocks on the surface contain limonite, which is similar to rust. The planet has large deserts with huge dust storms. You can create your own landscape of Mars. Here's how:

Materials Needed

1 shoe box
sand
pebbles
foil
spray bottle of water
2 steel wool cleaning pads
    (without soap)

Directions

1. Line the box with foil.
2. Fill it with sand.
3. Cut the steel wool into small pieces and mix with sand.
4. Place rocks and pebbles on top.
5. Make dried-out river beds using your fingers.
6. Spray water to cover sand and keep wet for a few days.
7. Record with descriptions below.

Day 1	Day 2	Day 3
Day 4	Day 4	Day 6

Name _____

Jupiter

Jupiter is the largest planet in our solar system. It has sixteen moons. Jupiter is the second brightest planet— only Venus is brighter.

Jupiter is bigger and heavier than all of the other planets together. It is covered with thick clouds. Many loose rocks and dust particles form a ring around Jupiter.

One of the most fascinating things about Jupiter is its Great Red Spot. The Great Red Spot of Jupiter is a huge storm in the atmosphere. It looks like a red ball. This giant storm is larger than Earth! Every six days it goes completely around Jupiter.

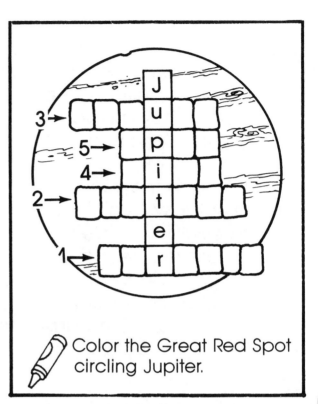

Color the Great Red Spot circling Jupiter.

Unscramble and write in puzzle.

1 → Jupiter is the _____ planet in our solar system. 2 → Jupiter

```
e t s l r g a
5 7 6 1 3 4 2
```

has _____ moons. 3 → Jupiter is covered with thick

```
t n x s e i e
4 7 3 1 5 2 6
```

_____. 4 → Loose rocks and dust form a _____ around

```
d s o c l u
5 6 3 1 2 4
```

```
g i r n
4 2 1 3
```

Jupiter. 5 → The Great Red _____ of Jupiter is a huge storm.

```
t S o p
4 1 3 2
```

Circle and Write.

Jupiter is the second   largest / brightest   planet.

Jupiter is _____ and   lighter / heavier   than all planets together.
       bigger   redder

SCIENCE

Name _____

Saturn

Saturn is probably most famous for its rings. The rings which circle Saturn are made of billions of tiny pieces of ice and dust. Although these rings are very wide, they are very thin. If you look at the rings from the side, they are almost too thin to be seen.

Saturn is the second largest planet in our solar system. It is so big that 758 Earths could fit inside it!

Saturn is covered by clouds. Strong, fast winds move the clouds quickly across the planet.

Saturn has 22 moons! Its largest moon is called Titan.

Draw 22 moons around Saturn!

Circle.

Saturn is most famous for its   spots.   rings.

Write.

Saturn's rings are made of _____ and _____.

mud   ice   dust   moons

Check.

Saturn's rings are   ☐ red, yellow and purple.
                      ☐ wide, but thin.

Underline.

Saturn ₒₒₒ is the second largest planet in our solar system.
is big enough to hold 758 Earths inside it.
is farther from the sun than any other planet.
is covered by fast, strong winds.
has 22 moons.

Unscramble.

Saturn's largest moon is called _____.

i T a n t
2 1 4 5 3

Name _____

Uranus

Did you know that Uranus was first thought to be a comet? Many scientists studied the mystery "comet." It was soon decided that Uranus was a planet. It was the first planet to be discovered through a telescope.

Scientists believe that Uranus is made of rock and metal with gas and ice surrounding it.

Even through a telescope, Uranus is not easy to see. That is because it is almost two billion miles from the sun that lights it. It takes Uranus 84 Earth years to orbit the sun!

Scientists know that Uranus has five moons and is circled by nine thin rings. But there are still many mysteries about this faraway planet.

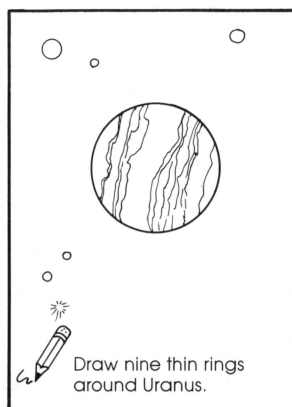

Draw nine thin rings around Uranus.

SCIENCE

Circle.

Uranus was first thought to be a   moon.
                                     comet.

Write.

Uranus was the first planet to be discovered through a _____.

telescope   TV

Check.

Scientists believe that Uranus is made of:

☐ rock   ☐ oil   ☐ metal   ☐ oceans   ☐ gas   ☐ ice

Match.

two billion miles   . . .the number of Uranus' moons

84 Earth years   . . .the distance of Uranus from the sun

five   . . .the number of Uranus' rings

nine   . . .the time it takes Uranus to orbit the sun

Name _____

Neptune

Neptune is the eighth planet from the sun. It is difficult to see Neptune—even through a telescope. It is almost three billion miles from Earth.

Scientists believe that Neptune is much like Uranus—made of rock, iron, ice and gases.

Neptune has two moons. Scientists believe that it may also have rings.

Neptune is so far away from the sun that it takes 164 Earth years for it to orbit the sun just once!

Neptune is a cold and distant planet that scientists still know very little about.

Draw 2 moons around Neptune.

Write, Circle or Unscramble.

N eptune is the   sixth / eighth   planet from the sun.

E arth is almost three _____ miles from Neptune.
million   billion

P eople know   very little / very much   about Neptune.

T elescopes are used to see Neptune.   **Yes   No**

U ranus and Neptune are made of: rock   soap   gases   ice

N eptune is a _____ and _____ planet.
warm   cold   distant   near

E very orbit around the _____ takes Neptune 164 Earth years.
u   s   n
2   1   3

Name _____

Constellations of the Zodiac

Astronomers have divided the sky into 88 constellations. The letters in the blocks below will spell out the names of 12 constellations found in the sky. The beginning letter of each constellation is in the star. Draw straight lines between the letters to find the name of each constellation. No lines will cross. Write the name of each constellation at the bottom of the page.

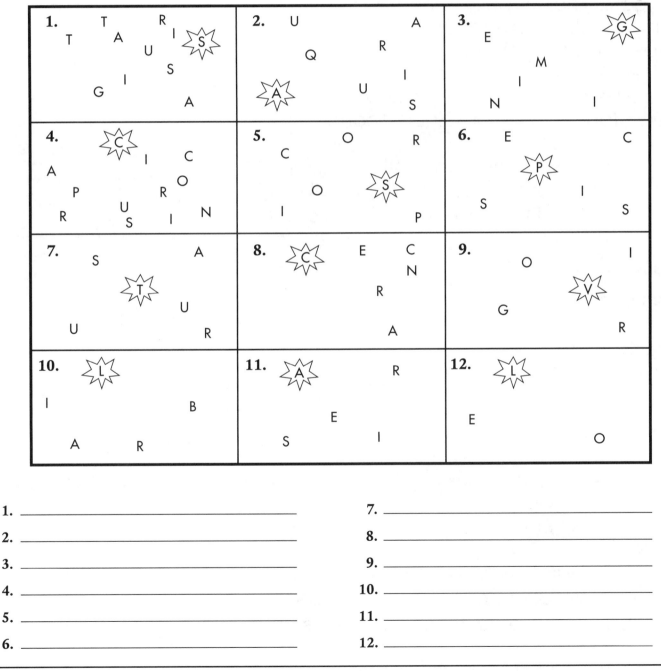

1. _____
2. _____
3. _____
4. _____
5. _____
6. _____

7. _____
8. _____
9. _____
10. _____
11. _____
12. _____

SCIENCE

Name _____

Constellations

On a clear night, you can see about two thousand stars in the sky. Scientists can use giant telescopes to see billions of stars.

Stars in groups form pictures called constellations. These constellations have been recognized for years. Ancient people named many constellations for animals, heroes and mythical creatures. Many of these names are still used.

Some constellations can be seen every night of the year. Others change with the seasons.

Since all stars are constantly moving, these same constellations that we now see will be changed thousands of years from now.

Connect the stars to form the constellation called the Little Dipper.

Write.

Stars in groups form pictures called _____.

telescopes   constellations

Check.

Ancient people named many constellations for:

☐ animals   ☐ heroes   ☐ oceans   ☐ mythical creatures

Match.

Billions of stars can be seen.

About two thousand stars can be seen.

Yes or No

Some constellations can be seen every night.	Yes	No
Some constellations change with the seasons.	Yes	No
In thousands of years, all constellations will be the same.	Yes	No

Name _____

Leaning into Summer

Why isn't it summer all year long? The seasons change because the Earth is tilted like the leaning Tower of Pisa. As the Earth orbits the sun, it stays tilting in the same direction in space.

Let's look at the seasons in the Northern Hemisphere. When the North Pole is tilting toward the sun, the days become warmer and longer. It is summer. Six months later, the North Pole tilts away from the sun. The days become cooler and shorter. It is winter.

Label the Northern Hemisphere's seasons on the chart below. Write a make-believe weather forecast for each season. Each forecast should show what the weather is like in your region for that season.

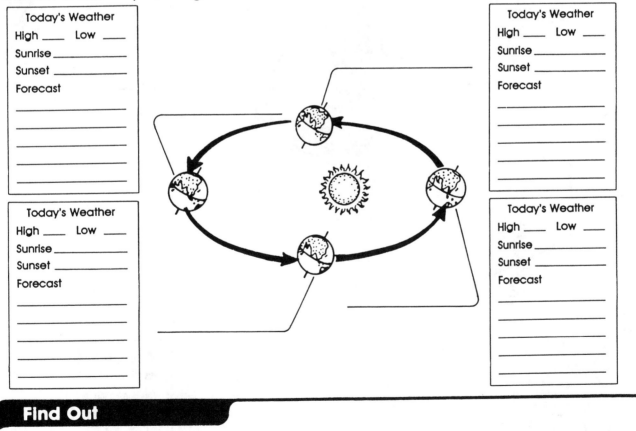

Today's Weather

High _____ Low _____

Sunrise _____

Sunset _____

Forecast

_____

_____

_____

_____

_____

Today's Weather

High _____ Low _____

Sunrise _____

Sunset _____

Forecast

_____

_____

_____

_____

_____

Today's Weather

High _____ Low _____

Sunrise _____

Sunset _____

Forecast

_____

_____

_____

_____

_____

Today's Weather

High _____ Low _____

Sunrise _____

Sunset _____

Forecast

_____

_____

_____

_____

_____

SCIENCE

Find Out

Where is the "land of the midnight sun"? Why does it have that name?

Name _____

The Moon's "Faces"

As the moon orbits the Earth, we often see different amounts of the moon's lighted part. Sometimes it looks like a circle, half-circle, or thin, curved sliver. These different shapes are the moon's **phases**.

Cut out the moon's phases as seen from Earth at the bottom of the page. Paste them in the correct box. Label the pictures using the words in the Word Bank. Use your science book to help you.

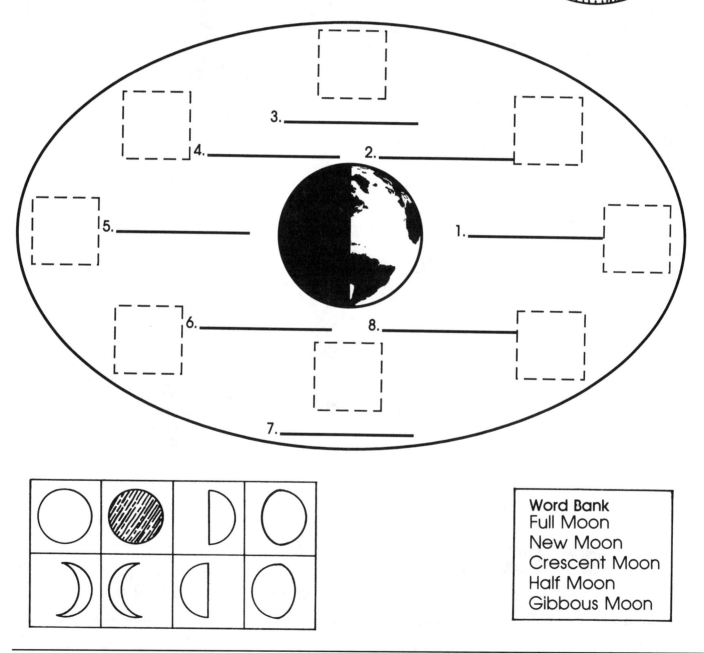

Word Bank
Full Moon
New Moon
Crescent Moon
Half Moon
Gibbous Moon

230

Name _____

Fatty Foods

Many of the foods we eat contain fat.
Try this fat test on several foods.

Materials Needed

6" x 6" pieces of brown paper bags (one per student)
6 containers each containing 1/4 cup of the following:
    water, oil, peanut butter, soft cheese,
    orange juice, soft margarine
6 toothpicks (one in each container)

Directions

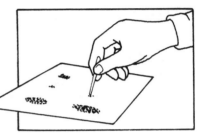

- Predict which foods contain fat on the chart below.
- Use the toothpick from each container to make a spot on your bag. Be careful to use small amounts so they won't run together.
- Wait several minutes and check the spots. Those with fat will leave a greasy spot.
- Record your observations.

Name of Food	I Predict . . .		I Observed . . .	
	Fat	No Fat	Fat	No Fat

Which food seemed to have the most fat? Why?_____

Which food surprised you? _____

Which of the foods do you eat often? _____

What could you eat instead of the fatty foods? _____

On the back of this page, draw the path of these foods through the digestive system.

SCIENCE

Name _____

My Body Homework

To keep your body working and looking its best, you should start good habits now and keep them as you grow older. Use this checklist to keep yourself on track for the next week. Keep it on your bathroom mirror or next to your bed where it will remind you to do your "homework!"

	Sun.	Mon.	Tues.	Wed.	Thurs.	Fri.	Sat.
I slept at least 8 hours.							
I ate a healthy breakfast.							
I brushed my teeth this morning.							
I ate a healthy lunch.							
I washed my hands after using the bathroom.							
I exercised at least 30 minutes today.							
I drank at least 6 glasses of water.							
I stood and sat up straight.							
I ate a healthy dinner.							
I bathed.							
I brushed my teeth this evening.							

Name _____

What I Look for in a Friend

What I Look for in a Friend	What I Do Not Look for in a Friend
1.	1.
2.	2.
3.	3.
4.	4.

SOCIAL STUDIES

Name _____

Story Plan About Friends

Setting

Where the story takes place _____

_____

When the story takes place _____

_____

Characters in the story _____

_____

The problem in the story is _____

_____

_____

_____

Steps to solve the problem:

First, the friends _____

_____

Next, the friends _____

_____

Finally, the friends _____

_____

The story ends _____

_____

_____

_____

Name _____

Your Family

1. What is a family? _____
   _____
   _____
   _____

2. What is the purpose of a family? _____
   _____
   _____
   _____

3. Who in your family do you go to . . .
   when you are sick? _____
   for help with homework? _____
   for advice? _____
   when you are afraid? _____
   when you want something? _____
   when you are unhappy? _____
   when you have had a bad day? _____
   Have you always gone to the same person in each situation or do you go
   to different people in the family at different times? _____
   Explain your answer. _____
   _____
   _____

4. What does your family do for recreation? _____
   _____
   _____

5. Compare your family with others. How is it the same? How is it different?
   _____
   _____

6. Do you think families around the world are like families you know?
   Explain your answer. _____
   _____
   _____

SOCIAL STUDIES

Name _____

What Do You See?

Look at the pictures below. Write three sentences about each one concerning
(1) the appearance of the person(s), (2) the means of transportation and
(3) the landscape.

_____
_____
_____
_____
_____
_____

_____
_____
_____
_____
_____
_____

_____
_____
_____
_____
_____

Draw a picture in the box of you
going somewhere. Write three
sentences describing yourself.

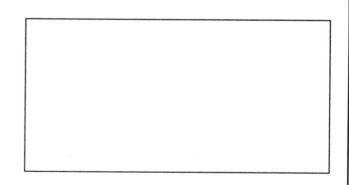

_____
_____
_____

Name _____

The Secret Message

One morning in late June, Sally, Jim, and Lee Cruise found a very strange note on the breakfast table. It looked like a secret code. Suddenly, Lee realized that it was a rebus. Each line contained one word in the message. Help the Cruise children read the rebus.

L + (✈ − j) + 's = _____

s + (🐝 − b) = _____

(🪤 − rap) + (🐔 − n) = _____

(🦄 − 🌽) + t + (🛏 − b) = _____

(📎 − pler) + (⭕ − ir) + s = _____

Then Mom and Dad yelled, "Surprise! Do you want to go?"

The excited children answered their parents' question with a rebus of their own. Fill in the missing blanks.

Y + (♜♝♞ − CH − S) = _____ !

SOCIAL STUDIES

Name _____

The Best Way to Tell It

There are many vehicles that can be used to convey a message, such as a telephone, a fax machine, a radio, etc. Tell by which vehicle you think the information below would best be delivered. In some instances, there may be more than one choice.

You will be late coming home from school.

_____

How you looked when you were a baby

_____

An urgent need for help _____

How the world looked 5,000,000 years ago _____

The first Thanksgiving _____

National news _____

A make-believe story _____

Asking someone to visit your home on their vacation _____

A garage sale _____

Something that happened "once upon a time" _____

A funny experience _____

What you saw _____

A baseball game _____

An adventure in space _____

A series of strange events and their solutions _____

Tell someone you missed them. _____

_____

Your dog ran away. _____

_____

A true story _____

_____

Name _____

It Says the Same Thing Differently

Translate and write the rebus message. Then do what it tells you to do on this line:

_____

W + [V] - P + [tent] - NT   [yoyo] - YO + [jar] - N

_____   _____

[nail] + [people] - ILN   [man] + [water] - TE + [door] - OOR

_____   _____

Use the Code Key below to translate the message under it.

A	B	C	D	E	F	G	H	I	J	K	L	M	N	O	P	Q	R	S	T	U	V	W	X	Y	Z

Make a code of your own. Fill in the Code Key below with a symbol to represent each letter. Write a direction using your code.

A	B	C	D	E	F	G	H	I	J	K	L	M	N	O	P	Q	R	S	T	U	V	W	X	Y	Z

_____

_____

_____

Name _____

Symbol-Sign Communication

Here are some familiar symbol-signs:

Handicapped

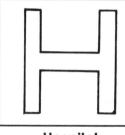

Hospital

No Parking

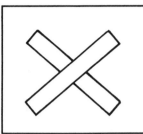

Railroad Crossing

Design, draw and color symbol-signs for the following:

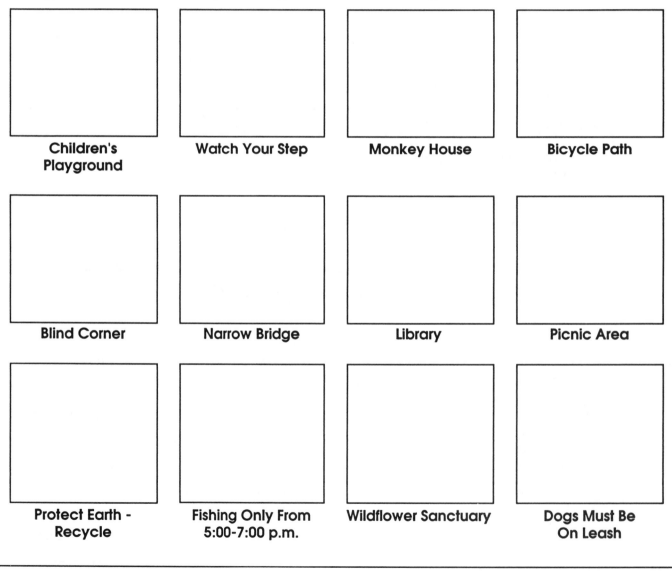

Children's Playground

Watch Your Step

Monkey House

Bicycle Path

Blind Corner

Narrow Bridge

Library

Picnic Area

Protect Earth - Recycle

Fishing Only From 5:00-7:00 p.m.

Wildflower Sanctuary

Dogs Must Be On Leash

Name _____

Land Ho!

Read each clue. Find the matching word in the Word Bank. Write it in the puzzle.

Across

1. Opposite of south
4. Raised land smaller than mountain
5. Opposite of east
6. A very high hill
10. Water with land all around it
11. Water is on three sides of this landform
12. Opposite of west
14. A very large piece of land

Down

2. Large body of salt water
3. Flat land that is higher than the land around it
7. Water is all around this land
8. Very dry, sandy land
9. A large stream of water
11. Flat land
13. Opposite of north

Word Bank

continent	lake	plain
desert	mountain	plateau
east	north	river
hill	ocean	south
island	peninsula	west

Daily Learning Drills Grade 3

SOCIAL STUDIES

Name _____

The Long Climb

Mom, Dad, Sally, Lee, and Jim started their vacation by visiting some places in the state of New York.

They decided to visit the Statue of Liberty. Two sets of parallel stairways rise from the statue's base to its crown. First Dad gave the children clues so they could find out how many steps are in each stairway.

Clue 1: The number is between 160 and 170.
Clue 2: It is an even number.
Clue 3: If you add the 3 digits in the number, the answer is 15. How many steps are in each stairway? _____

Next, Dad asked them to figure out the statue's height in inches from its base to its torch.

Clue 1: The number is less than 1,820 and more than 1,800.
Clue 2: It is an odd number.
Clue 3: The sum of the digits is 13.

The Statue of Liberty is _____ inches tall.

Finally, Dad had them compute the statue's weight in tons.

Clue 1: The number is between 200 and 250.
Clue 2: It is divisible by 5.
Clue 3: The sum of the digits is 9.

The Statue of Liberty weighs _____ tons.

Extra: The Statue of Liberty weighs _____ pounds.

Name _____

Music in the Air

While in New York City, the Cruise family saw a famous play on Broadway. Both Sally and Lee thought it was funny, and Jim really enjoyed the music.

To find out the name of the musical, read the sentence hidden in the chart below. Look up, down and sideways, connecting all the letters into words as you go.

N	N	I	Y	P	K
I	A	S	A	L	R
E	N	E	W	Y	O
T	E	H	T	F	O
H	E	N	A	M	E

End →

Start →

Write the sentence here: _____

_____

SOCIAL STUDIES

Name _____

A Family Tree

The Cruise family stopped at Ellis Island, an old immigration station located in the New York Harbor. Mom and Dad reminded the children that America is a land of immigrants. Immigrants are individuals and families from other countries who have decided to live in America.

Mom told the children that people can show who belongs in their family by drawing a family tree. Each branch represents a member of the family.

Sally, Lee, and Jim decided that they would like to make a family tree. It would include their names; the names of their parents; both sets of grandparents, the Cruises and the Flyers; their dad's sister, Alice; her husband, John Jones; and their two children, Molly and Mark.

How many branches would the tree need? _____

Complete the family tree by drawing a branch for each family member. Write each person's name on a branch.

Name _____

Plymouth Rock

In Plymouth, Massachusetts, the Cruise family was able to see the famous rock which marks the Pilgrims' landing in America in 1620. The graphite boulder with the date carved on it is named "Plymouth Rock." It lies near the water's edge.

Lee decided to play with some of the other rocks in the bay. The rocks he chose were all about the same size.

First, Lee placed the rocks flat on the ground and started forming a triangle. It looked like this:

If Lee continued to follow the pattern and added rocks at the bottom of the triangle until he formed ten rows, how many rocks would he need? _____

Next, Lee created a four-sided hollow box. Each side was three rocks high and three rocks across like this:

How many rocks did Lee use? _____

Finally, Lee stacked rocks in a three-sided pyramid like the one shown here:

How many rocks did it take to form the pyramid? _____

SOCIAL STUDIES

Name _____

A Relaxing Ride

In Pennsylvania, the Cruise family visited Pennsylvania Dutch country. They rode through beautiful farmlands in a horse and buggy.

The horse and buggy followed a path from the farmhouse to the barn. Look carefully at the paths and count how many different ways they could travel.

They could travel _____ ways to get from the farmhouse to the barn.

Name _____

Our Capital

Washington, D.C., our nation's capital, has many popular tourist attractions.

Sally Cruise really wanted to visit the Lincoln Memorial because she had studied about our 16th President in school this year.

As she looked up at the large statue of Lincoln, Sally looked closely at the base. She noticed that it looked like it was made up of many rectangular shapes.

Count all the rectangles shown in the base of the statue. Do not count any shaded areas. _____

Daily Learning Drills Grade 3

SOCIAL STUDIES

Name _____

The White House

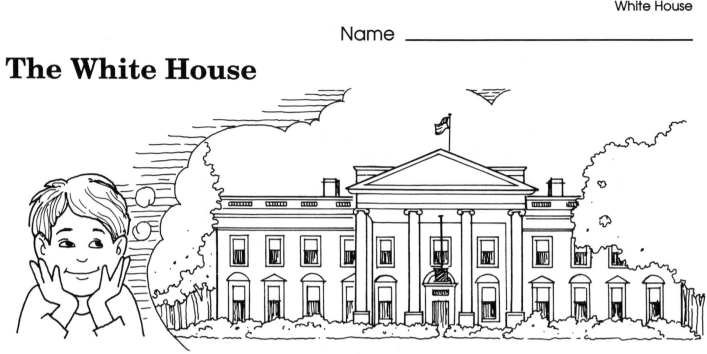

Jim Cruise really enjoyed his family's visit to the White House. Everything seemed so large and majestic. He remembered studying about some of the important events that have taken place there. Jim recalled that the White House has been the home of every President in American history except George Washington.

Jim has even thought about becoming the President of the U.S. himself. He knows that the President of the United States may not serve more than two terms in office. A term is four years.

Help Jim answer questions about his possible future election.

Our 42nd President was elected in 1992. If each future President is only elected to **one** term of four years, which President would Jim become if he were elected in the year 2040? _____

Our 42nd President was elected in 1992. If each future President is elected to **two** terms in office, which President would Jim become if he were elected in the year 2040? _____

Our 42nd President was elected in 1992. If in the future, all but two Presidents serve two terms, what President would Jim become if he were elected in the year 2040? _____

Name _____

Where's Our Mummy?

Chicago, Illinois, is a city with many interesting things to do. The Cruise family visited a zoo, an aquarium, a museum, and a planetarium.

The last place they went was the Field Museum of Natural History. Everyone agreed that their favorite exhibit was the Egyptian mummies. They learned that scientists today have discovered how the Egyptians of long ago made the mummies.

As they looked around at the mummy cases, each family member chose a favorite mummy. Use the clues to match each family member with his or her favorite mummy.

Clue 1: Mom liked a mummy on one end.

Clue 2: Dad liked the mummy that stood between Sally's and Lee's.

Clue 3: Jim's favorite mummy stood to the left of Sally's.

Clue 4: Mom's favorite mummy was separated from Dad's by two mummies.

_____'s   _____'s   _____'s   _____'s   _____'s
favorite   favorite   favorite   favorite   favorite

SOCIAL STUDIES

Name _____

Frontier Town

Dodge City, Kansas is an old western frontier town which attracts many tourists. On Front Street, each family member imagined himself or herself riding into town over 120 years ago. Dad thought about how tired he would have been just finishing a long cattle drive. Jim and Lee pictured themselves atop horses and not their ten-speed bikes. Mom and Sally thought about riding horses wearing long, full dresses on a hot, summer day.

As they looked at the buildings in town, they noticed signs posted in each window. The businesses were open only on certain days of the week.

Read the signs to help the family figure out which day of the week Dodge City really is a "Ghost Town," because all the stores are closed.

The day of the week on which

all of the shops are closed is _____ .

Your State

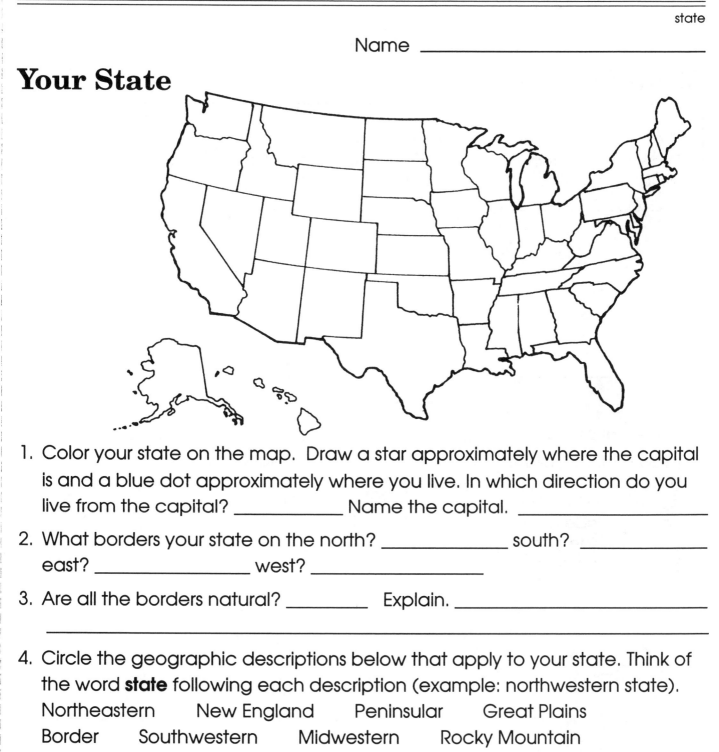

1. Color your state on the map. Draw a star approximately where the capital is and a blue dot approximately where you live. In which direction do you live from the capital? _____ Name the capital. _____

2. What borders your state on the north? _____ south? _____ east? _____ west? _____

3. Are all the borders natural? _____ Explain. _____
   _____

4. Circle the geographic descriptions below that apply to your state. Think of the word **state** following each description (example: northwestern state).
   Northeastern   New England   Peninsular   Great Plains
   Border   Southwestern   Midwestern   Rocky Mountain
   Inland Northwestern   Gulf Coast   Middle Atlantic   Southeastern

5. Write the names of several points of interest in your state. _____
   _____

6. Select one of the points of interest you would like to visit. Write a sentence or two about it. On the map, put a red dot approximately where it is located.
   _____

SOCIAL STUDIES

Name _____

State Symbols

My state is _____ .

Draw pictures of three of the state's symbols: bird, flower and tree.
Write the name of each symbol on the line under it.

Bird _____   **Flower** _____   **Tree** _____

Other state symbols: _____

Draw a picture of the
state flag. If the flag is
different on each side,
draw one side here and
the other side on the
back of this paper.

State Flag

State Seal

Write a description of the state seal.

_____

_____

_____

_____

_____

Draw the seal in the circle to the left. If the
two sides are different, draw the other side
on the back of this paper.

Name _____

Briefly Addressed

Write the postal abbreviation for each state.

1. Washington	_____	26. Oregon	_____
2. California	_____	27. Idaho	_____
3. Nevada	_____	28. Arizona	_____
4. Montana	_____	29. Wyoming	_____
5. Utah	_____	30. Colorado	_____
6. New Mexico	_____	31. North Dakota	_____
7. South Dakota	_____	32. Nebraska	_____
8. Kansas	_____	33. Oklahoma	_____
9. Texas	_____	34. Minnesota	_____
10. Iowa	_____	35. Missouri	_____
11. Arkansas	_____	36. Louisiana	_____
12. Wisconsin	_____	37. Illinois	_____
13. Mississippi	_____	38. Indiana	_____
14. Ohio	_____	39. Kentucky	_____
15. Tennessee	_____	40. Alabama	_____
16. Pennsylvania	_____	41. New York	_____
17. Vermont	_____	42. New Hampshire	_____
18. Maine	_____	43. Massachusetts	_____
19. Rhode Island	_____	44. Connecticut	_____
20. New Jersey	_____	45. Delaware	_____
21. Maryland	_____	46. Virginia	_____
22. West Virginia	_____	47. North Carolina	_____
23. South Carolina	_____	48. Georgia	_____
24. Florida	_____	49. Michigan	_____
25. Alaska	_____	50. Hawaii	_____

SOCIAL STUDIES

Daily Learning Drills Grade 3

Name _____

Baseball, U.S.A.

Locate the cities that have Major League Baseball teams on the map. Draw the symbol for each where it belongs.

National League
EAST
★ Philadelphia, PA (Phillies)
⚾ St. Louis, MO (Cardinals)
M Montreal (Expos)
🐻 Chicago, IL (Cubs)
☠ Pittsburgh, PA (Pirates)
🐟 Miami , FL (Marlins)
🍎 New York, NY (Mets)

WEST
G San Francisco, CA (Giants)
⚒ Atlanta, GA (Braves)
LA Los Angeles, CA (Dodgers)
✗ Houston, TX (Astros)
🔴 Cincinnati, OH (Reds)
P San Diego, CA (Padres)
⛰ Denver, CO (Rockies)

American League
EAST
T Toronto (Blue Jays)
NY New York, NY (Yankees)
🐯 Detroit, MI (Tigers)
🐦 Baltimore, MD (Orioles)
🧦 Boston, MA (Red Sox)
ᒻ Cleveland, OH (Indians)
B Milwaukee, WI (Brewers)

WEST
🧦 Chicago, IL (White Sox)
♛ Kansas City, KS (Royals)
R Arlington, TX (Rangers)
O Anaheim, CA (Angels)
🐟 Seattle, WA (Mariners)
A Oakland, CA (A's)
⦿⦿ Minneapolis, MN (Twins)

Name _____

North, South, East, and West

Pretend you are flying in an airplane with the wind blowing sharply in your face. You are flying from Chicago to Nashville. In what direction are you traveling?

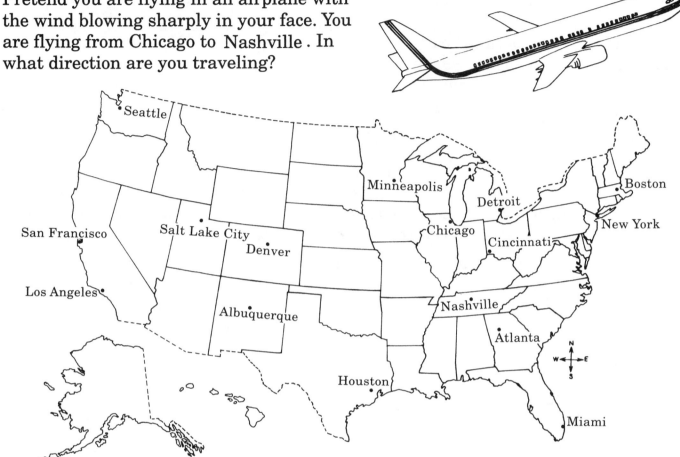

If you said, "south," to the above question, you are correct!

Write the direction you would be traveling for each set of cities. Use the four cardinal directions—north, south, east, and west.

Atlanta to Los Angeles _____

Seattle to Los Angeles _____

San Francisco to Nashville _____

Denver to Salt Lake City _____

Cincinnati to Detroit _____

Chicago to Nashville _____

Houston to Minneapolis _____

Miami to New York _____

Detroit to New York _____

Boston to Minneapolis _____

Atlanta to Albuquerque _____

Nashville to Miami _____

SOCIAL STUDIES

Name _____

Drawing a Compass Rose

The maps of the early explorers were beautiful pieces of art. Their maps would often have pictures of fire-breathing dragons and sea monsters warning of dangers where they were traveling.

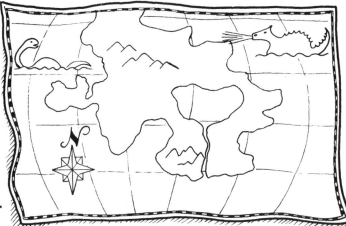

In a corner of their map would be a beautiful **compass rose**. The compass rose indicated the four **cardinal directions**—north, south, east, and west.

Follow the steps below to draw a compass rose in the upper right-hand corner of the map. Indicate the cardinal directions on your rose.

After completing the compass rose, draw a map of your own make-believe land.

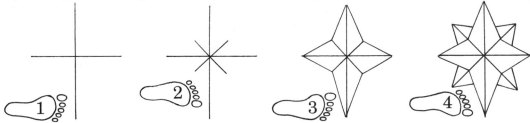

Name _____

Making a Compass

A compass is a magnet that can identify geographic direction. It is very easy to make your own compass and a lot of fun too!

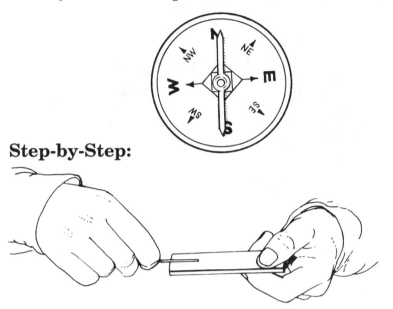

Step-by-Step:

You will need:
magnet
steel sewing needle
piece of thin plastic foam
    (from fast-food packaging)
shallow glass or plastic bowl
masking tape
water

1. Pull the sewing needle toward you across the magnet. Repeat this 20 times. Be sure to always pull in the same direction.

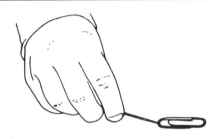

2. Test your needle on a steel object. If it is not yet magnetized, repeat step #1, until it is.

3. Tape the needle to a small piece of plastic foam.

4. Float your magnet in a dish of water.

What did you find out?

Wait for your floating needle to stop spinning. In what direction is it pointing?

_____

Try giving the floating needle a little spin. Wait for it to stop spinning. Now what direction is it pointing? _____

SOCIAL STUDIES

Name _____

Dream Town

You are the city planner and have been chosen to map out a new "dream town." What will make your community a great place to live?

Your new town will have shopping malls, parks, factories, streets, railroads, an airport, and whatever else you would like to add.

You will need:
large piece of white drawing paper or poster board
crayons or markers
ruler

Step-by-Step:
1. Cut out the Map Key and glue it on a corner of the large sheet of paper.
2. Draw the natural features like rivers, oceans, lakes, and hills or mountains.
3. Draw the streets and highways.
4. Draw the homes, factories, shopping centers, police station, etc., using the symbols from the Map Key.

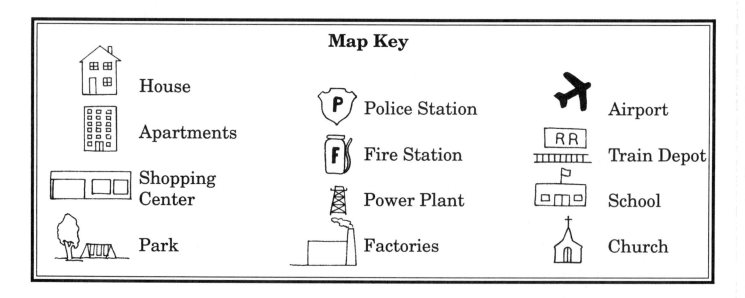

Map Key

House

Apartments

Shopping Center

Park

Police Station

Fire Station

Power Plant

Factories

Airport

Train Depot

School

Church

Name _____

A Walk Around Town

Let's take a walk around the town of Forest Grove. Use a marker or crayon to trace your route.

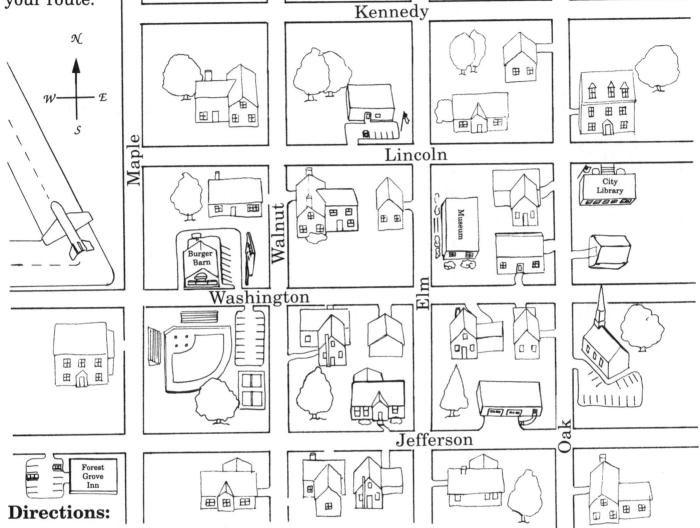

Directions:

1. Begin your walking tour at Forest Grove Inn.
2. Walk two blocks east to Elm Street.
3. Turn north on Elm Street. Walk to the Museum.
4. Go 1/2 block north to the corner of Elm and Lincoln.
5. Turn east on Lincoln. Walk until you come to the City Library.
6. Go south on Oak Street until you reach Washington Street.
7. Turn west on Washington and walk 2 1/2 blocks to the Burger Barn.
8. Lunch is over. Take the shortest way back to Forest Grove Inn.

Name _____

Near School

Geographers can tell us how places are the same and how they are different. Where you live is different from where your friend lives. Maybe you live southwest of school while your friend lives north of the school.

Write the names and draw pictures of landmarks that are found near your school. Place each one on the chart in its correct location relative to your school.

Northwest	North	Northeast
West	School	East
Southwest	South	Southeast

Name _____

Do You Have the Time?

The earth spins on its axis in a west to east direction. This causes our day to begin with the sun rising in the east and setting in the west. Different areas of the United States can have different amounts of daylight at the same moment in time. For instance, when the sun is rising in New York, it is still dark in California.

A **time zone** is an area in which everyone has the same time. Every zone is one hour different from its neighbor. There are 24 time zones around the world. There are six time zones in the United States. The map above shows the four zones that cover the 48 contiguous states.

When it is 6 o'clock in New York, what time is it in . . .

Chicago? _____   Los Angeles? _____   Denver? _____

What is the name of the time zone in which you live? _____

Name three other states in your time zone. _____

_____   _____

SOCIAL STUDIES

Name _____

They Showed the Way

Meriwether Lewis and William Clark were chosen by President Jefferson to find a route to the Pacific Ocean. They had to draw maps of the land, record weather conditions and write about the plants and animals that they found along the way. People wanted to know what it was like west of the Mississippi River. On May 14, 1804 they started their expedition. They arrived at the Pacific Ocean on November 7, 1805. They set up a camp which they named Fort Clatsop.

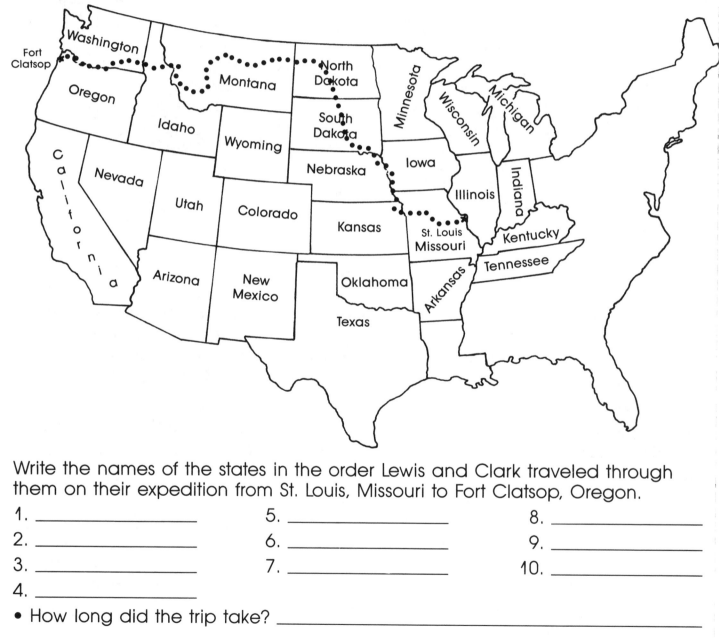

Write the names of the states in the order Lewis and Clark traveled through them on their expedition from St. Louis, Missouri to Fort Clatsop, Oregon.

1. _____   5. _____   8. _____

2. _____   6. _____   9. _____

3. _____   7. _____   10. _____

4. _____

• How long did the trip take? _____

Name _____

Totem Poles

Many Native American tribes painted symbols to tell stories. Others weaved designs into blankets to remind them of legends. The tribes in Washington State and parts of Alaska carved their family crests into trees. We call these totem poles. You can make a personal totem pole too. Draw your totem pole on another sheet of paper.

1. For the bottom of your totem pole, draw a human figure. It could be you.

2. On the top of the human figure, draw a symbol of your father's occupation.

3. Above that, draw a symbol to depict your mother. The symbol could show her occupation or it could show something she does that has special meaning to you.

4. Next draw a favorite animal, which will be your family's crest. It could be your family pet or an animal your family especially likes, such as a special bird.

5. The next section should include a symbol of the type of job you want to do when you become an adult.

6. Next think of a hobby that you really enjoy, such as a sport, music, or computers. Draw this.

7. On top of your totem pole, draw a symbol that stands for something very important to you.

8. Now go back and color your totem pole.

9. Then think of a way to make your totem pole out of scraps of construction paper, tissue paper, and other odds and ends.

10. Use your design to create a 3-D totem pole. Give it to your teacher for display.

SOCIAL STUDIES

Name _____

The Makah and Nootka Whalers

Although many tribes of the Northwest Coastal area used whales as a source of food and supplies, only the Makah and Nootka tribes actually hunted them at sea. These Indians trained and purified themselves for three months before the hunt. Then they set out in canoes. When a whale was spotted, the chief had the honor of striking with the first harpoon. All others then joined in until the whale was exhausted and eventually died. Finally, the Indians tied the mouth shut so the whale's lungs couldn't fill with water and sink, and the whale was towed back to shore.

Imagine the difficulty of hunting an animal the size of a whale! To help you visualize this incredible feat, use encyclopedias to find the length in meters of the whales listed below. Then write these lengths in feet and list a comparison to help you imagine the size.

Type of Whale	Length in Meters	Length in Feet	That's about as long as ...
blue			
humpback			
killer			
sperm			

Fun Fact: An entire tribe could live a whole year on only 2-4 whales!

Name _____

Native American Drum

The Eastern Woodland tribes lived in the woods and depended greatly on hunting. They practiced dances and songs from the time they were children. The drum was an important part of their ceremonies. Children learned to make their own drums using the five steps below. Number the steps for making a drum in the correct order. Then draw a picture to illustrate each step. Draw your completed drum in the last box.

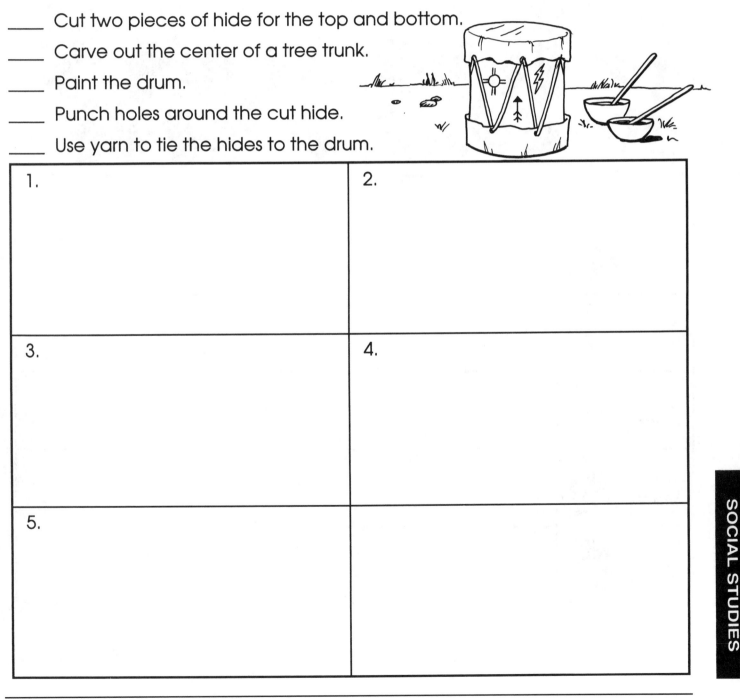

____ Cut two pieces of hide for the top and bottom.

____ Carve out the center of a tree trunk.

____ Paint the drum.

____ Punch holes around the cut hide.

____ Use yarn to tie the hides to the drum.

1.	2.
3.	4.
5.	

SOCIAL STUDIES

Name _____

The Hunters

Although they farmed and ate other foods besides meat, hunting was very important to most Woodland Indians, especially during the winter.

The information below shows the game that was caught by two Eastern Woodland tribes. Use the imformation to complete a double bar graph comparing the successes of the two tribes. Be sure to use a different color for each tribe.

Iroquois Tribe   **Mohawk Tribe**

* Each print represents 4 animals caught.

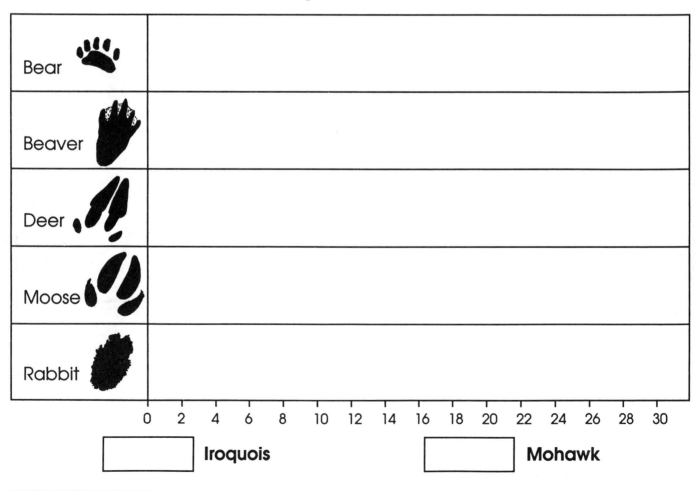

Name _____

Southwest Symbols

The tribes who lived in this area made pictures called pictographs to tell stories of hunting, farming, trading, traveling and battling with other tribes.

You can write an Indian story on another sheet of paper using symbols for the most important parts. Be sure to use words between the symbols to create complete sentences! The key has been started for you, but add your own symbols as you use them in the story.

Ex: As the [sun symbol] rose into the sky, the great [warrior symbol] rode off toward the [mountains symbol]

Symbol Key

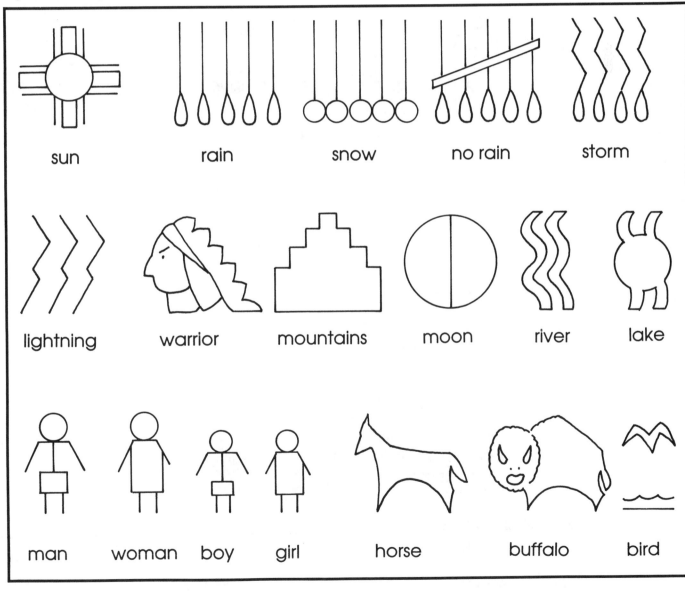

sun	rain	snow	no rain	storm

| lightning | warrior | mountains | moon | river | lake |

| man | woman | boy | girl | horse | buffalo | bird |

SOCIAL STUDIES

Daily Learning Drills Grade 3

Name _____

The Buffalo Hunters

The Plains Indians' survival depended on the buffalo. They killed only as many as they needed and wasted none of the animal.

Below is a list of some buffalo body parts. Make a logical guess as to the function of each. Then use an encyclopedia to find the actual uses. You may be very surprised!

Your Logical Guess

clothing, tepees, drums •   • teeth

decorations •   • brain

bowls for cooking •   • tongue

cups, spoons •   • hide

jewelry •   • large intestine

strings on bows •   • horns

bags for storage •   • muscles

ropes, belts •   • stomach

food •   • hair

tanning mixture •   • tail
for leather

Name another buffalo part and its function. _____

Fun Fact: The Plains Indians had over 500 uses for the buffalo.

Name _____

Canada, Geographically Speaking

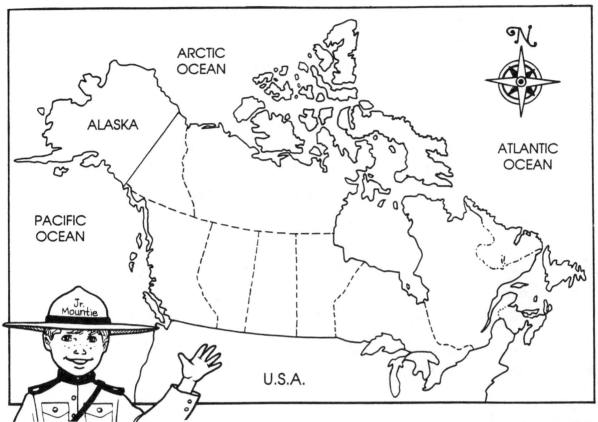

Unlike the United States, Canada is not divided into states. Follow the directions to label the ten provinces and two territories that make up Canada.

1. The Yukon Territory is connected to Alaska. The Northwest Territory is the large area to its east. Label them.
2. British Columbia is south of Yukon. Label the province and color it yellow.
3. East of British Columbia is Alberta. Label it and color it red.
4. The province between Alberta and Manitoba is called Saskatchewan. This is where Big Foot supposedly lives. Draw him there and label the provinces.
5. Winnepeg is a city in Manitoba. Label the city and color the province brown.
6. The province north of the Great Lakes is Ontario. Color it orange.
7. The largest province is Quebec. Label the province and color it green.
8. New Brunswick borders Quebec on the southeast, and Nova Scotia is attached to it. Label them and color them purple.
9. Nestled above the two provinces is Prince Edward Island. Color this province black.
10. The last province is Newfoundland. This province borders Quebec and includes the large island near it. Label both parts.

Name _____

Montreal, the Heart of French Canada

Canada's largest province, Quebec, is unique because most of its inhabitants speak French. The people there have long been referred to as French-Canadians. They are quite proud of their French heritage, often referring to themselves as "pure wool."

Montreal is Quebec's most famous city and is often called the "Heart of French Canada." By day or night, it is an exciting city with fine universities, the National Hockey League (Montreal Canadiens), incredible museums, and the one-of-a-kind *Cirque du Soleil*.

Cirque du Soleil means Circus of the Sun. This circus is unique because it only has human performers; no animals. Quebec funds a school called the École Nationale de Cirque. With an enrollment of 20 youngsters, the school provides an academic education while the students learn the arts of the big top on the trapeze, stilts, trampoline, and tightrope.

Pretend that you are a student at the school. Write about what a typical day is like for you. Draw yourself performing below.

Name _____

Bolivia

Bolivia is located in South America and is about twice the size of Texas. Children here go to school from 9 a.m. to 4 p.m. They have a long vacation in June and July, but for them this is winter break. They have another long break from October to December. This is summer in Bolivia!

Think about yourself during summer and winter vacations. Then, follow these directions:

1. Write your name in the chart below.
2. Draw yourself during summer break in the first box.
3. Draw something Porfirio might do in July.
4. Draw yourself during winter break in the third box.
5. Draw something Porfirio might do in December.
6. Color each picture.

What do you notice about the pictures? Why are the seasons opposite? Write your answers on the back.

	_____ (your name)	Porfirio (Bolivian boy)
July	1.	2.
December	3.	4.

SOCIAL STUDIES

Name _____

Animals in the Rainforest

Brazil is located in South America. Many of its people are very poor. This country is partially covered by rainforests in which thousands of different plants and animals live. However, many of these animals could become extinct because of the destruction of the rainforests for their lumber. Follow the directions below to discover some of the animals that live in the rainforest.

1. Draw a jungle pig (called a tapir) hiding in the leaves.
2. Draw a jaguar lying on the ground.
3. Draw a parrot in the trees.
4. Draw an anaconda snake on the riverbank.
5. Draw spiders on the trees and on the ground.
6. Draw fish in the river.
7. Draw an alligator in the river.
8. Draw butterflies in the air.
9. Draw an Indian in the trees.
10. Color your rainforest and its animals.

Name _____

Chewing Pleasures

Chewing gum is probably something you enjoy. Did you ever wonder about its history? Chewing gummy substances dates back hundreds of years. Early Greeks and American Indians chewed resin from the bark of trees. In the mid-1800s, sweetened paraffin wax came to be favored over resin.

Today gum has an "international flavor." Gum base, the chewy ingredient, comes mainly from the Amazon Valley in Brazil. Natural resins, which make the gum feel better when you chew it, come from southern United States.

Exact recipes are top-secret information. Manufacturers are continually improving their products. They also have to design appealing packages so you will want to buy them! That is why companies put baseball cards in some of the packages.

Some people have been against chewing gum. They thought it kept students from concentrating in school. Others thought that if you swallowed gum it would clog up your stomach. Research says that chewing gum actually reduces tension and improves concentration. Gum is a low-calorie snack and it helps prevent tooth decay and promotes sweeter breath.

Interview people to find out why they chew gum. Each space equals one person's answer.

Why We Chew Gum										
Enjoyment										
Tastes Good										
Helps Concentration										
Freshens Breath										
Cleans Teeth										
	1	2	3	4	5	6	7	8	9	10

Compile your information and make a group graph.

SOCIAL STUDIES

Name _____

Central America

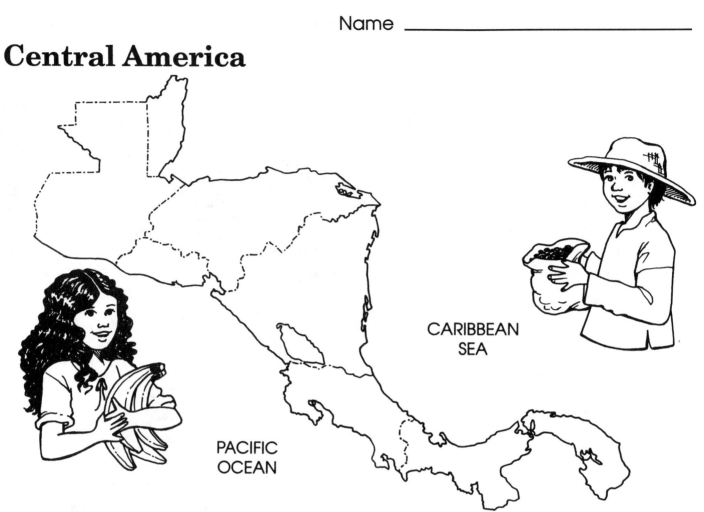

CARIBBEAN
SEA

PACIFIC
OCEAN

The land connecting North and South America is called Central America. This is where Costa Rica and six other countries are located. Follow the directions below to label the countries and some of their products.

1. Draw a cotton plant in Belize. It's the northernmost country.

2. Draw a cotton plant in Guatemala. It borders Belize.

3. El Salvador grows many coffee beans. Draw a cup of coffee in this country that is southeast of Guatemala.

4. Silver is mined in Honduras, north of El Salvador. Color this country silver.

5. Nicaragua contains gold mines. Color this country bordering Honduras gold.

6. Children from Costa Rica love the bananas grown there. Draw a banana.

7. Panama's fishermen catch many shrimp. Draw some shrimp in this southern-most country. If you look closely, you will see a break in the land through which ships can pass. This is the Panama Canal. Label it also.

The U.S. helped clear the land that was once where the canal is now. Why do you think they wanted to help? Write your answer on the back of this paper.

Name _____

The Emerald Isle

Ireland is often called the Emerald Isle because of its rolling green farmland and countryside. This is why we wear green on St. Patrick's Day, an Irish holiday. Sean and Kathleen want you to follow the directions below to make today a special Irish day.

1. Write the name of three crayons that have a green tint. _____

   _____

2. Name two people wearing green today. _____

   _____

3. Write three words you can spell with the letters in IRELAND. _____

   _____

4. Write the title of a book that has the word *green* in it. _____

   _____

5. Name four green animals. _____

   _____

6. What do scientists call trees that stay green all winter? _____

7. List two things in your classroom that are entirely green. _____

8. Name your favorite green food. _____

9. Draw a leprechaun on the back of your paper.

10. Use only green crayons for the rest of the school day.

Daily Learning Drills Grade 3

SOCIAL STUDIES

Name _____

Number, Please!

The population of Israel is a mixture of people from over 70 countries. Use the telephone puzzle below to dial and meet a few!

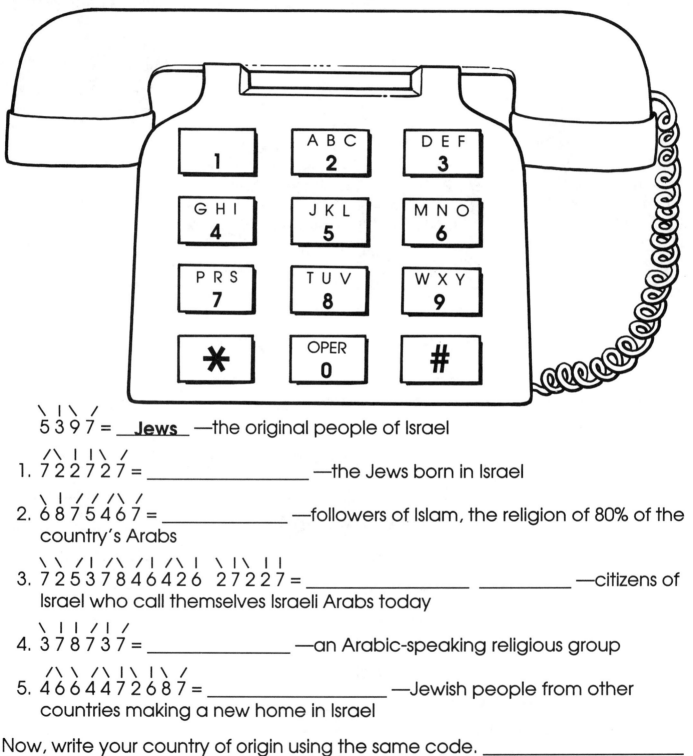

\ I \ /
5 3 9 7 = __Jews__ —the original people of Israel

/\ I I \ /
1. 7 2 2 7 2 7 = _____ —the Jews born in Israel

\ I / / /\ /
2. 6 8 7 5 4 6 7 = _____ —followers of Islam, the religion of 80% of the country's Arabs

\ \ / I /\ / I /\ I \ I \ I I
3. 7 2 5 3 7 8 4 6 4 2 6 2 7 2 2 7 = _____ _____ —citizens of Israel who call themselves Israeli Arabs today

\ I I / I /
4. 3 7 8 7 3 7 = _____ —an Arabic-speaking religious group

/\ \ /\ \ I \ I \ /
5. 4 6 6 4 4 7 2 6 8 7 = _____ —Jewish people from other countries making a new home in Israel

Now, write your country of origin using the same code. _____

Name _____

A Journey to Japan

Follow the directions to complete the map of Japan, Mieko's homeland.

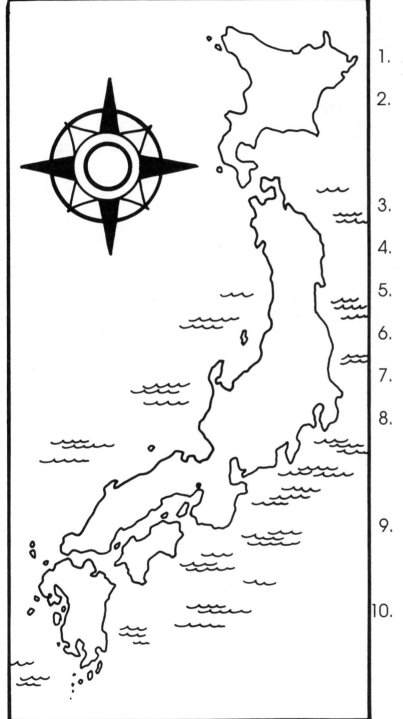

1. Add the eight directional letters to the compass rose.
2. Label the islands in capital letters:
   KYUSHU – southernmost
   HOKKAIDO – northernmost
   HONSHU – south of Hokkaido
   SHIKOKU – north of Kyushu
3. Add a red ★ and label the capital city, Tokyo.
4. Draw a mountain at Mount Fuji's location.
5. Label **Nagasaki** by the dot on Kyushu Island.
6. Label the **Sea of Japan** and the **Pacific Ocean**. Add blue waves.
7. Label **Osaka** by the dot on Honshu Island.
8. Outline the islands in these colors:
   Hokkaido – orange
   Honshu – green
   Shikoku – red
   Kyushu – yellow
9. Along the northern edge of the box, label the map **JAPAN**, using a different color for each letter.
10. Draw the flag of Japan.

SOCIAL STUDIES

Name _____

Written Japanese

When Laura visited a Japanese classroom, she could not read anything that was written. She learned that written Japanese is considered to be one of the most difficult writing systems in the world. It is a combination of Japanese phonetic symbols as well as Chinese characters. Each character is a symbol that stands for a complete word or syllable. However difficult, almost all Japanese people 15 years of age or older can read and write.

Use the following Japanese characters to write a story about a big man. Use the characters in your story whenever possible.

大	人	木	森	山	門
big	man	tree	forest	mountain	gate

The 大 人

_____

_____

_____

_____

_____

_____

_____

_____

Name _____

Raising a Family in Kenya

As members of the more progressive Njoroge Tribe, Omar's parents have a dream. They want to see their four children through secondary school. That will require great sacrifice for them as their coffee crop only earned them $120 after expenses last year.

Omar and his family live a very simple life. Omar's father raises coffee plants on their one-acre farm. Omar's mother and father work very hard to earn the money to send Omar and his brother and two sisters to school. It costs $75 a year for primary school for each child. To earn more money, Omar's father works as a stonemason for $5 a day. Omar's mother works at a larger farm for $2 a day.

1. How many days will Omar's father have to work as a stonemason to pay for one year of Omar's primary school? (Hint: Count by 5's.) _____

2. How many days will Omar's father have to work to pay for the other 3 children's primary school each year? (Hint: Add your answer from #1 three times.) _____

3. One pair of children's shoes cost $10. How many days will Omar's mother have to work to buy him a pair of shoes? (Hint: Count by 2's.) _____

4. How many days will Omar's mother have to work to buy the other 3 children new pairs of shoes? (Hint: Add your answer to #3 three times.) _____

5. How much will it cost to buy shoes for all four children. (Hint: Count by 10's.) _____

SOCIAL STUDIES

Name _____

Tortillas, Anyone?

Juan lives in Mexico. The main food crop grown there is corn. Even though it is grown on half of Mexico's cultivated land, corn is still imported because the demand for it is so high. Since ancient times, corn has been used to make flat pancakes called tortillas. Sometimes they are folded and  stuffed with different foods to make tacos. Throughout Mexico, you will see stands on the street serving tortillas and tacos. Juan's mother folds the tortillas and fills them with meat, goat cheese, beans, hot sauce, and lettuce.

Scientists have been unable to trace the ancestry of modern corn directly to a wild plant. But they do know that Indians in what is now Central or Southern Mexico gathered corn from wild plants about 10,000 years ago. About 5000 B.C., the Indians learned how to grow their own corn. That is how it came to be called Indian corn.

The words in dark type below make each of the sentences untrue. Rewrite the sentences so they are true. On another sheet of paper, draw all the things you would want to include in a super delicious taco. Be creative!

1. Tacos are made from **wheat bread**.

   _____

2. The Indians that gathered corn from wild plants lived in **northern Mexico**.

   _____

3. Tortillas are made from **wheat**.

   _____

4. The stands on the streets of Mexico serve **hot dogs.**

   _____

5. Corn is often called **Italian** corn.

   _____

6. About **10,000** B.C., Indians learned to grow corn themselves.

   _____

7. Much corn is **exported** to Mexico.

   _____

8. Corn is used to make flat **sandwiches** called tortillas.

   _____

Name _____

Life in the Village

Juan's house is made of clay. The clay was mixed together with straw and water and shaped into bricks. His roof is made of red tiles that are sloped to let the rain run off easily.

In the back of Juan's house is a shady patio. It has a wall around it to form a courtyard. At night, the cow and burro join the chickens and turkeys there.

The house has a hard-packed dirt floor. Juan's mother or father builds a cooking fire on the floor. It is built near the door so the smoke can go out the door and windows on either side of the door. That is where Juan's mother makes the tortillas that he loves. It is 10-year-old Maria's job to sweep the floor and bring cool water to drink from the village fountain. She helps her mother wash the family's clothes in the river.

Juan helps his father with his clay animals that he makes to sell at the village market during fiestas. Some day Juan wants to be a potter like his father. Juan has already sold some vases at the market. On a sheet of white paper, draw and decorate a colorful vase that Juan might have made.

Draw a picture of Juan's house and yard below. Reread the paragraphs above to include as much detail as possible. When you draw the front door, draw what you can see inside of it.

SOCIAL STUDIES

Name _____

New Zealand

canton ⌐

New Zealand is an island southeast of Australia. The people there speak English because most of their ancestors were from England. Children there, as in the U.S., face their flag when they say their pledge. You can make a New Zealand flag by following the directions below.

1. In the middle of the small box (the canton), draw a red stripe from the top to the bottom.

2. Draw a red stripe across the middle of the canton area.

3. Still in the canton area, draw a red stripe diagonally from corner to corner.

4. Draw a red stripe diagonally the other way.

5. Color white stripes on both sides of the red stripes.

6. Draw four stars to the right of the canton.

7. Color the stars red.

8. Outline the stars in white.

9. Color the entire background blue.

10. Look at a British flag. What do you notice?

Name _____

Operation Bootstrap

Puerto Rico is a small island located about 1,000 miles southeast of Florida. The people there are U.S. citizens though they cannot vote in presidential elections and do not pay federal income taxes. The country is poor, but their program "Operation Bootstrap" is helping manufacturing to grow. José has been given the task of making a bar graph about his country's employment. Follow the directions to help him complete the graph.

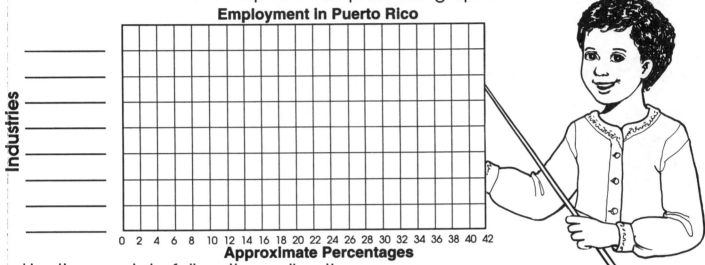

Employment in Puerto Rico

Industries

0 2 4 6 8 10 12 14 16 18 20 22 24 26 28 30 32 34 36 38 40 42

Approximate Percentages

Use the graph to follow these directions.

1. Agriculture accounts for 5 percent of all employment. Label it and fill in the bar graph.
2. Construction employs about the same percentage of people as agriculture.
3. Finance, insurance and real estate is one category. It employs 2 percent less people than does agriculture. Label it and fill in the bar graph.
4. Government employs the highest number of workers. It employs 42 percent of all workers. Label this category and fill in the bar graph.
5. Manufacturing accounts for a high amount of employment, but it employs 21 percent less than the government does. Label and fill in the bar graph.
6. Wholesale and retail trade employs about 13 percent more people than does construction. Label and fill in the bar graph.
7. Transportation and communication employs 1 percent less than agriculture does. Label and fill in the bar graph.
8. The last category is utilities and mining. It employs 2 percent less people than transportation and communication. Label and fill in the bar graph.

SOCIAL STUDIES

Name _____

Chinese Lion Dance

Children in Taiwan go to school from Monday through Saturday! They study all of the subjects that you do, including physical education. They sometimes learn the Chinese Lion Dance, which is done with two or more children carrying a costume like the one below. Complete the picture above by following the directions.

1. Color its face green.
2. Color its mouth red.
3. Color its nose purple.
4. Color its hair yellow.
5. Draw and color the rest of the lion's body.
6. Draw the legs of two children underneath the lion costume.

On the back of this paper, design another lion costume. Use at least five crayons to color your design.

Name _____

Desert Attire

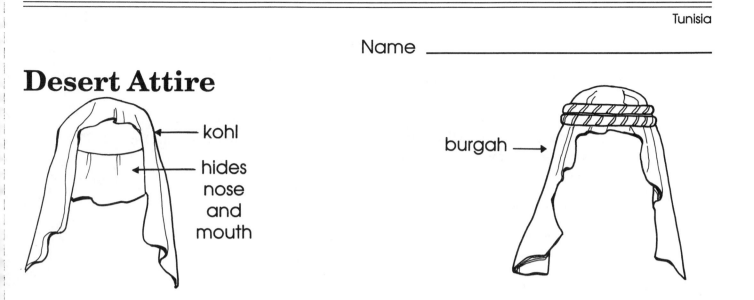

kohl

hides nose and mouth

burgah →

Tunisia is located in northeastern Africa. Much of the land is desert, so the people must protect themselves from sun and blowing sand. For this reason, many children wear special head coverings like the ones pictured. Finish the picture above by following the directions.

1. Use pencil to draw a boy wearing the burgah.
2. Draw a girl wearing the kohl.
3. Draw a white robe on the boy.
4. Draw a black robe on the girl.
5. Draw desert sand under their feet.
6. Draw the blazing sun.
7. Draw a camel nearby.
8. Color the boy and the girl.

It is an Arabian custom for the girls to keep their noses and mouths covered. Why do you think they do this?

SOCIAL STUDIES

Name _____

Everybody Grows Rice

Although Asian countries grow ninety percent of the world's rice, it is grown in many other countries, including the United States. Write the names of the rice-producing countries in the puzzle.

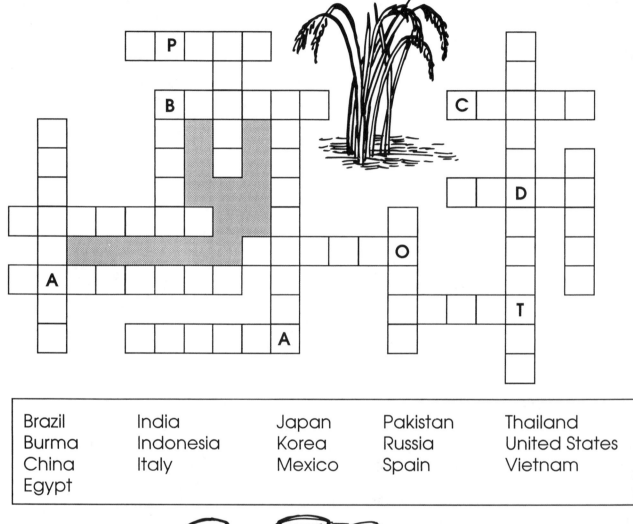

Brazil	India	Japan	Pakistan	Thailand
Burma	Indonesia	Korea	Russia	United States
China	Italy	Mexico	Spain	Vietnam
Egypt				

A N O W D Find out more about one of these rice-producing countries. Draw and label a map showing the regions in that country where rice is grown. Label the capital city. Show the type of dress worn by the people of the country.

Name _____

Hip, Hip, Hooray for Holidays

Choose a word from the Word Box to complete each sentence. Then write the word in the puzzle.

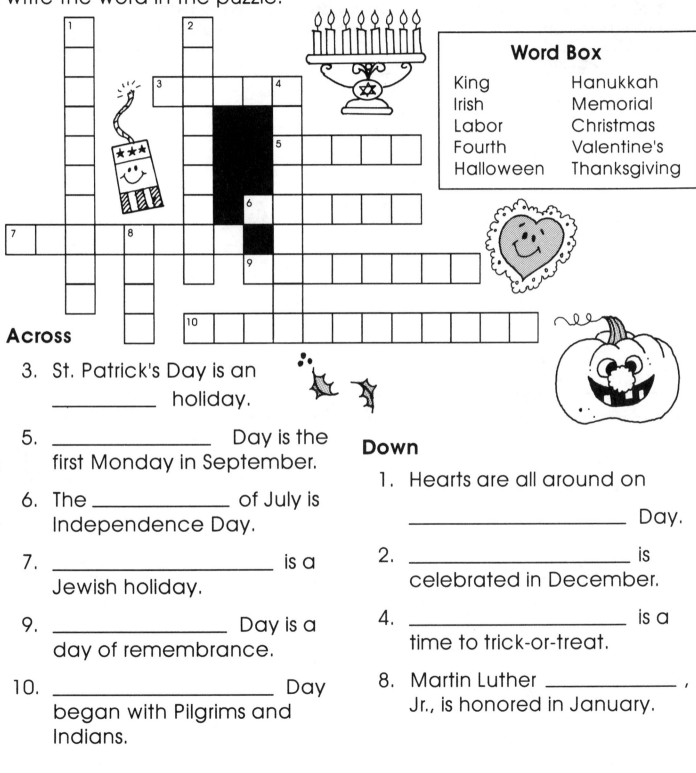

Word Box

King	Hanukkah
Irish	Memorial
Labor	Christmas
Fourth	Valentine's
Halloween	Thanksgiving

Across

3. St. Patrick's Day is an _____ holiday.

5. _____ Day is the first Monday in September.

6. The _____ of July is Independence Day.

7. _____ is a Jewish holiday.

9. _____ Day is a day of remembrance.

10. _____ Day began with Pilgrims and Indians.

Down

1. Hearts are all around on _____ Day.

2. _____ is celebrated in December.

4. _____ is a time to trick-or-treat.

8. Martin Luther _____, Jr., is honored in January.

SOCIAL STUDIES

Name _____

Let's Celebrate!

In each calendar month below, write all the holidays you and your family celebrate and their dates. Include family celebrations like birthdays and anniversaries and national, religious, state and community holidays.

January	February	March

April	May	June

July	August	September

October	November	December

Answer Key

A World of Its Own
Connect the words in alphabetical order

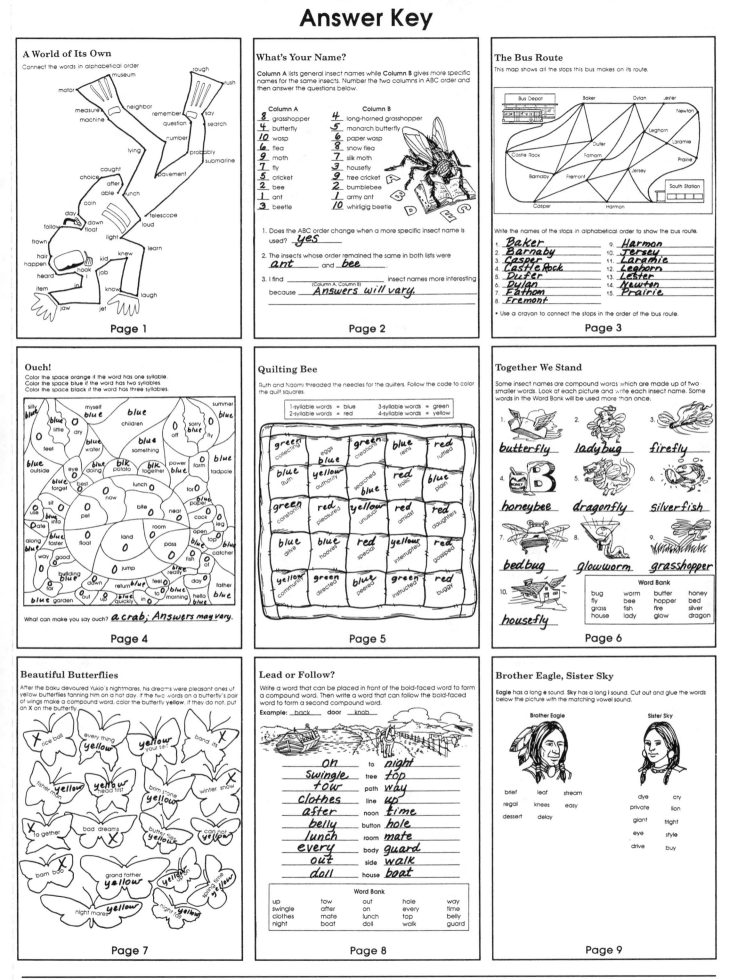

Page 1

What's Your Name?
Column A lists general insect names while **Column B** gives more specific names for the same insects. Number the two columns in ABC order and then answer the questions below.

Column A		Column B	
8	grasshopper	4	long-horned grasshopper
4	butterfly	5	monarch butterfly
10	wasp	6	paper wasp
6	flea	8	snow flea
9	moth	7	silk moth
7	fly	3	housefly
5	cricket	9	tree cricket
2	bee	2	bumblebee
1	ant	1	army ant
3	beetle	10	whirligig beetle

1. Does the ABC order change when a more specific insect name is used? _yes_

2. The insects whose order remained the same in both lists were _ant_ and _bee_.

3. I find _____ (Column A, Column B) insect names more interesting because _Answers will vary._

Page 2

The Bus Route
This map shows all the stops this bus makes on its route.

Write the names of the stops in alphabetical order to show the bus route.
1. Baker
2. Barnaby
3. Casper
4. Castle Rock
5. Dufer
6. Dylan
7. Fathom
8. Fremont
9. Harmon
10. Jersey
11. Laramie
12. Leghorn
13. Lester
14. Newton
15. Prairie

• Use a crayon to connect the stops in the order of the bus route.

Page 3

Ouch!
Color the space orange if the word has one syllable.
Color the space blue if the word has two syllables.
Color the space black if the word has three syllables.

What can make you say ouch? _a crab; Answers may vary._

Page 4

Quilting Bee
Ruth and Naomi threaded the needles for the quilters. Follow the code to color the quilt squares.

1-syllable words = blue	3-syllable words = green
2-syllable words = red	4-syllable words = yellow

Page 5

Together We Stand
Some insect names are compound words which are made up of two smaller words. Look at each picture and write each insect name. Some words in the Word Bank will be used more than once.

1. butterfly
2. ladybug
3. firefly
4. honeybee
5. dragonfly
6. silverfish
7. bedbug
8. glowworm
9. grasshopper
10. housefly

Word Bank
bug	worm	butter	honey
fly	bee	hopper	bed
grass	fish	fire	silver
house	lady	glow	dragon

Page 6

Beautiful Butterflies
After the baku devoured Yukio's nightmares, his dreams were pleasant ones of yellow butterflies fanning him on a hot day. If the two words on a butterfly's pair of wings make a compound word, color the butterfly **yellow**. If they do not, put an **X** on the butterfly.

X rice ball
every thing — yellow
yellow your self
band its — X
fisher man — X
yellow head first
brim stone — yellow
winter snow — X
X to gether
bad dreams — X
butter flies — yellow
can not — yellow
X bam boo
grand father — yellow
moon up — yellow
spring time — yellow
yellow
night mares — yellow
night fall — yellow

Page 7

Lead or Follow?
Write a word that can be placed in front of the bold-faced word to form a compound word. Then write a word that can follow the bold-faced word to form a second compound word.

Example: _back_ **door** _knob_

on	**to**	night
Swingle	**tree**	top
tow	**path**	way
clothes	**line**	up
after	**noon**	time
belly	**button**	hole
lunch	**room**	mate
every	**body**	guard
out	**side**	walk
doll	**house**	boat

Word Bank
up	tow	out	hole	way
swingle	after	on	every	time
clothes	mate	lunch	top	belly
night	boat	doll	walk	guard

Page 8

Brother Eagle, Sister Sky
Eagle has a long **e** sound. **Sky** has a long **i** sound. Cut out and glue the words below the picture with the matching vowel sound.

Brother Eagle | Sister Sky

brief   leaf   stream   dye   cry
regal   knees   easy   private   lion
dessert delay   giant   fright
                               eye   style
                               drive   buy

Page 9

Daily Learning Drills Grade 3

The Money Box

When Xiao Sheng put the pearl in the money box with its one remaining coin, the coin multiplied and the box brimmed over with gold coins.
Cut out and glue the coins that have the same vowel sound as coin in and around the money box.

Coins: joyful, sailed, coiled, boxing, rejoice, destroy, 'toys, oyster, spoil, boys, enjoy, oil, convoy, foil

Phonics Fun

Help Richard with his phonics by following these directions.

Circle the short o words in black.
Underline the short i words in pink.
Put a red box around the short e words.
Draw an olive green X over the short o words.
Draw a green line over the long e words.
Draw a wavy gray line over the long a words.
Put a white X over the long i words.
Draw a gold circle over the long o words.

Beast — Holly olive
Hansel black
plane
kids
Kettle
teacher
Noah gold
Matthew black
banner black
Mancino black
stage
best
Richard
wished
liar white
smell
smile white
bike olive
Gretel
flg
piece
Polk gold
class black
sky olive

The Puzzling Printout

Professor Gizmo built his own computer. But sometimes the professor was a little absent-minded, and he would push the wrong buttons. Today he printed some "Funny Food Facts."

Read each silly sentence. Cross out the noun that doesn't make sense. Find a noun in another sentence that fits but still makes a silly sentence. Write it over the crossed-off word. The first one is done for you.

Funny Food Facts

meatloaf (from sentence #7)
1. Lazy people eat chili. jellybeans - 5
2. The Easter Bunny's favorite vegetables are chicken. chicken - 2
3. The best fruit to drink is strawberries. watermelon - 8
4. If you're scared, don't eat dough. chili
5. Jellybeans must be a cold food. milkshakes - 9
6. Dancing cows make blueberries. club sandwiches - 10
7. Cavemen ate meatloaf. dough - 4
8. Bread is rich because it has watermelon. blueberries - 6
9. Milkshakes are an unhappy fruit. strawberries - 3
10. Club sandwiches grow on the floor of a barn.

Nouns in the Clouds

Look at the list of words. If a word is a common noun, copy it in the cloud titled common nouns. If it is a proper noun, change its first letters to capital letters and copy it in the cloud titled proper nouns.

1. ohio
2. dr simon
3. ocean
4. president lincoln
5. dog
6. jane
7. new york
8. ice cream
9. mount everest
10. columbus
11. teacher
12. second avenue
13. circus
14. sheriff

Common Nouns | Proper Nouns

common nouns: Ocean, dog, ice cream, teacher, circus, sheriff

proper nouns: Ohio, Dr. Simon, President Lincoln, Jane, New York, Mount Everest, Columbus, Second Avenue

Pencil in the Plural

Write the plural for each of the nouns below.

wish (Example)	hobby	sheep	day
wishes	hobbies	sheep	days
deer	bluff	child	boss
deer	bluffs	children	bosses
rash	cookie	match	knife
rashes	cookies	matches	knives
car	success	pony	foot
cars	successes	ponies	feet
kiss	city	couch	mouse
kisses	cities	couches	mice
woman	half	mirror	trout
women	halves	mirrors	trout
person	tooth	dress	girl
persons	teeth	dresses	girls

Bright and Beautiful

Color the space yellow if you have to only add an s to make the word plural.
Color the space orange if you have to add es to make the word plural.
Color the space blue if you have to change the last letter and then add es to make the word plural.

(coloring words: strawberry, shelf, baby blue, blackberry, half, cherry, goody, puppy, loaf, ox, moon, mix, dress, page, clock, leaf, box, fox, flower, grass, wind, glass, raspberry, pony, sky, elf, kitty, body, blueberry, scarf)

What is this ocean creature? a squid

P.J.'s Cup

Change the underlined word to show possession by adding an apostrophe or apostrophe and s. Write the possessive form on the line.

	possessive
Example → The balloon string is long.	balloon's
1. The three cats paws were wet.	1. cats'
2. Mary pencil was broken.	2. Mary's
3. Both boys grades were good.	3. boys'
4. This house is Cliff house.	4. Cliff's
5. Tony aunt came to visit.	5. Tony's
6. Some flowers leaves were large.	6. flowers'
7. We saw two bears tracks.	7. bears'
8. The children room was messy.	8. children's
9. My sister birthday is today.	9. sister's
10. The clowns acts made us laugh.	10. clowns'
11. Charlie Brown filled Snoopy dish.	11. Snoopy's
12. Mark joined the game with the boys.	12. boys
13. The baseball players uniforms are clean.	13. players'
14. The dog dish was empty.	14. dog's

Be a Star!

Follow the rules to color each design.

Rule 1: Add ed to most verbs to show the past tense. Color these words blue.
Rule 2: If the verb ends in e, drop the e and add ed. Color these words green.
Rule 3: If the verb has a short vowel followed by a single consonant, double the final consonant and add ed. Color these words white.
Rule 4: If the verb ends in y, change the y to i and add ed. Color these words yellow.

(words: need blue, call blue, cry yellow, watch blue, drop white, hunt blue, tremple green, hoot blue, slip white, gather blue, move green, tremble green, lean blue, live green, smile green, look blue, sparkle green, stop white, listen blue, walk blue)

Hop – Hopped – Hopping!

Help bouncy Bong hop to his special piece of liver. If you can add an 'ed' or 'ing' to a word, color that piece of liver brown. Do not color the other pieces.

(words: cheer, demand, gather, pretend, cemetery, ribbon, fudge, necklace, dinosaur, creepy, gulp, friend, stomach, thief, whisper, remember, exclaim, horrible, gym, frosty, science, mural, attack, toboggan, peace, downhill, hatchet, carnation, workshop, season, snowbank, rooftop, squish, skill, sketch)

Bong is certainly a frog of action. All of the words he hopped on are verbs or action words

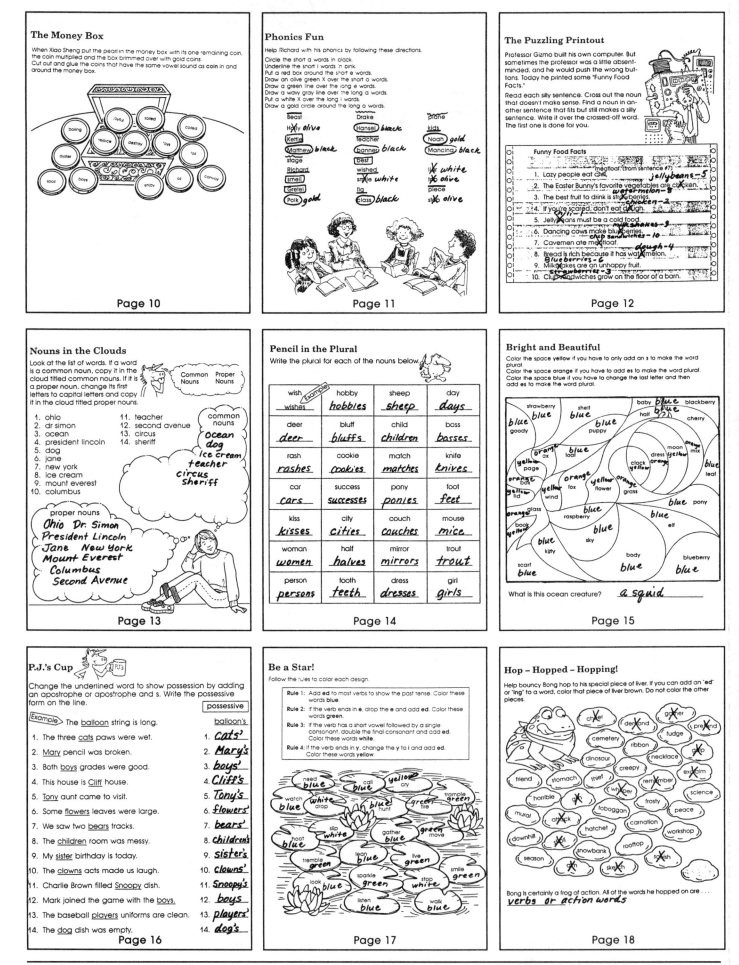

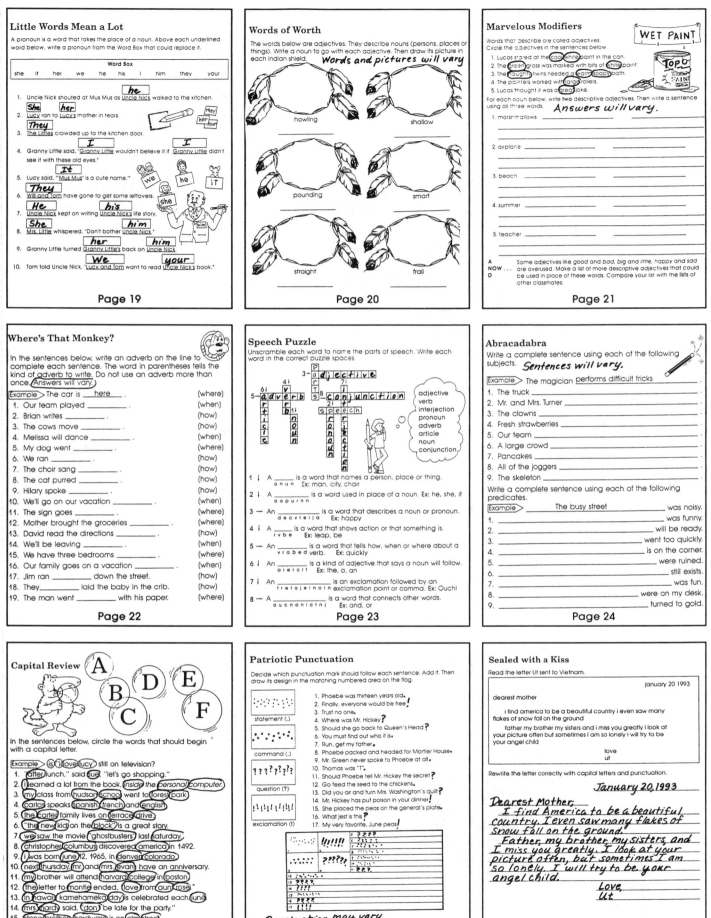

Little Words Mean a Lot

A pronoun is a word that takes the place of a noun. Above each underlined word below, write a pronoun from the Word Box that could replace it.

Word Box

she   it   her   we   he   his   I   him   they   your

1. Uncle Nick shouted at Mus Mus as Uncle Nick [**he**] walked to the kitchen.
2. Lucy [**She**] ran to Lucy's [**her**] mother in tears.
3. The Littles [**They**] crowded up to the kitchen door.
4. Granny Little said, "Granny Little [**I**] wouldn't believe it if Granny Little [**I**] didn't see it with these old eyes."
5. Lucy said, "Mus Mus [**It**] is a cute name."
6. Will and Tom [**They**] have gone to get some leftovers.
7. Uncle Nick [**He**] kept on writing Uncle Nick's [**his**] life story.
8. Mrs. Little [**She**] whispered, "Don't bother Uncle Nick [**him**]."
9. Granny Little turned Granny Little's [**her**] back on Uncle Nick [**him**].
10. Tom told Uncle Nick, "Lucy and Tom [**We**] want to read Uncle Nick's [**your**] book."

Page 19

Words of Worth

The words below are adjectives. They describe nouns (persons, places or things). Write a noun to go with each adjective. Then draw its picture in each Indian shield.

Words and pictures will vary

howling   shallow   pounding   smart   straight   frail

Page 20

Marvelous Modifiers

Words that describe are called adjectives. Circle the adjectives in the sentences below.

1. Lucas stared at the (cool) (white) paint in the can.
2. The (green) grass was marked with bits of (white) paint.
3. The (naughty) twins needed a (warm) (soapy) bath.
4. The painters worked with (large) rollers.
5. Lucas thought it was a (great) joke.

For each noun below, write two descriptive adjectives. Then write a sentence using all three words. *Answers will vary.*

1. marshmallows
2. airplane
3. beach
4. summer
5. teacher

A NOW ... AD Some adjectives like good and bad, big and little, happy and sad are overused. Make a list of more descriptive adjectives that could be used in place of these words. Compare your list with the lists of other classmates.

Page 21

Where's That Monkey?

In the sentences below, write an adverb on the line to complete each sentence. The word in parentheses tells the kind of adverb to write. Do not use an adverb more than once. (Answers will vary.)

Example > The car is ___here___ . (where)
1. Our team played _____ . (when)
2. Brian writes _____ . (how)
3. The cows move _____ . (how)
4. Melissa will dance _____ . (when)
5. My dog went _____ . (where)
6. We ran _____ . (how)
7. The choir sang _____ . (how)
8. The cat purred _____ . (how)
9. Hilary spoke _____ . (how)
10. We'll go on our vacation _____ . (when)
11. The sign goes _____ . (where)
12. Mother brought the groceries _____ . (where)
13. David read the directions _____ . (how)
14. We'll be leaving _____ . (when)
15. We have three bedrooms _____ . (where)
16. Our family goes on a vacation _____ . (when)
17. Jim ran _____ down the street. (how)
18. They_____ laid the baby in the crib. (how)
19. The man went _____ with his paper. (where)

Page 22

Speech Puzzle

Unscramble each word to name the parts of speech. Write each word in the correct puzzle spaces.

Puzzle answers: parts of speech; adjective; adverb; conjunction; noun; pronoun; article; interjection

adjective
verb
interjection
pronoun
adverb
article
noun
conjunction

1↓ A _____ is a word that names a person, place or thing.
   o n u n   Ex: man, city, chair
2↓ A _____ is a word used in place of a noun. Ex: he, she, it
   a o p u r n n
3— An _____ is a word that describes a noun or pronoun.
   d e c v t i e i j a   Ex: happy
4↓ A _____ is a word that shows action or that something is.
   r v b e   Ex: leap, be
5— An _____ is a word that tells how, when or where about a
   v r a b e d   verb. Ex: quickly
6↓ An _____ is a kind of adjective that says a noun will follow.
   a i e r c l t   Ex: the, a, an
7↓ An _____ is an exclamation followed by an
   t r e t o j e i n c i n   exclamation point or comma. Ex: Ouch!
8— A _____ is a word that connects other words.
   a u c n o n i c t n j   Ex: and, or

Page 23

Abracadabra

Write a complete sentence using each of the following subjects. *Sentences will vary.*

Example > The magician performs difficult tricks

1. The truck _____
2. Mr. and Mrs. Turner _____
3. The clowns _____
4. Fresh strawberries _____
5. Our team _____
6. A large crowd _____
7. Pancakes _____
8. All of the joggers _____
9. The skeleton _____

Write a complete sentence using each of the following predicates.

Example > The busy street _____ was noisy.

1. _____ was funny.
2. _____ will be ready.
3. _____ went too quickly.
4. _____ is on the corner.
5. _____ were ruined.
6. _____ still exists.
7. _____ was fun.
8. _____ were on my desk.
9. _____ turned to gold.

Page 24

Capital Review

In the sentences below, circle the words that should begin with a capital letter.

Example > (is) (i) love (lucy) still on television?

1. (after) lunch," said (sue), "let's go shopping."
2. (i) learned a lot from the book, (inside) (the) (personal) (computer).
3. (my) class from (hudson) (school) went to (forest) (park).
4. (carlos) speaks (spanish), (french) and (english).
5. (the) (carter) family lives on (terrace) (drive).
6. "(the) (new) kid on the (block)" is a great story.
7. (we) saw the movie "(ghostbusters)" last (saturday).
8. (christopher) (columbus) discovered (america) in 1492.
9. (i) was born (june) 12, 1965, in (denver), (colorado).
10. (next) (thursday), (mr.) and (mrs.) (evans) have an anniversary.
11. (my) brother will attend (harvard) (college) in (boston).
12. (the) letter to (montie) ended, "(love) (from) (aunt) (rose)."
13. (in) (hawaii) (kamehameka) (day) is celebrated each (june).
14. (mrs.) (hardy) said, "(don)'t be late for the party."
15. (stone) (brother) (hardware) is on (elm) (street).

Page 25

Patriotic Punctuation

Decide which punctuation mark should follow each sentence. Add it. Then draw its design in the matching numbered area on the flag.

statement (.)
command (.)
question (?)
exclamation (!)

1. Phoebe was thirteen years old.
2. Finally, everyone would be free!
3. Trust no one.
4. Where was Mr. Hickey?
5. Should she go back to Queen's Head?
6. You must find out who it is.
7. Run, get my father.
8. Phoebe packed and headed for Mortier House.
9. Mr. Green never spoke to Phoebe at all.
10. Thomas was "T".
11. Should Phoebe tell Mr. Hickey the secret?
12. Go feed the seed to the chickens.
13. Did you air and turn Mrs. Washington's quilt?
14. Mr. Hickey has put poison in your dinner!
15. She placed the peas on the general's plate.
16. What jest is this?
17. My very favorite, June peas!

Punctuation may vary.

Page 26

Sealed with a Kiss

Read the letter Ut sent to Vietnam.

january 20 1993

dearest mother

i find america to be a beautiful country i even saw many flakes of snow fall on the ground

father my brother my sisters and i miss you greatly i look at your picture often but sometimes i am so lonely i will try to be your angel child

love
ut

Rewrite the letter correctly with capital letters and punctuation.

January 20, 1993

Dearest Mother,
   I find America to be a beautiful country. I even saw many flakes of snow fall on the ground.
   Father, my brother, my sisters, and I miss you greatly. I look at your picture often, but sometimes I am so lonely. I will try to be your angel child.

Love,
Ut

Page 27

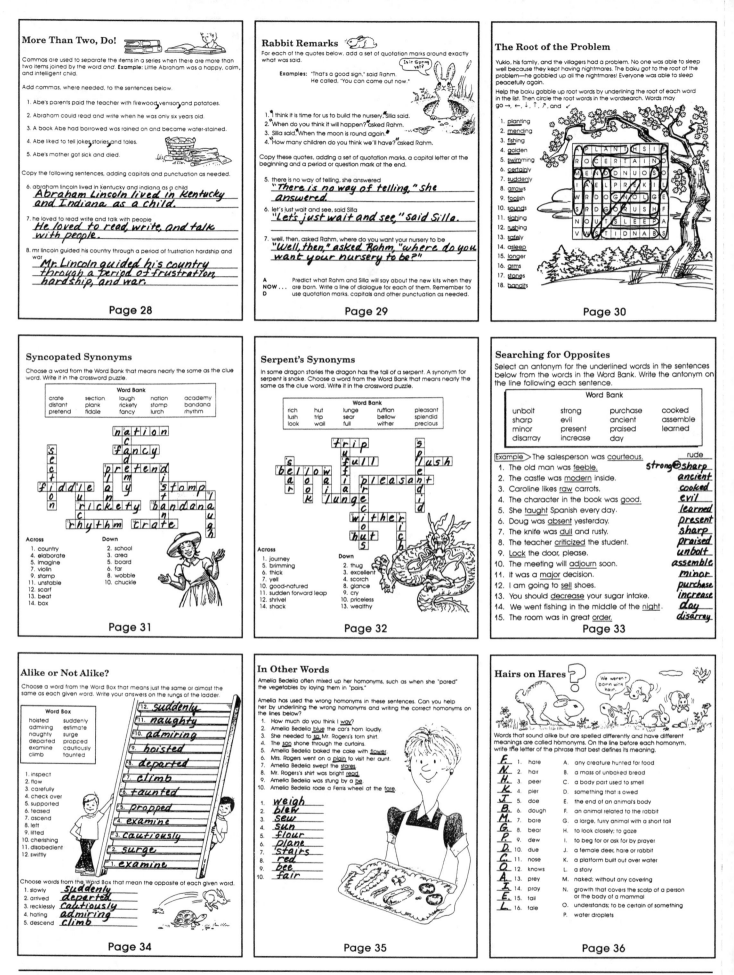

More Than Two, Do!

Commas are used to separate the items in a series when there are more than two items joined by the word and. Example: Little Abraham was a happy, calm, and intelligent child.

Add commas, where needed, to the sentences below.

1. Abe's parents paid the teacher with firewood, venison, and potatoes.
2. Abraham could read and write when he was only six years old.
3. A book Abe had borrowed was rained on and became water-stained.
4. Abe liked to tell jokes, stories, and tales.
5. Abe's mother got sick and died.

Copy the following sentences, adding capitals and punctuation as needed.

6. abraham lincoln lived in kentucky and indiana as a child

Abraham Lincoln lived in Kentucky and Indiana as a child.

7. he loved to read write and talk with people

He loved to read, write, and talk with people.

8. mr lincoln guided his country through a period of frustration hardship and war

Mr. Lincoln guided his country through a period of frustration, hardship, and war.

Page 28

Rabbit Remarks

For each of the quotes below, add a set of quotation marks around exactly what was said.

Examples: "That's a good sign," said Rahm.
He called, "You can come out now."

Is it Spring yet?

1. "I think it is time for us to build the nursery," Silla said.
2. "When do you think it will happen?" asked Rahm.
3. Silla said, "When the moon is round again."
4. "How many children do you think we'll have?" asked Rahm.

Copy these quotes, adding a set of quotation marks, a capital letter at the beginning and a period or question mark at the end.

5. there is no way of telling, she answered

"There is no way of telling," she answered.

6. let's just wait and see, said Silla

"Let's just wait and see," said Silla.

7. well, then, asked Rahm, where do you want your nursery to be

"Well, then," asked Rahm, "where do you want your nursery to be?"

A
NOW . . .
D
Predict what Rahm and Silla will say about the new kits when they are born. Write a line of dialogue for each of them. Remember to use quotation marks, capitals and other punctuation as needed.

Page 29

The Root of the Problem

Yukio, his family, and the villagers had a problem. No one was able to sleep well because they kept having nightmares. The baku got to the root of the problem—he gobbled up all the nightmares! Everyone was able to sleep peacefully again.

Help the baku gobble up root words by underlining the root of each word in the list. Then circle the root words in the wordsearch. Words may go →, ←, ↓, ↑, ↗, and ↘.

1. planting
2. mending
3. fishing
4. golden
5. swimming
6. certainly
7. suddenly
8. arrows
9. foolish
10. sounds
11. sighing
12. rushing
13. safely
14. asleep
15. longer
16. arms
17. stones
18. bandits

Page 30

Syncopated Synonyms

Choose a word from the Word Bank that means nearly the same as the clue word. Write it in the crossword puzzle.

Word Bank

crate	section	laugh	nation	academy
distant	plank	rickety	stomp	bandana
pretend	fiddle	fancy	lurch	rhythm

Across
1. country
4. elaborate
6. imagine
7. violin
9. stamp
11. unstable
12. scarf
13. beat
14. box

Down
2. school
3. area
5. board
6. far
8. wobble
10. chuckle

Page 31

Serpent's Synonyms

In some dragon stories the dragon has the tail of a serpent. A synonym for serpent is snake. Choose a word from the Word Bank that means nearly the same as the clue word. Write it in the crossword puzzle.

Word Bank

rich	hut	lunge	ruffian	pleasant
lush	trip	sear	bellow	splendid
look	wail	full	wither	precious

Across
1. journey
5. brimming
6. thick
7. yell
10. good-natured
11. sudden forward leap
12. shrivel
14. shack

Down
2. thug
3. excellent
4. scorch
8. glance
9. cry
10. priceless
13. wealthy

Page 32

Searching for Opposites

Select an antonym for the underlined words in the sentences below from the words in the Word Bank. Write the antonym on the line following each sentence.

Word Bank

unbolt	strong	purchase	cooked
sharp	evil	ancient	assemble
minor	present	praised	learned
disarray	increase	day	

Example ▷ The salesperson was courteous. → *rude*
1. The old man was feeble. *strong*
2. The castle was modern inside. *ancient*
3. Caroline likes raw carrots. *cooked*
4. The character in the book was good. *evil*
5. She taught Spanish every day. *learned*
6. Doug was absent yesterday. *present*
7. The knife was dull and rusty. *sharp*
8. The teacher criticized the student. *praised*
9. Lock the door, please. *unbolt*
10. The meeting will adjourn soon. *assemble*
11. It was a major decision. *minor*
12. I am going to sell shoes. *purchase*
13. You should decrease your sugar intake. *increase*
14. We went fishing in the middle of the night. *day*
15. The room was in great order. *disarray*

Page 33

Alike or Not Alike?

Choose a word from the Word Box that means just the same or almost the same as each given word. Write your answers on the rungs of the ladder.

Word Box

hoisted	suddenly
admiring	estimate
naughty	surge
departed	propped
examine	cautiously
climb	taunted

1. inspect
2. flow
3. carefully
4. check over
5. supported
6. teased
7. ascend
8. left
9. lifted
10. cherishing
11. disobedient
12. swiftly

12. *suddenly*
11. *naughty*
10. *admiring*
9. *hoisted*
8. *departed*
7. *climb*
6. *taunted*
5. *propped*
4. *examine*
3. *cautiously*
2. *surge*
1. *examine*

Choose words from the Word Box that mean the opposite of each given word.

1. slowly *suddenly*
2. arrived *departed*
3. recklessly *cautiously*
4. hating *admiring*
5. descend *climb*

Page 34

In Other Words

Amelia Bedelia often mixed up her homonyms, such as when she "pared" the vegetables by laying them in "pairs."

Amelia has used the wrong homonyms in these sentences. Can you help her by underlining the wrong homonyms and writing the correct homonyms on the lines below?

1. How much do you think is way?
2. Amelia Bedelia blue the car's horn loudly.
3. She needed to so Mr. Rogers's torn shirt.
4. The son shone through the curtains.
5. Amelia Bedelia baked the cake with flower.
6. Mrs. Rogers went on a plain to visit her aunt.
7. Amelia Bedelia swept the stares.
8. Mr. Rogers's shirt was bright read.
9. Amelia Bedelia was stung by a be.
10. Amelia Bedelia rode a Ferris wheel at the fare.

1. *weigh*
2. *blew*
3. *sew*
4. *sun*
5. *flour*
6. *plane*
7. *stairs*
8. *red*
9. *bee*
10. *fair*

Page 35

Hairs on Hares

We weren't born with hair.

Words that sound alike but are spelled differently and have different meanings are called homonyms. On the line before each homonym, write the letter of the phrase that best defines its meaning.

F. 1. hare
N. 2. hair
H. 3. peer
K. 4. pier
J. 5. doe
B. 6. dough
M. 7. bare
G. 8. bear
P. 9. dew
D. 10. due
C. 11. nose
O. 12. knows
A. 13. prey
I. 14. pray
E. 15. tail
L. 16. tale

A. any creature hunted for food
B. a mass of unbaked bread
C. a body part used to smell
D. something that is owed
E. the end of an animal's body
F. an animal related to the rabbit
G. a large, furry animal with a short tail
H. to look closely; to gaze
I. to beg for or ask for by prayer
J. a female deer, hare or rabbit
K. a platform built out over water
L. a story
M. naked; without any covering
N. growth that covers the scalp of a person or the body of a mammal
O. understands; to be certain of something
P. water droplets

Page 36

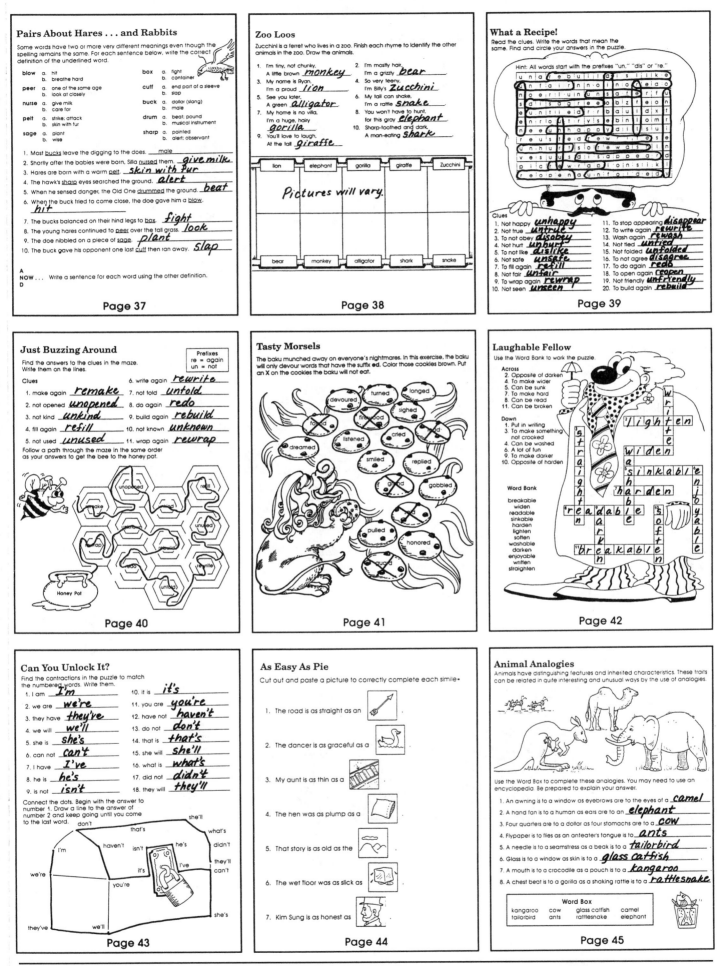

Pairs About Hares . . . and Rabbits

Some words have two or more very different meanings even though the spelling remains the same. For each sentence below, write the correct definition of the underlined word.

blow   a. hit
  b. breathe hard

peer   a. one of the same age
  b. look at closely

nurse   a. give milk
  b. care for

pelt   a. strike; attack
  b. skin with fur

sage   a. plant
  b. wise

box   a. fight
  b. container

cuff   a. end part of a sleeve
  b. slap

buck   a. dollar (slang)
  b. male

drum   a. beat; pound
  b. musical instrument

sharp   a. pointed
  b. alert; observant

1. Most bucks leave the digging to the does. __male__
2. Shortly after the babies were born, Silla nursed them. __give milk__
3. Hares are born with a warm pelt. __skin with fur__
4. The hawk's sharp eyes searched the ground. __alert__
5. When he sensed danger, the Old One drummed the ground. __beat__
6. When the buck tried to come close, the doe gave him a blow. __hit__
7. The bucks balanced on their hind legs to box. __fight__
8. The young hares continued to peer over the tall grass. __look__
9. The doe nibbled on a piece of sage. __plant__
10. The buck gave his opponent one last cuff then ran away. __slap__

A
NOW . . . Write a sentence for each word using the other definition.
D

Page 37

Zoo Loos

Zucchini is a ferret who lives in a zoo. Finish each rhyme to identify the other animals in the zoo. Draw the animals.

1. I'm tiny, not chunky,
A little brown __monkey__
2. My name is Ryan,
I'm a proud __lion__
5. See you later,
A green __alligator__
7. My home is no villa,
I'm a huge, hairy __gorilla__
9. You'll love to laugh,
At the tall __giraffe__
3. I'm mostly hair,
I'm a grizzly __bear__
4. So very teeny,
I'm Billy's __Zucchini__
6. My tail can shake,
I'm a rattle __snake__
8. You won't have to hunt,
for this gray __elephant__
10. Sharp-toothed and dark,
A man-eating __shark__

lion	elephant	gorilla	giraffe	Zucchini
bear	monkey	alligator	shark	snake

Pictures will vary.

Page 38

What a Recipe!

Read the clues. Write the words that mean the same. Find and circle your answers in the puzzle.

Hint: All words start with the prefixes "un," "dis" or "re."

Clues
1. Not happy __unhappy__
2. Not true __untrue__
3. To not obey __disobey__
4. Not hurt __unhurt__
5. To not like __dislike__
6. Not safe __unsafe__
7. To fill again __refill__
8. Not fair __unfair__
9. To wrap again __rewrap__
10. Not seen __unseen__
11. To stop appearing __disappear__
12. To write again __rewrite__
13. Wash again __rewash__
14. Not tied __untied__
15. Not folded __unfolded__
16. To not agree __disagree__
17. To do again __redo__
18. To open again __reopen__
19. Not friendly __unfriendly__
20. To build again __rebuild__

Page 39

Just Buzzing Around

Find the answers to the clues in the maze. Write them on the lines.

Prefixes
re = again
un = not

Clues
1. make again __remake__
2. not opened __unopened__
3. not kind __unkind__
4. fill again __refill__
5. not used __unused__
6. write again __rewrite__
7. not told __untold__
8. do again __redo__
9. build again __rebuild__
10. not known __unknown__
11. wrap again __rewrap__

Follow a path through the maze in the same order as your answers to get the bee to the honey pot.

Honey Pot

Page 40

Tasty Morsels

The baku munched away on everyone's nightmares. In this exercise, the baku will only devour words that have the suffix ed. Color those cookies brown. Put an X on the cookies the baku will not eat.

Page 41

Laughable Fellow

Use the Word Bank to work the puzzle.

Across
2. Opposite of darken
4. To make wider
5. Can be sunk
6. Can be read
8. To make hard
11. Can be broken

Down
1. Put in writing
3. To make something not crooked
4. Can be washed
6. A lot of fun
9. To make dark
10. Opposite of harden

Word Bank

breakable
widen
readable
sinkable
harden
lighten
soften
washable
darken
enjoyable
written
straighten

Page 42

Can You Unlock It?

Find the contractions in the puzzle to match the numbered words. Write them.

1. I am __I'm__
2. we are __we're__
3. they have __they've__
4. we will __we'll__
5. she is __she's__
6. can not __can't__
7. I have __I've__
8. he is __he's__
9. is not __isn't__
10. it is __it's__
11. you are __you're__
12. have not __haven't__
13. do not __don't__
14. that is __that's__
15. she will __she'll__
16. what is __what's__
17. did not __didn't__
18. they will __they'll__

Connect the dots. Begin with the answer to number 1. Draw a line to the answer of number 2 and keep going until you come to the last word.

don't
she'll
that's
what's
haven't
he's
didn't
I'm
isn't
it's
they'll
can't
we're
I've
you're
she's
they've
we'll

Page 43

As Easy As Pie

Cut out and paste a picture to correctly complete each simile.

1. The road is as straight as an
2. The dancer is as graceful as a
3. My aunt is as thin as a
4. The hen was as plump as a
5. That story is as old as the
6. The wet floor was as slick as
7. Kim Sung is as honest as

Page 44

Animal Analogies

Animals have distinguishing features and inherited characteristics. These traits can be related in quite interesting and unusual ways by the use of analogies.

Use the Word Box to complete these analogies. You may need to use an encyclopedia. Be prepared to explain your answer.

1. An awning is to a window as eyebrows are to the eyes of a __camel__
2. A hand fan is to a human as ears are to an __elephant__
3. Four quarters are to a dollar as four stomachs are to a __cow__
4. Flypaper is to flies as an anteater's tongue is to __ants__
5. A needle is to a seamstress as a beak is to a __tailorbird__
6. Glass is to a window as skin is to a __glass catfish__
7. A mouth is to a crocodile as a pouch is to a __kangaroo__
8. A chest beat is to a gorilla as a shaking rattle is to a __rattlesnake__

Word Box
kangaroo   cow   glass catfish   camel
tailorbird   ants   rattlesnake   elephant

Page 45

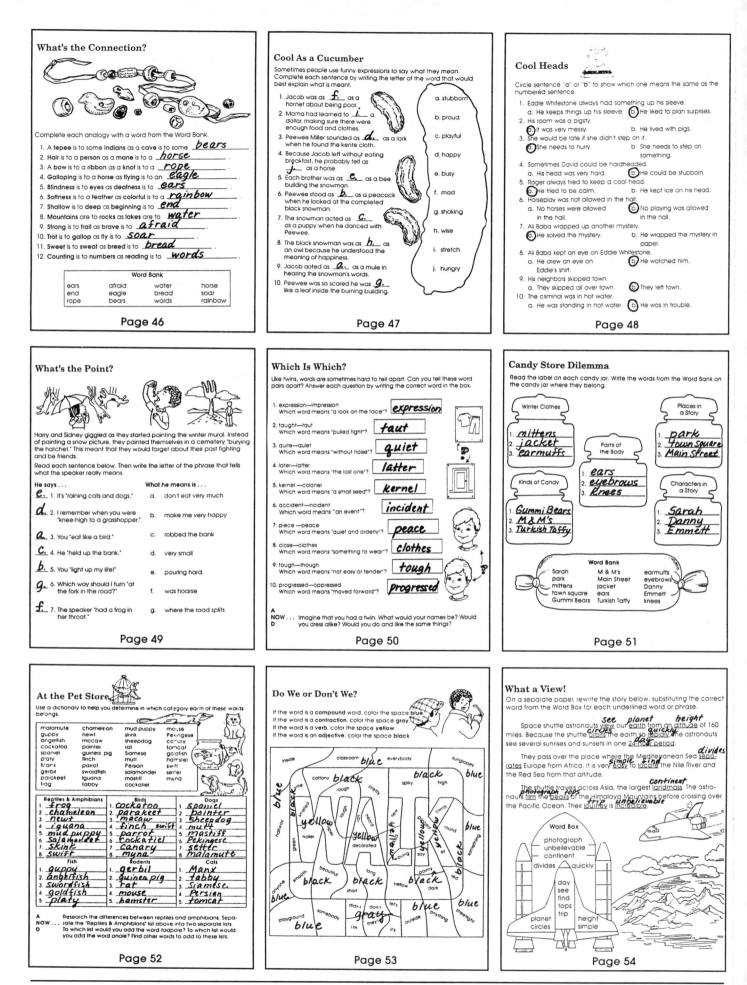

What's the Connection?

Complete each analogy with a word from the Word Bank.

1. A tepee is to some Indians as a cave is to some **bears**
2. Hair is to a person as a mane is to a **horse**
3. A bow is to a ribbon as a knot is to a **rope**
4. Galloping is to a horse as flying is to an **eagle**
5. Blindness is to eyes as deafness is to **ears**
6. Softness is to a feather as colorful is to a **rainbow**
7. Shallow is to deep as beginning is to **end**
8. Mountains are to rocks as lakes are to **water**
9. Strong is to frail as brave is to **afraid**
10. Trot is to gallop as fly is to **soar**
11. Sweet is to sweat as breed is to **bread**
12. Counting is to numbers as reading is to **words**

Word Bank			
ears	afraid	water	horse
end	eagle	bread	soar
rope	bears	words	rainbow

Page 46

Cool As a Cucumber

Sometimes people use funny expressions to say what they mean. Complete each sentence by writing the letter of the word that would best explain what is meant.

1. Jacob was as **f** as a hornet about being poor.
2. Mama had learned to **i** a dollar, making sure there were enough food and clothes.
3. Peewee Miller sounded as **d** as a lark when he found the kente cloth.
4. Because Jacob left without eating breakfast, he probably felt as **j** as a horse.
5. Each brother was as **e** as a bee building the snowman.
6. Peewee stood as **b** as a peacock when he looked at the completed black snowman.
7. The snowman acted as **c** as a puppy when he danced with Peewee.
8. The black snowman was as **h** as an owl because he understood the meaning of happiness.
9. Jacob acted as **a** as a mule in hearing the snowman's words.
10. Peewee was so scared he was **g** like a leaf inside the burning building.

a. stubborn
b. proud
c. playful
d. happy
e. busy
f. mad
g. shaking
h. wise
i. stretch
j. hungry

Page 47

Cool Heads

Circle sentence "a" or "b" to show which one means the same as the numbered sentence.

1. Eddie Whitestone always had something up his sleeve.
   a. He keeps things up his sleeve. **(b)** He liked to plan surprises.
2. His room was a pigsty.
   (a) It was very messy. b. He lived with pigs.
3. She would be late if she didn't step on it.
   (a) She needs to hurry. b. She needs to step on something.
4. Sometimes David could be hardheaded.
   a. His head was very hard. **(b)** He could be stubborn.
5. Roger always tried to keep a cool head.
   (a) He tried to be calm. b. He kept ice on his head.
6. Horseplay was not allowed in the hall.
   a. No horses were allowed in the hall. **(b)** No playing was allowed in the hall.
7. Ali Baba wrapped up another mystery.
   (a) He solved the mystery. b. He wrapped the mystery in paper.
8. Ali Baba kept an eye on Eddie Whitestone.
   a. He drew an eye on Eddie's shirt. **(b)** He watched him.
9. His neighbors skipped town.
   a. They skipped all over town. **(b)** They left town.
10. The criminal was in hot water.
    a. He was standing in hot water. **(b)** He was in trouble.

Page 48

What's the Point?

Harry and Sidney giggled as they started painting the winter mural. Instead of painting a snow picture, they painted themselves in a cemetery "burying the hatchet." This meant that they would forget about their past fighting and be friends.

Read each sentence below. Then write the letter of the phrase that tells what the speaker really means.

He says . . .

e 1. It's "raining cats and dogs."
d 2. I remember when you were "knee-high to a grasshopper."
a 3. You "eat like a bird."
c 4. He "held up the bank."
b 5. You "light up my life!"
g 6. Which way should I turn "at the fork in the road?"
f 7. The speaker "had a frog in her throat."

What he means is . . .

a. don't eat very much
b. make me very happy
c. robbed the bank
d. very small
e. pouring hard
f. was hoarse
g. where the road splits

Page 49

Which Is Which?

Like twins, words are sometimes hard to tell apart. Can you tell these word pairs apart? Answer each question by writing the correct word in the box.

1. expression—impression
   Which word means "a look on the face"? **expression**
2. taught—taut
   Which word means "pulled tight"? **taut**
3. quite—quiet
   Which word means "without noise"? **quiet**
4. later—latter
   Which word means "the last one"? **latter**
5. kernel—colonel
   Which word means "a small seed"? **kernel**
6. accident—incident
   Which word means "an event"? **incident**
7. piece—peace
   Which word means "quiet and orderly"? **peace**
8. close—clothes
   Which word means "something to wear"? **clothes**
9. tough—though
   Which word means "not easy or tender"? **tough**
10. progressed—oppressed
    Which word means "moved forward"? **progressed**

A
NOW . . . Imagine that you had a twin. What would your names be? Would
D   you dress alike? Would you do and like the same things?

Page 50

Candy Store Dilemma

Read the label on each candy jar. Write the words from the Word Bank on the candy jar where they belong.

Winter Clothes
1. mittens
2. jacket
3. earmuffs

Parts of the Body
1. ears
2. eyebrows
3. knees

Kinds of Candy
1. Gummi Bears
2. M & M's
3. Turkish Taffy

Places in a Story
1. park
2. town square
3. Main Street

Characters in a Story
1. Sarah
2. Danny
3. Emmett

Word Bank		
Sarah	M & M's	earmuffs
park	Main Street	eyebrows
mittens	jacket	Danny
town square	ears	Emmett
Gummi Bears	Turkish Taffy	knees

Page 51

At the Pet Store

Use a dictionary to help you determine in which category each of these words belongs.

malamute	chameleon	mud puppy	mouse
guppy	newt	skink	Pekingese
angelfish	macaw	sheepdog	canary
cockatoo	pointer	rat	tomcat
spaniel	guinea pig	Siamese	goldfish
platy	finch	mutt	hamster
Manx	parrot	Persian	swift
gerbil	swordfish	salamander	setter
parakeet	iguana	mastiff	myna
frog	tabby	cockatiel	

Reptiles & Amphibians
1. frog
2. chameleon
3. newt
4. iguana
5. mud puppy
6. salamander
7. skink
8. swift

Birds
1. cockatoo
2. parakeet
3. macaw
4. finch
5. parrot
6. cockatiel
7. canary
8. myna

Dogs
1. spaniel
2. pointer
3. sheepdog
4. mutt
5. mastiff
6. Pekingese
7. setter
8. malamute

Fish
1. guppy
2. angelfish
3. swordfish
4. goldfish
5. platy

Rodents
1. gerbil
2. guinea pig
3. rat
4. mouse
5. hamster

Cats
1. Manx
2. tabby
3. Siamese
4. Persian
5. tomcat

A
NOW . . . Research the differences between reptiles and amphibians. Separate the "Reptiles & Amphibians" list above into two separate lists. To which list would you add the word tadpole? To which list would you add the word anole? Find other words to add to these lists.

Page 52

Do We or Don't We?

If the word is a **compound word**, color the space blue.
If the word is a **contraction**, color the space gray.
If the word is a **verb**, color the space yellow.
If the word is an **adjective**, color the space black.

Page 53

What a View!

On a separate paper, rewrite the story below, substituting the correct word from the Word Box for each underlined word or phrase.

Space shuttle astronauts *view* our *earth* from an *altitude* of 160 miles. Because the shuttle *orbits* the earth so *rapidly*, the astronauts see several sunrises and sunsets in one *24-hour period*.

They pass over the place where the Mediterranean Sea *separates* Europe from Africa. It is very *easy* to *locate* the Nile River and the Red Sea from that altitude.

The shuttle travels across Asia, the largest *landmass*. The astronauts *film* the *peaks* of the Himalaya Mountains before crossing over the Pacific Ocean. Their *journey* is *incredible*.

Word Box	
photograph	
unbelievable	
continent	
divides	quickly
day	see
find	tops
trip	
planet	height
circles	simple

Page 54

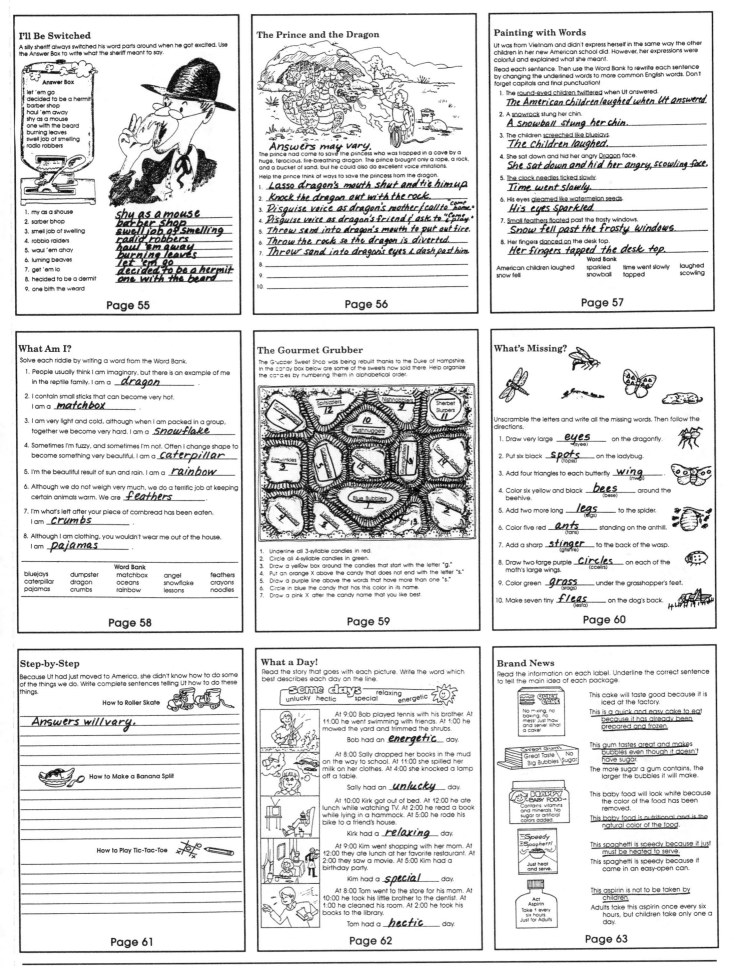

I'll Be Switched

A silly sheriff always switched his word parts around when he got excited. Use the Answer Box to write what the sheriff meant to say.

Answer Box

let 'em go
decided to be a hermit
barber shop
haul 'em away
shy as a mouse
one with the beard
burning leaves
swell job of smelling
radio robbers

1. my as a shouse — *shy as a mouse*
2. sarber bhop — *barber shop*
3. smell job of swelling — *swell job of smelling*
4. robbio raiders — *radio robbers*
5. waul 'em ahay — *haul 'em away*
6. luming beaves — *burning leaves*
7. get 'em lo — *let 'em go*
8. hecided to be a dermit — *decided to be a hermit*
9. one blth the weard — *one with the beard*

Page 55

The Prince and the Dragon

Answers may vary.

The prince had come to save the princess who was trapped in a cave by a huge, ferocious, fire-breathing dragon. The prince brought only a rope, a rock, and a bucket of sand, but he could also do excellent voice imitations.

Help the prince think of ways to save the princess from the dragon.

1. *Lasso dragon's mouth shut and tie him up*
2. *Knock the dragon out with the rock.*
3. *Disguise voice as dragon's mother & call to "come home".*
4. *Disguise voice as dragon's friend & ask to "come & play".*
5. *Throw sand into dragon's mouth to put out fire.*
6. *Throw the rock so the dragon is diverted.*
7. *Throw sand into dragon's eyes & dash past him.*
8. _____
9. _____
10. _____

Page 56

Painting with Words

Ut was from Vietnam and didn't express herself in the same way the other children in her new American school did. However, her expressions were colorful and explained what she meant.

Read each sentence. Then use the Word Bank to rewrite each sentence by changing the underlined words to more common English words. Don't forget capitals and final punctuation!

1. The round-eyed children twittered when Ut answered.
   The American children laughed when Ut answered
2. A snowrock stung her chin.
   A snowball stung her chin.
3. The children screeched like bluejays.
   The children laughed.
4. She sat down and hid her angry Dragon face.
   She sat down and hid her angry, scowling face.
5. The clock needles ticked slowly.
   Time went slowly.
6. His eyes gleamed like watermelon seeds.
   His eyes sparkled.
7. Small feathers floated past the frosty windows.
   Snow fell past the frosty windows.
8. Her fingers danced on the desk top.
   Her fingers tapped the desk top.

Word Bank

American children laughed | sparkled | time went slowly | laughed
snow fell | snowball | tapped | scowling

Page 57

What Am I?

Solve each riddle by writing a word from the Word Bank.

1. People usually think I am imaginary, but there is an example of me in the reptile family. I am a *dragon*.
2. I contain small sticks that can become very hot. I am a *matchbox*.
3. I am very light and cold, although when I am packed in a group, together we become very hard. I am a *snowflake*.
4. Sometimes I'm fuzzy, and sometimes I'm not. Often I change shape to become something very beautiful. I am a *caterpillar*.
5. I'm the beautiful result of sun and rain. I am a *rainbow*.
6. Although we do not weigh very much, we do a terrific job at keeping certain animals warm. We are *feathers*.
7. I'm what's left after your piece of cornbread has been eaten. I am *crumbs*.
8. Although I am clothing, you wouldn't wear me out of the house. I am *pajamas*.

Word Bank

bluejays | dumpster | matchbox | angel | feathers
caterpillar | dragon | oceans | snowflake | crayons
pajamas | crumbs | rainbow | lessons | noodles

Page 58

The Gourmet Grubber

The Grubber Sweet Shop was being rebuilt thanks to the Duke of Hampshire. In the candy box below are some of the sweets now sold there. Help organize the candies by numbering them in alphabetical order.

1. Underline all 3-syllable candies in red.
2. Circle all 4-syllable candies in green.
3. Draw a yellow box around the candies that start with the letter "g."
4. Put an orange X above the candy that does not end with the letter "s."
5. Draw a purple line above the words that have more than one "s."
6. Circle in blue the candy that has this color in its name.
7. Draw a pink X after the candy name that you like best.

Page 59

What's Missing?

Unscramble the letters and write all the missing words. Then follow the directions.

1. Draw very large *eyes* (syee) on the dragonfly.
2. Put six black *spots* (topss) on the ladybug.
3. Add four triangles to each butterfly *wing* (nwgi).
4. Color six yellow and black *bees* (bese) around the beehive.
5. Add two more long *legs* (elgs) to the spider.
6. Color five red *ants* (tans) standing on the anthill.
7. Add a sharp *stinger* (gtisrne) to the back of the wasp.
8. Draw two large purple *circles* (ccelirs) on each of the moth's large wings.
9. Color green *grass* (srags) under the grasshopper's feet.
10. Make seven tiny *fleas* (lesfa) on the dog's back.

Page 60

Step-by-Step

Because Ut had just moved to America, she didn't know how to do some of the things we do. Write complete sentences telling Ut how to do these things.

How to Roller Skate

Answers will vary.

How to Make a Banana Split

How to Play Tic-Tac-Toe

Page 61

What a Day!

Read the story that goes with each picture. Write the word which best describes each day on the line.

some days
unlucky | hectic | special | relaxing | energetic

At 9:00 Bob played tennis with his brother. At 11:00 he went swimming with friends. At 1:00 he mowed the yard and trimmed the shrubs.
Bob had an *energetic* day.

At 8:00 Sally dropped her books in the mud on the way to school. At 11:00 she spilled her milk on her clothes. At 4:00 she knocked a lamp off a table.
Sally had an *unlucky* day.

At 10:00 Kirk got out of bed. At 12:00 he ate lunch while watching TV. At 2:00 he read a book while lying in a hammock. At 5:00 he rode his bike to a friend's house.
Kirk had a *relaxing* day.

At 9:00 Kim went shopping with her mom. At 12:00 they ate lunch at her favorite restaurant. At 2:00 they saw a movie. At 5:00 Kim had a birthday party.
Kim had a *special* day.

At 8:00 Tom went to the store for his mom. At 10:00 he took his little brother to the dentist. At 1:00 he cleaned his room. At 2:00 he took his books to the library.
Tom had a *hectic* day.

Page 62

Brand News

Read the information on each label. Underline the correct sentence to tell the main idea of each package.

Instant Cake — No mixing, no baking, no mess! Just thaw and serve! What a cake!
- This cake will taste good because it is iced at the factory.
- <u>This is a quick and easy cake to eat because it has already been prepared and frozen.</u>

Great Gum — Great Taste, Big Bubbles, No Sugar
- <u>This gum tastes great and makes bubbles even though it doesn't have sugar.</u>
- The more sugar a gum contains, the larger the bubbles it will make.

Happy Baby Food — Contains: vitamins and minerals. No sugar or artificial colors added.
- This baby food will look white because the color of the food has been removed.
- <u>This baby food is nutritional and is the natural color of the food.</u>

Speedy Spaghetti — Just heat and serve.
- <u>This spaghetti is speedy because it just must be heated to serve.</u>
- This spaghetti is speedy because it came in an easy-open can.

Act Aspirin — Take 1 every six hours. Just for Adults
- <u>This aspirin is not to be taken by children.</u>
- Adults take this aspirin once every six hours, but children take only one a day.

Page 63

Next ...

Read each sentence. Write two sentences which tell two different things that could happen.

1. The smoke from the oven rose in the air toward the smoke detector.
next: *Answers will vary.*

2. The crowd cheered wildly as the football player ran toward the goal line.
next: 1. _____ 2. _____

3. Bob and Kelly were on their way to the movie when Kelly realized she had left her money at home.
next: 1. _____ 2. _____

4. The diver was looking for the old sunken ship when he spotted a huge grey mass ahead.
next: 1. _____ 2. _____

5. When Rob arrived for the museum tour, he found that the tour had started ten minutes earlier.
next: 1. _____ 2. _____

6. Just as Sam was to go on stage for the class play, he realized he had forgotten his lines.
next: 1. _____ 2. _____

Page 64

Horsing Around

Horses are beautiful and are very smart animals. They have excellent senses of smell, sight, and hearing.

Study this diagram of a horse. Write the names of its body parts shown by solving each puzzle.

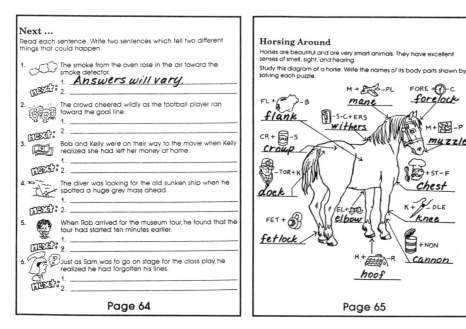

M + [ ] – PL — *mane*
FORE + [ ] – C — *forelock*
FL [ ] – B — *flank*
[ ] – S – C + ERS — *withers*
M + [ ] – P — *muzzle*
CR + [ ] – S — *croup*
[ ] – TOR + K — *dock*
[ ] + ST – F — *chest*
K + [ ] – DLE — *knee*
EL + [ ] — *elbow*
FET + [ ] — *fetlock*
[ ] + NON — *cannon*
H + [ ] – R — *hoof*

Page 65

Forgetful Fred

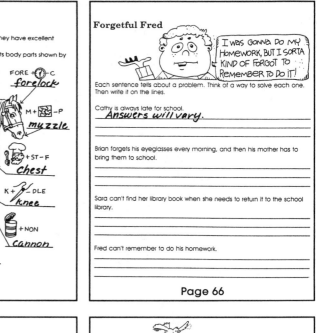

I WAS GONNA DO MY HOMEWORK, BUT I SORTA KIND OF FORGOT TO REMEMBER TO DO IT!

Each sentence tells about a problem. Think of a way to solve each one. Then write it on the lines.

Cathy is always late for school.
Answers will vary.

Brian forgets his eyeglasses every morning, and then his mother has to bring them to school.

Sara can't find her library book when she needs to return it to the school library.

Fred can't remember to do his homework.

Page 66

Think About It!

Arthur, the director of a play, had to handle many problems. Think about each problem and then write what you would have done to help each character solve it.

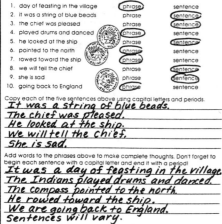

Can you hear me?
Sue Ellen didn't talk loudly enough.
Answers will vary.

Huh?
Buster could not remember what to say.

Whoops!
Muffy kept dropping the basket filled with cranberries.

Page 67

Is That a Fact!

Read each sentence. If it states a fact, write the word **fact** on the line. If it states an opinion, write the word **opinion** on the line.

1. Eighth graders are too old to be rolling snowballs. — *opinion*
2. A town square is part of a town. — *fact*
3. Enough snow can fall in one night to become a foot deep. — *fact*
4. Mr. Wetzel sells the best candy in the world. — *opinion*
5. A fence is usually strong enough to stop a snowball. — *fact*
6. Winter is the season after fall and before spring. — *fact*
7. Everyone likes to play in the snow. — *opinion*
8. Warm weather will make snow melt. — *fact*
9. Emmett always makes the biggest and best snowballs. — *opinion*
10. It is hard for wild animals to find food in the snow. — *fact*

Page 68

Now Really!

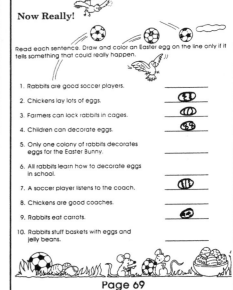

Read each sentence. Draw and color an Easter egg on the line only if it tells something that could really happen.

1. Rabbits are good soccer players. _____
2. Chickens lay lots of eggs. [egg]
3. Farmers can lock rabbits in cages. [egg]
4. Children can decorate eggs. [egg]
5. Only one colony of rabbits decorates eggs for the Easter Bunny. _____
6. All rabbits learn how to decorate eggs in school. _____
7. A soccer player listens to the coach. [egg]
8. Chickens are good coaches. _____
9. Rabbits eat carrots. [egg]
10. Rabbits stuff baskets with eggs and jelly beans. _____

Page 69

A Penny for Your Thoughts

A **phrase** is an *incomplete* thought—it doesn't make sense all by itself. A **sentence**, on the other hand, is a *complete* thought.

Circle **phrase** or **sentence** to show whether each group of words below is an incomplete or a complete thought.

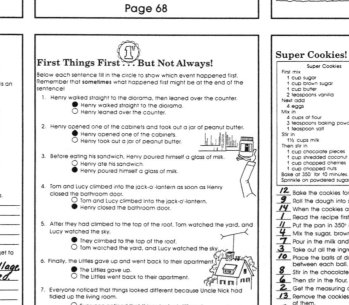

1. day of feasting in the village — (phrase) sentence
2. it was a string of blue beads — phrase (sentence)
3. the chief was pleased — phrase (sentence)
4. played drums and danced — (phrase) sentence
5. he looked at the ship — phrase (sentence)
6. pointed to the north — (phrase) sentence
7. rowed toward the ship — (phrase) sentence
8. we will tell the chief — phrase (sentence)
9. she is sad — phrase (sentence)
10. going back to England — (phrase) sentence

Copy each of the five sentences above using capital letters and periods.
It was a string of blue beads.
The chief was pleased.
He looked at the ship.
We will tell the chief.
She is sad.

Add words to the phrases above to make complete thoughts. Don't forget to begin each sentence with a capital letter and end it with a period!
It was a day of feasting in the village.
The Indians played drums and danced.
The compass pointed to the north.
He rowed toward the ship.
We are going back to England.
Sentences will vary.

Page 70

First Things First . . . But Not Always!

Below each sentence fill in the circle to show which event happened first. Remember that **sometimes** what happened first might be at the end of the sentence!

1. Henry walked straight to the diorama, then leaned over the counter.
● Henry walked straight to the diorama.
○ Henry leaned over the counter.

2. Henry opened one of the cabinets and took out a jar of peanut butter.
● Henry opened one of the cabinets.
○ Henry took out a jar of peanut butter.

3. Before eating his sandwich, Henry poured himself a glass of milk.
○ Henry ate his sandwich.
● Henry poured himself a glass of milk.

4. Tom and Lucy climbed into the jack-o'-lantern as soon as Henry closed the bathroom door.
○ Tom and Lucy climbed into the jack-o'-lantern.
● Henry closed the bathroom door.

5. After they had climbed to the top of the roof, Tom watched the yard, and Lucy watched the sky.
● They climbed to the top of the roof.
○ Tom watched the yard, and Lucy watched the sky.

6. Finally, the Littles gave up and went back to their apartment.
● The Littles gave up.
○ The Littles went back to their apartment.

7. Everyone noticed that things looked different because Uncle Nick had tidied up the living room.
○ Everyone noticed that things looked different.
● Uncle Nick tidied up the living room.

Page 71

Super Cookies!

Super Cookies
First mix
1 cup sugar
1 cup brown sugar
1 cup butter
2 teaspoons vanilla
Next add
4 eggs
Mix in
4 cups of flour
3 teaspoons baking powder
1 teaspoon salt
Stir in
1½ cups milk
Then stir in
1 cup chocolate pieces
1 cup shredded coconut
1 cup chopped cherries
1 cup chopped nuts
Bake at 350° for 10 minutes.
Sprinkle on powdered sugar.

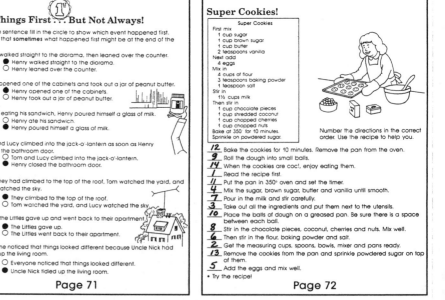

Number the directions in the correct order. Use the recipe to help you.

12 Bake the cookies for 10 minutes. Remove the pan from the oven.
9 Roll the dough into small balls.
14 When the cookies are cool, enjoy eating them.
1 Read the recipe first.
11 Put the pan in 350° oven and set the timer.
4 Mix the sugar, brown sugar, butter and vanilla until smooth.
7 Pour in the milk and stir carefully.
3 Take out all the ingredients and put them next to the utensils.
10 Place the balls of dough on a greased pan. Be sure there is a space between each ball.
8 Stir in the chocolate pieces, coconut, cherries and nuts. Mix well.
6 Then stir in the flour, baking powder and salt.
2 Get the measuring cups, spoons, bowls, mixer and pans ready.
13 Remove the cookies from the pan and sprinkle powdered sugar on top of them.
5 Add the eggs and mix well.

• Try the recipe!

Page 72

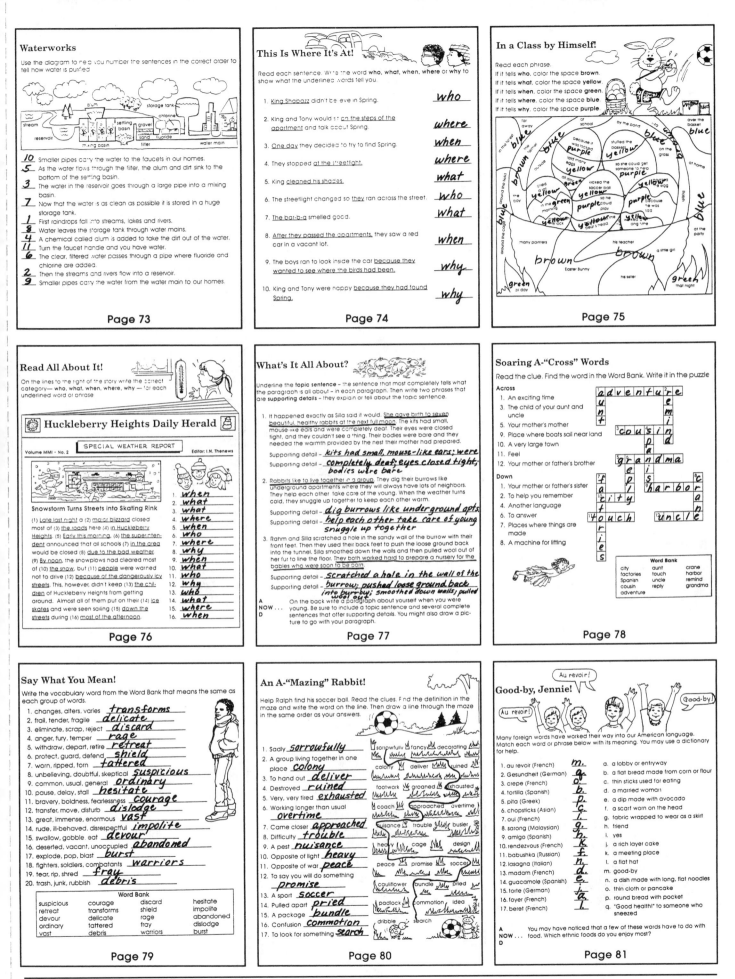

Waterworks — Page 73

Use the diagram to help you number the sentences in the correct order to tell how water is purified.

10 Smaller pipes carry the water to the faucets in our homes.
5 As the water flows through the filter, the alum and dirt sink to the bottom of the settling basin.
3 The water in the reservoir goes through a large pipe into a mixing basin.
7 Now that the water is as clean as possible it is stored in a huge storage tank.
1 First raindrops fall into streams, lakes and rivers.
8 Water leaves the storage tank through water mains.
4 A chemical called alum is added to take the dirt out of the water.
11 Turn the faucet handle and you have water.
6 The clear, filtered water passes through a pipe where fluoride and chlorine are added.
2 Then the streams and rivers flow into a reservoir.
9 Smaller pipes carry the water from the water main to our homes.

This Is Where It's At! — Page 74

Read each sentence. Write the word who, what, when, where or why to show what the underlined words tell you.

1. King Shabazz didn't believe in Spring. — *who*
2. King and Tony would sit on the steps of the apartment and talk about Spring. — *where*
3. One day they decided to try to find Spring. — *when*
4. They stopped at the streetlight. — *where*
5. King cleaned his shades. — *what*
6. The streetlight changed so they ran across the street. — *who*
7. The bar-b-q smelled good. — *what*
8. After they passed the apartments, they saw a red car in a vacant lot. — *when*
9. The boys ran to look inside the car because they wanted to see where the birds had been. — *why*
10. King and Tony were happy because they had found Spring. — *why*

In a Class by Himself! — Page 75

Read each phrase.
If it tells who, color the space brown.
If it tells what, color the space yellow.
If it tells when, color the space green.
If it tells where, color the space blue.
If it tells why, color the space purple.

Read All About It! — Page 76

On the lines to the right of the story write the correct category — who, what, when, where, why — for each underlined word or phrase.

Huckleberry Heights Daily Herald
SPECIAL WEATHER REPORT
Volume MMI · No. 2   Editor: I.N. Thenews

Snowstorm Turns Streets into Skating Rink

(1) Late last night a (2) major blizzard closed most of the (3) roads here (4) in Huckleberry Heights. (5) Early this morning, (6) the superintendent announced that all schools (7) in the area would be closed (8) due to the bad weather. (9) By noon, the snowplows had cleared most of (10) the snow, but (11) people were warned not to drive (12) because of the dangerously icy streets. This, however, didn't keep (13) the children of Huckleberry Heights from getting around. Almost all of them put on their (14) ice skates and were seen sailing (15) down the streets during (16) most of the afternoon.

1. when
2. what
3. where
4. when
5. when
6. who
7. where
8. why
9. when
10. what
11. who
12. why
13. who
14. what
15. where
16. when

What's It All About? — Page 77

Underline the topic sentence – the sentence that most completely tells what the paragraph is all about – in each paragraph. Then write two phrases that are supporting details – they explain or tell about the topic sentence.

1. It happened exactly as Silla said it would. She gave birth to seven beautiful, healthy rabbits at the next full moon. The kits had small, mouse-like ears and were completely deaf. Their eyes were closed tight, and they couldn't see a thing. Their bodies were bare and they needed the warmth provided by the nest their mother had prepared.

Supporting detail - *kits had small, mouse-like ears; were completely deaf; eyes closed tight;*
Supporting detail - *bodies were bare*

2. Rabbits like to live together in a group. They dig their burrows like underground apartments where they will always have lots of neighbors. They help each other take care of the young. When the weather turns cold, they snuggle up together to keep each other warm.

Supporting detail - *dig burrows like underground apts.*
Supporting detail - *help each other take care of young; snuggle up together*

3. Rahm and Silla scratched a hole in the sandy wall of the burrow with their front feet. Then they used their back feet to push the loose ground back into the tunnel. Silla smoothed down the walls and then pulled wool out of her fur to line the floor. They both worked hard to prepare a nursery for the babies who were soon to be born.

Supporting detail - *scratched a hole in the wall of the burrow; pushed loose ground back into burrow; smoothed down walls; pulled wool out*

A NOW ... D On the back write a paragraph about yourself when you were young. Be sure to include a topic sentence and several complete sentences that offer supporting details. You might also draw a picture to go with your paragraph.

Soaring A-"Cross" Words — Page 78

Read the clue. Find the word in the Word Bank. Write it in the puzzle

Across
1. An exciting time
3. The child of your aunt and uncle
5. Your mother's mother
9. Place where boats sail near land
10. A very large town
11. Feel
12. Your mother or father's brother

Down
1. Your mother or father's sister
2. To help you remember
4. Another language
6. To answer
7. Places where things are made
8. A machine for lifting

Crossword answers:
1. adventure
3. cousin
5. grandma
9. harbor
10. city
11. touch
12. uncle
(Down) aunt, remind, factories, reply, Spanish, crane

Word Bank
city, factories, Spanish, cousin, adventure, aunt, touch, uncle, reply, crane, harbor, remind, grandma

Say What You Mean! — Page 79

Write the vocabulary word from the Word Bank that means the same as each group of words.

1. changes, alters, varies — *transforms*
2. frail, tender, fragile — *delicate*
3. eliminate, scrap, reject — *discard*
4. anger, fury, temper — *rage*
5. withdraw, depart, retire — *retreat*
6. protect, guard, defend — *shield*
7. worn, ripped, torn — *tattered*
8. unbelieving, doubtful, skeptical — *suspicious*
9. common, usual, plain — *ordinary*
10. pause, delay, stall — *hesitate*
11. bravery, boldness, fearlessness — *courage*
12. transfer, move, shift — *dislodge*
13. great, immense, enormous — *vast*
14. rude, ill-behaved, disrespectful — *impolite*
15. swallow, gobble, eat — *devour*
16. deserted, vacant, unoccupied — *abandoned*
17. explode, pop, blast — *burst*
18. fighters, soldiers, combatants — *warriors*
19. tear, rip, shred — *fray*
20. trash, junk, rubbish — *debris*

Word Bank
suspicious, retreat, devour, ordinary, vast, courage, transforms, delicate, tattered, debris, discard, shield, rage, fray, warriors, hesitate, impolite, abandoned, dislodge, burst

An A-"Mazing" Rabbit! — Page 80

Help Ralph find his soccer ball. Read the clues. Find the definition in the maze and write the word on the line. Then draw a line through the maze in the same order as your answers.

1. Sadly — *sorrowfully*
2. A group living together in one place — *colony*
3. To hand out — *deliver*
4. Destroyed — *ruined*
5. Very, very tired — *exhausted*
6. Working longer than usual — *overtime*
7. Came closer — *approached*
8. Difficulty — *trouble*
9. A pest — *nuisance*
10. Opposite of light — *heavy*
11. Opposite of war — *peace*
12. To say you will do something — *promise*
13. A sport — *soccer*
14. Pulled apart — *pried*
15. A package — *bundle*
16. Confusion — *commotion*
17. To look for something — *search*

Good-by, Jennie! — Page 81

Au revoir!   Au revoir!   Good-by!

Many foreign words have worked their way into our American language. Match each word or phrase below with its meaning. You may use a dictionary for help.

1. au revoir (French) — *m*
2. Gesundheit (German) — *q*
3. crepe (French) — *o*
4. tortilla (Spanish) — *b*
5. pita (Greek) — *p*
6. chopsticks (Asian) — *c*
7. oui (French) — *i*
8. sarong (Malaysian) — *g*
9. amigo (Spanish) — *h*
10. rendezvous (French) — *k*
11. babushka (Russian) — *f*
12. lasagna (Italian) — *n*
13. madam (French) — *d*
14. guacamole (Spanish) — *e*
15. torte (German) — *j*
16. foyer (French) — *a*
17. beret (French) — *l*

a. a lobby or entryway
b. a flat bread made from corn or flour
c. thin sticks used for eating
d. a married woman
e. a dip made with avocado
f. a scarf worn on the head
g. fabric wrapped to wear as a skirt
h. friend
i. yes
j. a rich layer cake
k. a meeting place
l. a flat hat
m. good-by
n. a dish made with long, flat noodles
o. thin cloth or pancake
p. round bread with pocket
q. "Good health!" to someone who sneezed

A NOW D You may have noticed that a few of these words have to do with food. Which ethnic foods do you enjoy most?

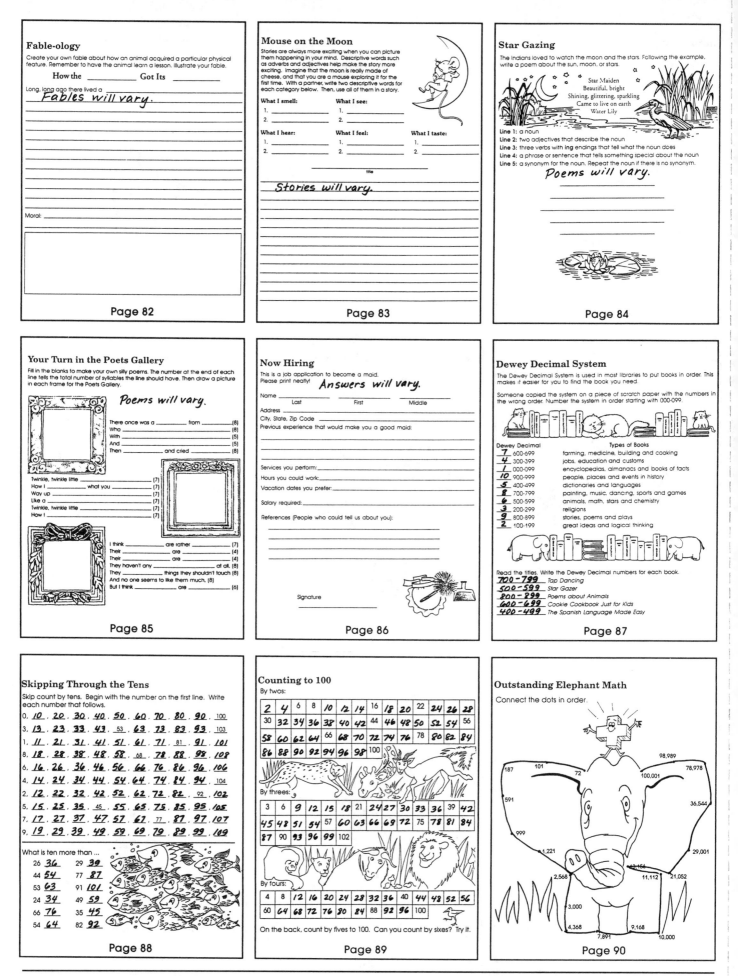

Fable-ology

Create your own fable about how an animal acquired a particular physical feature. Remember to have the animal learn a lesson. Illustrate your fable.

How the _____ Got Its _____

Long, long ago there lived a _____
Fables will vary.

Moral: _____

Page 82

Mouse on the Moon

Stories are always more exciting when you can picture them happening in your mind. Descriptive words such as adverbs and adjectives help make the story more exciting. Imagine that the moon is really made of cheese, and that you are a mouse exploring it for the first time. With a partner, write two descriptive words for each category below. Then, use all of them in a story.

What I smell:
1. _____
2. _____

What I see:
1. _____
2. _____

What I hear:
1. _____
2. _____

What I feel:
1. _____
2. _____

What I taste:
1. _____
2. _____

_____ title

Stories will vary.

Page 83

Star Gazing

The Indians loved to watch the moon and the stars. Following the example, write a poem about the sun, moon, or stars.

Star Maiden
Beautiful, bright
Shining, glittering, sparkling
Came to live on earth
Water Lily

Line 1: a noun
Line 2: two adjectives that describe the noun
Line 3: three verbs with ing endings that tell what the noun does
Line 4: a phrase or sentence that tells something special about the noun
Line 5: a synonym for the noun. Repeat the noun if there is no synonym.

Poems will vary.

Page 84

Your Turn in the Poets Gallery

Fill in the blanks to make your own silly poems. The number at the end of each line tells the total number of syllables the line should have. Then draw a picture in each frame for the Poets Gallery.

Poems will vary.

There once was a _____ from _____ (8)
Who _____ (8)
With _____ (5)
And _____ (5)
Then _____ and cried _____ (8)

Twinkle, twinkle little _____ (7)
How I _____ what you _____ (7)
Way up _____ (7)
Like a _____ (7)
Twinkle, twinkle little _____ (7)
How I _____ (7)

I think _____ are rather _____ (7)
Their _____ are _____ (4)
Their _____ are _____ (4)
They haven't any _____ at all. (8)
They _____ things they shouldn't touch (8)
And no one seems to like them much. (8)
But I think _____ are _____ (6)

Page 85

Now Hiring

This is a job application to become a maid.
Please print neatly!

Answers will vary.

Name _____
Last   First   Middle
Address _____
City, State, Zip Code _____
Previous experience that would make you a good maid:
_____
_____

Services you perform: _____
Hours you could work: _____
Vacation dates you prefer: _____

Salary required: _____

References (People who could tell us about you):
_____
_____

Signature
_____

Page 86

Dewey Decimal System

The Dewey Decimal System is used in most libraries to put books in order. This makes it easier for you to find the book you need.

Someone copied the system on a piece of scratch paper with the numbers in the wrong order. Number the system in order starting with 000-099.

Dewey Decimal		Types of Books
7	600-699	farming, medicine, building and cooking
4	300-399	jobs, education and customs
1	000-099	encyclopedias, almanacs and books of facts
10	900-999	people, places and events in history
5	400-499	dictionaries and languages
8	700-799	painting, music, dancing, sports and games
6	500-599	animals, math, stars and chemistry
3	200-299	religions
9	800-899	stories, poems and plays
2	100-199	great ideas and logical thinking

Read the titles. Write the Dewey Decimal numbers for each book.

700-799 Tap Dancing
500-599 Star Gazer
800-899 Poems about Animals
600-699 Cookie Cookbook Just for Kids
400-499 The Spanish Language Made Easy

Page 87

Skipping Through the Tens

Skip count by tens. Begin with the number on the first line. Write each number that follows.

0, **10**, **20**, **30**, **40**, **50**, **60**, **70**, **80**, **90**, 100
3, **13**, **23**, **33**, **43**, 53, **63**, **73**, **83**, **93**, 103
1, **11**, **21**, **31**, **41**, **51**, **61**, **71**, 81, **91**, **101**
8, **18**, **28**, **38**, **48**, **58**, 68, **78**, **88**, **98**, **108**
6, **16**, **26**, **36**, **46**, **56**, **66**, **76**, **86**, **96**, **106**
4, **14**, **24**, **34**, **44**, **54**, 64, **74**, **84**, **94**, 104
2, **12**, **22**, **32**, **42**, **52**, **62**, **72**, **82**, 92, **102**
5, **15**, **25**, **35**, 45, **55**, **65**, **75**, **85**, **95**, **105**
7, **17**, **27**, **37**, **47**, **57**, **67**, 77, **87**, **97**, **107**
9, **19**, **29**, **39**, **49**, **59**, **69**, **79**, **89**, **99**, **109**

What is ten more than ...

26 **36**   29 **39**
44 **54**   77 **87**
53 **63**   91 **101**
24 **34**   49 **59**
66 **76**   35 **45**
54 **64**   82 **92**

Page 88

Counting to 100

By twos:

2	4	6	8	10	12	14	16	18	20	22	24	26	28
30	32	34	36	38	40	42	44	46	48	50	52	54	56
58	60	62	64	66	68	70	72	74	76	78	80	82	84
86	88	90	92	94	96	98	100						

By threes:

3	6	9	12	15	18	21	24	27	30	33	36	39	42
45	48	51	54	57	60	63	66	69	72	75	78	81	84
87	90	93	96	99	102								

By fours:

4	8	12	16	20	24	28	32	36	40	44	48	52	56
60	64	68	72	76	80	84	88	92	96	100			

On the back, count by fives to 100. Can you count by sixes? Try it.

Page 89

Outstanding Elephant Math

Connect the dots in order.

187   101   72   100,001   98,989   78,978
591   36,544
999   29,001
1,221
2,568   12,156   11,112   21,052
3,000
4,368   7,891   9,168   10,000

Page 90

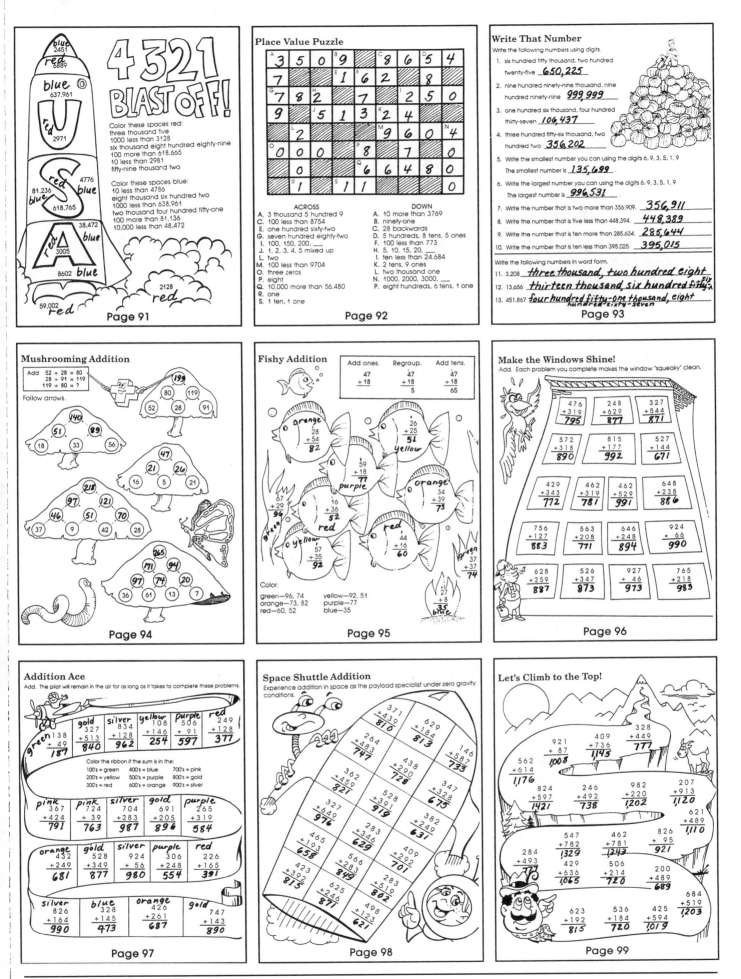

4321 BLAST OFF!

(rocket labels) blue 2451, red 6889, blue 637,961, red 2971, 81,236 red, blue 618,765, 4776 blue, 38,472 blue, red 3005, A blue, 8602 blue, 2128 red, 59,002 red

Color these spaces red:
three thousand five
1000 less than 3128
six thousand eight hundred eighty-nine
100 more than 618,665
10 less than 2981
fifty-nine thousand two

Color these spaces blue:
10 less than 4786
eight thousand six hundred two
1000 less than 638,961
two thousand four hundred fifty-one
100 more than 81,136
10,000 less than 48,472

Page 91

Place Value Puzzle

A3	5	0	9		C8	6	D5	4
7			E1	F6	2			8
G7	H8	2		7		I2	5	0
9		J5	1	3	K2	4		
	L2				M9	6	0	N4
O0	0	0		P8		7		0
	0			Q6	6	4	8	0
R1		S1	1					0

ACROSS
A. 3 thousand 5 hundred 9
C. 100 less than 8754
E. one hundred sixty-two
G. seven hundred eighty-two
I. 100, 150, 200, ___
J. 1, 2, 3, 4, 5 mixed up
L. two
M. 100 less than 9704
O. three zeros
P. eight
Q. 10,000 more than 56,480
R. one
S. 1 ten, 1 one

DOWN
A. 10 more than 3769
B. ninety-one
C. 28 backwards
D. 5 hundreds, 8 tens, 5 ones
F. 100 less than 773
H. 5, 10, 15, 20, ___
I. ten less than 24,684
K. 2 tens, 9 ones
L. two thousand one
N. 1000, 2000, 3000, ___
P. eight hundreds, 6 tens, 1 one

Page 92

Write That Number

Write the following numbers using digits.

1. six hundred fifty thousand, two hundred twenty-five 650,225
2. nine hundred ninety-nine thousand, nine hundred ninety-nine 999,999
3. one hundred six thousand, four hundred thirty-seven 106,437
4. three hundred fifty-six thousand, two hundred two 356,202
5. Write the smallest number you can using the digits 6, 9, 3, 5, 1, 9 The smallest number is 135,699.
6. Write the largest number you can using the digits 6, 9, 3, 5, 1, 9 The largest number is 996,531.
7. Write the number that is two more than 356,909. 356,911
8. Write the number that is five less than 448,394. 448,389
9. Write the number that is ten more than 285,634. 285,644
10. Write the number that is ten less than 395,025. 395,015

Write the following numbers in word form.

11. 3,208 three thousand, two hundred eight
12. 13,656 thirteen thousand, six hundred fifty-six
13. 451,867 four hundred fifty-one thousand, eight hundred sixty-seven

Page 93

Mushrooming Addition

Add 52 + 28 = 80
28 + 91 = 119
119 + 80 = ?

Follow arrows.

Page 94

Fishy Addition

Add ones.	Regroup.	Add tens.
47 +18	47 +18 5	47 +18 65

orange 28 +54 82
26 +25 51 yellow
59 +18 77 purple
67 +29 96 green
16 +36 52 red
34 +39 73 orange
57 +35 92 yellow
44 +16 60 red
37 +37 74 green
27 +8 35 blue

Color.
green—96, 74
orange—73, 82
red—60, 52
yellow—92, 51
purple—77
blue—35

Page 95

Make the Windows Shine!

Add. Each problem you complete makes the window "squeaky" clean.

476 +319 795	248 +629 877	327 +544 871
572 +318 890	815 +177 992	527 +144 671
429 +343 772	462 +319 781	462 +529 991	648 +238 886
756 +127 883	563 +208 771	646 +248 894	924 +66 990
628 +259 887	526 +347 873	927 +46 973	765 +218 983

Page 96

Addition Ace

Add. The pilot will remain in the air for as long as it takes to complete these problems.

green 138 +49 187
gold 327 +513 840
silver 834 +128 962
yellow 108 +146 254
purple 506 +91 597
red 249 +128 377

Color the ribbon if the sum is in the:
100's = green   400's = blue   700's = pink
200's = yellow   500's = purple   800's = gold
300's = red   600's = orange   900's = silver

pink 367 +424 791
pink 724 +39 763
silver 704 +283 987
gold 691 +205 896
purple 265 +319 584

orange 432 +249 681
gold 528 +349 877
silver 924 +56 980
purple 306 +248 554
red 226 +165 391

silver 826 +164 990
blue 328 +145 473
orange 426 +261 687
gold 747 +143 890

Page 97

Space Shuttle Addition

Experience addition in space as the payload specialist under zero gravity conditions.

371 +439 810
629 +184 813
146 +587 733
264 +483 747
438 +290 728
347 +328 675
362 +459 821
528 +391 919
382 +249 631
327 +649 976
283 +346 629
409 +292 701
465 +193 658
566 +283 849
283 +519 802
423 +392 815
625 +246 871
498 +123 621

Page 98

Let's Climb to the Top!

921 +87 1,008
409 +736 1,145
328 +449 777
562 +614 1,176
824 +597 1,421
246 +492 738
982 +220 1,202
207 +913 1,120
621 +489 1,110
284 +493 777
547 +782 1,329
462 +781 1,243
826 +95 921
429 +636 1,065
506 +214 720
200 +489 689
684 +519 1,203
623 +192 815
536 +184 720
425 +594 1,019

Page 99

Picnic Problems

Help the ant find a path to the picnic. Work the problems. Shade the box if an answer has a 9 in it.

836 + 90 = 926	536 + 248 = 784	952 + 8 = 960	362 + 47 = 409	486 + 293 = 779	368 + 529 = 897
789 526 + 214 = 1,529	2846 + 6478 = 9324	932 + 365 = 1297	374 + 299 = 773	835 + 552 = 1387	956 874 + 65 = 1895
4768 + 2894 = 7662	38 456 + 3894 = 4,388	4507 + 2743 = 7,250	404 + 289 = 693	1843 + 6752 = 8595	4367 + 3571 = 7938
639 + 77 = 716	587 342 + 679 = 1,608	5379 1865 + 2348 = 9592	450 + 145 = 595	594 + 278 = 872	459 + 367 = 826
29 875 + 2341 = 3,245	387 379 + 5614 = 6,030	462 379 + 248 = 1,089			

Page 100

Bubble Math

Add the problems inside these bubbles.

These bubbles all popped in order from least to greatest. Number from 1 to 20 in the order in which they popped starting with the smallest sum.

Page 101

Yummy Additions

Add ones. Regroup.	Add tens. Regroup.	Add hundreds. Regroup.	Add thousands. Regroup.
7465 + 4978 = 3	7465 + 4978 = 43	7465 + 4978 = 443	7465 + 4978 = 12443

Do the problems. Color an answer containing a 3–brown, 4–red, 5–yellow.

6591 + 5569 = 12160
6843 + 7568 = 14,411 red
9224 + 7878 = 17,102
2549 + 9577 = 12,126
9853 + 8798 = 18,651 yellow
2698 + 8499 = 11,197
3849 + 7261 = 11,110
6456 + 4948 = 11,404 red
7767 + 9899 = 17,666 brown
8796 + 8975 = 17,771
9764 + 7459 = 17,223
5678 + 6984 = 12,662
9653 + 1568 = 11,221

Page 102

Mountaintop Getaway

Work all problems. Find a path to the cabin by shading in all answers that have a 3 in them.

98 − 52 = 46	46 − 12 = 34	68 − 17 = 51
79 − 53 = 26	65 − 23 = 42	86 − 32 = 54
59 − 45 = 14	75 − 64 = 11	67 − 24 = 43	97 − 54 = 43	55 − 43 = 12
87 − 65 = 22	44 − 32 = 12	57 − 24 = 33	88 − 25 = 63	75 − 61 = 14	48 − 26 = 22
69 − 25 = 44	95 − 24 = 71	48 − 13 = 35	58 − 16 = 42	35 − 13 = 22	39 − 17 = 22

SECRET PATHS

Page 103

Hats, Hats, Hats

Calculate the difference in each hat below.

736 − 629 = 107
466 − 327 = 139
837 − 529 = 308
742 − 428 = 314
784 − 565 = 219
673 − 458 = 215
648 − 426 = 222
982 − 665 = 317
947 − 729 = 218
543 − 426 = 117
928 − 619 = 309
847 − 628 = 219
427 − 318 = 109
524 − 318 = 206
245 − 126 = 119
852 − 328 = 524
545 − 221 = 324

Page 104

Soaring to the Stars

Connect the dots to form two stars. Begin one star with the subtraction problem whose difference is 100 and end with the problem whose difference is 109. Begin the other with 110 and end with 120. Color the pictures.

953 − 839 = 114
493 − 378 = 115
774 − 658 = 116
751 − 638 = 113
364 − 247 = 117
570 − 458 = 112
839 − 728 = 111
446 − 327 = 119
844 − 726 = 118
384 − 279 = 105
383 − 273 = 110
696 − 576 = 120
590 − 487 = 103
575 − 471 = 104
653 − 547 = 106
493 − 386 = 107
359 − 257 = 102
862 − 754 = 108
190 − 89 = 101
359 − 259 = 100
585 − 476 = 109

Page 105

Dino-Might

Whenever you're using "kid transportation," what is the best thing to do? To find out, work the problems. Then write the letters on the matching blanks.

A L W A Y S
195 92 265 195 185 45

W E A R A
265 171 195 183 195

H E L M E T !
181 171 92 93 171 191 74

A: 348 − 153 = 195	L: 765 − 673 = 92	S: 427 − 382 = 45	M: 568 − 475 = 93
T: 637 − 446 = 191	H: 878 − 697 = 181	Y: 548 − 363 = 185	W: 748 − 483 = 265
E: 824 − 653 = 171	R: 439 − 256 = 183	I: 447 − 373 = 74	

Page 106

Find the Hidden Instrument

Solve each problem. Color each shape according to the key below.

482
529 − 373 = 156 purple
484 − 364 = 120 blue
543 − 382 = 761 yellow
428
732 − 561 = 171 red
896 − 135 = 761 yellow
513 − 321 = 192 purple
954 − 392 = 562
642 − 462 = 180 blue
629 − 583 = 46 green
705 − 443 = 262 yellow
548 − 283 = 265
926 − 564 = 362
635 − 573 = 62
529 − 364 = 165 yellow
439 − 275 = 164
853 − 552 = 331 orange
614 − 453 = 161
626 − 394 = 232 orange
843 − 392 = 451 purple
328 − 182 = 146 green

If the difference in the ten's column is:
1 = color red
2 = color blue
3 = color orange
4 = color green
5 = color purple
6 = color yellow
7 = color red
8 = color blue
9 = color purple

Page 107

Sailing Through Subtraction

Start at the bottom and work your way up the sails.

542 − 383 = 159	638 − 453 = 185	836 − 478 = 358	737 − 448 = 289
243 − 154 = 89	567 − 384 = 183	984 − 643 = 341	468 − 399 = 69
674 − 342 = 182	674 − 495 = 179	374 − 185 = 189	246 − 158 = 88
852 − 464 = 388	736 − 557 = 179	642 − 557 = 85	435 − 286 = 149

Page 108

Daily Learning Drills Grade 3

300

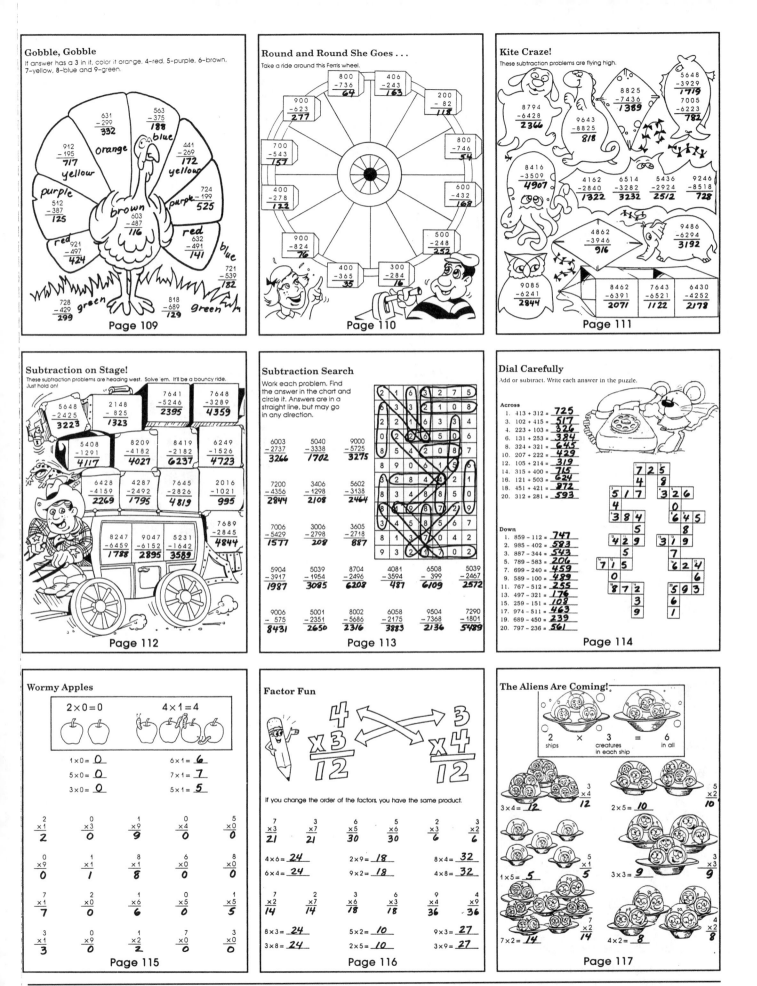

Gobble, Gobble
If answer has a 3 in it, color it orange, 4-red, 5-purple, 6-brown, 7-yellow, 8-blue and 9-green.

$631 - 299 = 332$
$563 - 375 = 188$ blue
$912 - 195 = 717$ yellow orange
$441 - 269 = 172$ yellow
$512 - 387 = 125$ purple
$724 - 199 = 525$ purple
$603 - 487 = 116$ brown
$921 - 497 = 424$ red
$632 - 491 = 141$ red blue
$721 - 539 = 182$
$728 - 429 = 299$ green
$818 - 689 = 129$ green

Page 109

Round and Round She Goes . . .
Take a ride around this Ferris wheel.

$800 - 736 = 64$
$406 - 243 = 163$
$200 - 82 = 118$
$900 - 623 = 277$
$700 - 543 = 157$
$800 - 746 = 54$
$400 - 278 = 122$
$600 - 432 = 168$
$900 - 824 = 76$
$500 - 248 = 252$
$400 - 365 = 35$
$300 - 284 = 16$

Page 110

Kite Craze!
These subtraction problems are flying high.

$5648 - 3929 = 1719$
$8794 - 6428 = 2366$
$8825 - 7436 = 1389$
$7005 - 6223 = 782$
$9643 - 8825 = 818$
$8416 - 3509 = 4907$
$4162 - 2840 = 1322$
$6514 - 3282 = 3232$
$5436 - 2924 = 2512$
$9246 - 8518 = 728$
$4862 - 3946 = 916$
$9486 - 6294 = 3192$
$9085 - 6241 = 2844$
$8462 - 6391 = 2071$
$7643 - 6521 = 1122$
$6430 - 4252 = 2178$

Page 111

Subtraction on Stage!
These subtraction problems are heading west. Solve 'em. It'll be a bouncy ride. Just hold on!

$5648 - 2425 = 3223$
$2148 - 825 = 1323$
$7641 - 5246 = 2395$
$7648 - 3289 = 4359$
$5408 - 1291 = 4117$
$8209 - 4182 = 4027$
$8419 - 2182 = 6237$
$6249 - 1526 = 4723$
$6428 - 4159 = 2269$
$4287 - 2492 = 1795$
$7645 - 2826 = 4819$
$2016 - 1021 = 995$
$8247 - 6459 = 1788$
$9047 - 6152 = 2895$
$5231 - 1642 = 3589$
$7689 - 2845 = 4844$

Page 112

Subtraction Search
Work each problem. Find the answer in the chart and circle it. Answers are in a straight line, but may go in any direction.

$6003 - 2737 = 3266$
$5040 - 3338 = 1702$
$9000 - 5725 = 3275$
$7200 - 4356 = 2844$
$3406 - 1298 = 2108$
$5602 - 3138 = 2464$
$7006 - 5429 = 1577$
$3006 - 2798 = 208$
$3605 - 2718 = 887$
$5904 - 3917 = 1987$
$5039 - 1954 = 3085$
$8704 - 2496 = 6208$
$4081 - 3594 = 487$
$6508 - 399 = 6109$
$5039 - 2467 = 2572$
$9006 - 575 = 8431$
$5001 - 2351 = 2650$
$8002 - 5686 = 2316$
$6058 - 2175 = 3883$
$9504 - 7368 = 2136$
$7290 - 1801 = 5489$

Page 113

Dial Carefully
Add or subtract. Write each answer in the puzzle.

Across
1. $413 + 312 = 725$
3. $102 + 415 = 517$
4. $223 + 103 = 326$
6. $131 + 253 = 384$
8. $324 + 321 = 645$
10. $207 + 222 = 429$
12. $105 + 214 = 319$
14. $315 + 400 = 715$
16. $121 + 503 = 624$
18. $451 + 421 = 872$
20. $312 + 281 = 593$

Down
1. $859 - 112 = 747$
2. $985 - 402 = 583$
3. $887 - 344 = 543$
5. $789 - 583 = 206$
7. $699 - 240 = 459$
9. $589 - 100 = 489$
11. $767 - 512 = 255$
13. $497 - 321 = 176$
15. $259 - 151 = 108$
17. $974 - 511 = 463$
19. $689 - 450 = 239$
20. $797 - 236 = 561$

Page 114

Wormy Apples

$2 \times 0 = 0$ $4 \times 1 = 4$

$1 \times 0 = 0$ $6 \times 1 = 6$
$5 \times 0 = 0$ $7 \times 1 = 7$
$3 \times 0 = 0$ $5 \times 1 = 5$

$2 \times 1 = 2$ $0 \times 3 = 0$ $1 \times 9 = 9$ $0 \times 4 = 0$ $5 \times 0 = 0$
$0 \times 9 = 0$ $1 \times 1 = 1$ $8 \times 1 = 8$ $6 \times 0 = 0$ $8 \times 0 = 0$
$7 \times 1 = 7$ $2 \times 0 = 0$ $1 \times 6 = 6$ $0 \times 5 = 0$ $1 \times 5 = 5$
$3 \times 1 = 3$ $0 \times 9 = 0$ $1 \times 2 = 2$ $7 \times 0 = 0$ $3 \times 0 = 0$

Page 115

Factor Fun

$\times \frac{4}{3} = 12$ $\times \frac{3}{4} = 12$

If you change the order of the factors, you have the same product.

$7 \times 3 = 21$ $3 \times 7 = 21$ $6 \times 5 = 30$ $5 \times 6 = 30$ $3 \times 2 = 6$ $2 \times 3 = 6$
$4 \times 6 = 24$ $2 \times 9 = 18$ $8 \times 4 = 32$
$6 \times 4 = 24$ $9 \times 2 = 18$ $4 \times 8 = 32$
$7 \times 2 = 14$ $2 \times 7 = 14$ $3 \times 6 = 18$ $6 \times 3 = 18$ $9 \times 4 = 36$ $4 \times 9 = 36$
$8 \times 3 = 24$ $5 \times 2 = 10$ $9 \times 3 = 27$
$3 \times 8 = 24$ $2 \times 5 = 10$ $3 \times 9 = 27$

Page 116

The Aliens Are Coming!

$2 \times 3 = 6$
ships   creatures in each ship   in all

$3 \times 4 = 12$ 12
$2 \times 5 = 10$ 10
$1 \times 5 = 5$ 5
$3 \times 3 = 9$ 9
$7 \times 2 = 14$ 14
$4 \times 2 = 8$ 8

Page 117

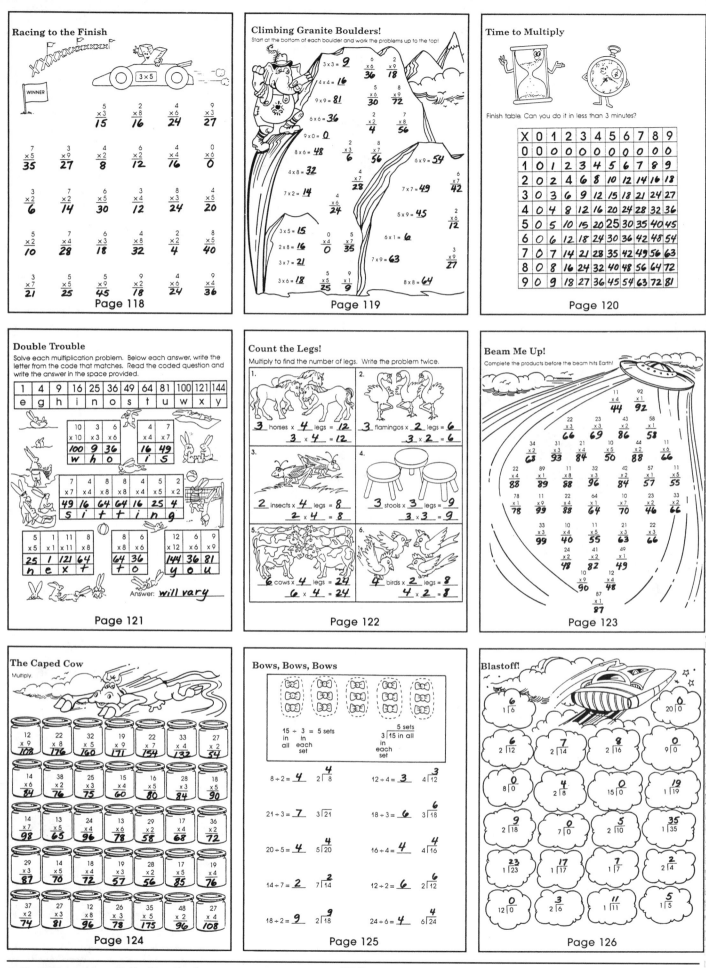

Racing to the Finish

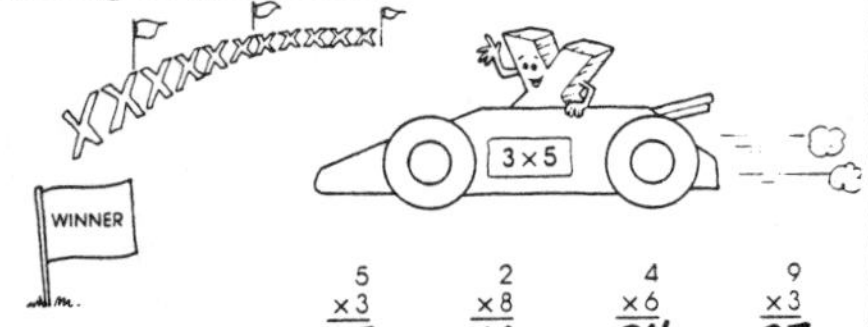

		5 × 3 = 15	2 × 8 = 16	4 × 6 = 24	9 × 3 = 27
7 × 5 = 35	3 × 9 = 27	4 × 2 = 8	6 × 2 = 12	4 × 4 = 16	0 × 6 = 0
3 × 2 = 6	7 × 2 = 14	6 × 5 = 30	3 × 4 = 12	8 × 3 = 24	4 × 5 = 20
5 × 2 = 10	7 × 4 = 28	6 × 3 = 18	4 × 8 = 32	2 × 2 = 4	8 × 5 = 40
3 × 7 = 21	5 × 5 = 25	5 × 9 = 45	9 × 2 = 18	4 × 6 = 24	9 × 4 = 36

Page 118

Climbing Granite Boulders!

Start at the bottom of each boulder and work the problems up to the top!

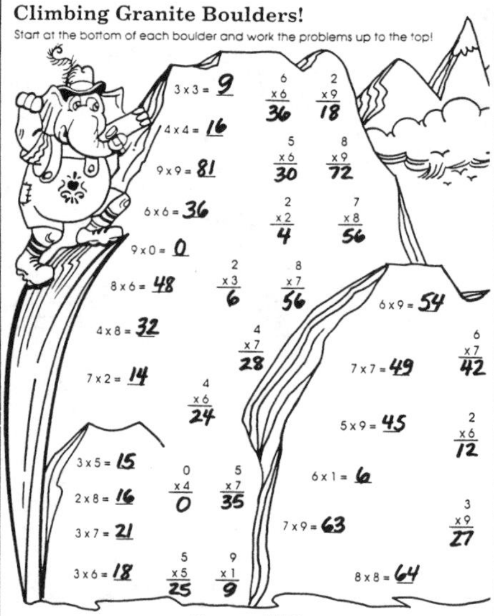

3 x 3 = 9; 6 x 6 = 36; 2 x 9 = 18; 4 x 4 = 16; 9 x 9 = 81; 5 x 6 = 30; 8 x 9 = 72; 6 x 6 = 36; 2 x 2 = 4; 7 x 8 = 56; 9 x 0 = 0; 2 x 3 = 6; 8 x 7 = 56; 8 x 6 = 48; 6 x 9 = 54; 4 x 8 = 32; 4 x 7 = 28; 6 x 7 = 42; 7 x 2 = 14; 7 x 7 = 49; 4 x 6 = 24; 5 x 9 = 45; 2 x 6 = 12; 3 x 5 = 15; 6 x 1 = 6; 2 x 8 = 16; 0 x 4 = 0; 5 x 7 = 35; 3 x 7 = 21; 7 x 9 = 63; 3 x 9 = 27; 5 x 5 = 25; 9 x 1 = 9; 3 x 6 = 18; 8 x 8 = 64

Page 119

Time to Multiply

Finish table. Can you do it in less than 3 minutes?

X	0	1	2	3	4	5	6	7	8	9
0	0	0	0	0	0	0	0	0	0	0
1	0	1	2	3	4	5	6	7	8	9
2	0	2	4	6	8	10	12	14	16	18
3	0	3	6	9	12	15	18	21	24	27
4	0	4	8	12	16	20	24	28	32	36
5	0	5	10	15	20	25	30	35	40	45
6	0	6	12	18	24	30	36	42	48	54
7	0	7	14	21	28	35	42	49	56	63
8	0	8	16	24	32	40	48	56	64	72
9	0	9	18	27	36	45	54	63	72	81

Page 120

Double Trouble

Solve each multiplication problem. Below each answer, write the letter from the code that matches. Read the coded question and write the answer in the space provided.

1	4	9	16	25	36	49	64	81	100	121	144
e	g	h	i	n	o	s	t	u	w	x	y

10 x 10	3 x 3	6 x 6
100	9	36
w	h	o

4 x 4	7 x 7
16	49
i	s

7 x 7	4 x 4	8 x 8	8 x 8	4 x 4	5 x 5	2 x 2
49	16	64	64	16	25	4
s	i	t	t	i	n	g

5 x 5	1 x 1	11 x 11	8 x 8
25	1	121	64
n	e	x	t

8 x 8	6 x 6
64	36
t	o

12 x 12	6 x 6	9 x 9
144	36	81
y	o	u

Answer: will vary

Page 121

Count the Legs!

Multiply to find the number of legs. Write the problem twice.

1.

3 horses x 4 legs = 12
3 x 4 = 12

2.

3 flamingos x 2 legs = 6
3 x 2 = 6

3.

2 insects x 4 legs = 8
2 x 4 = 8

4.

3 stools x 3 legs = 9
3 x 3 = 9

5.
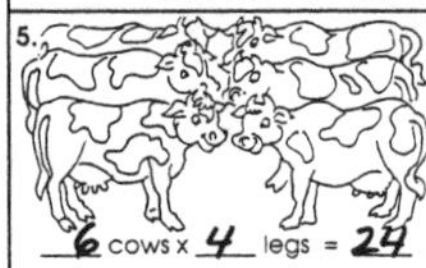
6 cows x 4 legs = 24
6 x 4 = 24

6.

4 birds x 2 legs = 8
4 x 2 = 8

Page 122

Beam Me Up!

Complete the products before the beam hits Earth!

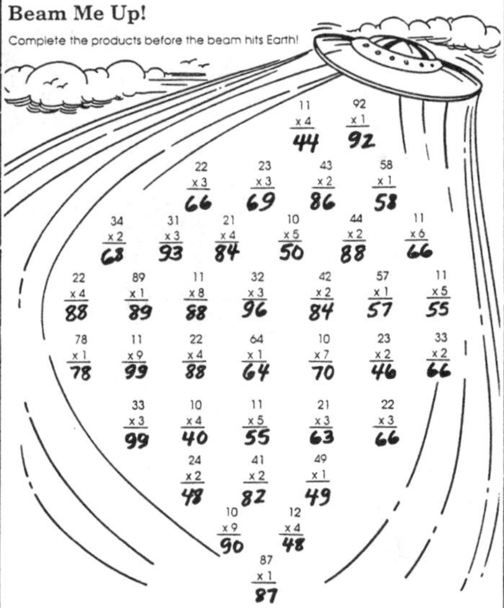

11 x 4 = 44; 92 x 1 = 92
22 x 3 = 66; 23 x 3 = 69; 43 x 2 = 86; 58 x 1 = 58
34 x 2 = 68; 31 x 3 = 93; 21 x 4 = 84; 10 x 5 = 50; 44 x 2 = 88; 11 x 6 = 66
22 x 4 = 88; 89 x 1 = 89; 11 x 8 = 88; 32 x 3 = 96; 42 x 2 = 84; 57 x 1 = 57; 11 x 5 = 55
78 x 1 = 78; 11 x 9 = 99; 22 x 4 = 88; 64 x 1 = 64; 10 x 7 = 70; 23 x 2 = 46; 33 x 2 = 66
33 x 3 = 99; 10 x 4 = 40; 11 x 5 = 55; 21 x 3 = 63; 22 x 3 = 66
24 x 2 = 48; 41 x 2 = 82; 49 x 1 = 49
10 x 9 = 90; 12 x 4 = 48
87 x 1 = 87

Page 123

The Caped Cow

Multiply.

12 x 9 = 108	22 x 8 = 176	32 x 5 = 160	19 x 9 = 171	22 x 7 = 154	33 x 4 = 132	27 x 2 = 54
14 x 6 = 84	38 x 2 = 76	25 x 3 = 75	15 x 4 = 60	16 x 5 = 80	28 x 3 = 84	18 x 5 = 90
14 x 7 = 98	13 x 5 = 65	24 x 4 = 96	13 x 6 = 78	29 x 2 = 58	17 x 4 = 68	36 x 2 = 72
29 x 3 = 87	14 x 5 = 70	18 x 4 = 72	19 x 3 = 57	28 x 2 = 56	17 x 5 = 85	19 x 4 = 76
37 x 2 = 74	27 x 3 = 81	12 x 8 = 96	26 x 3 = 78	35 x 5 = 175	48 x 2 = 96	27 x 4 = 108

Page 124

Bows, Bows, Bows

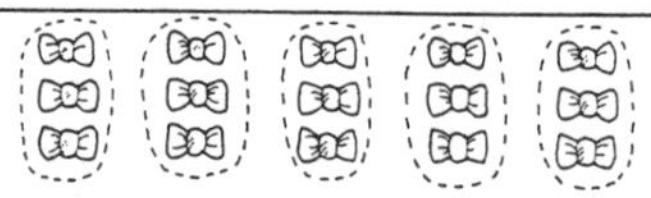

15 ÷ 3 = 5 sets (15 in all; 3 in each set)
3)15 in all = 5 sets (3 in each set)

8 ÷ 2 = 4	2)8 = 4	12 ÷ 4 = 3	4)12 = 3
21 ÷ 3 = 7	3)21 = 7	18 ÷ 3 = 6	3)18 = 6
20 ÷ 5 = 4	5)20 = 4	16 ÷ 4 = 4	4)16 = 4
14 ÷ 7 = 2	7)14 = 2	12 ÷ 2 = 6	2)12 = 6
18 ÷ 2 = 9	2)18 = 9	24 ÷ 6 = 4	6)24 = 4

Page 125

Blastoff!

1)6 = 6			20)0 = 0
2)12 = 6	2)14 = 7	2)16 = 8	9)0 = 0
8)0 = 0	2)8 = 4	15)0 = 0	1)19 = 19
2)18 = 9	7)0 = 0	2)10 = 5	1)35 = 35
1)23 = 23	1)17 = 17	1)7 = 7	2)4 = 2
12)0 = 0	2)6 = 3	1)11 = 11	1)5 = 5

Page 126

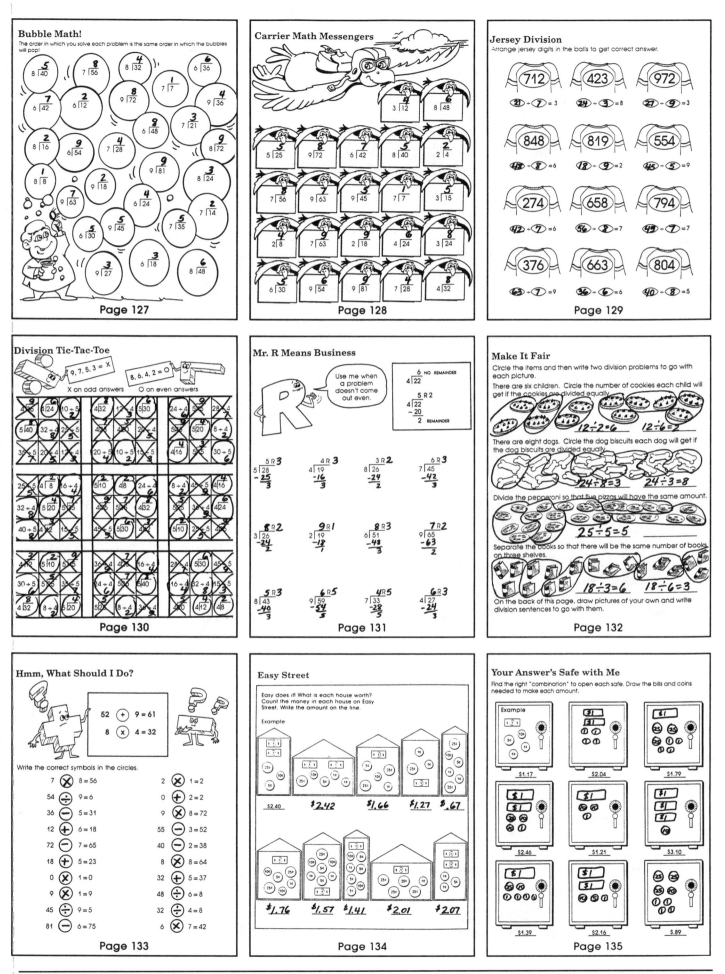

Page 127 — Bubble Math!

Page 128 — Carrier Math Messengers

Page 129 — Jersey Division

Page 130 — Division Tic-Tac-Toe

Page 131 — Mr. R Means Business

Page 132 — Make It Fair

Page 133 — Hmm, What Should I Do?

Page 134 — Easy Street

Page 135 — Your Answer's Safe with Me

303   Daily Learning Drills Grade 3

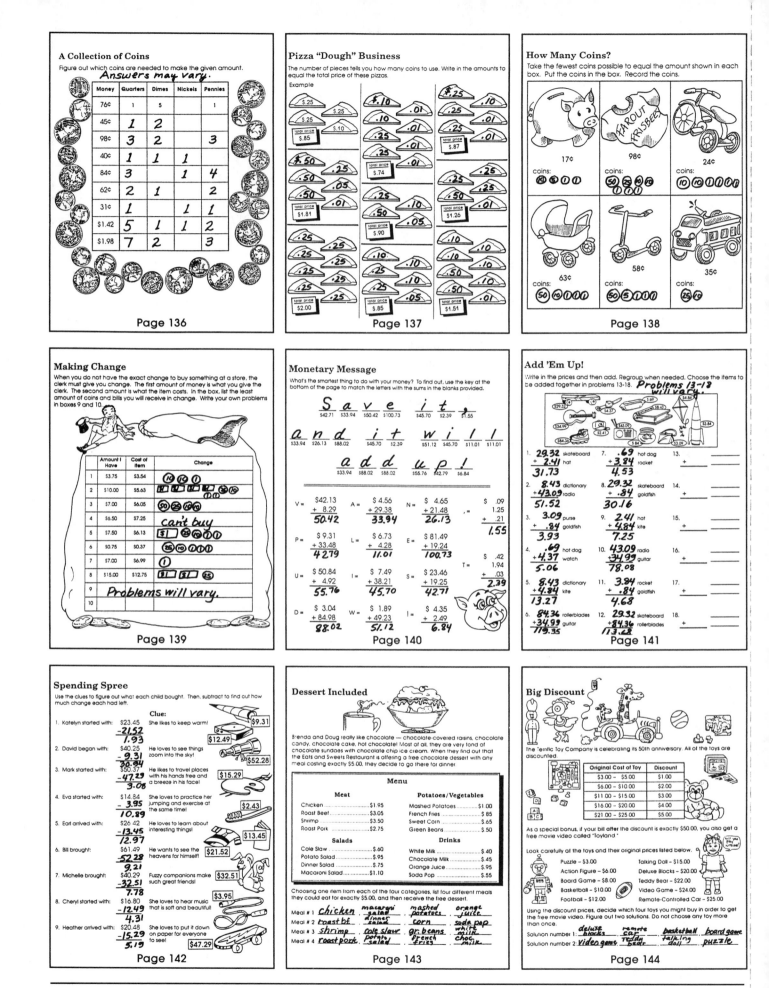

A Collection of Coins

Figure out which coins are needed to make the given amount.

Answers may vary.

Money	Quarters	Dimes	Nickels	Pennies
76¢	1	5		1
45¢	1	2		
98¢	3	2		3
40¢	1	1	1	
84¢	3		1	4
62¢	2	1		2
31¢	1		1	1
$1.42	5	1	1	2
$1.98	7	2		3

Page 136

Pizza "Dough" Business

The number of pieces tells you how many coins to use. Write in the amounts to equal the total price of these pizzas.

Example

Page 137

How Many Coins?

Take the fewest coins possible to equal the amount shown in each box. Put the coins in the box. Record the coins.

17¢   98¢   24¢

63¢   58¢   35¢

Page 138

Making Change

When you do not have the exact change to buy something at a store, the clerk must give you change. The first amount of money is what you give the clerk. The second amount is what the item costs. In the box, list the least amount of coins and bills you will receive in change. Write your own problems in boxes 9 and 10.

	Amount I Have	Cost of Item	Change
1	$3.75	$3.54	
2	$10.00	$5.63	
3	$7.00	$6.05	
4	$6.50	$7.25	can't buy
5	$7.50	$6.13	
6	$0.75	$0.37	
7	$7.00	$6.99	
8	$15.00	$12.75	
9			Problems will vary.
10			

Page 139

Monetary Message

What's the smartest thing to do with your money? To find out, use the key at the bottom of the page to match the letters with the sums in the blanks provided.

S a v e   i t ,
$42.71 $33.94 $50.42 $100.73 $45.70 $2.39 $1.55

a n d   i t   w i l l
$33.94 $26.13 $88.02 $45.70 $2.39 $51.12 $45.70 $11.01 $11.01

a d d   u p !
$33.94 $88.02 $88.02 $55.76 $42.79 $6.84

V =	A =	N =	$ .09
$42.13 + 8.29 = 50.42	$4.56 + 29.38 = 33.94	$4.65 + 21.48 = 26.13	1.25 .21 , = 1.55

P =	L =	E =	
$9.31 + 33.48 = 42.79	$6.73 + 4.28 = 11.01	$81.49 + 19.24 = 100.73	$ .42 T = 1.94 .03 = 2.39

U =	I =	S =
$50.84 + 4.92 = 55.76	$7.49 + 38.21 = 45.70	$23.46 + 19.25 = 42.71

D =	W =	I =
$3.04 + 84.98 = 88.02	$1.89 + 49.23 = 51.12	$4.35 + 2.49 = 6.84

Page 140

Add 'Em Up!

Write in the prices and then add. Regroup when needed. Choose the items to be added together in problems 13-18. **Problems 13-18 will vary.**

1. 29.32 skateboard
   + 2.41 hat
   31.73

2. 8.43 dictionary
   +43.09 radio
   51.52

3. 3.09 purse
   + .84 goldfish
   3.93

4. .69 hot dog
   +4.37 watch
   5.06

5. 8.43 dictionary
   +4.84 kite
   13.27

6. 84.36 rollerblades
   +34.99 guitar
   719.35

7. .69 hot dog
   + 3.84 rocket
   4.53

8. 29.32 skateboard
   + .84 goldfish
   30.16

9. 2.41 hat
   + 4.84 kite
   7.25

10. 43.09 radio
    +34.99 guitar
    78.08

11. 3.84 rocket
    + .84 goldfish
    4.68

12. 29.32 skateboard
    +84.36 rollerblades
    113.68

13. ___ + ___
14. ___ + ___
15. ___ + ___
16. ___ + ___
17. ___ + ___
18. ___ + ___

Page 141

Spending Spree

Use the clues to figure out what each child bought. Then, subtract to find out how much change each had left.

Clue:

1. Katelyn started with: $23.45
   -21.52
   1.93
   She likes to keep warm!

2. David began with: $40.25
   - 9.31
   30.94
   He loves to see things zoom into the sky!

3. Mark started with: $50.37
   -47.29
   3.08
   He likes to travel places with his hands free and a breeze in his face!

4. Eva started with: $14.84
   - 3.95
   10.89
   She loves to practice her jumping and exercise at the same time!

5. Earl arrived with: $26.42
   -13.45
   12.97
   He loves to learn about interesting things!

6. Bill brought: $61.49
   -52.28
   9.21
   He wants to see the heavens for himself!

7. Michelle brought: $40.29
   -32.51
   7.78
   Fuzzy companions make such great friends!

8. Cheryl started with: $16.80
   -12.49
   4.31
   She loves to hear music that is soft and beautiful!

9. Heather arrived with: $20.48
   -15.29
   5.19
   She loves to put it down on paper for everyone to see!

$9.31 $12.49 $52.28 $15.29 $2.43 $13.45 $21.52 $32.51 $3.95 $47.29

Page 142

Dessert Included

Brenda and Doug really like chocolate — chocolate-covered raisins, chocolate candy, chocolate cake, hot chocolate! Most of all, they are very fond of chocolate sundaes with chocolate chip ice cream. When they find out that the Eats and Sweets Restaurant is offering a free chocolate dessert with any meal costing exactly $5.00, they decide to go there for dinner.

Menu

Meat		Potatoes/Vegetables	
Chicken	$1.95	Mashed Potatoes	$1.00
Roast Beef	$3.05	French Fries	$.85
Shrimp	$3.50	Sweet Corn	$.65
Roast Pork	$2.75	Green Beans	$.50

Salads		Drinks	
Cole Slaw	$.60	White Milk	$.40
Potato Salad	$.95	Chocolate Milk	$.45
Dinner Salad	$.75	Orange Juice	$.95
Macaroni Salad	$1.10	Soda Pop	$.55

Choosing one item from each of the four categories, list four different meals they could eat for exactly $5.00, and then receive the free dessert.

Meal #1 chicken macaroni salad mashed potatoes orange juice
Meal #2 roast bf. dinner salad corn soda pop
Meal #3 shrimp cole slaw gr. beans white milk
Meal #4 roast pork potato salad french fries choc. milk

Page 143

Big Discount

The Terrific Toy Company is celebrating its 50th anniversary. All of the toys are discounted.

Original Cost of Toy	Discount
$3.00 – $5.00	$1.00
$6.00 – $10.00	$2.00
$11.00 – $15.00	$3.00
$16.00 – $20.00	$4.00
$21.00 – $25.00	$5.00

As a special bonus, if your bill after the discount is exactly $50.00, you also get a free movie video called "Toyland."

Look carefully at the toys and their original prices listed below.

Puzzle – $3.00
Action Figure – $6.00
Board Game – $8.00
Basketball – $10.00
Football – $12.00
Talking Doll – $15.00
Deluxe Blocks – $20.00
Teddy Bear – $22.00
Video Game – $24.00
Remote-Controlled Car – $25.00

Using the discount prices, decide which four toys you might buy in order to get the free movie video. Figure out two solutions. Do not choose any toy more than once.

Solution number 1: deluxe blocks remote car basketball board game
Solution number 2: video game Teddy bear talking doll puzzle

Page 144

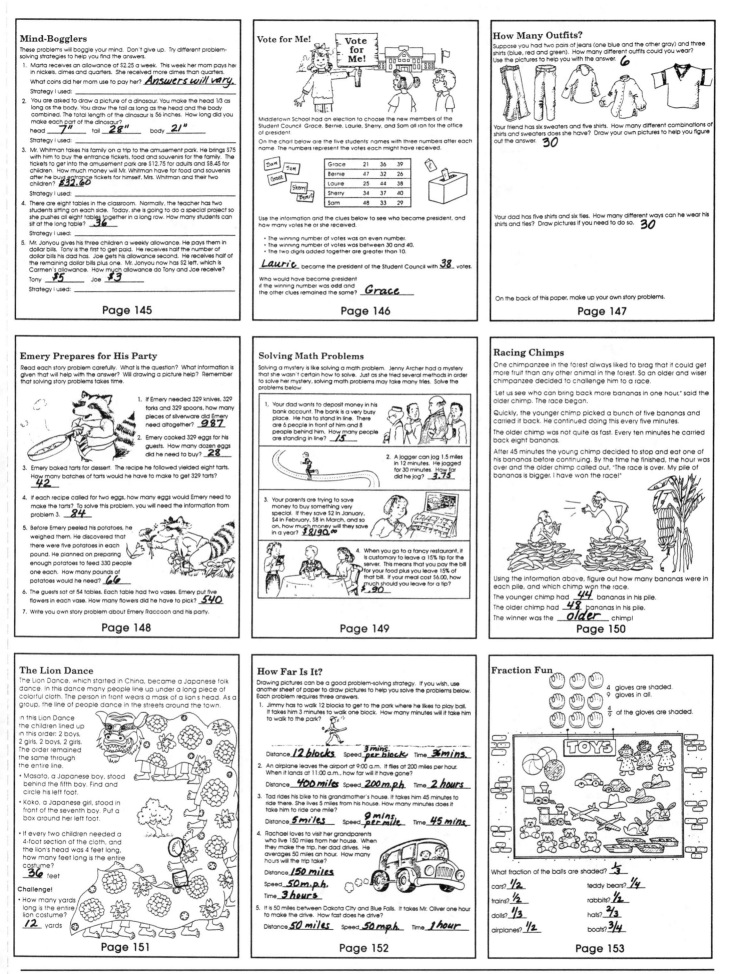

Mind-Bogglers

These problems will boggle your mind. Don't give up. Try different problem-solving strategies to help you find the answers.

1. Marta receives an allowance of $2.25 a week. This week her mom pays her in nickels, dimes and quarters. She received more dimes than quarters. What coins did her mom use to pay her? **Answers will vary.**
Strategy I used: _____

2. You are asked to draw a picture of a dinosaur. You make the head 1/3 as long as the body. You draw the tail as long as the head and the body combined. The total length of the dinosaur is 56 inches. How long did you make each part of the dinosaur?
head **7"**   tail **28"**   body **21"**
Strategy I used: _____

3. Mr. Whitman takes his family on a trip to the amusement park. He brings $75 with him to buy the entrance tickets, food and souvenirs for the family. The tickets to get into the amusement park are $12.75 for adults and $8.45 for children. How much money will Mr. Whitman have for food and souvenirs after he buys entrance tickets for himself, Mrs. Whitman and their two children? **$32.60**
Strategy I used: _____

4. There are eight tables in the classroom. Normally, the teacher has two students sitting on each side. Today, she is going to do a special project so she pushes all eight tables together in a long row. How many students can sit at the long table? **36**
Strategy I used: _____

5. Mr. Jonyou gives his three children a weekly allowance. He pays them in dollar bills. Tony is the first to get paid. He receives half the number of dollar bills his dad has. Joe gets his allowance second. He receives half of the remaining dollar bills plus one. Mr. Jonyou now has $2 left, which is Carmen's allowance. How much allowance do Tony and Joe receive?
Tony **$5**   Joe **$3**
Strategy I used: _____

Page 145

Vote for Me!

Vote for Me!

Middletown School had an election to choose the new members of the Student Council. Grace, Bernie, Laurie, Sherry, and Sam all ran for the office of president.

On the chart below are the five students' names with three numbers after each name. The numbers represent the votes each might have received.

Grace	21	36	39
Bernie	47	32	26
Laurie	25	44	38
Sherry	34	37	40
Sam	48	33	29

Use the information and the clues below to see who became president, and how many votes he or she received.

• The winning number of votes was an even number.
• The winning number of votes was between 30 and 40.
• The two digits added together are greater than 10.

Laurie became the president of the Student Council with **38** votes.

Who would have become president if the winning number was odd and the other clues remained the same? **Grace**

Page 146

How Many Outfits?

Suppose you had two pairs of jeans (one blue and the other gray) and three shirts (blue, red and green). How many different outfits could you wear? Use the pictures to help you find the answer. **6**

Your friend has six sweaters and five shirts. How many different combinations of shirts and sweaters does she have? Draw your own pictures to help you figure out the answer. **30**

Your dad has five shirts and six ties. How many different ways can he wear his shirts and ties? Draw pictures if you need to do so. **30**

On the back of this paper, make up your own story problems.

Page 147

Emery Prepares for His Party

Read each story problem carefully. What is the question? What information is given that will help with the answer? Will drawing a picture help? Remember that solving story problems takes time.

1. If Emery needed 329 knives, 329 forks and 329 spoons, how many pieces of silverware did Emery need altogether? **987**

2. Emery cooked 329 eggs for his guests. How many dozen eggs did he need to buy? **28**

3. Emery baked tarts for dessert. The recipe he followed yielded eight tarts. How many batches of tarts would he have to make to get 329 tarts? **42**

4. If each recipe called for two eggs, how many eggs would Emery need to make the tarts? To solve this problem, you will need the information from problem 3. **84**

5. Before Emery peeled his potatoes, he weighed them. He discovered that there were five potatoes in each pound. He planned on preparing enough potatoes to feed 330 people one each. How many pounds of potatoes would he need? **66**

6. The guests sat at 54 tables. Each table had two vases. Emery put five flowers in each vase. How many flowers did he have to pick? **540**

7. Write you own story problem about Emery Raccoon and his party.

Page 148

Solving Math Problems

Solving a mystery is like solving a math problem. Jenny Archer had a mystery that she wasn't certain how to solve. Just as she tried several methods in order to solve her mystery, solving math problems may take many tries. Solve the problems below.

1. Your dad wants to deposit money in his bank account. The bank is a very busy place. He has to stand in line. There are 6 people in front of him and 8 people behind him. How many people are standing in line? **15**

2. A jogger can jog 1.5 miles in 12 minutes. He jogged for 30 minutes. How far did he jog? **3.75**

3. Your parents are trying to save money to buy something very special. If they save $2 in January, $4 in February, $8 in March, and so on, how much money will they save in a year? **$8190.00**

4. When you go to a fancy restaurant, it is customary to leave a 15% tip for the server. This means that you pay the bill for your food plus you leave 15% of that bill. If your meal cost $6.00, how much should you leave for a tip? **$.90**

Page 149

Racing Chimps

One chimpanzee in the forest always liked to brag that it could get more fruit than any other animal in the forest. So an older and wiser chimpanzee decided to challenge him to a race.

"Let us see who can bring back more bananas in one hour," said the older chimp. The race began.

Quickly, the younger chimp picked a bunch of five bananas and carried it back. He continued doing this every five minutes.

The older chimp was not quite as fast. Every ten minutes he carried back eight bananas.

After 45 minutes the young chimp decided to stop and eat one of his bananas before continuing. By the time he finished, the hour was over and the older chimp called out, "The race is over. My pile of bananas is bigger. I have won the race!"

Using the information above, figure out how many bananas were in each pile, and which chimp won the race.

The younger chimp had **44** bananas in his pile.
The older chimp had **48** bananas in his pile.
The winner was the **older** chimp!

Page 150

The Lion Dance

The Lion Dance, which started in China, became a Japanese folk dance. In this dance many people line up under a long piece of colorful cloth. The person in front wears a mask of a lion's head. As a group, the line of people dance in the streets around the town.

In this Lion Dance the children lined up in this order: 2 boys, 2 girls, 2 boys, 2 girls. The order remained the same through the entire line.

• Masato, a Japanese boy, stood behind the fifth boy. Find and circle his left foot.

• Koko, a Japanese girl, stood in front of the seventh boy. Put a box around her left foot.

• If every two children needed a 4-foot section of the cloth, and the lion's head was 4 feet long, how many feet long is the entire costume? **36** feet

Challenge!

• How many yards long is the entire lion costume? **12** yards

Page 151

How Far Is It?

Drawing pictures can be a good problem-solving strategy. If you wish, use another sheet of paper to draw pictures to help you solve the problems below. Each problem requires three answers.

1. Jimmy has to walk 12 blocks to get to the park where he likes to play ball. It takes him 3 minutes to walk one block. How many minutes will it take him to walk to the park?
Distance **12 blocks**   Speed **3 mins. per block**   Time **36 mins.**

2. An airplane leaves the airport at 9:00 a.m. It flies at 200 miles per hour. When it lands at 11:00 a.m., how far will it have gone?
Distance **400 miles**   Speed **200 m.p.h.**   Time **2 hours**

3. Tad rides his bike to his grandmother's house. It takes him 45 minutes to ride there. She lives 5 miles from his house. How many minutes does it take him to ride one mile?
Distance **5 miles**   Speed **9 mins. per mile**   Time **45 mins.**

4. Rachael loves to visit her grandparents who live 150 miles from her house. When they make the trip, her dad drives. He averages 50 miles an hour. How many hours will the trip take?
Distance **150 miles**   Speed **50 m.p.h.**   Time **3 hours**

5. It is 50 miles between Dakota City and Blue Falls. It takes Mr. Oliver one hour to make the drive. How fast does he drive?
Distance **50 miles**   Speed **50 mph**   Time **1 hour**

Page 152

Fraction Fun

4 gloves are shaded.
9 gloves in all.
4/9 of the gloves are shaded.

TOYS

What fraction of the balls are shaded? **1/3**
cars? **1/2**   teddy bears? **1/4**
trains? **1/2**   rabbits? **1/2**
dolls? **1/3**   hats? **3/3**
airplanes? **1/2**   boats? **3/4**

Page 153

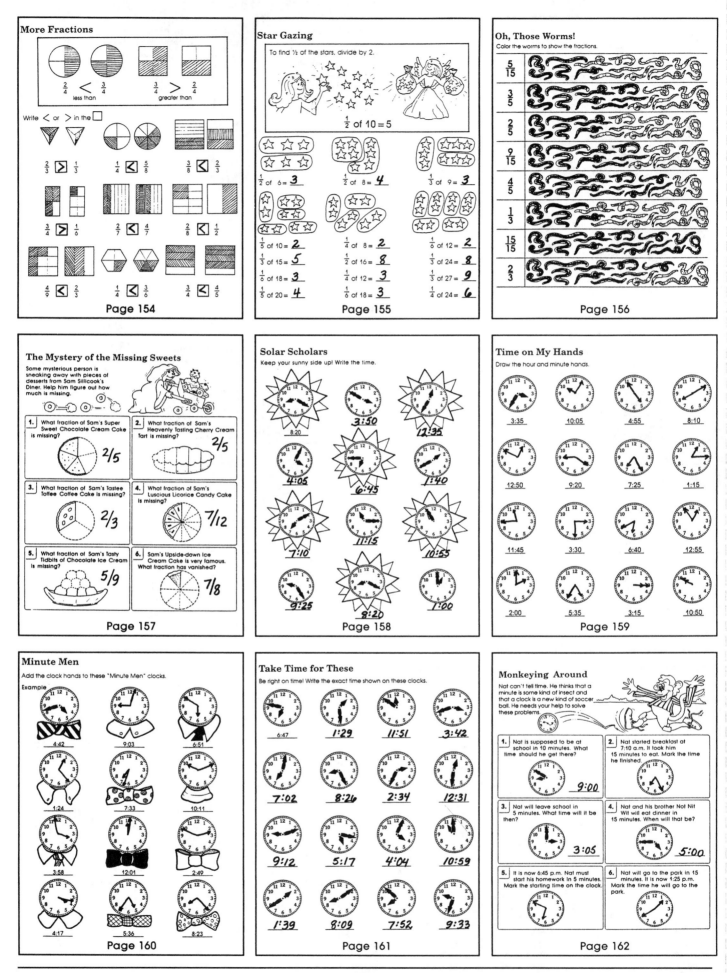

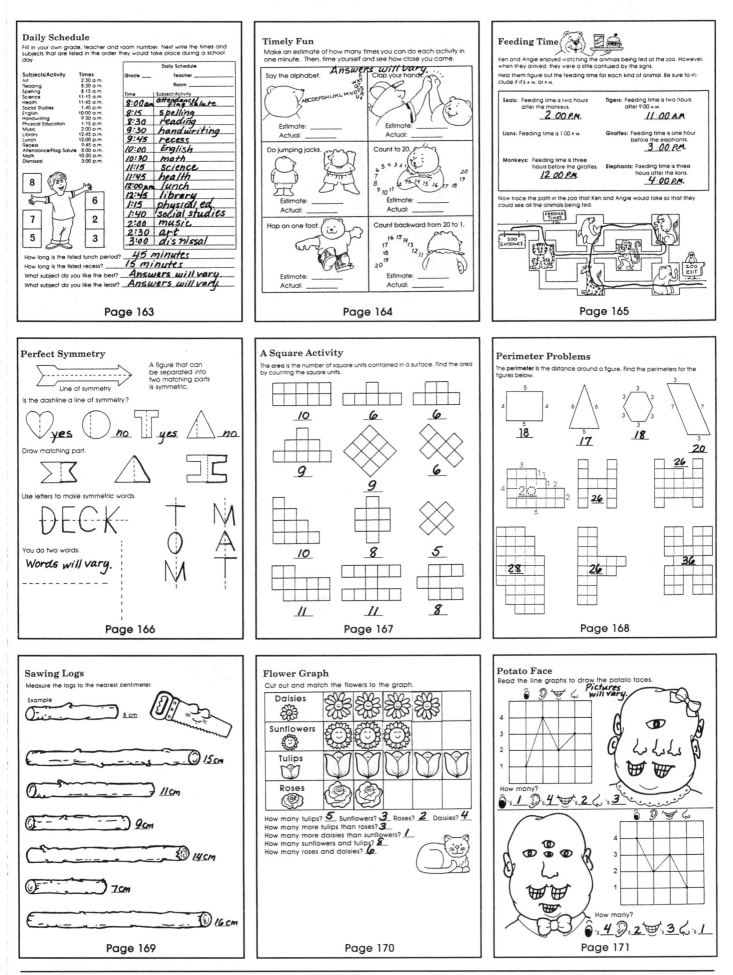

Daily Schedule

Fill in your own grade, teacher and room number. Next write the times and subjects that are listed in the order they would take place during a school day.

Subjects/Activity	Times
Art	2:30 p.m.
Reading	8:30 a.m.
Spelling	8:15 a.m.
Science	11:15 a.m.
Health	11:45 a.m.
Social Studies	1:40 p.m.
English	10:00 a.m.
Handwriting	9:30 a.m.
Physical Education	1:15 p.m.
Music	2:00 p.m.
Library	12:45 p.m.
Lunch	12:00 p.m.
Recess	9:45 a.m.
Attendance/Flag Salute	8:00 a.m.
Math	10:30 a.m.
Dismissal	3:00 p.m.

Daily Schedule

Grade _____ Teacher _____
Room _____

Time	Subject/Activity
8:00 am	attendance/flag salute
8:15	spelling
8:30	reading
9:30	handwriting
9:45	recess
10:00	English
10:30	math
11:15	science
11:45	health
12:00 pm	lunch
12:45	library
1:15	physical ed.
1:40	social studies
2:00	music
2:30	art
3:00	dismissal

How long is the listed lunch period? **45 minutes**
How long is the listed recess? **15 minutes**
What subject do you like the best? **Answers will vary.**
What subject do you like the least? **Answers will vary.**

Page 163

Timely Fun

Make an estimate of how many times you can do each activity in one minute. Then, time yourself and see how close you came. *Answers will vary.*

Say the alphabet: ABCDEFGHIJKLMNOPQRSTUVWXYZ
Estimate: _____
Actual: _____

Clap your hands.
Estimate: _____
Actual: _____

Do jumping jacks.
Estimate: _____
Actual: _____

Count to 20.
Estimate: _____
Actual: _____

Hop on one foot.
Estimate: _____
Actual: _____

Count backward from 20 to 1.
Estimate: _____
Actual: _____

Page 164

Feeding Time

Ken and Angie enjoyed watching the animals being fed at the zoo. However, when they arrived, they were a little confused by the signs.

Help them figure out the feeding time for each kind of animal. Be sure to include if it's A.M. or P.M.

Seals: Feeding time is two hours after the monkeys. **2:00 P.M.**

Tigers: Feeding time is two hours after 9:00 A.M. **11:00 A.M.**

Lions: Feeding time is 1:00 P.M.

Giraffes: Feeding time is one hour before the elephants. **3:00 P.M.**

Monkeys: Feeding time is three hours before the giraffes. **12:00 P.M.**

Elephants: Feeding time is three hours after the lions. **4:00 P.M.**

Now trace the path in the zoo that Ken and Angie would take so that they could see all the animals being fed.

Page 165

Perfect Symmetry

A figure that can be separated into two matching parts is symmetric.

Line of symmetry

Is the dashline a line of symmetry?

♡ **yes**   ○ **no**   T **yes**   △ **no**

Draw matching part.

Use letters to make symmetric words.

DECK   TOM   MAT

You do two words.

Words will vary.

Page 166

A Square Activity

The **area** is the number of square units contained in a surface. Find the area by counting the square units.

10   **6**   **6**

9   **9**   **6**

10   **8**   **5**

11   **11**   **8**

Page 167

Perimeter Problems

The **perimeter** is the distance around a figure. Find the perimeters for the figures below.

18   **17**   **18**   **20**

20   **26**   **26**

28   **26**   **36**

Page 168

Sawing Logs

Measure the logs to the nearest centimeter.

Example   8 cm

15 cm
11 cm
9 cm
14 cm
7 cm
16 cm

Page 169

Flower Graph

Cut out and match the flowers to the graph.

Daisies				
Sunflowers				
Tulips				
Roses				

How many tulips? **5** Sunflowers? **3** Roses? **2** Daisies? **4**
How many more tulips than roses? **3**
How many more daisies than sunflowers? **1**
How many sunflowers and tulips? **8**
How many roses and daisies? **6**

Page 170

Potato Face

Read the line graphs to draw the potato faces. *Pictures will vary.*

How many?
👁's **1** 👃's **4** 😁's **2** 👂's **3**

How many?
👁's **4** 👃's **2** 😁's **3** 👂's **1**

Page 171

Frog Bubbles

Color the picture.

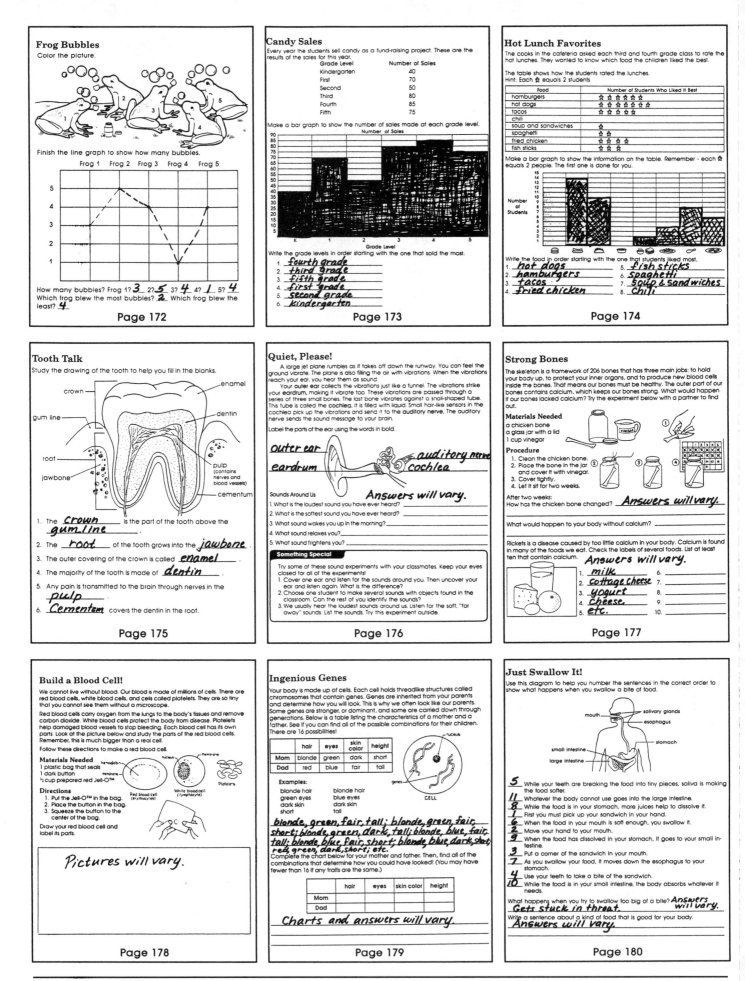

Finish the line graph to show how many bubbles.

How many bubbles? Frog 1? **3** 2? **5** 3? **4** 4? **1** 5? **4**
Which frog blew the most bubbles? **2** Which frog blew the least? **4**

Page 172

Candy Sales

Every year the students sell candy as a fund-raising project. These are the results of the sales for this year.

Grade Level	Number of Sales
Kindergarten	40
First	70
Second	50
Third	80
Fourth	85
Fifth	75

Make a bar graph to show the number of sales made at each grade level.

Write the grade levels in order starting with the one that sold the most.

1. _fourth grade_
2. _third grade_
3. _fifth grade_
4. _first grade_
5. _second grade_
6. _kindergarten_

Page 173

Hot Lunch Favorites

The cooks in the cafeteria asked each third and fourth grade class to rate the hot lunches. They wanted to know which food the children liked the best.

The table shows how the students rated the lunches.
Hint: Each ☆ equals 2 students

Food	Number of Students Who Liked It Best
hamburgers	☆ ☆ ☆ ☆ ☆ ☆
hot dogs	☆ ☆ ☆ ☆ ☆ ☆ ☆
tacos	☆ ☆ ☆ ☆ ☆
chili	
soup and sandwiches	☆
spaghetti	☆ ☆
fried chicken	☆ ☆ ☆ ☆
fish sticks	☆ ☆ ☆

Make a bar graph to show the information on the table. Remember - each ☆ equals 2 people. The first one is done for you.

Write the food in order starting with the one that students liked most.

1. _hot dogs_
2. _hamburgers_
3. _tacos_
4. _fried chicken_
5. _fish sticks_
6. _spaghetti_
7. _soup & sandwiches_
8. _chili_

Page 174

Tooth Talk

Study the drawing of the tooth to help you fill in the blanks.

crown, enamel, gum line, dentin, root, pulp (contains nerves and blood vessels), jawbone, cementum

1. The **crown** is the part of the tooth above the **gum line**.
2. The **root** of the tooth grows into the **jawbone**.
3. The outer covering of the crown is called **enamel**.
4. The majority of the tooth is made of **dentin**.
5. Any pain is transmitted to the brain through nerves in the **pulp**.
6. **Cementum** covers the dentin in the root.

Page 175

Quiet, Please!

A large jet plane rumbles as it takes off down the runway. You can feel the ground vibrate. The plane is also filling the air with vibrations. When the vibrations reach your ear, you hear them as sound.

Your outer ear collects the vibrations just like a funnel. The vibrations strike your eardrum, making it vibrate too. These vibrations are passed through a series of three small bones. The last bone vibrates against a snail-shaped tube. This tube is called the cochlea. It is filled with liquid. Small hair-like sensors in the cochlea pick up the vibrations and send it to the auditory nerve. The auditory nerve sends the sound message to your brain.

Label the parts of the ear using the words in bold.

outer ear, eardrum, auditory nerve, cochlea

Answers will vary.

Sounds Around Us
1. What is the loudest sound you have ever heard? _____
2. What is the softest sound you have ever heard? _____
3. What sound wakes you up in the morning? _____
4. What sound relaxes you? _____
5. What sound frightens you? _____

Something Special

Try some of these sound experiments with your classmates. Keep your eyes closed for all of the experiments!
1. Cover one ear and listen for the sounds around you. Then uncover your ear and listen again. What is the difference?
2. Choose one student to make several sounds with objects found in the classroom. Can the rest of you identify the sounds?
3. We usually hear the loudest sounds around us. Listen for the soft, "far away" sounds. List the sounds. Try this experiment outside.

Page 176

Strong Bones

The skeleton is a framework of 206 bones that has three main jobs: to hold your body up, to protect your inner organs, and to produce new blood cells inside the bones. That means our bones must be healthy. The outer part of our bones contains calcium, which keeps our bones strong. What would happen if our bones lacked calcium? Try the experiment below with a partner to find out.

Materials Needed
a chicken bone
a glass jar with a lid
1 cup vinegar

Procedure
1. Clean the chicken bone.
2. Place the bone in the jar and cover it with vinegar.
3. Cover tightly.
4. Let it sit for two weeks.

After two weeks:
How has the chicken bone changed? **Answers will vary.**

What would happen to your body without calcium? _____

Rickets is a disease caused by too little calcium in your body. Calcium is found in many of the foods we eat. Check the labels of several foods. List at least ten that contain calcium. **Answers will vary.**

1. _milk_   6. _____
2. _cottage cheese_   7. _____
3. _yogurt_   8. _____
4. _cheese_   9. _____
5. _etc._   10. _____

Page 177

Build a Blood Cell!

We cannot live without blood. Our blood is made of millions of cells. There are red blood cells, white blood cells, and cells called platelets. They are so tiny that you cannot see them without a microscope.

Red blood cells carry oxygen from the lungs to the body's tissues and remove carbon dioxide. White blood cells protect the body from disease. Platelets help damaged blood vessels to stop bleeding. Each blood cell has its own parts. Look at the picture below and study the parts of the red blood cells. Remember, this is much bigger than a real cell.

Follow these directions to make a red blood cell.

Materials Needed
1 plastic bag that seals
1 dark button
½ cup prepared red Jell-O™

Directions
1. Put the Jell-O in the bag.
2. Place the button in the bag.
3. Squeeze the button to the center of the bag.

Draw your red blood cell and label its parts.

Red blood cell (erythrocyte)
White blood cell (lymphocyte)
Platelets

Pictures will vary.

Page 178

Ingenious Genes

Your body is made up of cells. Each cell holds threadlike structures called chromosomes that contain genes. Genes are inherited from your parents and determine what we will look. This is why we often look like our parents. Some genes are stronger, or dominant, and some are carried down through generations. Below is a table listing the characteristics of a mother and a father. See if you can find all of the possible combinations for their children. There are 16 possibilities.

	hair	eyes	skin color	height
Mom	blonde	green	dark	short
Dad	red	blue	fair	tall

Examples:
blonde hair — blonde hair
green eyes — blue eyes
dark skin — dark skin
short — tall

blonde, green, fair, tall; blonde, green, fair, short; blonde, green, dark, tall; blonde, blue, fair, tall; blonde, blue, fair, short; blonde, blue, dark, short; red, green, dark, short; etc.

Complete the chart below for your mother and father. Then, find all of the combinations that determine how you could have looked! (You may have fewer than 16 if any traits are the same.)

	hair	eyes	skin color	height
Mom				
Dad				

Charts and answers will vary.

Page 179

Just Swallow It!

Use this diagram to help you number the sentences in the correct order to show what happens when you swallow a bite of food.

mouth, salivary glands, esophagus, stomach, small intestine, large intestine

5 While your teeth are breaking the food into tiny pieces, saliva is making the food softer.
11 Whatever the body cannot use goes into the large intestine.
8 While the food is in your stomach, more juices help to dissolve it.
1 First you must pick up your sandwich in your hand.
6 When the food in your mouth is soft enough, you swallow it.
2 Move your hand to your mouth.
9 When the food has dissolved in your stomach, it goes to your small intestine.
3 Put a corner of the sandwich in your mouth.
7 As you swallow your food, it moves down the esophagus to your stomach.
4 Use your teeth to take a bite of the sandwich.
10 While the food is in your small intestine, the body absorbs whatever it needs.

What happens when you try to swallow too big of a bite? **Answers will vary.** _Gets stuck in throat._

Write a sentence about a kind of food that is good for your body.
Answers will vary.

Page 180

Going Around in Circles!

The circulatory system is responsible for moving blood throughout your body. It is blood that carries food and oxygen to your body's cells and carries away carbon dioxide and other wastes. This system also carries disease-fighting substances that help prevent you from getting sick.

The main components of your body's circulatory system are: the heart, blood vessels, blood, and the lymphatic system. Your heart controls this system.

The heart is responsible for sending blood mixed with oxygen to the rest of your body through blood vessels called arteries. Blood vessels called veins return blood to your heart. Your veins look blue because the blood in them has no oxygen. Back toward the heart, the blood gathers more oxygen as it passes through your lungs and becomes red. This cycle occurs about one time every minute. It is your heart's constant pumping that keeps your blood circulating.

Use the information above to solve the puzzle.

Across
2. The _heart_ controls the circulatory system.
3. Blood without oxygen is _blue_.
6. Arteries carry blood mixed with _oxygen_ from the heart to the rest of your body.
7. _Veins_ carry blood to the heart.

Down
1. _Arteries_ carry blood away from the heart.
3. Blood is _red_ when it contains oxygen.
5. Blood gets oxygen from your _lungs_.

Page 181

Backbone or No Backbone?

Which part of your body helps you stand tall or sit up straight? It is your backbone. You are a member of a large group of animals that all have backbones. Animals with backbones are called vertebrates. Birds, fish, reptiles, amphibians, and mammals are all vertebrates.

Some animals do not have backbones. These animals are called invertebrates. Worms, centipedes, and insects are all invertebrates.

Classifying
Find the five vertebrates and five invertebrates hidden in the wordsearch. Then write them in the correct group.

Invertebrates
1. beetle
2. worm
3. spider
4. fly
5. moth

Vertebrates
1. lion
2. giraffe
3. whale
4. rabbit
5. frog

Your neighborhood has many animals in or near it. Add their names to the lists.

Invertebrates
6. Answers will vary.

Vertebrates
7.

Find Out
There are many more invertebrates than vertebrates. Nine out of ten animals is an invertebrate. Which group has the largest animals? Which group has the smallest animals?

Page 182

Insects in Winter

In the summertime, insects can be seen buzzing and fluttering around us. But as winter's cold weather begins, suddenly the insects seem to disappear. Do you know where they go?

Many insects, such as flies and mosquitoes, find a warm place to spend the winter. They live in cellars, barns, attics, caves and tree holes.

Beetles and ants try to dig deep into the ground. Some beetles stack up in piles under rocks or dead leaves.

In the fall, female grasshoppers and crickets lay their eggs and die. The eggs hatch in the spring.

Bees also try to protect themselves from the winter cold. Honeybees gather in a ball in the middle of their hive. The bees stay in this tight ball trying to stay warm.

Winter is very hard for insects, but each spring the survivors come out and the buzzing and fluttering begins again.

Write:
When cold weather begins, _insects_ seem to disappear.

Unscramble and check.
Mosquitoes and _flies_ find a warm place in:
quimsoeosi / stile
☐ beds ☑ barns ☑ caves ☑ cellars ☑ attics ☐ sweaters

Circle Yes or No.
In the winter, insects look for a warm place to live. **Yes** No
Noise, such as buzzing, can be heard all winter long. Yes **No**
Some beetles and ants dig deep into the ground. **Yes** No
Every insect finds a warm home for the winter. Yes **No**
Crickets and grasshoppers lay their eggs and die. **Yes** No
The honeybees gather in a ball in their hive. **Yes** No
Survivors of the cold weather come out each spring. **Yes** No

Page 183

Six-Legged Friends

The largest group of animals belongs to the group called invertebrates–or animals without backbones. This large group is the insect group.

Insects are easy to tell apart from other animals. Adult insects have three body parts and six legs. The first body part is the head. On the head are the mouth, eyes, and antennae. The second body part is the thorax. On it are the legs and wings. The third part is the abdomen. On it are small openings for breathing.

Color the body parts of the insect above.
head–red, thorax–yellow, abdomen–blue

Draw an insect below. Make your insect a one-of-a-kind. Be sure it has the correct number of body parts, legs, wings, and antennae. Fill in the information.

Pictures and answers will vary.

Insect's name _____ Warning: _____
Length _____
Where found _____
Food _____

Find Out
Many people think that spiders are insects. Spiders and insects are alike in many ways, but spiders are not insects. Find out how the two are different.

Page 184

Go Bats for Bats

Bats live all over the world. The bats found in the rainforest play an important role because they control insects and pollinate and disperse seeds for avocados, bananas, cashews, figs, peaches and other fruits. However, the bats that live in the rainforest are in danger due to the increasing destruction of their habitat. This could mean that our supply of fruits, nuts and spices could decrease and possibly vanish if the destruction continues. Read the description of each bat below. Notice how each one is different and has special features to help it survive. Put the letter of each description next to the bat it describes and the bat's food.

A. Notice the long nose and tongue this bat uses to sip into the durian blossom.
B. This bat's large ears and nose flap enable it to locate insects at night.
C. With its long feet and claws, this bat captures certain small prey.
D. The long snout on this bat helps it eat fruit like figs.

Food

Bats

Once you have matched up the bats and their food, cut all the pictures apart. Glue each bat to a piece of construction paper. Glue the food it eats to the back. Punch a hole in each piece of construction paper. Put a piece of string through each piece of paper and tie the bats to a hanger. Now, you have a bat mobile to hang from the ceiling.

Page 185

A Sampling of Snakes

The Snake House is a very popular place to visit at the zoo. There are many different types and sizes of snakes. Some snakes are poisonous while others are not. Some snakes are harmless to most creatures, and some are very dangerous.

The five snakes described here are held in the cages below.

Decide which snake belongs in each cage by using the clues given here and beneath the boxes. Then write each name in the correct cage.

The King Cobra is the longest poisonous snake in the world. One of these snakes measured almost 19 feet long. It comes from southeast Asia and the Philippines.

The Gaboon Viper, a very poisonous snake, has the longest fangs of all snakes (nearly 2 inches). It comes from southeast Asia.

The Reticulated Python is the longest snake of all. One specimen measured 32 feet 9½ inches. It comes from southeast Asia, Indonesia, and the Philippines. It crushes its prey to death.

The Black Mamba, the fastest-moving land snake, can move at speeds of 10–12 m.p.h. It lives in the eastern part of tropical Africa.

The Anaconda is almost twice as heavy as a reticulated python of the same length. One anaconda that was almost 28 feet long weighed nearly 500 pounds.

#1 Anaconda   #2 King Cobra   #3 Ret. Python   #4 Gaboon Viper   #5 Black Mamba

Clues:
- The snake in cage #5 moves the fastest on land.
- The longest snake of all is between the snake that comes from tropical Africa and the longest poisonous snake.
- The very heavy snake is to the left of the longest poisonous snake.

Page 186

From Egg to Tadpole to Frog

The poem below tells about the changes that occur in frogs during their life cycles. In every line, there is one word that doesn't make sense. Find the correct form in the Word Bank and write it in the puzzle. Hint: The correct word rhymes with it.

The Life Cycle of a Frog

There is jelly on the legs (13)
To protect the entire match. (11)
It takes tree to twenty-five days (7↓)
Until they're ready to catch. (5)

Out comes a polihog (18)
When the time is just bright. (8)
It breathes using hills (14)
And its size is very light. (4)

It loses its long scale (9)
After pegs begin to grow. (1)
Digestion changes strange (12)
In a process fast and glow. (2)

What helps a frog to seethe (3)
Is its thin and moist chin. (6↓)
It also uses rungs (15)
To let the hair in. (10)

Some frogs can skim like a duck. (6→)
And some can mop like a rabbit. (16)
Others climb bees like a squirrel (3→)
Which may seem a bunny habit. (17)

Word Bank
lungs	eggs	right	hatch
funny	air	slow	change
legs	tail	tree	breathe
gills	skin	slight	polliwog
swim	hop	three	batch

Page 187

The Mighty Bear

Bears are large and powerful animals. Depending on the type of bear, they can weigh from 60 to 2,000 pounds.

Listed below are four different kinds of bears. The lengths of these bears are 3 feet, 5 feet, 8 feet, and 9 feet. Use the clues to match each bear to its length. Write the answers in the blanks.

Clues:

Alaskan brown bear + American black bear = 14 feet

Polar bear + Alaskan brown bear = 17 feet

American black bear + Sun bear = 8 feet

The Alaskan brown bear is _9_ feet in length.
The American black bear is _5_ feet in length.
The polar bear is _8_ feet in length.
The sun bear is _3_ feet in length.

Page 188

Toadly Froggin' Around

Harry and Song Lee loved frogs and similar creatures. Read the information about frogs and toads. Then write true or false in front of each statement.

Frogs and Toads

Both frogs and toads are amphibians. Amphibians spend part of their lives as water animals and part as land animals. In the early stages of their lives, amphibians breathe through gills, while as adults they develop lungs. Most amphibians lay eggs near water. One of these newly hatched frogs and toads both have tails that they later lose. Both often have poison glands in their skin to protect them from their enemies.

Frogs and toads are different in several ways. Most toads are broader, darker, and flatter. Their skin is drier. Toads are usually covered with warts while frogs have smooth skin. Most toads live on land while most frogs prefer being in or near the water.

true 1. Both frogs and toads usually lay eggs near water.
false 2. Most frogs have drier skin than toads.
false 3. Very young amphibians breathe with lungs.
true 4. Frogs tend to be lighter in color.
false 5. An adult frog's tail helps support him while sitting.
true 6. Poison glands often protect frogs from an enemy.
true 7. A toad's skin is often bumpy.
true 8. Frogs and toads are both amphibians.

Page 189

Daily Learning Drills Grade 3

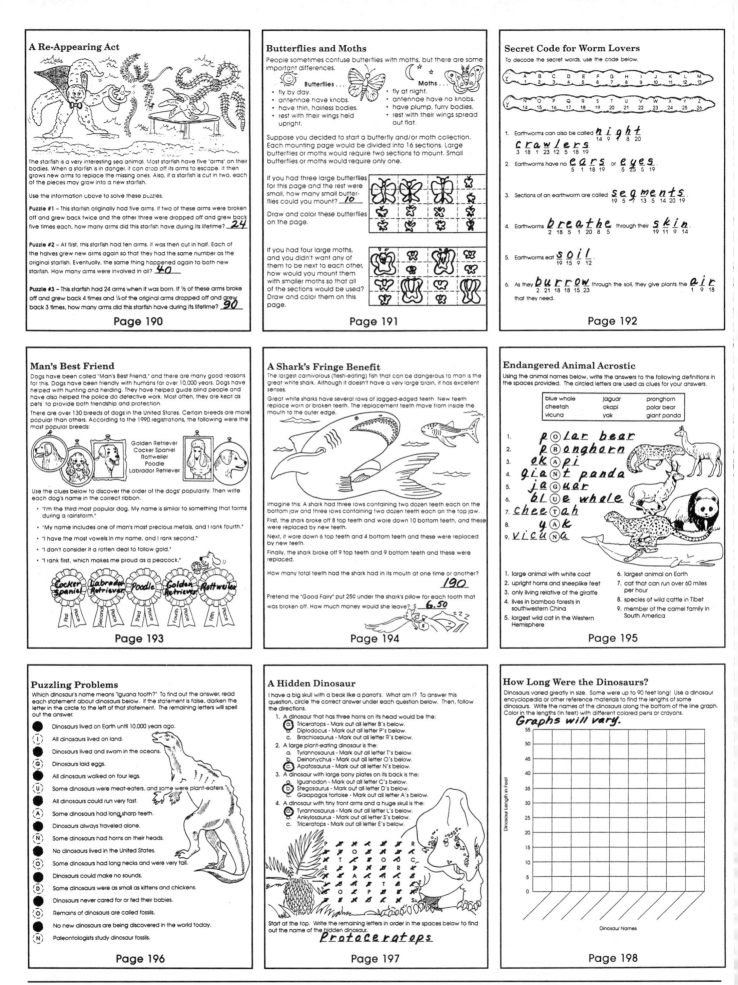

A Re-Appearing Act

The starfish is a very interesting sea animal. Most starfish have five "arms" on their bodies. When a starfish is in danger, it can drop off its arms to escape. It then grows new arms to replace the missing ones. Also, if a starfish is cut in two, each of the pieces may grow into a new starfish.

Use the information above to solve these puzzles.

Puzzle #1 – This starfish originally had five arms. If two of these arms were broken off and grew back twice and the other three were dropped off and grew back five times each, how many arms did this starfish have during its lifetime? **24**

Puzzle #2 – At first, this starfish had ten arms. It was then cut in half. Each of the halves grew new arms again so that they had the same number as the original starfish. Eventually, the same thing happened again to both new starfish. How many arms were involved in all? **40**

Puzzle #3 – This starfish had 24 arms when it was born. If ½ of these arms broke off and grew back 4 times and ¼ of the original arms dropped off and grew back 3 times, how many arms did this starfish have during its lifetime? **90**

Page 190

Butterflies and Moths

People sometimes confuse butterflies with moths, but there are some important differences.

Butterflies . . .
- fly by day.
- antennae have knobs.
- have thin, hairless bodies.
- rest with their wings held upright.

Moths . . .
- fly at night.
- antennae have no knobs.
- have plump, furry bodies.
- rest with their wings spread out flat.

Suppose you decided to start a butterfly and/or moth collection. Each mounting page would be divided into 16 sections. Large butterflies or moths would require two sections to mount. Small butterflies or moths would require only one.

If you had three large butterflies for this page and the rest were small, how many small butterflies could you mount? **10**

Draw and color these butterflies on the page.

If you had four large moths, and you didn't want any of them to be next to each other, how would you mount them with smaller moths so that all of the sections would be used? Draw and color them on this page.

Page 191

Secret Code for Worm Lovers

To decode the secret words, use the code below.

A	B	C	D	E	F	G	H	I	J	K	L	M
1	2	3	4	5	6	7	8	9	10	11	12	13

N	O	P	Q	R	S	T	U	V	W	X	Y	Z
14	15	16	17	18	19	20	21	22	23	24	25	26

1. Earthworms can also be called **night** (14 9 7 8 20) **crawlers** (3 18 1 23 12 5 18 19)

2. Earthworms have no **ears** (5 1 18 19) or **eyes** (5 25 5 19)

3. Sections of an earthworm are called **segments** (19 5 7 13 5 14 20 19)

4. Earthworms **breathe** (2 18 5 1 20 8 5) through their **skin** (19 11 9 14)

5. Earthworms eat **soil** (19 15 9 12)

6. As they **burrow** (2 21 18 18 15 23) through the soil, they give plants the **air** (1 9 18) that they need.

Page 192

Man's Best Friend

Dogs have been called "Man's Best Friend," and there are many good reasons for this. Dogs have been friendly with humans for over 10,000 years. Dogs have helped with hunting and herding. They have helped guide blind people and have also helped the police do detective work. Most often, they are kept as pets to provide both friendship and protection.

There are over 130 breeds of dogs in the United States. Certain breeds are more popular than others. According to the 1990 registrations, the following were the most popular breeds:

Golden Retriever
Cocker Spaniel
Rottweiler
Poodle
Labrador Retriever

Use the clues below to discover the order of the dogs' popularity. Then write each dog's name in the correct ribbon.

- "I'm the third most popular dog. My name is similar to something that forms during a rainstorm."
- "My name includes one of man's most precious metals, and I rank fourth."
- "I have the most vowels in my name, and I rank second."
- "I don't consider it a rotten deal to follow gold."
- "I rank first, which makes me proud as a peacock."

Cocker Spaniel — First Place
Labrador Retriever — Second Place
Poodle — Third Place
Golden Retriever — Fourth Place
Rottweiler — Fifth Place

Page 193

A Shark's Fringe Benefit

The largest carnivorous (flesh-eating) fish that can be dangerous to man is the great white shark. Although it doesn't have a very large brain, it has excellent senses.

Great white sharks have several rows of jagged-edged teeth. New teeth replace worn or broken teeth. The replacement teeth move from inside the mouth to the outer edge.

Imagine this. A shark had three rows containing two dozen teeth each on the bottom jaw and three rows containing two dozen teeth each on the top jaw.

First, the shark broke off 8 top teeth and wore down 10 bottom teeth, and these were replaced by new teeth.

Next, it wore down 6 top teeth and 4 bottom teeth and these were replaced by new teeth.

Finally, the shark broke off 9 top teeth and 9 bottom teeth and these were replaced.

How many total teeth had the shark had in its mouth at one time or another? **190**

Pretend the "Good Fairy" put 25¢ under the shark's pillow for each tooth that was broken off. How much money would she leave? $ **6.50**

Page 194

Endangered Animal Acrostic

Using the animal names below, write the answers to the following definitions in the spaces provided. The circled letters are used as clues for your answers.

blue whale	jaguar	pronghorn
cheetah	okapi	polar bear
vicuna	yak	giant panda

1. **p**olar bear
2. p**r**onghorn
3. ok**a**pi
4. gia**n**t panda
5. **j**aguar
6. b**l**ue whale
7. chee**t**ah
8. **ya**k
9. vicu**na**

1. large animal with white coat
2. upright horns and sheeplike feet
3. only living relative of the giraffe
4. lives in bamboo forests in southwestern China
5. largest wild cat in the Western Hemisphere
6. largest animal on Earth
7. cat that can run over 60 miles per hour
8. species of wild cattle in Tibet
9. member of the camel family in South America

Page 195

Puzzling Problems

Which dinosaur's name means "iguana tooth?" To find out the answer, read each statement about dinosaurs below. If the statement is false, darken the letter in the circle to the left of that statement. The remaining letters will spell out the answer.

- ● Dinosaurs lived on Earth until 10,000 years ago.
- (I) All dinosaurs lived on land.
- ● Dinosaurs lived and swam in the oceans.
- (G) Dinosaurs laid eggs.
- ● All dinosaurs walked on four legs.
- (U) Some dinosaurs were meat-eaters, and some were plant-eaters.
- ● All dinosaurs could run very fast.
- (A) Some dinosaurs had long, sharp teeth.
- ● Dinosaurs always traveled alone.
- (N) Some dinosaurs had horns on their heads.
- ● No dinosaurs lived in the United States.
- (O) Some dinosaurs had long necks and were very tall.
- ● Dinosaurs could make no sounds.
- (D) Some dinosaurs were as small as kittens and chickens.
- ● Dinosaurs never cared for or fed their babies.
- (O) Remains of dinosaurs are called fossils.
- ● No new dinosaurs are being discovered in the world today.
- (N) Paleontologists study dinosaur fossils.

Page 196

A Hidden Dinosaur

I have a big skull with a beak like a parrot's. What am I? To answer this question, circle the correct answer under each question below. Then, follow the directions.

1. A dinosaur that has three horns on its head would be:
   (a.) Triceratops - Mark out all letter B's below.
   b. Diplodocus - Mark out all letter P's below.
   c. Brachiosaurus - Mark out all letter R's below.

2. A large plant-eating dinosaur is:
   a. Tyrannosaurus - Mark out all letter T's below.
   b. Deinonychus - Mark out all letter O's below.
   (c.) Apatosaurus - Mark out all letter N's below.

3. A dinosaur with large bony plates on its back is the:
   a. Iguanodon - Mark out all letter C's below.
   (b.) Stegosaurus - Mark out all letter D's below.
   c. Galapagos tortoise - Mark out all letter A's below.

4. A dinosaur with tiny front arms and a huge skull is the:
   (a.) Tyrannosaurus - Mark out all letter T's below.
   b. Ankylosaurus - Mark out all letter S's below.
   c. Triceratops - Mark out all letter E's below.

Start at the top. Write the remaining letters in order in the spaces below to find out the name of the hidden dinosaur.

Protoceratops

Page 197

How Long Were the Dinosaurs?

Dinosaurs varied greatly in size. Some were up to 90 feet long! Use a dinosaur encyclopedia or other reference materials to find the lengths of some dinosaurs. Write the names of the dinosaurs along the bottom of the line graph. Color in the lengths (in feet) with different colored pens or crayons.

Graphs will vary.

Dinosaur Length in Feet — 0, 5, 10, 15, 20, 25, 30, 35, 40, 45, 50, 55

Dinosaur Names

Page 198

Dinosaur Diagram

A Venn diagram is a great tool to use to compare things. Use the one below to compare two dinosaurs. Fill in the Iguanodon with characteristics common only to it. Fill in the Triceratops with characteristics common only to the Triceratops. Above **Same**, write characteristics that both dinosaurs share. Write a story about your findings on the lines below.

Answers will vary.

about 30 ft. long
lived during period
Cretaceous
plant-eater

no horns
walked on 2 legs

3 horns
walked on 4 legs

Different   Same   Different

Stories will vary

Page 199

A Dinosaur Tale

Study the dinosaurs illustrated below. Then complete each category with words that you associate with these animals. A few examples are already written under each heading. Use the words to compose a poem or short story about these dinosaurs. You can write your own composition or poem or you can share your ideas with other students and write a group composition or poem. Read your work aloud. *Words will vary.*

Nouns	Verbs	Adjectives
tail	walk	huge
teeth	run	spiked
head	eat	sharp

Title: _____

Compositions and poems will vary.

Page 200

Get a Clue!

Get a Clue! is a fun way to gain information about dinosaurs. To play, read the 16 clues below about a certain dinosaur. Use your science book or other resource materials and your own logical thinking to guess the name of the dinosaur. When you are finished, write your own clues about another dinosaur. Give it to another student to see if he/she can guess the answer.

I am a dinosaur.
1. My name means "three-horned face."
2. My skull is 7 or 8 feet long.
3. I have a beaked mouth like a parrot.
4. I eat plants.
5. I walk on all four legs.
6. I am 30 feet long.
7. I weigh up to 10 tons.
8. I am one of the last dinosaurs to live.
9. I have 3 claws on my front feet.
10. I live in Canada and the U.S.
11. I have a thick neck frill.
12. I have 3 horns on my skull.
13. I am the best-known horned dinosaur.
14. I use my horns for protection.
15. I have a small hoof on each toe.
16. I was named by O. C. Marsh in 1889.

I am a *triceratops*.

Clues will vary.

I am a dinosaur.
1. _____
2. _____
3. _____
4. _____
5. _____
6. _____
7. _____
8. _____
9. _____
10. _____

I am a _____ .

Page 201

The End of the Dinosaurs

What could have killed all the dinosaurs? Scientists are not really sure. They have many different theories, or explanations, for why the dinosaurs died out.

Several theories are listed below. Each theory has a cause and an effect. A cause is "a change that happened on earth" and an effect is "what resulted from the change on earth." Draw a line from each cause to its effect.

Cause

| A huge meteor hit the earth, starting fires and making a thick cloud of dust and smoke that covered the earth. |
| Small, fast mammals that liked to eat eggs quickly spread around the world. |
| New kinds of flowering plants started to grow on the earth. These plants had poison in them that the dinosaurs could not taste. |
| When dinosaurs were living, the earth was warm all year long. Suddenly the earth became cooler with cold winter months. |

Effect

| Dinosaurs were cold-blooded and they couldn't find places to hibernate. They had no fur or feathers to keep them warm. They froze to death. |
| The sunlight was blocked and plants couldn't grow. The dinosaurs starved to death. |
| Fewer and fewer baby dinosaurs were born. |
| The dinosaurs ate poison without even knowing it and they died. |

Page 202

Animal Mysteries

As long as people have studied animals, there have been mysteries about why animals act in certain ways.

One mystery has to do with some animals' strange behavior before earthquakes. Horse and cattle stampedes, screeching seabirds, howling dogs, even animals coming out of hibernation early, are examples of this mysterious behavior.

Another mystery involves birds and ants. No one can explain why a bird will pick up an ant in its beak and rub the ant over its feathers again and again. This is called "anting," and birds have been known to do this for an hour without stopping.

One animal mystery is very sad. For hundreds of years, some whales have mysteriously swam from the ocean onto a beach where they would die. Reports of "beached whales" occur about five times a year somewhere in the world.

There are hundreds of other animal mysteries—such as how and why animals hibernate—that scientists have not solved. Can you think of another animal mystery?

3 Animal Mysteries

Write.
1. Some animals act strangely before an *earthquake*.

Check.
This strange behavior includes: ☐ laughing birds ☑ howling dogs ☑ horse and cattle stampedes ☐ barking whales ☑ leaving hibernation early ☑ screeching seabirds

Write.
2. This mystery is about *birds* rubbing *ants* over their feathers.

Write.
3. A sad mystery is about *whales* swimming onto a *beach* and dying.

• Write a solution to one of the animal mysteries.

Page 203

Hibernation

Have you ever wondered why some animals hibernate? Hibernation is a long sleep that some animals go into for the winter.

Animals get their warmth and energy from food. Some animals cannot find enough food in the winter. They must eat large amounts of food in the fall. Their bodies store this food as fat. Then in winter, they sleep in hibernation. Since their bodies need much less food during hibernation, they can stay alive without eating new food during the winter.

Some animals that hibernate are: bats, chipmunks, bears, snakes and turtles.

Underline.
Hibernation   is a sleep that some animals go into for the winter.   is the time of year to gather food for the winter.

Yes or No.
Animals get their warmth and energy from food.   (Yes) No
Some animals cannot find enough food in the winter.   (Yes) No
Animals hibernate because they are lazy.   Yes (No)
Animals need less food while they are hibernating.   (Yes) No

Match.
Animals that hibernate . . .
   eat and store food ⟶ in the winter.
   go to sleep ⟶ in the fall.

Color the animals that hibernate.

Page 204

Rain in the Rainforest

At least 80 inches of rain falls and thundershowers may occur for 200 or more days each year in a rainforest. Rainforests need a lot of rain so that the plants native to them do not dry out. Fill in the precipitation graph below with the average rainfall of a typical tropical rainforest. The amounts are listed beneath the graph.

0 2 4 6 8 10 12 14 16 18 20 22 24 26 28 30

JANUARY
FEBRUARY
MARCH
APRIL
MAY
JUNE
JULY
AUGUST
SEPTEMBER
OCTOBER
NOVEMBER
DECEMBER

J F M A M J J A S O N D
24" 20" 13" 11" 10" 7" 8" 9" 9" 11" 14" 18"

What was the total rainfall for the year in this rainforest? *154"*
What is the total rainfall for a year in your area? _____

Page 205

Lightning

Lightning is a flash of light caused by electricity in the sky. Clouds are made of many water droplets. All of these droplets together contain a large electrical charge. Sometimes these clouds set off a huge spark of electricity called lightning. Lightning travels very fast. As it cuts through the air, it can cause thunder.

Lightning takes various forms. Some lightning looks like a zigzag in the sky. Sheet lightning spreads and lights the sky. Ball lightning looks like a ball of fire.

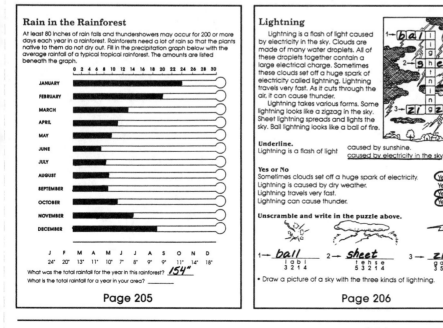

1 - b a l l
2 - s h e e t
3 - z i g z a g

Underline.
Lightning is a flash of light   caused by sunshine.   caused by electricity in the sky.

Yes or No
Sometimes clouds set off a huge spark of electricity.   (Yes) No
Lightning is caused by dry weather.   Yes (No)
Lightning travels very fast.   (Yes) No
Lightning can cause thunder.   (Yes) No

Unscramble and write in the puzzle above.
1 - *ball* (l a b l / 3 2 1 4)
2 - *sheet* (t e h s e / 5 3 2 1 4)
3 - *zigzag* (g a i z g z / 3 5 2 1 8 4)

• Draw a picture of a sky with the three kinds of lightning.

Page 206

A Funnel Cloud—Danger!

Did you know that a tornado is the most violent windstorm on Earth? A tornado is a whirling, twisting storm that is shaped like a funnel.

A tornado usually occurs in the spring on a hot day. It begins with thunderclouds and thunder. A cloud becomes very dark. The bottom of the cloud begins to twist and form a funnel. Rain and lightning begin. The funnel cloud drops from the dark storm clouds. It moves down toward the ground.

A tornado is very dangerous. It can destroy almost everything in its path.

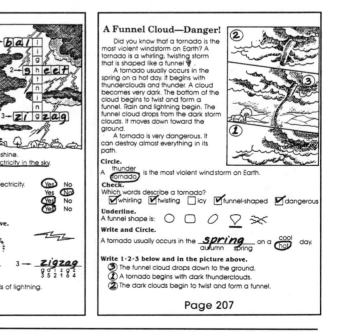

Circle.
A (tornado) is the most violent windstorm on Earth.

Check.
Which words describe a tornado? ☑ whirling ☑ twisting ☐ icy ☑ funnel-shaped ☑ dangerous

Underline.
A funnel shape is: ◯ ▭ ⬭ ▽ ⟩⟨

Write and Circle.
A tornado usually occurs in the *spring* on a *cool* day.   (autumn / spring)   (hot) day.

Write 1-2-3 below and in the picture above.
3 The funnel cloud drops down to the ground.
1 A tornado begins with dark thunderclouds.
2 The dark clouds begin to twist and form a funnel.

Page 207

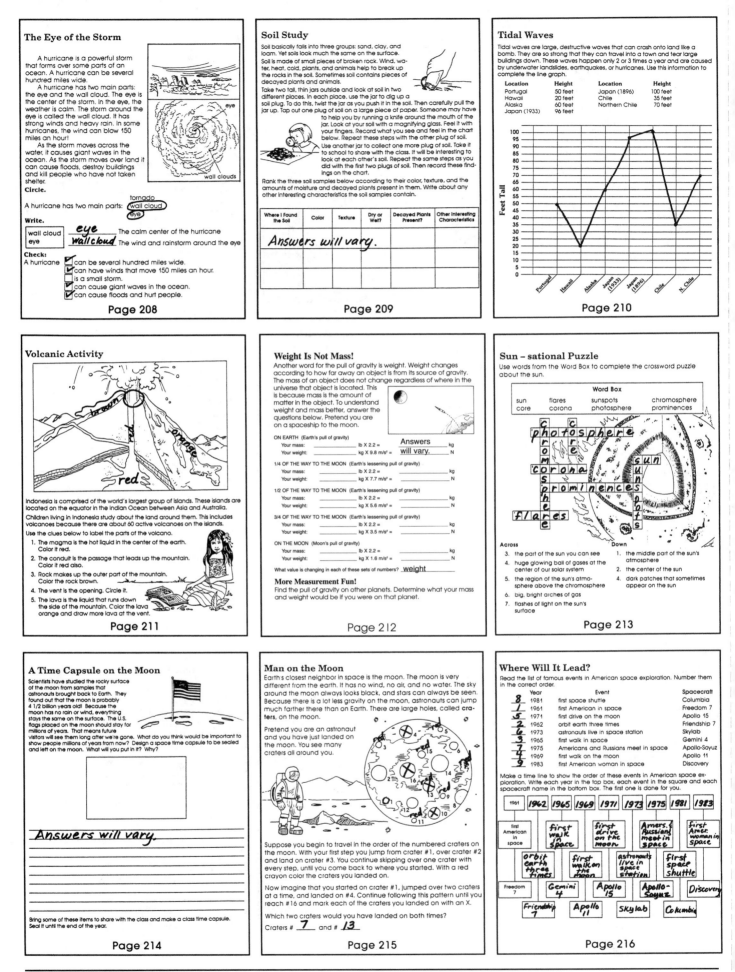

The Eye of the Storm

A hurricane is a powerful storm that forms over some parts of an ocean. A hurricane can be several hundred miles wide.

A hurricane has two main parts: the eye and the wall cloud. The eye is the center of the storm. In the eye, the weather is calm. The storm around the eye is called the wall cloud. It has strong winds and heavy rain. In some hurricanes, the wind can blow 150 miles an hour!

As the storm moves across the water, it causes giant waves in the ocean. As the storm moves over land it can cause floods, destroy buildings and kill people who have not taken shelter.

Circle.

A hurricane has two main parts: ⟨wall cloud⟩ tornado ⟨eye⟩

Write.

| wall cloud | eye | The calm center of the hurricane |
| eye | wall cloud | The wind and rainstorm around the eye |

Check:
A hurricane
- ☑ can be several hundred miles wide.
- ☑ can have winds that move 150 miles an hour.
- ☐ is a small storm.
- ☑ can cause giant waves in the ocean.
- ☑ can cause floods and hurt people.

Page 208

Soil Study

Soil basically falls into three groups: sand, clay, and loam. Yet soils look much the same on the surface.

Soil is made of small pieces of broken rock. Wind, water, heat, cold, plants, and animals help to break up the rocks in the soil. Sometimes soil contains pieces of decayed plants and animals.

Take two tall, thin jars outside and look at soil in two different places. In each place, use a jar to dig up a soil plug. To do this, twist the jar as you push it in the soil. Then carefully pull the jar up. Tap out one plug of soil on a large piece of paper. Someone may have to help you by running a knife around the mouth of the jar. Look at soil with a magnifying glass. Feel it with your fingers. Record what you see and feel in the chart below. Repeat these steps with the other plug of soil.

Use another jar to collect one more plug of soil. Take it to school to share with the class. It will be interesting to look at each other's soil. Repeat the same steps as you did with the first two plugs of soil. Then record these findings on the chart.

Rank the three soil samples below according to their color, texture, and the amounts of moisture and decayed plants present in them. Write about any other interesting characteristics the soil samples contain.

Where I Found the Soil	Color	Texture	Dry or Wet?	Decayed Plants Present?	Other Interesting Characteristics
Answers will vary.					

Page 209

Tidal Waves

Tidal waves are large, destructive waves that can crash onto land like a bomb. They are so strong that they can travel into a town and tear large buildings down. These waves happen only 2 or 3 times a year and are caused by underwater landslides, earthquakes, or hurricanes. Use this information to complete the line graph.

Location	Height	Location	Height
Portugal	50 feet	Japan (1896)	100 feet
Hawaii	20 feet	Chile	35 feet
Alaska	60 feet	Northern Chile	70 feet
Japan (1933)	96 feet		

Page 210

Volcanic Activity

Indonesia is comprised of the world's largest group of islands. These islands are located on the equator in the Indian Ocean between Asia and Australia.

Children living in Indonesia study about the land around them. This includes volcanoes because there are about 60 active volcanoes on the islands.

Use the clues below to label the parts of the volcano.

1. The magma is the hot liquid in the center of the earth. Color it red.
2. The conduit is the passage that leads up the mountain. Color it red also.
3. Rock makes up the outer part of the mountain. Color the rock brown.
4. The vent is the opening. Circle it.
5. The lava is the liquid that runs down the side of the mountain. Color the lava orange and draw more lava at the vent.

Page 211

Weight Is Not Mass!

Another word for the pull of gravity is weight. Weight changes according to how far away an object is from its source of gravity. The mass of an object does not change regardless of where in the universe that object is located. This is because mass is the amount of matter in the object. To understand weight and mass better, answer the questions below. Pretend you are on a spaceship to the moon.

ON EARTH (Earth's pull of gravity)
Your mass: _____ lb X 2.2 = _____ kg
Your weight: _____ kg X 9.8 m/s² = _____ N

Answers will vary.

1/4 OF THE WAY TO THE MOON (Earth's lessening pull of gravity)
Your mass: _____ lb X 2.2 = _____ kg
Your weight: _____ kg X 7.7 m/s² = _____ N

1/2 OF THE WAY TO THE MOON (Earth's lessening pull of gravity)
Your mass: _____ lb X 2.2 = _____ kg
Your weight: _____ kg X 5.6 m/s² = _____ N

3/4 OF THE WAY TO THE MOON (Earth's lessening pull of gravity)
Your mass: _____ lb X 2.2 = _____ kg
Your weight: _____ kg X 3.5 m/s² = _____ N

ON THE MOON (Moon's pull of gravity)
Your mass: _____ lb X 2.2 = _____ kg
Your weight: _____ kg X 1.6 m/s² = _____ N

What value is changing in each of these sets of numbers? **weight**

More Measurement Fun!
Find the pull of gravity on other planets. Determine what your mass and weight would be if you were on that planet.

Page 212

Sun – sational Puzzle

Use words from the Word Box to complete the crossword puzzle about the sun.

Word Box
sun, flares, sunspots, chromosphere, core, corona, photosphere, prominences

Across
3. the part of the sun you can see
4. huge glowing ball of gases at the center of our solar system
5. the region of the sun's atmosphere above the chromosphere
6. big, bright arches of gas
7. flashes of light on the sun's surface

Down
1. the middle part of the sun's atmosphere
2. the center of the sun
4. dark patches that sometimes appear on the sun

Page 213

A Time Capsule on the Moon

Scientists have studied the rocky surface of the moon from samples that astronauts brought back to Earth. They found out that the moon is probably 4 1/2 billion years old! Because the moon has no rain or wind, everything stays the same on its surface. The U.S. flags placed on the moon should stay for millions of years. That means future visitors will see them long after we're gone. What do you think would be important to show people millions of years from now? Design a space time capsule to be sealed and left on the moon. What will you put in it? Why?

Answers will vary.

Bring some of these items to share with the class and make a class time capsule. Seal it until the end of the year.

Page 214

Man on the Moon

Earth's closest neighbor in space is the moon. The moon is very different from the earth. It has no wind, no air, and no water. The sky around the moon always looks black, and stars can always be seen. Because there is a lot less gravity on the moon, astronauts can jump much farther there than on Earth. There are large holes, called **craters**, on the moon.

Pretend you are an astronaut and you have just landed on the moon. You see many craters all around you.

Suppose you begin to travel in the order of the numbered craters on the moon. With your first step you jump from crater #1, over crater #2 and land on crater #3. You continue skipping over one crater with every step, until you come back to where you started. With a red crayon color the craters you landed on.

Now imagine that you started on crater #1, jumped over two craters at a time, and landed on #4. Continue following this pattern until you reach #16 and mark each of the craters you landed on with an X.

Which two craters would you have landed on both times?
Craters # **7** and # **13**

Page 215

Where Will It Lead?

Read the list of famous events in American space exploration. Number them in the correct order.

	Year	Event	Spacecraft
8	1981	first space shuttle	Columbia
1	1961	first American in space	Freedom 7
5	1971	first drive on the moon	Apollo 15
2	1962	orbit earth three times	Friendship 7
6	1973	astronauts live in space station	Skylab
3	1965	first walk in space	Gemini 4
7	1975	Americans and Russians meet in space	Apollo-Soyuz
4	1969	first walk on the moon	Apollo 11
9	1983	first American woman in space	Discovery

Make a time line to show the order of these events in American space exploration. Write each year in the top box, each event in the square and each spacecraft name in the bottom box. The first one is done for you.

Page 216

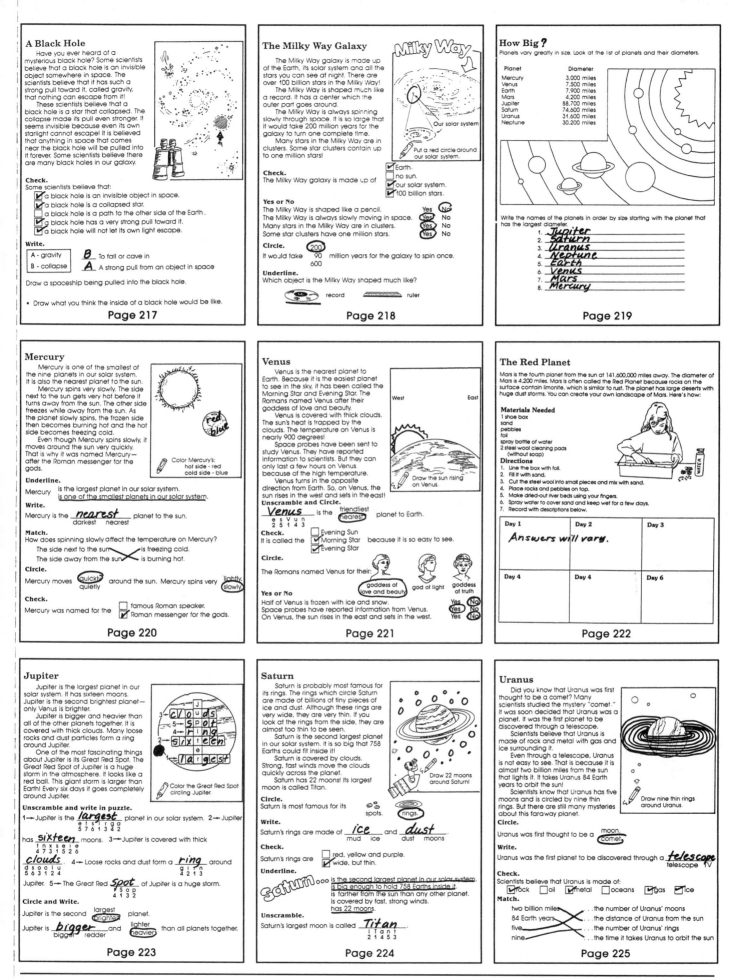

A Black Hole

Have you ever heard of a mysterious black hole? Some scientists believe that a black hole is an invisible object somewhere in space. The scientists believe that it has such a strong pull toward it, called gravity, that nothing can escape from it!

These scientists believe that a black hole is a star that collapsed. The collapse made its pull even stronger. It seems invisible because even its own starlight cannot escape! It is believed that anything in space that comes near the black hole will be pulled into it forever. Some scientists believe there are many black holes in our galaxy.

Check.
Some scientists believe that:
- ☑ a black hole is an invisible object in space.
- ☑ a black hole is a collapsed star.
- ☐ a black hole is a path to the other side of the Earth.
- ☑ a black hole has a very strong pull toward it.
- ☑ a black hole will not let its own light escape.

Write.
A - gravity
B - collapse

B To fall or cave in
A A strong pull from an object in space

Draw a spaceship being pulled into the black hole.

• Draw what you think the inside of a black hole would be like.

Page 217

The Milky Way Galaxy

The Milky Way galaxy is made up of the Earth, its solar system and all the stars you can see at night. There are over 100 billion stars in the Milky Way!

The Milky Way is shaped much like a record. It has a center which the outer part goes around.

The Milky Way is always spinning slowly through space. It is so large that it would take 200 million years for the galaxy to turn one complete time.

Many stars in the Milky Way are in clusters. Some star clusters contain up to one million stars!

Put a red circle around our solar system.

Check.
The Milky Way galaxy is made up of
- ☑ Earth.
- ☐ no sun.
- ☑ our solar system.
- ☑ 100 billion stars.

Yes or No
The Milky Way is shaped like a pencil. Yes (No)
The Milky Way is always slowly moving in space. (Yes) No
Many stars in the Milky Way are in clusters. (Yes) No
Some star clusters have one million stars. (Yes) No

Circle.
It would take (200) 600 million years for the galaxy to spin once.

Underline.
Which object is the Milky Way shaped much like?
record   ruler

Page 218

How Big?

Planets vary greatly in size. Look at the list of planets and their diameters.

Planet	Diameter
Mercury	3,000 miles
Venus	7,500 miles
Earth	7,900 miles
Mars	4,200 miles
Jupiter	88,700 miles
Saturn	74,600 miles
Uranus	31,600 miles
Neptune	30,200 miles

Write the names of the planets in order by size starting with the planet that has the largest diameter.
1. Jupiter
2. Saturn
3. Uranus
4. Neptune
5. Earth
6. Venus
7. Mars
8. Mercury

Page 219

Mercury

Mercury is one of the smallest of the nine planets in our solar system. It is also the nearest planet to the sun.

Mercury spins very slowly. The side next to the sun gets very hot before it turns away from the sun. The other side freezes while away from the sun. As the planet slowly spins, the frozen side then becomes burning hot and the hot side becomes freezing cold.

Even though Mercury spins slowly, it moves around the sun very quickly. That is why it was named Mercury—after the Roman messenger for the gods.

Color Mercury's:
hot side - red
cold side - blue

Underline.
Mercury is the largest planet in our solar system.
is one of the smallest planets in our solar system.

Write.
Mercury is the _nearest_ planet to the sun.
darkest nearest

Match.
How does spinning slowly affect the temperature on Mercury?
The side next to the sun ⤬ is freezing cold.
The side away from the sun ⤬ is burning hot.

Circle.
Mercury moves (quickly) quietly around the sun. Mercury spins very lightly (slowly).

Check.
Mercury was named for the
- ☐ famous Roman speaker.
- ☑ Roman messenger for the gods.

Page 220

Venus

Venus is the nearest planet to Earth. Because it is the easiest planet to see in the sky, it has been called the Morning Star and Evening Star. The Romans named Venus after their goddess of love and beauty.

Venus is covered with thick clouds. The sun's heat is trapped by the clouds. The temperature on Venus is nearly 900 degrees!

Space probes have been sent to study Venus. They have reported information to scientists. But they can only last a few hours on Venus because of the high temperature.

Venus turns in the opposite direction from Earth. So, on Venus, the sun rises in the west and sets in the east!

West   East

Draw the sun rising on Venus.

Unscramble and Circle.
Venus is the friendliest (nearest) planet to Earth.
e s V u n
2 5 1 4 3

Check.
It is called the
- ☐ Evening Sun
- ☑ Morning Star because it is so easy to see.
- ☑ Evening Star

Circle.
The Romans named Venus for their:
(goddess of love and beauty) god of light goddess of truth

Yes or No
Half of Venus is frozen with ice and snow. Yes (No)
Space probes have reported information from Venus. (Yes) No
On Venus, the sun rises in the east and sets in the west. Yes (No)

Page 221

The Red Planet

Mars is the fourth planet from the sun at 141,600,000 miles away. The diameter of Mars is 4,200 miles. Mars is often called the Red Planet because rocks on the surface contain limonite, which is similar to rust. The planet has large deserts with huge dust storms. You can create your own landscape of Mars. Here's how:

Materials Needed
1 shoe box
sand
pebbles
foil
spray bottle of water
2 steel wool cleaning pads
(without soap)

Directions
1. Line the box with foil.
2. Fill it with sand.
3. Cut the steel wool into small pieces and mix with sand.
4. Place rocks and pebbles on top.
5. Make dried-out river beds using your fingers.
6. Spray water to cover sand and keep wet for a few days.
7. Record with descriptions below.

Day 1	Day 2	Day 3
Answers will vary.		
Day 4	Day 4	Day 6

Page 222

Jupiter

Jupiter is the largest planet in our solar system. It has sixteen moons. Jupiter is the second brightest planet— only Venus is brighter.

Jupiter is bigger and heavier than all of the other planets together. It is covered with thick clouds. Many loose rocks and dust particles form a ring around Jupiter.

One of the most fascinating things about Jupiter is its Great Red Spot. The Great Red Spot of Jupiter is a huge storm in the atmosphere. It looks like a red ball. This giant storm is larger than Earth! Every six days it goes completely around Jupiter.

Color the Great Red Spot circling Jupiter.

Unscramble and write in puzzle.
1→ Jupiter is the _largest_ planet in our solar system. 2→ Jupiter
e t s i r g a
5 7 6 1 3 4 2

has _sixteen_ moons. 3→ Jupiter is covered with thick
t n x s e i e
4 7 3 1 5 2 6

clouds. 4→ Loose rocks and dust form a _ring_ around
d s o c l u   g i r n
5 6 3 1 2 4   4 2 1 3

Jupiter. 5→ The Great Red _spot_ of Jupiter is a huge storm.
S o p t
4 1 3 2

Circle and Write.
Jupiter is the second largest (brightest) planet.
Jupiter is _bigger_ and lighter (heavier) than all planets together.
bigger redder

Page 223

Saturn

Saturn is probably most famous for its rings. The rings which circle Saturn are made of billions of tiny pieces of ice and dust. Although these rings are very wide, they are very thin. If you look at the rings from the side, they are almost too thin to be seen.

Saturn is the second largest planet in our solar system. It is so big that 758 Earths could fit inside it.

Saturn is covered by clouds. Strong, fast winds move the clouds quickly across the planet.

Saturn has 22 moons! Its largest moon is called Titan.

Draw 22 moons around Saturn!

Circle.
Saturn is most famous for its   spots. (rings.)

Write.
Saturn's rings are made of _ice_ and _dust_.
mud ice   dust moons

Check.
Saturn's rings are
- ☐ red, yellow and purple.
- ☑ wide, but thin.

Underline.
Saturn... is the second largest planet in our solar system.
is big enough to hold 758 Earths inside it.
is farther from the sun than any other planet.
is covered by fast, strong winds.
has 22 moons.

Unscramble.
Saturn's largest moon is called _Titan_.
i T a n t
2 1 4 5 3

Page 224

Uranus

Did you know that Uranus was first thought to be a comet? Many scientists studied the mystery "comet." It was soon decided that Uranus was a planet. It was the first planet to be discovered through a telescope.

Scientists believe that Uranus is made of rock and metal with gas and ice surrounding it.

Even through a telescope, Uranus is not easy to see. That is because it is almost two billion miles from the sun that lights it. It takes Uranus 84 Earth years to orbit the sun!

Scientists know that Uranus has five moons and is circled by nine thin rings. But there are still many mysteries about this faraway planet.

Draw nine thin rings around Uranus.

Circle.
Uranus was first thought to be a moon. (comet.)

Write.
Uranus was the first planet to be discovered through a _telescope_.
telescope TV

Check.
Scientists believe that Uranus is made of:
- ☑ rock ☐ oil ☑ metal ☐ oceans ☑ gas ☑ ice

Match.
two billion miles ⤬ . . . the number of Uranus' moons
84 Earth years ⤬ . . . the distance of Uranus from the sun
five . . . the number of Uranus' rings
nine . . . the time it takes Uranus to orbit the sun

Page 225

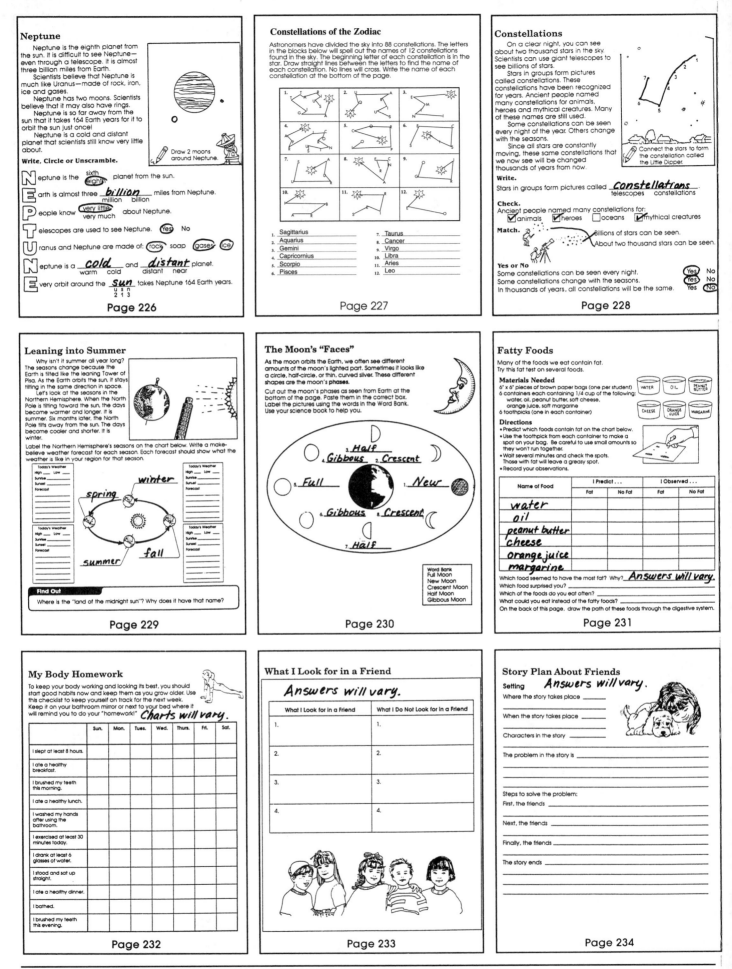

Neptune

Neptune is the eighth planet from the sun. It is difficult to see Neptune—even through a telescope. It is almost three billion miles from Earth.

Scientists believe that Neptune is much like Uranus—made of rock, iron, ice and gases.

Neptune has two moons. Scientists believe that it may also have rings.

Neptune is so far away from the sun that it takes 164 Earth years for it to orbit the sun just once!

Neptune is a cold and distant planet that scientists still know very little about.

Draw 2 moons around Neptune.

Write, Circle or Unscramble.

N eptune is the ~~sixth~~ **eighth** planet from the sun.

E arth is almost three **billion** miles from Neptune.

P eople know (very little) about Neptune.

T elescopes are used to see Neptune. (Yes) No

U ranus and Neptune are made of: (rock) soap (gases) (ice)

N eptune is a **cold** and **distant** planet.

E very orbit around the **sun** takes Neptune 164 Earth years.

Page 226

Constellations of the Zodiac

Astronomers have divided the sky into 88 constellations. The letters in the blocks below will spell out the names of 12 constellations found in the sky. The beginning letter of each constellation is in the star. Draw straight lines between the letters to find the name of each constellation. No lines will cross. Write the name of each constellation at the bottom of the page.

1. Sagittarius
2. Aquarius
3. Gemini
4. Capricornius
5. Scorpio
6. Pisces
7. Taurus
8. Cancer
9. Virgo
10. Libra
11. Aries
12. Leo

Page 227

Constellations

On a clear night, you can see about two thousand stars in the sky. Scientists can use giant telescopes to see billions of stars.

Stars in groups form pictures called constellations. These constellations have been recognized for years. Ancient people named many constellations for animals, heroes and mythical creatures. Many of these names are still used.

Some constellations can be seen every night of the year. Others change with the seasons.

Since all stars are constantly moving, these same constellations that we now see will be changed thousands of years from now.

Connect the stars to form the constellation called the Little Dipper.

Write.

Stars in groups form pictures called **Constellations**.
telescopes constellations

Check.

Ancient people named many constellations for:
☑ animals ☑ heroes ☐ oceans ☑ mythical creatures

Match.

Billions of stars can be seen.
About two thousand stars can be seen.

Yes or No

Some constellations can be seen every night. (Yes) No
Some constellations change with the seasons. (Yes) No
In thousands of years, all constellations will be the same. Yes (No)

Page 228

Leaning into Summer

Why isn't it summer all year long? The seasons change because the Earth is tilted like the leaning Tower of Pisa. As the Earth orbits the sun, it stays tilting in the same direction in space.

Let's look at the seasons in the Northern Hemisphere. When the North Pole is tilting toward the sun, the days become warmer and longer. It is summer. Six months later, the North Pole tilts away from the sun. The days become cooler and shorter. It is winter.

Label the Northern Hemisphere's seasons on the chart below. Write a make-believe weather forecast for each season. Each forecast should show what the weather is like in your region for that season.

winter spring summer fall

Find Out

Where is the "land of the midnight sun"? Why does it have that name?

Page 229

The Moon's "Faces"

As the moon orbits the Earth, we often see different amounts of the moon's lighted part. Sometimes it looks like a circle, half-circle, or thin, curved silver. These different shapes are the moon's **phases**.

Cut out the moon's phases as seen from Earth at the bottom of the page. Paste them in the correct box. Label the pictures using the words in the Word Bank. Use your science book to help you.

1. Full
2. Gibbous 3. Half 4. Crescent
5. New
6. Gibbous 7. Half Crescent

Word Bank
Full Moon
New Moon
Crescent Moon
Half Moon
Gibbous Moon

Page 230

Fatty Foods

Many of the foods we eat contain fat. Try this fat test on several foods.

Materials Needed
6" x 6" pieces of brown paper bags (one per student)
6 containers each containing 1/4 cup of the following: water, oil, peanut butter, soft cheese, orange juice, soft margarine
6 toothpicks (one in each container)

Directions
- Predict which foods contain fat on the chart below.
- Use the toothpick from each container to make a spot on your bag. Be careful to use small amounts so they won't run together.
- Wait several minutes and check the spots. Those with fat will leave a greasy spot.
- Record your observations.

Name of Food	I Predict...		I Observed...	
	Fat	No Fat	Fat	No Fat
water				
oil				
peanut butter				
cheese				
orange juice				
margarine				

Which food seemed to have the most fat? Why? **Answers will vary.**
Which food surprised you?
Which of the foods do you eat often?
What could you eat instead of the fatty foods?
On the back of this page, draw the path of these foods through the digestive system.

Page 231

My Body Homework

To keep your body working and looking its best, you should start good habits now and keep them as you grow older. Use this checklist to keep yourself on track for the next week. Keep it on your bathroom mirror or next to your bed where it will remind you to do your "homework!" **Charts will vary.**

	Sun.	Mon.	Tues.	Wed.	Thurs.	Fri.	Sat.
I slept at least 8 hours.							
I ate a healthy breakfast.							
I brushed my teeth this morning.							
I ate a healthy lunch.							
I washed my hands after using the bathroom.							
I exercised at least 30 minutes today.							
I drank at least 6 glasses of water.							
I stood and sat up straight.							
I ate a healthy dinner.							
I bathed.							
I brushed my teeth this evening.							

Page 232

What I Look for in a Friend

Answers will vary.

What I Look for in a Friend	What I Do Not Look for in a Friend
1.	1.
2.	2.
3.	3.
4.	4.

Page 233

Story Plan About Friends

Setting **Answers will vary.**
Where the story takes place _____

When the story takes place _____

Characters in the story _____

The problem in the story is _____

Steps to solve the problem:
First, the friends _____

Next, the friends _____

Finally, the friends _____

The story ends _____

Page 234

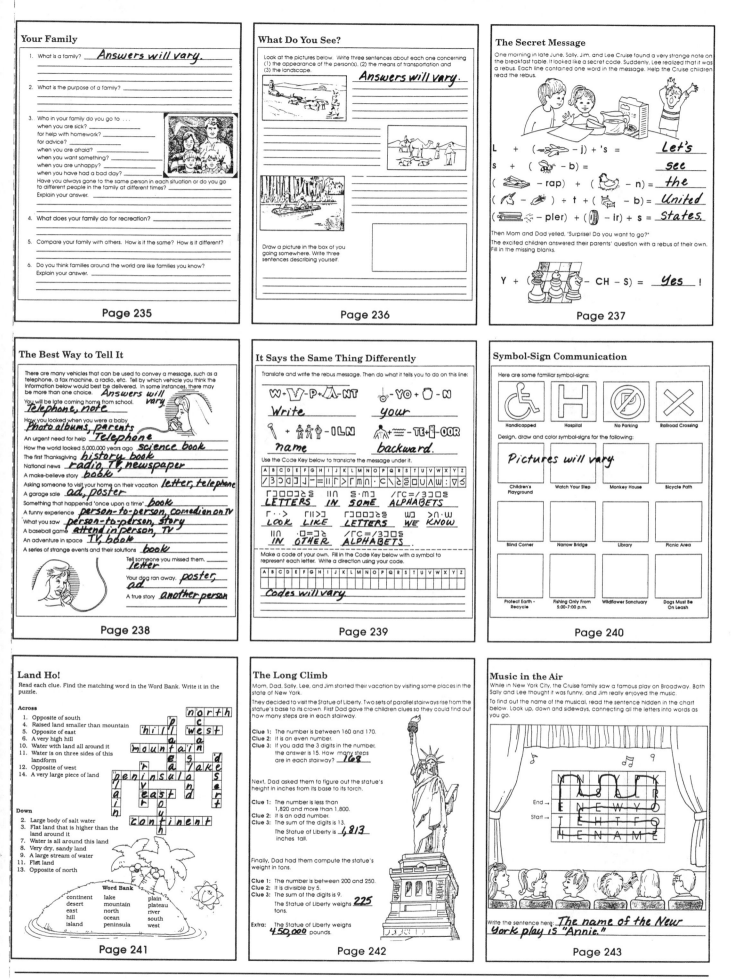

Your Family

1. What is a family? *Answers will vary.*
2. What is the purpose of a family?
3. Who in your family do you go to . . .
   when you are sick?
   for help with homework?
   for advice?
   when you are afraid?
   when you want something?
   when you are unhappy?
   when you have had a bad day?
   Have you always gone to the same person in each situation or do you go to different people in the family at different times?
   Explain your answer.
4. What does your family do for recreation?
5. Compare your family with others. How is it the same? How is it different?
6. Do you think families around the world are like families you know? Explain your answer.

Page 235

What Do You See?

Look at the pictures below. Write three sentences about each one concerning (1) the appearance of the person(s), (2) the means of transportation and (3) the landscape. *Answers will vary.*

Draw a picture in the box of you going somewhere. Write three sentences describing yourself.

Page 236

The Secret Message

One morning in late June, Sally, Jim, and Lee Cruise found a very strange note on the breakfast table. It looked like a secret code. Suddenly, Lee realized that it was a rebus. Each line contained one word in the message. Help the Cruise children read the rebus.

L + (🛩 – j) + 's = *Let's*
s + (🐝 – b) = *see*
(🩴 – rap) + (🐔 – n) = *the*
(🦄 – 🐁) + t + (🐝 – b) = *United*
(🦄🐁 – pler) + (🛞 – ir) + s = *States.*

Then Mom and Dad yelled, "Surprise! Do you want to go?"
The excited children answered their parents' question with a rebus of their own. Fill in the missing blanks.

Y + (♟♜♞ – CH – S) = *Yes* !

Page 237

The Best Way to Tell It

There are many vehicles that can be used to convey a message, such as a telephone, a fax machine, a radio, etc. Tell by which vehicle you think the information below would best be delivered. In some instances, there may be more than one choice. *Answers will vary.*

You'll be late coming home from school. *Telephone, note*
How you looked when you were a baby *Photo albums, parents*
An urgent need for help *Telephone*
How the world looked 5,000,000 years ago *science book*
The first Thanksgiving *history book*
National news *radio, TV, newspaper*
A make-believe story *book*
Asking someone to visit your home on their vacation *letter, telephone*
A garage sale *ad, poster*
Something that happened 'once upon a time' *book*
A funny experience *person-to-person, comedian on TV*
What you saw *person-to-person, story*
A baseball game *attend in person, TV*
An adventure in space *TV, book*
A series of strange events and their solutions *book*
Tell someone you missed them. *letter*
Your dog ran away. *poster, ad*
A true story *another person*

Page 238

It Says the Same Thing Differently

Translate and write the rebus message. Then do what it tells you to do on this line:

W + 🖤 – P + 🔺 – NT → *Write*
☉ – YO + ⭕ – N → *your*
🎤 + 👨‍👩‍👧‍👦 – ILN → *name*
👫 – TE + 🔟 – OOR → *backward.*

Use the Code Key below to translate the message under it.

A	B	C	D	E	F	G	H	I	J	K	L	M	N	O	P	Q	R	S	T	U	V	W	X	Y	Z

LETTERS IN SOME ALPHABETS
LOOK LIKE LETTERS WE KNOW
IN OTHER ALPHABETS.

Make a code of your own. Fill in the Code Key below with a symbol to represent each letter. Write a direction using your code.

A	B	C	D	E	F	G	H	I	J	K	L	M	N	O	P	Q	R	S	T	U	V	W	X	Y	Z

Codes will vary

Page 239

Symbol-Sign Communication

Here are some familiar symbol-signs:

Handicapped   Hospital   No Parking   Railroad Crossing

Design, draw and color symbol-signs for the following:

Pictures will vary

Children's Playground   Watch Your Step   Monkey House   Bicycle Path

Blind Corner   Narrow Bridge   Library   Picnic Area

Protect Earth - Recycle   Fishing Only From 5:00-7:00 p.m.   Wildflower Sanctuary   Dogs Must Be On Leash

Page 240

Land Ho!

Read each clue. Find the matching word in the Word Bank. Write it in the puzzle.

Across
1. Opposite of south
4. Raised land smaller than mountain
5. Opposite of east
6. A very high hill
10. Water with land all around it
11. Water is on three sides of this landform
12. Opposite of west
14. A very large piece of land

Down
2. Large body of salt water
3. Flat land that is higher than the land around it
7. Water is all around this land
8. Very dry, sandy land
9. A large stream of water
11. Flat land
13. Opposite of north

Word Bank
continent   lake   plain
desert   mountain   plateau
east   north   river
hill   ocean   south
island   peninsula   west

Puzzle answers: north, hill, west, mountain, lake, peninsula, east, continent, plateau, desert, ocean, river, plain, island

Page 241

The Long Climb

Mom, Dad, Sally, Lee, and Jim started their vacation by visiting some places in the state of New York.

They decided to visit the Statue of Liberty. Two sets of parallel stairways rise from the statue's base to its crown. First Dad gave the children clues so they could find out how many steps are in each stairway.

Clue 1: The number is between 160 and 170.
Clue 2: It is an even number.
Clue 3: If you add the 3 digits in the number, the answer is 15. How many steps are in each stairway? *168*

Next, Dad asked them to figure out the statue's height in inches from its base to its torch.

Clue 1: The number is less than 1,820 and more than 1,800.
Clue 2: It is an odd number.
Clue 3: The sum of the digits is 13.
The Statue of Liberty is *1,813* inches tall.

Finally, Dad had them compute the statue's weight in tons.

Clue 1: The number is between 200 and 250.
Clue 2: It is divisible by 5.
Clue 3: The sum of the digits is 9.
The Statue of Liberty weighs *225* tons.

Extra: The Statue of Liberty weighs *450,000* pounds.

Page 242

Music in the Air

While in New York City, the Cruise family saw a famous play on Broadway. Both Sally and Lee thought it was funny, and Jim really enjoyed the music.

To find out the name of the musical, read the sentence hidden in the chart below. Look up, down and sideways, connecting all the letters into words as you go.

Write the sentence here: *The name of the New York play is "Annie."*

Page 243

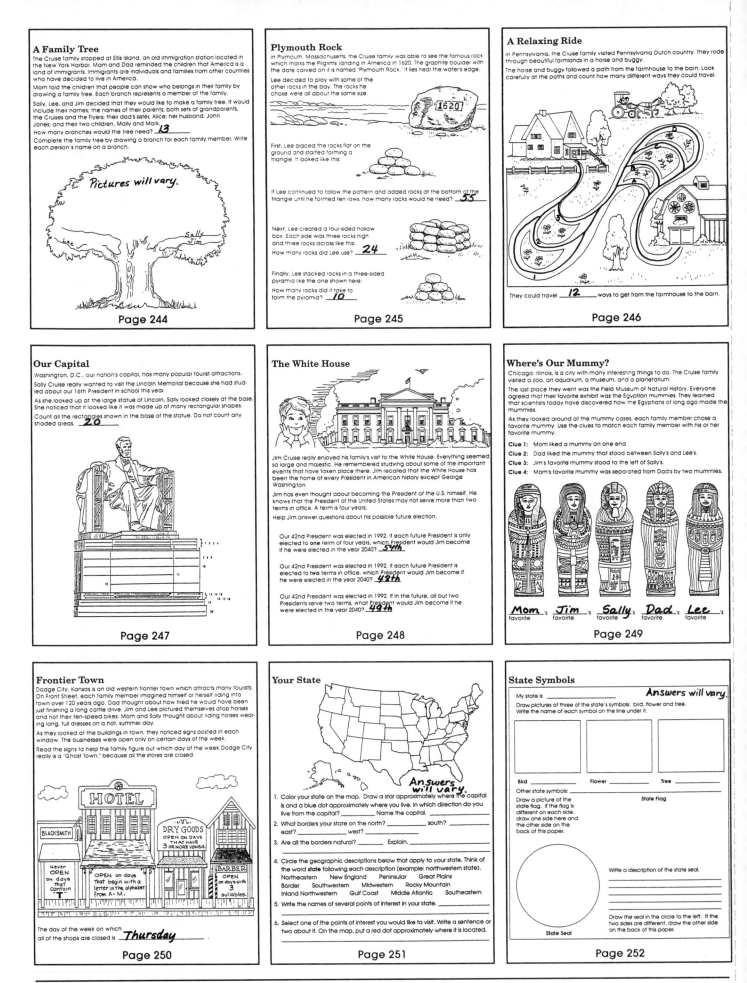

A Family Tree

The Cruise family stopped at Ellis Island, an old immigration station located in the New York Harbor. Mom and Dad reminded the children that America is a land of immigrants. Immigrants are individuals and families from other countries who have decided to live in America.

Mom told the children that people can show who belongs in their family by drawing a family tree. Each branch represents a member of the family.

Sally, Lee, and Jim decided that they would like to make a family tree. It would include the names of their parents; the names of their grandparents; both sets of grandparents; the Cruises and the Flyers; their dad's sister, Alice; her husband, John Jones; and their two children, Molly and Mark.

How many branches would the tree need? _13_

Complete the family tree by drawing a branch for each family member. Write each person's name on a branch.

Pictures will vary.

Page 244

Plymouth Rock

In Plymouth, Massachusetts, the Cruise family was able to see the famous rock which marks the Pilgrims' landing in America in 1620. The graphite boulder with the date carved on it is named "Plymouth Rock." It lies near the water's edge.

Lee decided to play with some of the other rocks in the bay. The rocks he chose were all about the same size.

First, Lee placed the rocks flat on the ground and started forming a triangle. It looked like this:

If Lee continued to follow the pattern and added rocks at the bottom of the triangle until he formed ten rows, how many rocks would he need? _55_

Next, Lee created a four-sided hollow box. Each side was three rocks high and three rocks across like this: How many rocks did Lee use? _24_

Finally, Lee stacked rocks in a three-sided pyramid like the one shown here: How many rocks did it take to form the pyramid? _10_

Page 245

A Relaxing Ride

In Pennsylvania, the Cruise family visited Pennsylvania Dutch country. They rode through beautiful farmlands in a horse and buggy.

The horse and buggy followed a path from the farmhouse to the barn. Look carefully at the paths and count how many different ways they could travel.

They could travel _12_ ways to get from the farmhouse to the barn.

Page 246

Our Capital

Washington, D.C., our nation's capital, has many popular tourist attractions.

Sally Cruise really wanted to visit the Lincoln Memorial because she had studied about our 16th President in school this year.

As she looked up at the large statue of Lincoln, Sally looked closely at the base. She noticed that it looked like it was made up of many rectangular shapes.

Count all the rectangles shown in the base of the statue. Do not count any shaded areas. _20_

Page 247

The White House

Jim Cruise really enjoyed his family's visit to the White House. Everything seemed so large and majestic. He remembered about some of the important events that have taken place there. Jim recalled that the White House has been the home of every President in American history except George Washington.

Jim has even thought about becoming the President of the U.S. himself. He knows that the President of the United States may not serve more than two terms in office. A term is four years.

Help Jim answer questions about his possible future election.

Our 42nd President was elected in 1992. If each future President is only elected to one term of four years, which President would Jim become if he were elected in the year 2040? _54th_

Our 42nd President was elected in 1992. If each future President is elected to two terms in office, which President would Jim become if he were elected in the year 2040? _48th_

Our 42nd President was elected in 1992. If in the future, all but two Presidents serve two terms, what President would Jim become if he were elected in the year 2040? _49th_

Page 248

Where's Our Mummy?

Chicago, Illinois, is a city with many interesting things to do. The Cruise family visited a zoo, an aquarium, a museum, and a planetarium.

The last place they went was the Field Museum of Natural History. Everyone agreed that their favorite exhibit was the Egyptian mummies. They learned that scientists today have discovered how the Egyptians of long ago made their mummies.

As they looked around at the mummy cases, each family member chose a favorite mummy. Use the clues to match each family member with his or her favorite mummy.

Clue 1: Mom liked a mummy on one end.
Clue 2: Dad liked the mummy that stood between Sally's and Lee's.
Clue 3: Jim's favorite mummy stood to the left of Sally's.
Clue 4: Mom's favorite mummy was separated from Dad's by two mummies.

Mom's favorite _Jim_'s favorite _Sally_'s favorite _Dad_'s favorite _Lee_'s favorite

Page 249

Frontier Town

Dodge City, Kansas, is an old western frontier town which attracts many tourists. On Front Street, each family member imagined himself or herself riding into town over 120 years ago. Dad thought about how tired he would have been just finishing a long cattle drive. Jim and Lee pictured themselves atop horses and not their ten-speed bikes. Mom and Sally thought about riding horses wearing long, full dresses on a hot, summer day.

As they looked at the buildings in town, they noticed signs posted in each window. The businesses were open only on certain days of the week.

Read the signs to help the family figure out which day of the week Dodge City really is a "Ghost Town," because all the stores are closed.

The day of the week on which all of the shops are closed is _Thursday_

Page 250

Your State

Answers will vary.

1. Color your state on the map. Draw a star approximately where the capital is and a blue dot approximately where you live. In which direction do you live from the capital? _____ Name the capital. _____

2. What borders your state on the north? _____ south? _____ east? _____ west? _____

3. Are all the borders natural? _____ Explain. _____

4. Circle the geographic descriptions below that apply to your state. Think of the word **state** following each description (example: northwestern state).
Northeastern   New England   Peninsular   Great Plains
Border   Southwestern   Midwestern   Rocky Mountain
Inland Northwestern   Gulf Coast   Middle Atlantic   Southeastern

5. Write the names of several points of interest in your state. _____

6. Select one of the points of interest you would like to visit. Write a sentence or two about it. On the map, put a red dot approximately where it is located. _____

Page 251

State Symbols

My state is _____   *Answers will vary.*

Draw pictures of three of the state's symbols: bird, flower and tree. Write the name of each symbol on the line under it.

Bird _____   Flower _____   Tree _____

Other state symbols: _____

Draw a picture of the state flag. If the flag is different on each side, draw one side here and the other side on the back of this paper.

State Flag

Write a description of the state seal.
_____

Draw the seal in the circle to the left. If the two sides are different, draw the other side on the back of this paper.

State Seal

Page 252

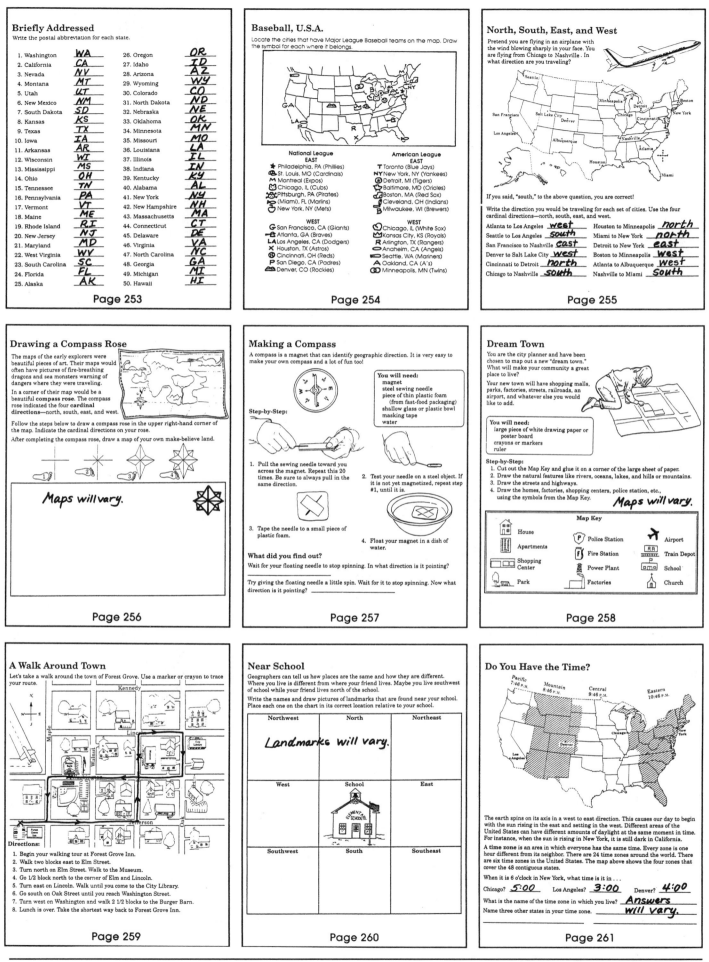

Briefly Addressed

Write the postal abbreviation for each state.

1. Washington — WA
2. California — CA
3. Nevada — NV
4. Montana — MT
5. Utah — UT
6. New Mexico — NM
7. South Dakota — SD
8. Kansas — KS
9. Texas — TX
10. Iowa — IA
11. Arkansas — AR
12. Wisconsin — WI
13. Mississippi — MS
14. Ohio — OH
15. Tennessee — TN
16. Pennsylvania — PA
17. Vermont — VT
18. Maine — ME
19. Rhode Island — RI
20. New Jersey — NJ
21. Maryland — MD
22. West Virginia — WV
23. South Carolina — SC
24. Florida — FL
25. Alaska — AK
26. Oregon — OR
27. Idaho — ID
28. Arizona — AZ
29. Wyoming — WY
30. Colorado — CO
31. North Dakota — ND
32. Nebraska — NE
33. Oklahoma — OK
34. Minnesota — MN
35. Missouri — MO
36. Louisiana — LA
37. Illinois — IL
38. Indiana — IN
39. Kentucky — KY
40. Alabama — AL
41. New York — NY
42. New Hampshire — NH
43. Massachusetts — MA
44. Connecticut — CT
45. Delaware — DE
46. Virginia — VA
47. North Carolina — NC
48. Georgia — GA
49. Michigan — MI
50. Hawaii — HI

Page 253

Baseball, U.S.A.

Locate the cities that have Major League Baseball teams on the map. Draw the symbol for each where it belongs.

National League
EAST
★ Philadelphia, PA (Phillies)
St. Louis, MO (Cardinals)
Montreal (Expos)
Chicago, IL (Cubs)
Pittsburgh, PA (Pirates)
Miami, FL (Marlins)
New York, NY (Mets)
WEST
G San Francisco, CA (Giants)
Atlanta, GA (Braves)
LA Los Angeles, CA (Dodgers)
X Houston, TX (Astros)
Cincinnati, OH (Reds)
P San Diego, CA (Padres)
Denver, CO (Rockies)

American League
EAST
T Toronto (Blue Jays)
NY New York, NY (Yankees)
Detroit, MI (Tigers)
Baltimore, MD (Orioles)
Boston, MA (Red Sox)
Cleveland, OH (Indians)
B Milwaukee, WI (Brewers)
WEST
Chicago, IL (White Sox)
Kansas City, KS (Royals)
R Arlington, TX (Rangers)
Anaheim, CA (Angels)
Seattle, WA (Mariners)
A Oakland, CA (A's)
Minneapolis, MN (Twins)

Page 254

North, South, East, and West

Pretend you are flying in an airplane with the wind blowing sharply into your face. You are flying from Chicago to Nashville. In what direction are you traveling?

If you said, "south," to the above question, you are correct!

Write the direction you would be traveling for each set of cities. Use the four cardinal directions—north, south, east, and west.

Atlanta to Los Angeles — west
Seattle to Los Angeles — south
San Francisco to Nashville — east
Denver to Salt Lake City — west
Cincinnati to Detroit — north
Chicago to Nashville — south

Houston to Minneapolis — north
Miami to New York — north
Detroit to New York — east
Boston to Minneapolis — west
Atlanta to Albuquerque — west
Nashville to Miami — south

Page 255

Drawing a Compass Rose

The maps of the early explorers were beautiful pieces of art. Their maps would often have pictures of fire-breathing dragons and sea monsters warning of dangers where they were traveling.

In a corner of their map would be a beautiful compass rose. The compass rose indicated the four **cardinal** directions—north, south, east, and west.

Follow the steps below to draw a compass rose in the upper right-hand corner of the map. Indicate the cardinal directions on your rose.

After completing the compass rose, draw a map of your own make-believe land.

Maps will vary.

Page 256

Making a Compass

A compass is a magnet that can identify geographic direction. It is very easy to make your own compass and a lot of fun too!

You will need:
magnet
steel sewing needle
piece of thin plastic foam (from fast-food packaging)
shallow glass or plastic bowl
masking tape
water

Step-by-Step:

1. Pull the sewing needle toward you across the magnet. Repeat this 20 times. Be sure to always pull in the same direction.

2. Test your needle on a steel object. If it is not yet magnetized, repeat step #1, until it is.

3. Tape the needle to a small piece of plastic foam.

4. Float your magnet in a dish of water.

What did you find out?

Wait for your floating needle to stop spinning. In what direction is it pointing?

_____

Try giving the floating needle a little spin. Wait for it to stop spinning. Now what direction is it pointing? _____

Page 257

Dream Town

You are the city planner and have been chosen to map out a new "dream town." What will make your community a great place to live?

Your new town will have shopping malls, parks, factories, streets, railroads, an airport, and whatever else you would like to add.

You will need:
large piece of white drawing paper or poster board
crayons or markers
ruler

Step-by-Step:
1. Cut out the Map Key and glue it on a corner of the large sheet of paper.
2. Draw the natural features like rivers, oceans, lakes, and hills or mountains.
3. Draw the streets and highways.
4. Draw the homes, factories, shopping centers, police station, etc., using the symbols from the Map Key.

Maps will vary.

Map Key

House	Police Station	Airport
Apartments	Fire Station	Train Depot
Shopping Center	Power Plant	School
Park	Factories	Church

Page 258

A Walk Around Town

Let's take a walk around the town of Forest Grove. Use a marker or crayon to trace your route.

Directions:
1. Begin your walking tour at Forest Grove Inn.
2. Walk two blocks east to Elm Street.
3. Turn north on Elm Street. Walk to the Museum.
4. Go 1/2 block north to the corner of Elm and Lincoln.
5. Turn east on Lincoln. Walk until you come to the City Library.
6. Go south on Oak Street until you reach Washington Street.
7. Turn west on Washington and walk 2 1/2 blocks to the Burger Barn.
8. Lunch is over. Take the shortest way back to Forest Grove Inn.

Page 259

Near School

Geographers can tell us how places are the same and how they are different. Where you live is different from where your friend lives. Maybe you live southwest of school while your friend lives north of the school.

Write the names and draw pictures of landmarks that are found near your school. Place each one on the chart in its correct location relative to your school.

Northwest	North	Northeast
	Landmarks will vary.	
West	**School**	**East**
Southwest	South	Southeast

Page 260

Do You Have the Time?

Pacific 7:46 P.M.   Mountain 8:46 P.M.   Central 9:46 P.M.   Eastern 10:46 P.M.

The earth spins on its axis in a west to east direction. This causes our day to begin with the sun rising in the east and setting in the west. Different areas of the United States can have different amounts of daylight at the same moment in time. For instance, when the sun is rising in New York, it is still dark in California.

A **time zone** is an area in which everyone has the same time. Every zone is one hour different from its neighbor. There are 24 time zones around the world. There are six time zones in the United States. The map above shows the four zones that cover the 48 contiguous states.

When it is 6 o'clock in New York, what time is it in ...

Chicago? 5:00   Los Angeles? 3:00   Denver? 4:00

What is the name of the time zone in which you live? Answers will vary.

Name three other states in your time zone. _____ _____

Page 261

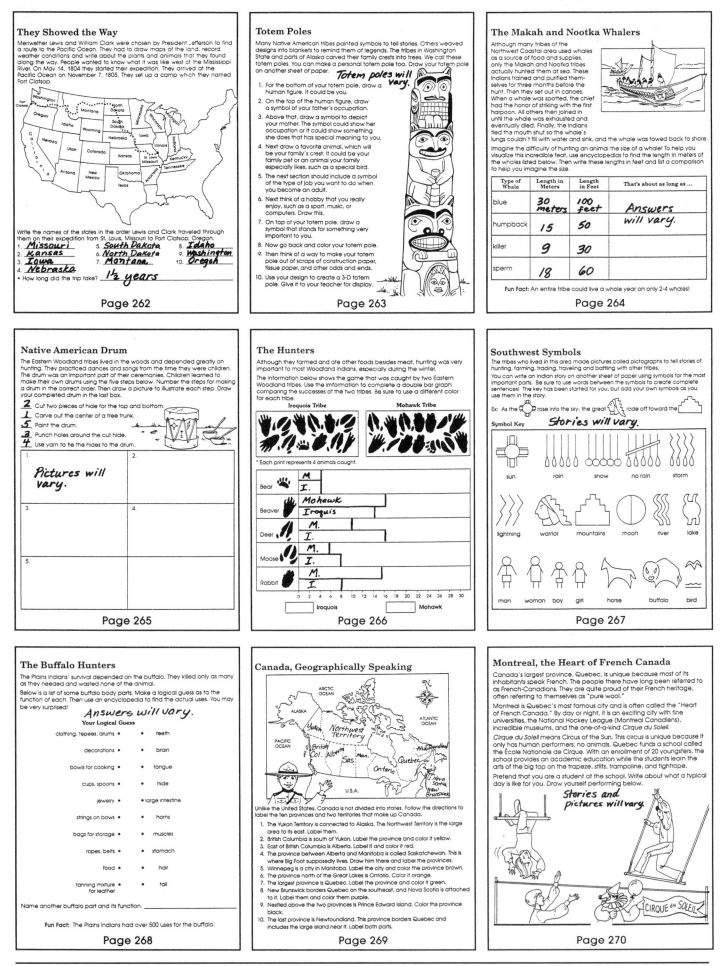

They Showed the Way

Meriwether Lewis and William Clark were chosen by President Jefferson to find a route to the Pacific Ocean. They had to draw maps of the land, record weather conditions and write about the plants and animals that they found along the way. People wanted to know what it was like west of the Mississippi River. On May 14, 1804 they started their expedition. They arrived at the Pacific Ocean on November 7, 1805. They set up a camp which they named Fort Clatsop.

Write the names of the states in the order Lewis and Clark traveled through them on their expedition from St. Louis, Missouri to Fort Clatsop, Oregon.

1. Missouri
2. Kansas
3. Iowa
4. Nebraska
5. South Dakota
6. North Dakota
7. Montana
8. Idaho
9. Washington
10. Oregon

• How long did the trip take? 1½ years

Page 262

Totem Poles

Many Native American tribes painted symbols to tell stories. Others weaved designs into blankets to remind them of legends. The tribes in Washington State and parts of Alaska carved their family crests into trees. We call these totem poles. You can make a personal totem pole too. Draw your totem pole on another sheet of paper.

Totem poles will vary.

1. For the bottom of your totem pole, draw a human figure. It could be you.
2. On the top of the human figure, draw a symbol of your father's occupation.
3. Above that, draw a symbol to depict your mother. The symbol could show her occupation or it could show something she does that has special meaning to you.
4. Next draw a favorite animal, which will be your family's crest. It could be your family pet or an animal your family especially likes, such as a special bird.
5. The next section should include a symbol of the type of job you want to do when you become an adult.
6. Next think of a hobby that you really enjoy, such as a sport, music, or computers. Draw this.
7. On top of your totem pole, draw a symbol that stands for something very important to you.
8. Now go back and color your totem pole.
9. Then think of a way to make your totem pole out of scraps of construction paper, tissue paper, and other odds and ends.
10. Use your design to create a 3-D totem pole. Give it to your teacher for display.

Page 263

The Makah and Nootka Whalers

Although many tribes of the Northwest Coastal area used whales as a source of food and supplies, only the Makah and Nootka tribes actually hunted them at sea. These Indians trained and purified themselves for three months before the hunt. Then they set out in canoes. When a whale was spotted, the chief had the honor of striking with the first harpoon. All others then joined in until the whale was exhausted and eventually died. Finally, the Indians tied the mouth shut so the whale's lungs couldn't fill with water and sink, and the whale was towed back to shore.

Imagine the difficulty of hunting an animal the size of a whale! To help you visualize this incredible feat, use encyclopedias to find the length in meters of the whales listed below. Then write these lengths in feet and list a comparison to help you imagine the size.

Type of Whale	Length in Meters	Length in Feet	That's about as long as ...
blue	30 meters	100 feet	Answers will vary.
humpback	15	50	
killer	9	30	
sperm	18	60	

Fun Fact: An entire tribe could live a whole year on only 2-4 whales!

Page 264

Native American Drum

The Eastern Woodland tribes lived in the woods and depended greatly on hunting. They practiced dances and songs from the time they were children. The drum was an important part of their ceremonies. Children learned to make their own drums using the five steps below. Number the steps for making a drum in the correct order. Then draw a picture to illustrate each step. Draw your completed drum in the last box.

2 Cut two pieces of hide for the top and bottom.
1 Carve out the center of a tree trunk.
5 Paint the drum.
3 Punch holes around the cut hide.
4 Use yarn to tie the hides to the drum.

1. Pictures will vary.	2.
3.	4.
5.	

Page 265

The Hunters

Although they farmed and ate other foods besides meat, hunting was very important to most Woodland Indians, especially during the winter.

The information below shows the game that was caught by two Eastern Woodland tribes. Use the information to complete a double bar graph comparing the successes of the two tribes. Be sure to use a different color for each tribe.

Iroquois Tribe   **Mohawk Tribe**

* Each print represents 4 animals caught.

Bear — M. / I.
Beaver — Mohawk / Iroquois
Deer — M. / I.
Moose — M. / I.
Rabbit — M. / I.

0 2 4 6 8 10 12 14 16 18 20 22 24 26 28 30

☐ Iroquois   ☐ Mohawk

Page 266

Southwest Symbols

The tribes who lived in this area made pictures called pictographs to tell stories of hunting, farming, trading, traveling and battling with other tribes.

You can write an Indian story on another sheet of paper using symbols for the most important details. Be sure to use words between the symbols to create complete sentences! The key has been started for you, but add your own symbols as you use them in the story.

Ex: As the ☼ rose into the sky, the great 🐟 rode off toward the ⛰.

Symbol Key   Stories will vary.

sun   rain   snow   no rain   storm

lightning   warrior   mountains   moon   river   lake

man   woman   boy   girl   horse   buffalo   bird

Page 267

The Buffalo Hunters

The Plains Indians' survival depended on the buffalo. They killed only as many as they needed and wasted none of the animal.

Below is a list of some buffalo body parts. Make a logical guess as to the function of each. Then use an encyclopedia to find the actual uses. You may be very surprised!

Answers will vary.

Your Logical Guess

clothing, tepees, drums • • teeth
decorations • • brain
bowls for cooking • • tongue
cups, spoons • • hide
jewelry • • large intestine
strings on bows • • horns
bags for storage • • muscles
ropes, belts • • stomach
food • • hair
tanning mixture for leather • • tail

Name another buffalo part and its function. _____

Fun Fact: The Plains Indians had over 500 uses for the buffalo.

Page 268

Canada, Geographically Speaking

Unlike the United States, Canada is not divided into states. Follow the directions below to label the ten provinces and two territories that make up Canada.

1. The Yukon Territory is connected to Alaska. The Northwest Territory is the large area to its east. Label them.
2. British Columbia is south of Yukon. Label the province and color it yellow.
3. East of British Columbia is Alberta. Label it and color it red.
4. The province between Alberta and Manitoba is called Saskatchewan. This is where Big Foot supposedly lives. Draw him there and label the provinces.
5. Winnepeg is a city in Manitoba. Label the city and color the province brown.
6. The province north of the Great Lakes is Ontario. Color it orange.
7. The largest province is Quebec. Label the province and color it green.
8. New Brunswick borders Quebec on the southeast, and Nova Scotia is attached to it. Label them and color them purple.
9. Nestled above the two provinces is Prince Edward Island. Color this province black.
10. The last province is Newfoundland. This province borders Quebec and includes the large island near it. Label both parts.

Page 269

Montreal, the Heart of French Canada

Canada's largest province, Quebec, is unique because most of its inhabitants speak French. The people there have long been referred to as French-Canadians. They are quite proud of their French heritage, often referring to themselves as "pure wool."

Montreal is Quebec's most famous city and is often called the "Heart of French Canada." By day or night, it is an exciting city with fine universities, the National Hockey League (Montreal Canadiens), incredible museums, and the one-of-a-kind *Cirque du Soleil.*

Cirque du Soleil means Circus of the Sun. This circus is unique because it only has human performers; no animals. Quebec funds a school called the École Nationale de Cirque. With an enrollment of 20 youngsters, the school provides an academic education while the students learn the arts of the big top on the trapeze, stilts, trampoline, and tightrope.

Pretend that you are a student at the school. Write about what a typical day is like for you. Draw yourself performing below.

Stories and pictures will vary.

CIRQUE du SOLEIL

Page 270

Bolivia

Bolivia is located in South America and is about twice the size of Texas. Children here go to school from 9 a.m. to 4 p.m. They have a long vacation in June and July, but for them this is winter break. They have another long break from October to December. This is summer in Bolivia!

Think about yourself during summer and winter vacations. Then, follow these directions:

1. Write your name in the chart below.
2. Draw yourself during summer break in the first box.
3. Draw something Porfirio might do in July.
4. Draw yourself during winter break in the third box.
5. Draw something Porfirio might do in December.
6. Color each picture.

What do you notice about the pictures? Why are the seasons opposite? Write your answers on the back.

	(your name)	Porfirio (Bolivian boy)
July	1. *Pictures will vary.*	2.
December	3.	4.

Page 271

Animals in the Rainforest

Pictures will vary

Brazil is located in South America. Many of its people are very poor. This country is partially covered by rainforests in which thousands of different plants and animals live. However, many of these animals could become extinct because of the destruction of the rainforests for their lumber. Follow the directions below to discover some of the animals that live in the rainforest.

1. Draw a jungle pig (called a tapir) hiding in the leaves.
2. Draw a jaguar lying on the ground.
3. Draw a parrot in the trees.
4. Draw an anaconda snake on the riverbank.
5. Draw spiders on the trees and on the ground.
6. Draw fish in the river.
7. Draw an alligator in the river.
8. Draw butterflies in the air.
9. Draw an Indian in the trees.
10. Color your rainforest and its animals.

Page 272

Chewing Pleasures

Chewing gum is probably something you enjoy. Did you ever wonder about its history? Chewing gummy substances dates back hundreds of years. Early Greeks and American Indians chewed resin from the bark of trees. In the mid-1800s, sweetened paraffin wax came to be favored over resin.

Today gum has an "international flavor." Gum base, the chewy ingredient, comes mainly from the Amazon Valley in Brazil. Natural resins, which make the gum feel better when you chew it, come from southern United States.

Exact recipes are top-secret information. Manufacturers are continually improving their products. They also have to design appealing packages so you will want to buy them! That is why companies put baseball cards in some of the packages.

Some people have been against chewing gum. They thought it kept students from concentrating in school. Others thought that if you swallowed gum it would clog up your stomach. Research says that chewing gum actually reduces tension and improves concentration. Gum is a low-calorie snack and it helps prevent tooth decay and promotes sweeter breath.

Interview people to find out why they chew gum. Each space equals one person's answer.

Graphs will vary.

Why We Chew Gum	1	2	3	4	5	6	7	8	9	10
Enjoyment										
Tastes Good										
Helps Concentration										
Freshens Breath										
Cleans Teeth										

Compile your information and make a group graph.

Page 273

Central America

The land connecting North and South America is called Central America. This is where Costa Rica and six other countries are located. Follow the directions below to label the countries and some of their products.

1. Draw a cotton plant in Belize. It's the northernmost country.
2. Draw a cotton plant in Guatemala. It borders Belize.
3. El Salvador grows many coffee beans. Draw a cup of coffee in this country that is southeast of Guatemala.
4. Silver is mined in Honduras, north of El Salvador. Color this country silver.
5. Nicaragua contains gold mines. Color this country bordering Honduras gold.
6. Children from Costa Rica love the bananas grown there. Draw a banana.
7. Panama's fishermen catch many shrimp. Draw some shrimp in this southernmost country. If you look closely, you will see a break in the land through which ships can pass. This is the Panama Canal. Label it also.

The U.S. helped clear the land that was once where the canal is now. Why do you think they wanted to help? Write your answer on the back of this paper.

Page 274

The Emerald Isle

Ireland is often called the Emerald Isle because of its rolling green farmland and countryside. This is why we wear green on St. Patrick's Day, an Irish holiday. Sean and Kathleen want you to follow the directions below to make today a special Irish day.

Answers will vary.

1. Write the name of three crayons that have a green tint. _____
2. Name two people wearing green today. _____
3. Write three words you can spell with the letters in IRELAND. _____
4. Write the title of a book that has the word *green* in it. _____
5. Name four green animals. _____
6. What do scientists call trees that stay green all winter? **evergreen**
7. List two things in your classroom that are entirely green. _____
8. Name your favorite green food. _____
9. Draw a leprechaun on the back of your paper.
10. Use only green crayons for the rest of the school day.

Page 275

Number, Please!

The population of Israel is a mixture of people from over 70 countries. Use the telephone puzzle below to dial and meet a few!

5397 = **Jews** —the original people of Israel

1. 722727 = **Sabras** —the Jews born in Israel
2. 6875467 = **Muslims** —followers of Islam, the religion of 80% of the country's Arabs
3. 72537846426 27227 = **Palestinian Arabs** —citizens of Israel who call themselves Israeli Arabs today
4. 378737 = **Druses** —an Arabic-speaking religious group
5. 4664472687 = **immigrants** —Jewish people from other countries making a new home in Israel

Now, write your country of origin using the same code. _____

Page 276

A Journey to Japan

Follow the directions to complete the map of Japan, Mieko's homeland.

1. Add the eight directional letters to the compass rose.
2. Label the islands in capital letters:
   KYUSHU – southernmost
   HOKKAIDO – northernmost
   HONSHU – south of Hokkaido
   SHIKOKU – north of Kyushu
3. Add a red ★ and label the capital city, Tokyo.
4. Draw a mountain at Mount Fuji's location.
5. Label **Nagasaki** by the dot on Kyushu Island.
6. Label the **Sea of Japan** and the **Pacific Ocean**. Add blue waves.
7. Label **Osaka** by the dot on Honshu Island.
8. Outline the islands in these colors:
   Hokkaido – orange
   Honshu – green
   Shikoku – red
   Kyushu – yellow
9. Along the northern edge of the box, label the map JAPAN, using a different color for each letter.
10. Draw the flag of Japan.

Page 277

Written Japanese

When Laura visited a Japanese classroom, she could not read anything that was written. She learned that written Japanese is considered to be one of the most difficult writing systems in the world. It is a combination of Japanese phonetic symbols as well as Chinese characters. Each character is a symbol that stands for a complete word or syllable. However difficult, almost all Japanese people 15 years of age or older can read and write.

Use the following Japanese characters to write a story about a big man. Use the characters in your story whenever possible.

大	人	木	森	山	門
big	man	tree	forest	mountain	gate

The 大 人

Stories will vary.

Page 278

Raising a Family in Kenya

As members of the more progressive Njoroge Tribe, Omar's parents have a dream. They want to see their four children through secondary school. That will require great sacrifice for them as their coffee crop only earned them $120 after expenses last year.

Omar and his family live a very simple life. Omar's father raises coffee plants on their one-acre farm. Omar's mother and father work very hard to earn the money to send Omar and his brother and two sisters to school. It costs $75 a year for primary school for each child. To earn more money, Omar's father works as a stonemason for $5 a day. Omar's mother works at a larger farm for $2 a day.

1. How many days will Omar's father have to work as a stonemason to pay for one year of Omar's primary school? (Hint: Count by 5's.) **15**
2. How many days will Omar's father have to work to pay for the other 3 children's primary school each year? (Hint: Add your answer from #1 three times.) **45**
3. One pair of children's shoes cost $10. How many days will Omar's mother have to work to buy him a pair of shoes? (Hint: Count by 2's.) **5**
4. How many days will Omar's mother have to work to buy the other 3 children new pairs of shoes? (Hint: Add your answer to #3 three times.) **15**
5. How much will it cost to buy shoes for all four children. (Hint: Count by 10's.) **$40**

Page 279

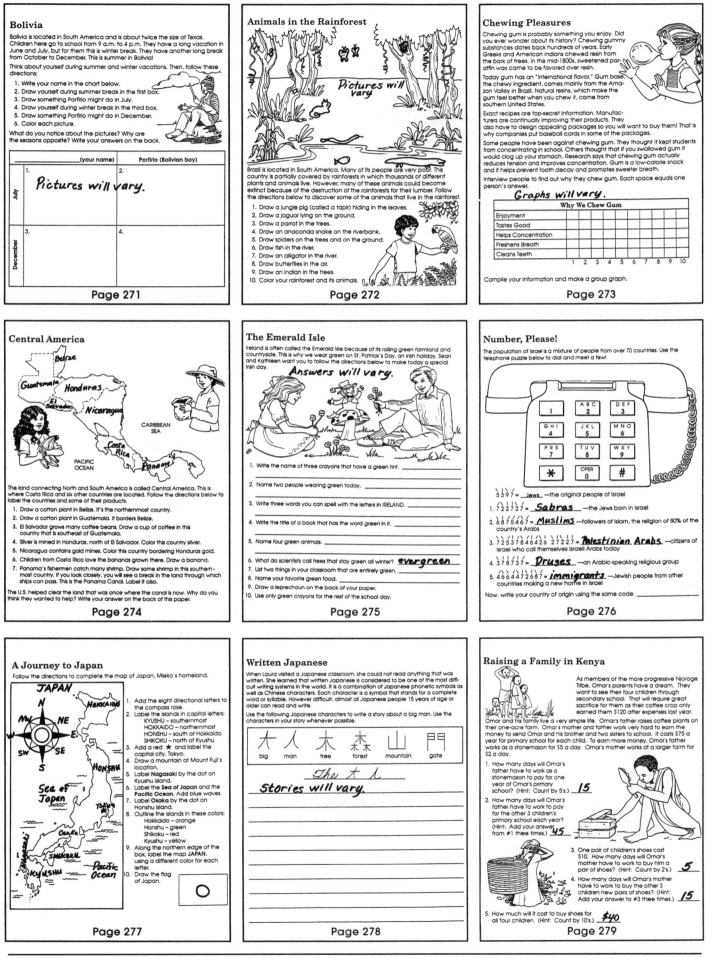

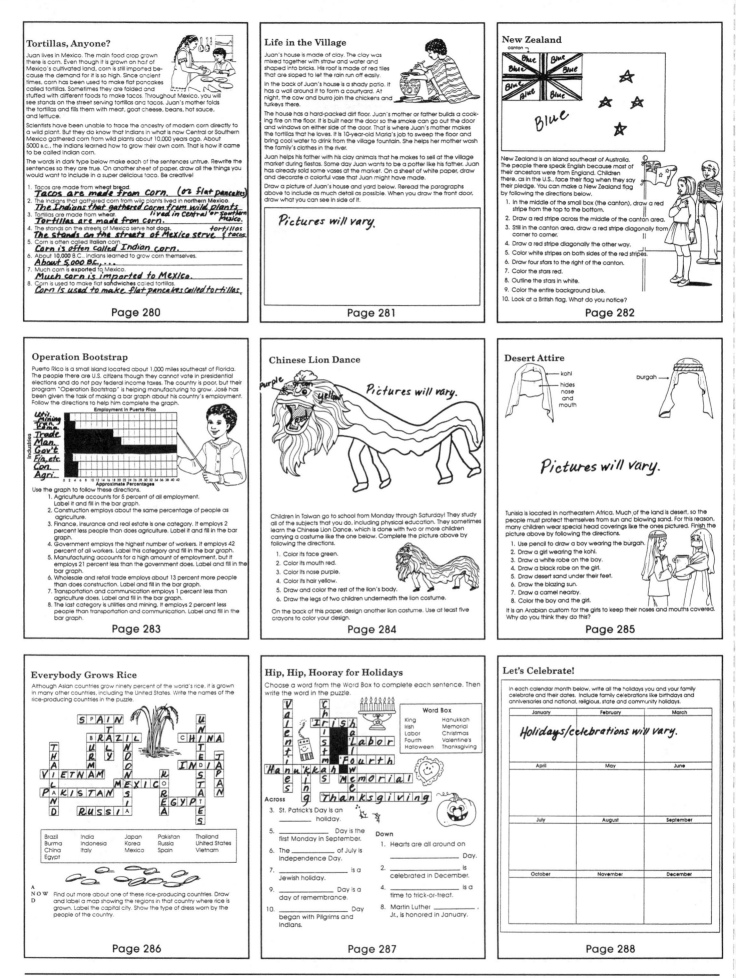

Tortillas, Anyone?

Juan lives in Mexico. The main food crop grown there is corn. Even though it is grown on half of Mexico's cultivated land, corn is still imported because the demand for it is so high. Since ancient times, corn has been used to make flat pancakes called tortillas. Sometimes they are folded and stuffed with different foods to make tacos. Throughout Mexico, you will see stands on the street serving tortillas and tacos. Juan's mother folds the tortillas and fills them with meat, goat cheese, beans, hot sauce, and lettuce.

Scientists have been unable to trace the ancestry of modern corn directly to a wild plant. But they do know that Indians in what is now Central or Southern Mexico gathered corn from wild plants about 10,000 years ago. About 5000 B.C., the Indians learned how to grow their own corn. That is how it came to be called Indian corn.

The words in dark type below make each of the sentences untrue. Rewrite the sentences so they are true. On another sheet of paper, draw all the things you would want to include in a super delicious taco. Be creative!

1. Tacos are made from **wheat bread**.
   Tacos are made from corn. (or flat pancakes)
2. The Indians that gathered corn from wild plants lived in **northern Mexico**.
   The Indians that gathered corn from wild plants lived in Central or southern Mexico.
3. Tortillas are made from **wheat**.
   Tortillas are made from corn.
4. The stands on the streets of Mexico serve **hot dogs**.
   The stands on the streets of Mexico serve tortillas & tacos.
5. Corn is often called **Italian corn**.
   Corn is often called Indian corn.
6. About **10,000 B.C.**, Indians learned to grow corn themselves.
   About 5,000 B.C...
7. Much corn is **exported** to Mexico.
   Much corn is imported to Mexico.
8. Corn is used to make flat **sandwiches** called tortillas.
   Corn is used to make flat pancakes called tortillas.

Page 280

Life in the Village

Juan's house is made of clay. The clay was mixed together with straw and water and shaped into bricks. His roof is made of red tiles that are sloped to let the rain run off easily.

In the back of Juan's house is a shady patio. It has a wall around it to form a courtyard. At night, the cow and burro join the chickens and turkeys there.

The house has a hard-packed dirt floor. Juan's mother or father builds a cooking fire on the floor. It is built near the door so the smoke can go out the door and windows on either side of the door. That is where Juan's mother makes the tortillas that he loves. It is 10-year-old Maria's job to sweep the floor and bring cool water to drink from the village fountain. She helps her mother wash the family's clothes in the river.

Juan helps his father with his clay animals that he makes to sell at the village market during fiestas. Some day Juan wants to be a potter like his father. Juan has already sold some vases at the market. On a sheet of white paper, draw and decorate a colorful vase that Juan might have made.

Draw a picture of Juan's house and yard below. Reread the paragraphs above to include as much detail as possible. When you draw the front door, draw what you can see in side of it.

Pictures will vary.

Page 281

New Zealand

Blue

New Zealand is an island southeast of Australia. The people there speak English because most of their ancestors were from England. Children there, as in the U.S., face the flag when they say their pledge. You can make a New Zealand flag by following the directions below.

1. In the middle of the small box (the canton), draw a red stripe from the top to the bottom.
2. Draw a red stripe across the middle of the canton area.
3. Still in the canton area, draw a red stripe diagonally from corner to corner.
4. Draw a red stripe diagonally the other way.
5. Color white stripes on both sides of the red stripes.
6. Draw four stars to the right of the canton.
7. Color the stars red.
8. Outline the stars in white.
9. Color the entire background blue.
10. Look at a British flag. What do you notice?

Page 282

Operation Bootstrap

Puerto Rico is a small island located about 1,000 miles southeast of Florida. The people there are U.S. citizens though they cannot vote in presidential elections and do not pay federal income taxes. The country is poor, but their program "Operation Bootstrap" is helping their country to grow. José has been given the task of making a bar graph about his country's employment. Follow the directions to help him complete the graph.

Employment in Puerto Rico

Use the graph to follow these directions.

1. Agriculture accounts for 5 percent of all employment. Label it and fill in the bar graph.
2. Construction employs about the same percentage of people as agriculture.
3. Finance, insurance and real estate is one category. It employs 2 percent less people than does agriculture. Label it and fill in the bar graph.
4. Government employs the highest number of workers. It employs 42 percent of all workers. Label this category and fill in the bar graph.
5. Manufacturing accounts for a high amount of employment, but it employs 21 percent less than the government does. Label and fill in the bar graph.
6. Wholesale and retail trade employs about 13 percent more people than does construction. Label and fill in the bar graph.
7. Transportation and communication employs 1 percent less than agriculture does. Label and fill in the bar graph.
8. The last category is utilities and mining. It employs 2 percent less people than transportation and communication. Label and fill in the bar graph.

Page 283

Chinese Lion Dance

Pictures will vary.

Children in Taiwan go to school from Monday through Saturday! They study all of the subjects that you do, including physical education. They sometimes learn the Chinese Lion Dance, which is done with two or more children carrying a costume like the one below. Complete the picture above by following the directions.

1. Color its face green.
2. Color its mouth red.
3. Color its nose purple.
4. Color its hair yellow.
5. Draw and color the rest of the lion's body.
6. Draw the legs of two children underneath the lion costume.

On the back of this paper, design another lion costume. Use at least five crayons to color your design.

Page 284

Desert Attire

kohl
hides nose and mouth

burgah

Pictures will vary.

Tunisia is located in northeastern Africa. Much of the land is desert, so the people must protect themselves from sun and blowing sand. For this reason, many children wear special head coverings like the ones pictured. Finish the picture above by following the directions.

1. Use pencil to draw a boy wearing the burgah.
2. Draw a girl wearing the kohl.
3. Draw a white robe on the boy.
4. Draw a black robe on the girl.
5. Draw desert sand under their feet.
6. Draw the blazing sun.
7. Draw a camel nearby.
8. Color the boy and the girl.

It is an Arabian custom for the girls to keep their noses and mouths covered. Why do you think they do this?

Page 285

Everybody Grows Rice

Although Asian countries grow ninety percent of the world's rice, it is grown in many other countries, including the United States. Write the names of the rice-producing countries in the puzzle.

SPAIN · BRAZIL · CHINA · UNITED STATES · THAILAND · BURMA · ITALY · INDIA · JAPAN · VIETNAM · MEXICO · KOREA · PAKISTAN · RUSSIA · EGYPT · INDONESIA

Brazil	India	Japan	Pakistan	Thailand
Burma	Indonesia	Korea	Russia	United States
China	Italy	Mexico	Spain	Vietnam
Egypt				

A NOW AND: Find out more about one of these rice-producing countries. Draw and label a map showing the regions in that country where rice is grown. Label the capital city. Show the type of dress worn by the people of the country.

Page 286

Hip, Hip, Hooray for Holidays

Choose a word from the Word Box to complete each sentence. Then write the word in the puzzle.

Word Box
King · Hanukkah · Irish · Memorial · Labor · Christmas · Fourth · Valentine's · Halloween · Thanksgiving

Valentines · Irish · Christmas · Labor · Fourth · Hanukkah · King · Memorial · Thanksgiving

Across
3. St. Patrick's Day is an _____ holiday.
5. _____ Day is the first Monday in September.
6. The _____ of July is Independence Day.
7. _____ is a Jewish holiday.
9. _____ Day is a day of remembrance.
10. _____ Day began with Pilgrims and Indians.

Down
1. Hearts are all around on _____ Day.
2. _____ is celebrated in December.
4. _____ is a time to trick-or-treat.
8. Martin Luther _____ Jr., is honored in January.

Page 287

Let's Celebrate!

In each calendar month below, write all the holidays you and your family celebrate and their dates. Include family celebrations like birthdays and anniversaries and national, religious, state and community holidays.

January	February	March
April	May	June
July	August	September
October	November	December

Holidays/celebrations will vary.

Page 288

Name _____

You're Invited!

Imagine that you are planning a slumber party. Think of ten friends you would like to invite and write their names on the invitations below. Then color the invitations.

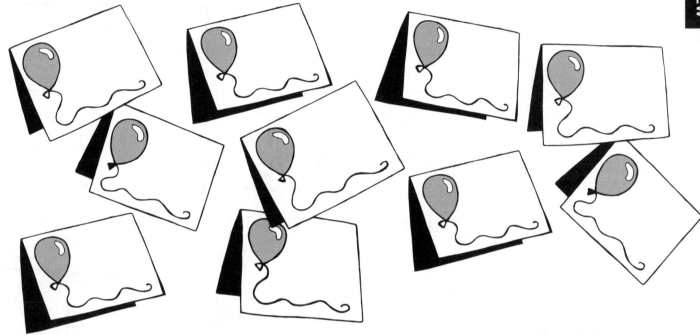

Now, alphabetize the names according to the first or last name.

_____

_____

_____

_____

_____

_____

_____

_____

_____

_____

Name _____

Seed Syllables

Say each word aloud. How many syllables do you hear? Write each word on the seed packet with the correct number.

carrot   parsley   lettuce

tomato   pumpkin   peas

zucchini   cucumber   squash

dill   celery   parsnips

beets   pepper   broccoli

Name _____

Crazy Compounds

Compound words are created by putting two smaller words together. Make compound words by drawing a line from each word in the left-hand columns to a word in the right-hand columns.

black	shake
eye	pipe
type	top
class	writer
milk	quake
bag	mate
north	brow
earth	way
work	knob
drive	west
door	shop

sun	stalk
button	shine
grape	keeper
corn	hole
sand	vine
stage	box
zoo	coach
pin	lace
butter	cushion
bird	house
shoe	fly

Daily Learning Drills Grade 3

Picnic Puzzlers

Name _____

Fill in each basket by writing the words from the Word Bank with the same vowel sound as the word on the basket. Remember, vowel combinations don't have to look the same to sound the same!

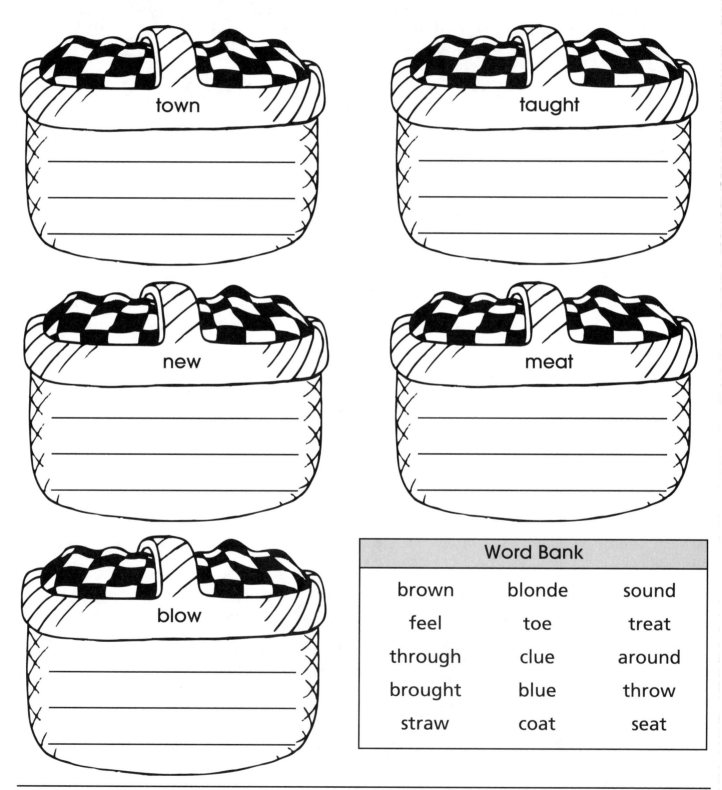

town

taught

new

meat

blow

Word Bank

brown	blonde	sound
feel	toe	treat
through	clue	around
brought	blue	throw
straw	coat	seat

Name _____

Silent Search

Some words contain letters that are "silent." These words can be tricky to spell. Watch carefully for the silent letters *e, kn, ght,* and *wr* in this story. Circle the words that have these silent letter combinations.

It was Saturday night! Jamie was having some friends over to spend the night. He had written letters inviting them to come. Everyone said they would be there.

There was a knock on the door! Jamie ran to answer it. All three friends were waiting on the porch. "Come in!" shouted Jamie. Simon, Ahman, and Lei came in carrying their sleeping bags. They put their things in Jamie's room.

Jamie's mother came in with cake and fruit juice. She cut the cake with a knife and served the boys a snack. She wrapped the extra pieces in plastic wrap for later. She knew they would be hungry again.

The boys watched videos and played board games. Then they ate the rest of their snacks. Finally, they turned out the lights and told scary stories to frighten each other. What a fun night!

Name _____

Name it!

A **proper noun** names a special person, animal, place, or thing. It begins with a capital letter. Read the common noun and proper noun in each brick. Write another proper noun to match.

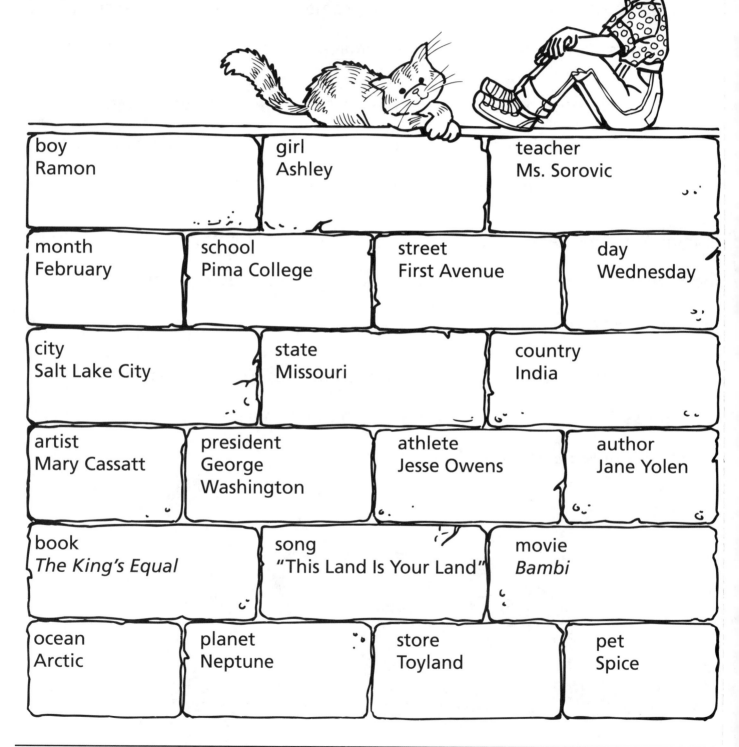

boy Ramon	girl Ashley	teacher Ms. Sorovic

month February	school Pima College	street First Avenue	day Wednesday

city Salt Lake City	state Missouri	country India

artist Mary Cassatt	president George Washington	athlete Jesse Owens	author Jane Yolen

book *The King's Equal*	song "This Land Is Your Land"	movie *Bambi*

ocean Arctic	planet Neptune	store Toyland	pet Spice

Name _____

Mouse-Mice

A **singular noun** names one person, animal, place, or thing.
A **plural noun** names more than one.

Most nouns are made plural by adding *s*.
    Examples: house-houses, shark-sharks

Some nouns have irregular, or strange, plural forms.
You need to memorize them.
    Examples: elf-elves, fish-fish

Read each plural noun. Write the matching
singular noun.

1. _____ mice
2. _____ lice
3. _____ men
4. _____ women
5. _____ children
6. _____ wolves
7. _____ halves
8. _____ shelves
9. _____ leaves
10. _____ teeth
11. _____ feet
12. _____ geese

13. _____ octopi
14. _____ cacti
15. _____ fungi
16. _____ potatoes
17. _____ tomatoes
18. _____ heroes
19. _____ echoes
20. _____ dice
21. _____ oxen
22. _____ deer
23. _____ moose
24. _____ sheep

Daily Learning Drills Grade 3

Name _____

Find the Verbs

A **verb** is an action word. *Sing*, *race*, and *understand* are verbs.

Read these sentences. Underline the verbs.
Some sentences have more than one.
Then make the verbs fit in the puzzle.
Note: There will be one extra word space in the puzzle.
     Write your own verb in it.

1. My mom and I <u>drive</u> to the toy store to <u>buy</u> a bike.

2. We look at all the mountain bikes.

3. I find one that I like.

4. My mom tells me to try it.

5. I worry about the narrow store aisles.

6. I start to ride slowly.

7. My bike wobbles.

8. Suddenly I crash into some toys.

9. We both laugh.

10. My mom helps me clean up the toys.

11. Then we take my new bike home.

Name _____

Pronoun Match-up

A **pronoun** is a word that takes the place of a noun.

Draw lines to match each noun to the pronoun that can take its place. On the blank lines, write your name.

A **subject pronoun** takes the place of a noun in the subject part of a sentence.

Tamara can ride a unicycle.
She can ride a unicycle.

Noun	Subject Pronoun
Greg and Sarah •	• He
Melinda •	• They
My cousin and I •	• I
Mr. Weisberg •	• She
The towering pine tree •	• We
_____ •	• It

Noun	Object Pronoun
my family and I •	• it
the bus •	• her
Valerie •	• us
the flowers •	• me
Peter •	• them
_____ •	• him

An **object pronoun** takes the place of a noun that follows a verb or a word such as *to, from, of*, or *by*.

Please give this note to Mike.
Please give this note to him.

A **possessive pronoun** takes the place of a possessive noun.

Dan and Claire's grandpa is visiting.
Their grandpa is visiting.

Possessive Noun	Possessive Pronoun
the dinosaur's •	• her
John's •	• his
Aunt Nancy's •	• its
the students' •	• our
my friends' and my •	• their

Name _____

Describe it!

An **adjective** is a word that describes a noun (person, animal, place, or thing). *Blue, delicious, fuzzy,* and *smart* are adjectives.

Look at these nouns. Write an adjective to describe each.
Finish drawing the picture and color it.
You may use the cartoon faces as a guide.

happy

sad

angry

worried

surprised

silly

tired

Name _____

Punctuation Puzzler

Punctuation and capitalization are important to understanding what you read. Rewrite these sentences, putting in the correct capitalization and punctuation.

1. hurry and deliver this pizza

   _____

2. i have collected 1324 stamps

   _____

3. how long should i walk your dog mr. hill

   _____

4. you are doing a great job he said

   _____

5. watch out don't crash your model plane she cried

   _____

6. i went to the store to buy some comics

   _____

7. boating is julies favorite hobby

   _____

8. where can you buy the newest copy of zoo magazine

   _____

9. how many stitches should I knit to complete that row

   _____

10. i need to weed the tulips today said mother

    _____

Name _____

Science Fair

Proofread this story Sean wrote. Check off each step as you do it.

☐ Underline three times the 6 letters that should be capitalized. (e̲̲̲)
☐ Write the 4 missing periods. (.)
☐ Write the 2 missing question marks. (?)
☐ Write the 2 missing sets of quotation marks. (" ")

"Hey, Mom!" I called out. Guess what I am going to do for the Science Fair.

"You're not doing a vinegar and baking soda experiment, are you   " she asked.

I go to Thomas edison Elementary School. Every January my school holds its Science Fair. And every january I do a vinegar and baking soda experiment.

I used to find my experiments in science books   In first grade, I made a balloon inflate. In second grade, i created an erupting volcano!

this year I tried my own experiment. I read that when vinegar and baking soda react, they produce heat along with carbon dioxide   So I poured vinegar in a jar and measured its temperature. I predicted that when I added the baking soda, the new liquid mixture would be hotter   Can you guess what happened   The temperature was about 15° cooler!

that's not right! I yelled. "It's supposed to be hotter."

Then I thought about it   The vinegar and baking soda must give off their own heat to make heat. maybe that is why they ended up colder.

Name _____

American Tall Tales

A **comma** (,) tells the reader to pause.

Use a comma to separate words in a series of three or more items.
Paul Bunyan, John Henry, and Slue-Foot Sue are tall-tale characters.
Tall-tale characters are larger, mightier, smarter, or bolder than regular folks.

Read these sentences. Write the missing commas.

1. Paul Bunyan was the biggest strongest and friendliest lumberjack ever.

2. Babe the Blue Ox was shaking shivering and shuddering when Paul Bunyan found him in a blue snowstorm.

3. Johnny Appleseed wore a tin pot on his head a sack for a shirt and no shoes on his feet.

4. Pennsylvania Ohio and Indiana are filled with the apple trees he planted.

5. John Henry was a strong brawny and muscular baby who was born with a hammer in his hand.

6. Stormalong could steer his boat through the wind rain or waves of any storm.

7. Bears cougars and wolves lived in the Tennessee woods with Davy Crockett.

8. Sally Ann Whirlwind could out-run out-swim and out-wrestle any critter when she was just a little girl.

9. Pecos Bill his wife Slue-Foot Sue and his horse Widow-Maker lived in the Southwest.

10. Pecos Bill picked up a rattlesnake tied it in a loop and used it for a lasso.

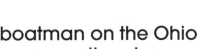

11. Mike Fink was the best keelboatman on the Ohio the Mississippi the Missouri   or any other river.

Name _____

What Big Teeth You Have!

Use **quotation marks** (" ") to show the exact words a speaker says.
"Tina," called Brandon, *"guess which animal uses its teeth to hold onto its mon*
"A bird?" guessed Tina.

Read this conversation.
Write quotation marks around the exact words being said.

1. Jose chimed in, Birds don't have teeth.

2. Oh, yeah, said Tina. I forgot.

3. What book are you reading? asked Michelle.

4. *What Big Teeth You Have!* answered Brandon.

5. Michelle scowled. I don't have big teeth!

6. No, laughed Brandon. That's the title of the book.

7. Oh! said Michelle. I was afraid you were being rude.

8. So, asked Tina, which animal uses its teeth to hold onto its mom?

9. A flying fox, replied Brandon.

10. Birds don't have teeth and foxes don't fly, said Jose.

11. Brandon responded, A flying fox is a type of bat.

12. Hmm, said Jose, I never knew that.

13. Which animal has the most teeth? asked Tina.

14. I'm not sure, answered Brandon. It says a tiger
    shark may use up 12,000 teeth in five years.

15. Wow! exclaimed Tina, Jose, and Michelle in unison.

Name _____

Up, Up, and Away!

Look at the words on the kite tails. Choose a synonym for each word from the Word Bank and write it on the correct tail piece. Can you think of others?

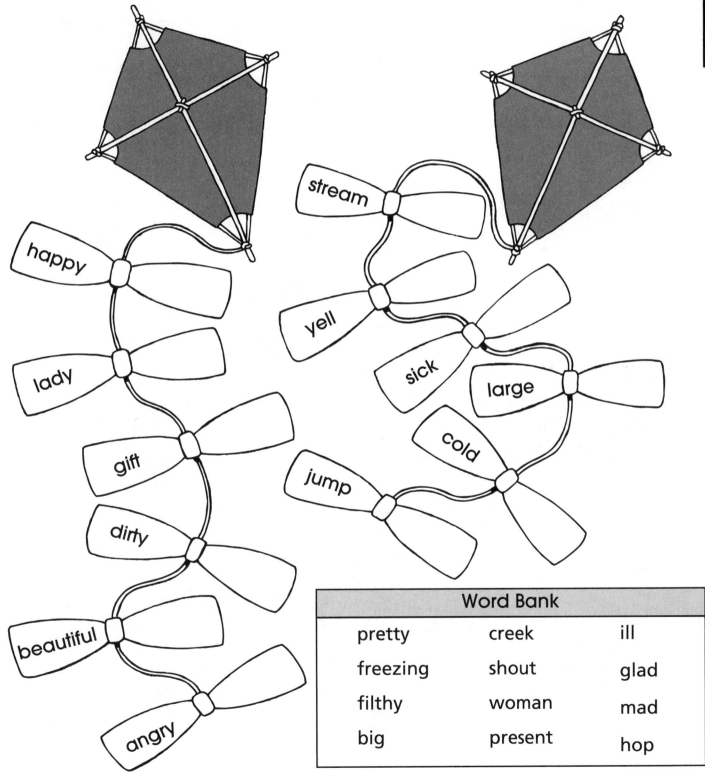

happy

lady

gift

dirty

beautiful

angry

stream

yell

sick

large

cold

jump

Word Bank		
pretty	creek	ill
freezing	shout	glad
filthy	woman	mad
big	present	hop

Daily Learning Drills Grade 3

Name _____

Here Come the "Ant"onyms!

Antonyms are words with opposite meanings, for example, *hot* and *cold*.
Write each word from the Word Bank on the correct "antonym ant."

Word Bank					
careful	save	sour	fat	dirty	pretty
cry	far	poor	under	winter	low

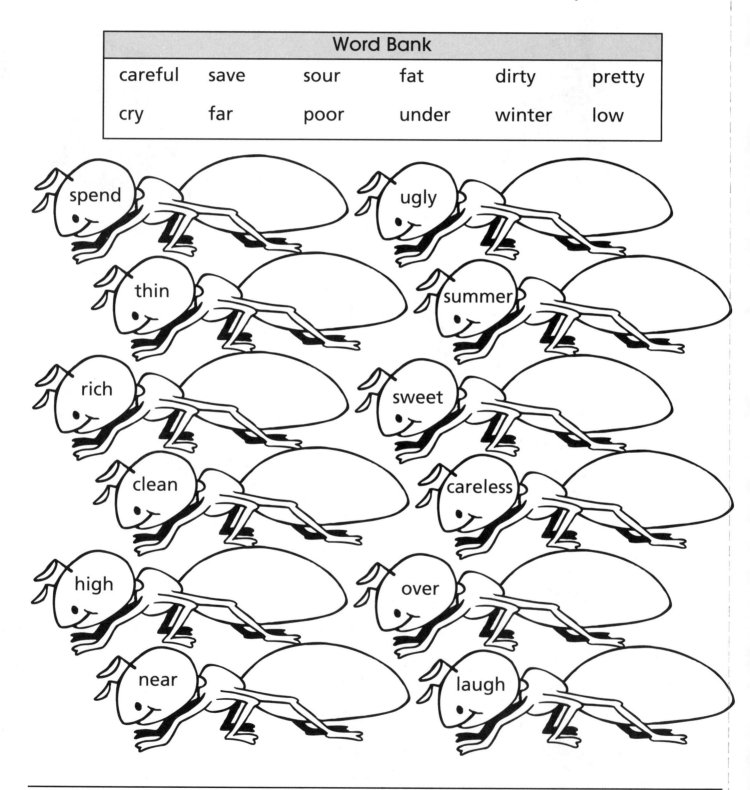

Name _____

Homophone Match–up

Homophones are words that sound alike but have different spellings and meanings. They are also called **homonyms**.

Draw lines to match each word to its correct meaning.

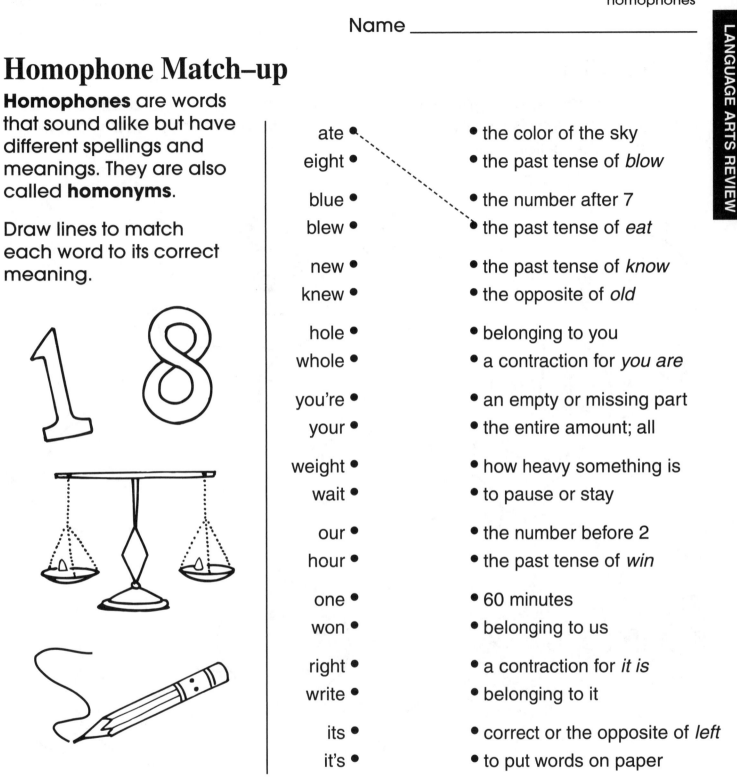

ate •	• the color of the sky
eight •	• the past tense of *blow*
blue •	• the number after 7
blew •	• the past tense of *eat*
new •	• the past tense of *know*
knew •	• the opposite of *old*
hole •	• belonging to you
whole •	• a contraction for *you are*
you're •	• an empty or missing part
your •	• the entire amount; all
weight •	• how heavy something is
wait •	• to pause or stay
our •	• the number before 2
hour •	• the past tense of *win*
one •	• 60 minutes
won •	• belonging to us
right •	• a contraction for *it is*
write •	• belonging to it
its •	• correct or the opposite of *left*
it's •	• to put words on paper

Think of another homophone pair. Write each word and its meaning.

_____

_____

Daily Learning Drills Grade 3

Name _____

Caterpillar Crawl

While camping you might see some interesting insects! Add prefixes and suffixes to the words below to make new words. Write each new word in a section of the caterpillar. The first one is started for you.

Name _____

What's the Answer?

A **contraction** is a shortened form of two or more words.
An **apostrophe** (') takes the place of the missing letters.

Examples: *it is → it's*   *of the clock → o'clock*   *he would → he'd*

Read these riddles and answers. Underline the contraction in each line.
Write its missing apostrophe where it belongs.
Then write the two words that make up the contraction.

Riddles

1. Whats the difference between a dog and a flea? _____

2. Why wont anyone play cards with this cat? _____

3. Why isnt the mayonnaise ever ready? _____

4. Why dont sea gulls fly over bays? _____

5. Whos smarter—a reptile or a fish? _____

6. Why doesnt a pro hockey player ever tell jokes? _____

Answers

1. A dog can have fleas, but a flea cant have dogs! _____

2. Because shes a cheetah! _____

3. Because its always dressing! _____

4. Because then theyd be bagels! _____

5. Fish, because theyre always in schools! _____

6. Hes worried the ice might crack up. _____

Write a riddle you know. Make it have a contraction in the question or the answer.

_____

_____

Name _____

A Sparkler Story

Read the story and then answer the questions below.

Carl was so excited! His cousins were coming to the annual Fourth of July barbeque. He hadn't seen them in over a year!

Carl's father bought ten boxes of sparklers. Each box cost $1.15. Then he went to the market and bought hot dogs, buns, chips, watermelon, and corn on the cob.

Pretty soon Carl's cousins arrived, and they all ran outside to play. Everyone had a wonderful time. But Carl couldn't wait for the fireworks. He sneaked around the side of the house and opened a box of sparklers. He lit one and it sparkled and crackled in his hand. As he waved it in the air, he noticed a tiny being sitting on the bush. Carl couldn't believe his eyes, so he blew out the sparkler to get a better look. But the being disappeared! Carl decided it must have been his imagination, so he lit another sparkler. As soon as the sparkler crackled to life, the being appeared again—this time on Carl's shoulder!

1. How long had it been since Carl had seen his cousins?

_____

2. How much did Carl's father spend on sparklers? _____

3. What food did Carl's father buy for the barbeque?

_____

4. Why did Carl go around the side of the house?

_____

On another sheet of paper, write about what happened next. Who was this tiny being? Did Carl tell his cousins about it? Finish the story.

Name _____

Build a Castle

Draw a castle by following the directions below.

The castle of the Third Count of Cracklewoods is located in the center of an oval island. The main part of the castle is a cube-shaped building with an arched door in the front. On either side of the door is a pentagon-shaped window. A rectangular drawbridge is lowered out from the door to let in visitors. On the left of the main building is the Tower of Joy. It is a tall cylinder topped with a cone. There are four triangle windows on the tower, facing out. On the right of the main building is the Tower of Triumph. This tower is shaped like a rectangular solid topped with a pyramid. It is the Knight's room, the Count's son. This tower has three round windows facing out. Two triangular flags fly from the top of this tower whenever the knight is home. That's when the castle is filled with happiness, and everyone dances and sings!

Name _____

A Goat Dairy Farm

A **sentence** is a group of words that tells a complete thought.
The words in a sentence are in an order that makes sense.
A sentence begins with a capital letter and ends with
a period (.), question mark (?), or exclamation mark (!).

Write the words in the correct order to make sentences.

1. a   class   field   on   Our   trip.   went

_____

2. a   dairy   farm.   visited   We

_____

3. goats   milk   there.   They

_____

4. cheese.   is   make   milk   The   to   used

_____

5. cheese   crackers.   on   some   tasted   We

_____

6. a   baby   each   goat.   got   hold   Then   to   we

_____

_____

7. days   goats   old!   only   The   tiny   two   were

_____

_____

Name _____

Who? What? Where? When?

Write *A* before the phrase if it tells *who*.
Write *B* before the phrase if it tells *what*.
Write *C* before the phrase if it tells *where*.
Write *D* before the phrase if it tells *when*.

1. _____ in the garden

2. _____ before the sun came up

3. _____ the farmer in his overalls

4. _____ the rain came down hard

5. _____ weeds sprouted

6. _____ early in the summer

7. _____ a hard-working gardener

8. _____ seven rows of peas

9. _____ near the cornfield

10. _____ a scraggly scarecrow

11. _____ after the snow arrived

12. _____ tall rows of beautiful flowers

13. _____ out in the backyard

14. _____ the boys and girls

15. _____ the carrots

16. _____ in the afternoon

17. _____ the hungry bunny

18. _____ over the fence

19. _____ the broken fence

20. _____ the rusted hoe

21. _____ before the frost

22. _____ among the carrots

Name _____

Missing Object

What does the magician
need? To find out, color the
squares with answers that
are products of 5. Write the
name of the picture you
color in the blank.

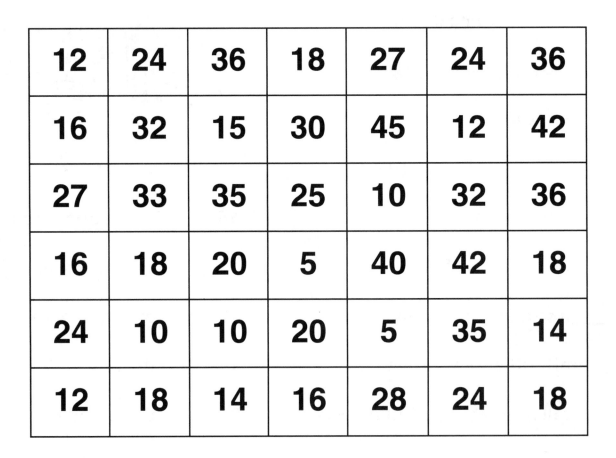

12	24	36	18	27	24	36
16	32	15	30	45	12	42
27	33	35	25	10	32	36
16	18	20	5	40	42	18
24	10	10	20	5	35	14
12	18	14	16	28	24	18

The magician needs his _____.

Name _____

Wall of Numbers

Write the numeral that matches the number words on each brick. Then color the bricks following the Color Key.

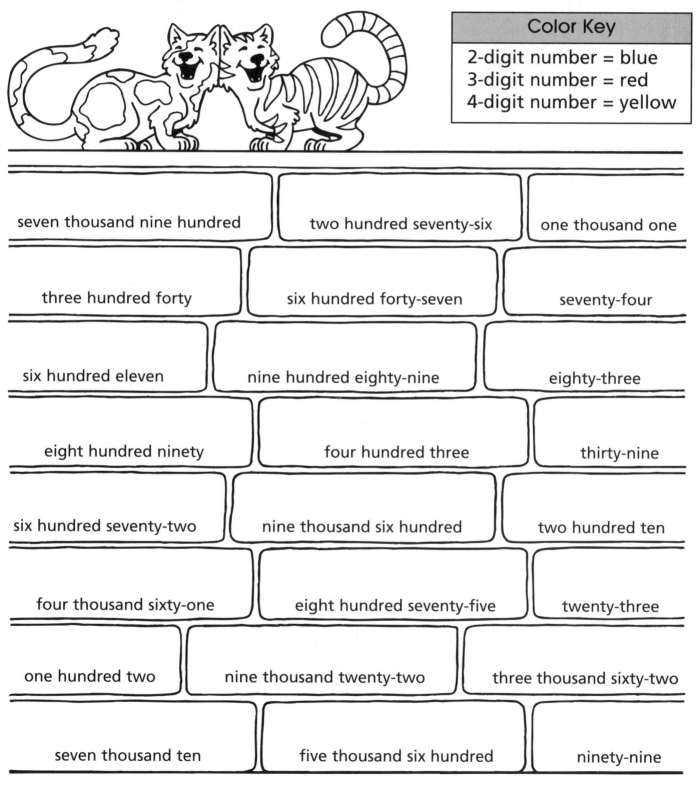

**Color Key**

2-digit number = blue
3-digit number = red
4-digit number = yellow

seven thousand nine hundred

two hundred seventy-six

one thousand one

three hundred forty

six hundred forty-seven

seventy-four

six hundred eleven

nine hundred eighty-nine

eighty-three

eight hundred ninety

four hundred three

thirty-nine

six hundred seventy-two

nine thousand six hundred

two hundred ten

four thousand sixty-one

eight hundred seventy-five

twenty-three

one hundred two

nine thousand twenty-two

three thousand sixty-two

seven thousand ten

five thousand six hundred

ninety-nine

nullMATH REVIEW

Daily Learning Drills Grade 3

Name _____

Missing Numbers

Find the missing number for each problem.

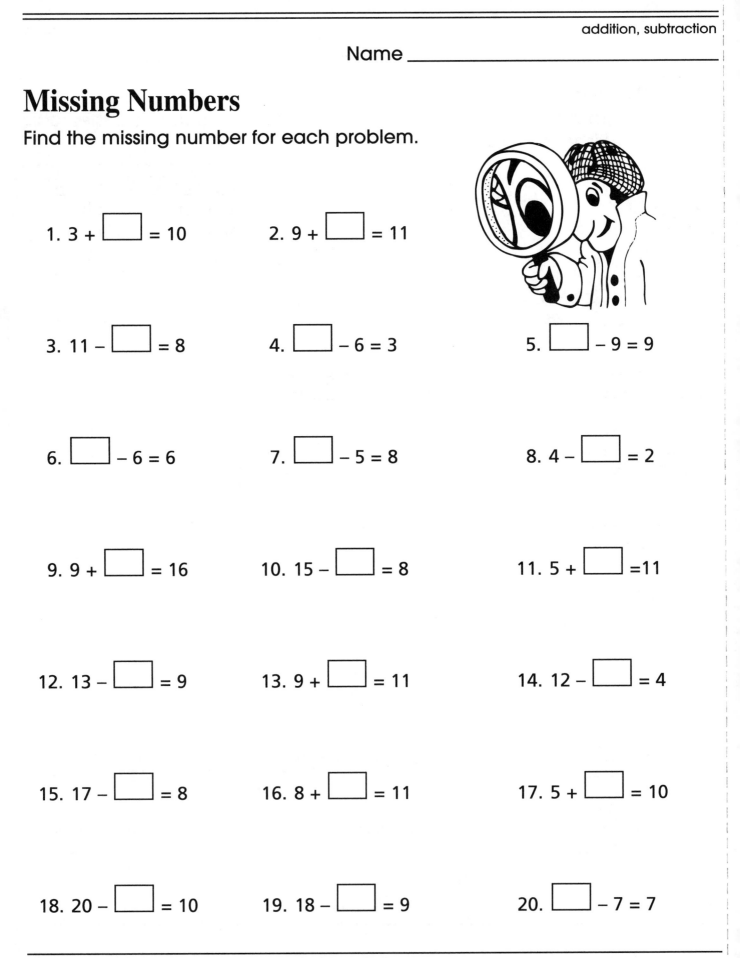

1. $3 + \boxed{} = 10$

2. $9 + \boxed{} = 11$

3. $11 - \boxed{} = 8$

4. $\boxed{} - 6 = 3$

5. $\boxed{} - 9 = 9$

6. $\boxed{} - 6 = 6$

7. $\boxed{} - 5 = 8$

8. $4 - \boxed{} = 2$

9. $9 + \boxed{} = 16$

10. $15 - \boxed{} = 8$

11. $5 + \boxed{} = 11$

12. $13 - \boxed{} = 9$

13. $9 + \boxed{} = 11$

14. $12 - \boxed{} = 4$

15. $17 - \boxed{} = 8$

16. $8 + \boxed{} = 11$

17. $5 + \boxed{} = 10$

18. $20 - \boxed{} = 10$

19. $18 - \boxed{} = 9$

20. $\boxed{} - 7 = 7$

Name _____

Math Parade

Add the numbers to solve each problem.

1.
```
  679
  816
+  11
```

2.
```
  784
   43
+ 123
```

3.
```
  634
  122
+ 441
```

4.
```
  249
  617
+  73
```

5.
```
  538
   72
+  34
```

6.
```
  321
  111
+ 203
```

7.
```
   43
  876
+ 311
```

8.
```
  765
    7
+ 276
```

9.
```
  $2.99
  $1.34
+ $3.55
```

10.
```
  $1.27
  $6.76
+ $ .33
```

11.
```
   $.89
  $1.66
+ $8.99
```

12.
```
  $3.45
  $2.77
+ $1.76
```

Daily Learning Drills Grade 3

Name _____

Zany Zeros!

Subtract to solve each problem. Check your work by adding.
Make sure to watch for the zeros! The first one is done for you.

1.
$$
\begin{array}{r}
700 \\
- 455 \\
\hline
245
\end{array}
\qquad
\begin{array}{r}
245 \\
+ 455 \\
\hline
700
\end{array}
$$

2.
$$
\begin{array}{r}
502 \\
- 133 \\
\hline
\end{array}
$$

3.
$$
\begin{array}{r}
601 \\
- \ \ 88 \\
\hline
\end{array}
$$

4.
$$
\begin{array}{r}
709 \\
- 328 \\
\hline
\end{array}
$$

5.
$$
\begin{array}{r}
903 \\
- 437 \\
\hline
\end{array}
$$

6.
$$
\begin{array}{r}
506 \\
- 456 \\
\hline
\end{array}
$$

7.
$$
\begin{array}{r}
\$7.02 \\
-\$2.63 \\
\hline
\end{array}
$$

8.
$$
\begin{array}{r}
\$5.00 \\
-\$3.27 \\
\hline
\end{array}
$$

9.
$$
\begin{array}{r}
\$4.50 \\
-\$1.71 \\
\hline
\end{array}
$$

10.
$$
\begin{array}{r}
\$6.04 \\
-\$3.76 \\
\hline
\end{array}
$$

11.
$$
\begin{array}{r}
600 \\
- 399 \\
\hline
\end{array}
$$

12.
$$
\begin{array}{r}
201 \\
- \ \ 99 \\
\hline
\end{array}
$$

Fact Toss

Practice your math facts by writing the answers to the problems below. Time yourself to see how fast you can finish!

1. 2389
   +1457

2. 8532
   + 2430

3. 4003
   + 2356

4. 1212
   + 5461

5. 6733
   + 1499

6. 7352
   − 2451

7. 6062
   + 1311

8. 1709
   + 1000

9. 8334
   − 3421

10. 4561
    − 3250

11. 1781
    − 773

12. 2901
    − 1800

13. 7542
    − 3651

14. 3503
    + 1491

Name _____

Circus Dogs

Fill in the missing factors.

A. 7 x ___ = 49

5 x ___ = 35

4 x ___ = 24

B. 6 x ___ = 54

6 x ___ = 0

4 x ___ = 12

C. 3 x ___ = 21

5 x ___ = 25

3 x ___ = 9

D. 4 x ___ = 28

5 x ___ = 15

5 x ___ = 45

E. 5 x ___ = 30

6 x ___ = 18

7 x ___ = 63

F. 6 x ___ = 48

5 x ___ = 30

6 x ___ = 54

G. 5 x ___ = 35

7 x ___ = 56

5 x ___ = 40

H. 7 x ___ = 28

7 x ___ = 7

6 x ___ = 6

I. 6 x ___ = 36

7 x ___ = 14

5 x ___ = 5

J. 5 x ___ = 20

5 x ___ = 10

4 x ___ = 32

Name _____

Keeping on Target

Multiply to find the answers. Write the answers in the darts.

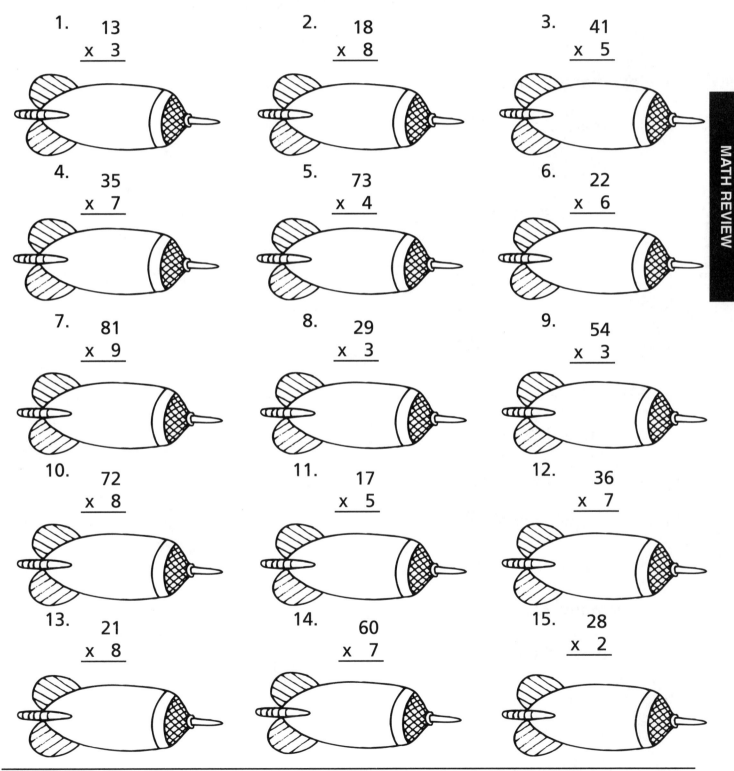

1. 13
    x 3

2. 18
    x 8

3. 41
    x 5

4. 35
    x 7

5. 73
    x 4

6. 22
    x 6

7. 81
    x 9

8. 29
    x 3

9. 54
    x 3

10. 72
    x 8

11. 17
    x 5

12. 36
    x 7

13. 21
    x 8

14. 60
    x 7

15. 28
    x 2

Daily Learning Drills Grade 3

Name _____

Roar with Pride!

Here's another way to think about division problems! Rewrite each question as a number sentence and solve the problem.

For example: How many 9's in 27?

$$27 \div 9 = 3$$

1. How many 8's in 56? _____

2. How many 2's in 12? _____

3. How many 6's in 36? _____

4. How many 5's in 25? _____

5. How many 3's in 27? _____

6. How many 4's in 24? _____

7. How many 10's in 100? _____

8. How many 7's in 49? _____

9. How many 12's in 36? _____

10. How many 1's in 1? _____

11. How many 1's in 9? _____

12. How many 11's in 33? _____

13. How many 20's in 100? _____

14. How many 4's in 16? _____

15. How many 7's in 35? _____

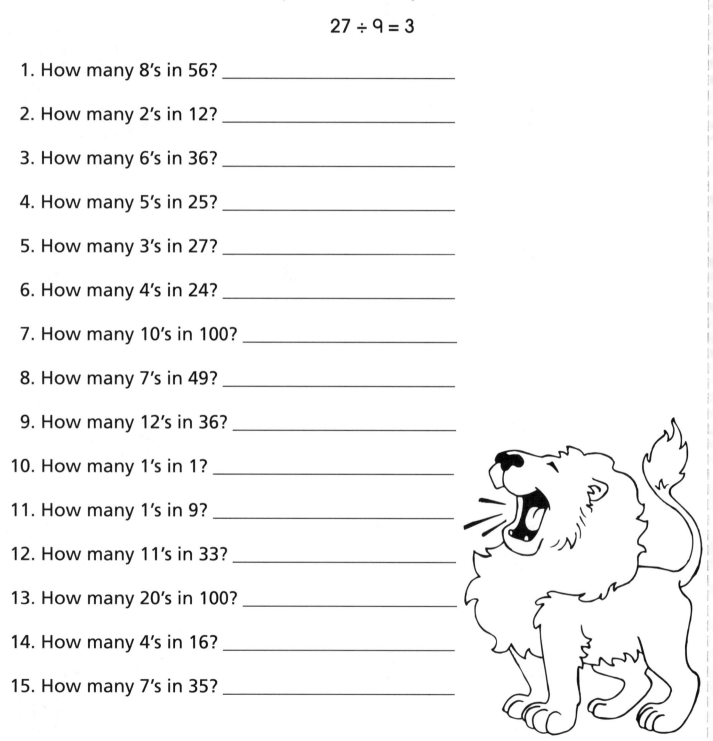

Name _____

Rising Remainders

Solve each problem. Write the remainder on the balloon.

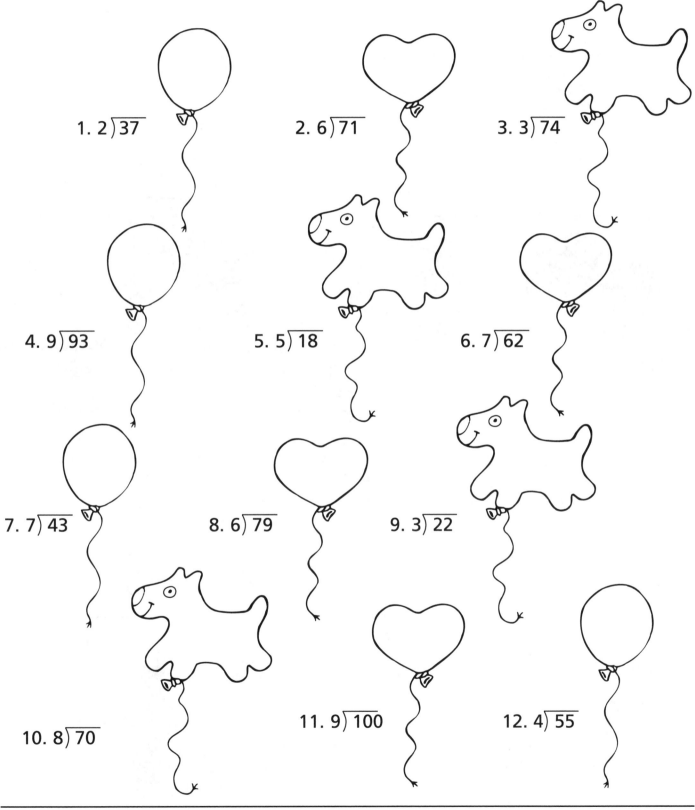

1. $2\overline{)37}$

2. $6\overline{)71}$

3. $3\overline{)74}$

4. $9\overline{)93}$

5. $5\overline{)18}$

6. $7\overline{)62}$

7. $7\overline{)43}$

8. $6\overline{)79}$

9. $3\overline{)22}$

10. $8\overline{)70}$

11. $9\overline{)100}$

12. $4\overline{)55}$

Daily Learning Drills Grade 3

Name _____

Money Matters

There are so many things to buy at the fair! Do you have enough money?
Circle Yes or No.

1. $1.85 $.50 $.10   You have $2.25
   Yes   No

2. $.35 $1.15 $.75   You have $2.50
   Yes   No

3. $.30 $1.35 $.40   You have $2.00
   Yes   No

4. $1.00 $.80 $.50   You have $2.50
   Yes   No

Name _____

Loose Change

Use the fewest coins possible. Draw coins to show each amount.

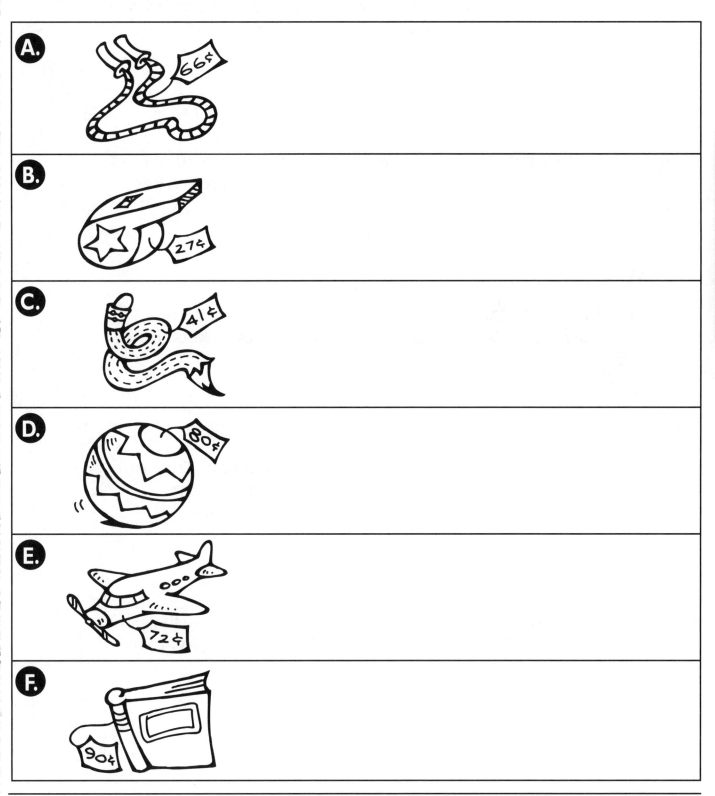

Daily Learning Drills Grade 3

Name _____

At the Carnival

Read each problem carefully. Then solve the problem, showing your work.

1. Fred played the ring-toss game. He tossed 27 rings. One-third of the rings landed on the ground. How many rings landed on the bottles?

   Answer: _____

2. Charlotte worked at the refreshment stand. She served 30 glasses of lemonade, 15 glasses of milk, and 45 glasses of water. What fraction of people ordered water that day?

   Answer: _____

3. A book of tickets for the rides cost $5.50, and there were 8 tickets in each book. Shane's dad wanted to buy 24 tickets. How much did it cost him?

   Answer: _____

4. For the baseball toss, they ordered 522 stuffed animals. They got 75 bears, 48 turtles, 110 dogs, and 215 cats. The rest of the animals were rabbits. How many rabbits did they order?

   Answer: _____

5. Kristin loved the roller coaster! She rode 5 times the first day. She came back 6 more days and rode it 3 times each day. How many times did she ride in all?

   Answer: _____

Name _____

Math Trails

Calculate how far each person hiked at Golden Canyon.
Use the trail sign to help you.

Golden Canyon Trails

White Elk Trail...................1 km
Blue Heron Trail ....3 km
Red Robin Trail..................6 km
Orange Sunset Trail ....8 km
Green Meadow Trail........4 km

**All trails start here
and circle back around.
km = kilometers**

1. During the week, Pete walked White Elk Trail once and Blue Heron Trail three times. How many km did he walk?

   Answer: _____

2. Shay walked the Blue Heron Trail every day that week. How many km did she walk?

   Answer: _____

3. On Sunday, Sui walked Green Meadow Trail. On Monday, she walked Orange Sunset Trail. Which day did she walk the longest? How much farther did she walk?

   Answer: _____

4. Mel walked half of Red Robin Trail and half of Green Meadow Trail. How far did he walk all together?

   Answer: _____

5. Suzanne walked each trail twice during the week. How far did she walk?

   Answer: _____

Name _____

Fun with Fractions

Read each problem carefully. Then solve the problem, showing your work.

1. Ryan read a book for 1/2 hour and Echo read a book for 3/4 of an hour. Who read longer, Ryan or Echo?

   Answer: _____

2. Sally picked 18 cucumbers. She gave 1/3 of them to her neighbor. How many cucumbers did she keep?

   Answer: _____

3. Don hit 32 home runs this summer. Alan hit 1/2 that many. How many home runs did Alan hit?

   Answer: _____

4. At the swimming pool, Ken swam for 45 minutes. Dustin swam only 1/3 of that time. How long did Dustin swim?

   Answer: _____

5. There were 48 red, white, and blue boats in the parade at the lake. 1/2 of them were red and 1/4 of them were white. How many were blue?

   Answer: _____

Name _____

On Top

The **numerator** is the number above the line in a fraction. It names the number of parts or objects being thought about. Circle the numerator in each fraction.

A. ①/2 **B.** 2/3 **C.** 2/2 **D.** 3/4

E. 1/3 **F.** 2/4 **G.** 1/4 **H.** 5/6

Color the number of parts shown in each numerator.

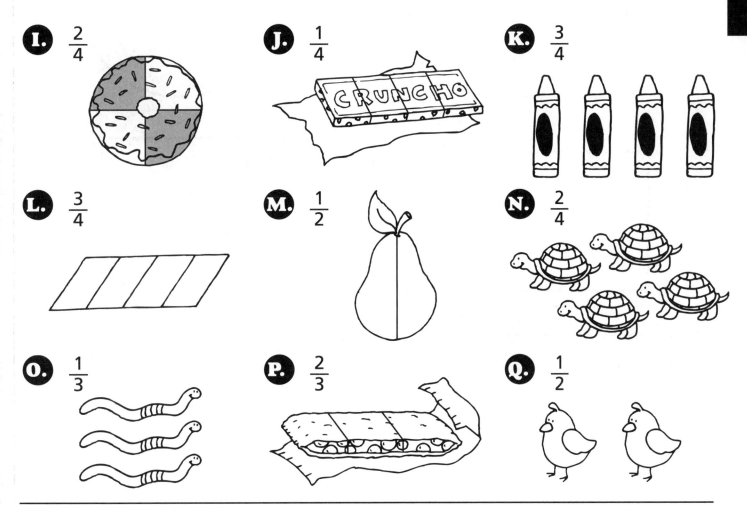

I. 2/4

J. 1/4

K. 3/4

L. 3/4

M. 1/2

N. 2/4

O. 1/3

P. 2/3

Q. 1/2

Daily Learning Drills Grade 3

Name _____

The Shape of Things

Divide and shade in each shape for the fraction shown.

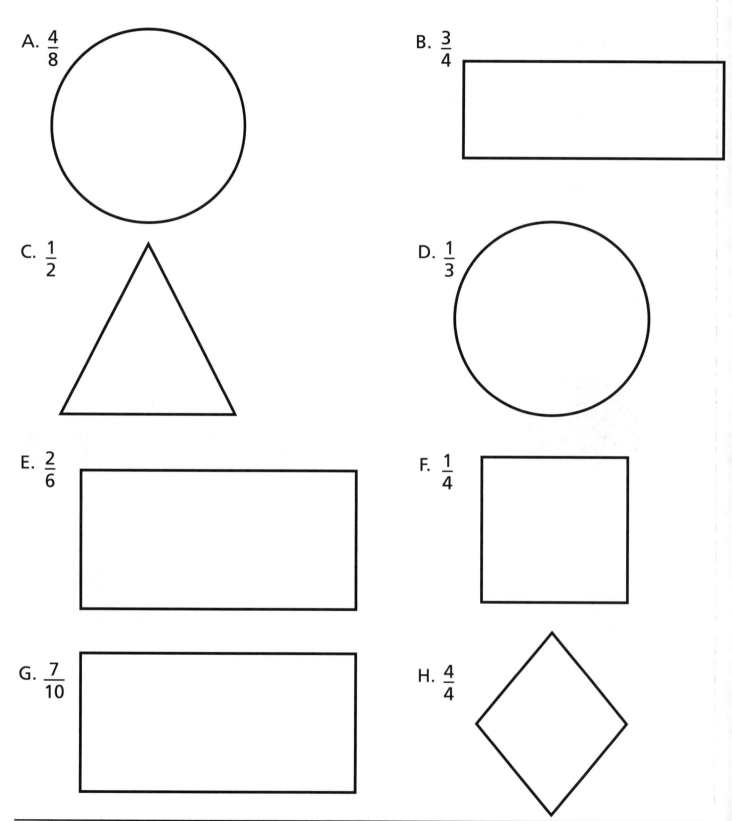

A. $\frac{4}{8}$

B. $\frac{3}{4}$

C. $\frac{1}{2}$

D. $\frac{1}{3}$

E. $\frac{2}{6}$

F. $\frac{1}{4}$

G. $\frac{7}{10}$

H. $\frac{4}{4}$

Name _____

Time Out

Look carefully at each clock. Then write the exact time on the line.

1. _____8:05_____   2. _____   3. _____

4. _____   5. _____   6. _____

7. _____   8. _____   9. _____

MATH REVIEW

Name _____

In the Area

1 centimeter

1 square centimeter

___

The **area** of a shape tells how many square centimeters will cover it. The square centimeter is used to measure area.

Write the area of each shape on the blank line. The first one is done for you.

A.

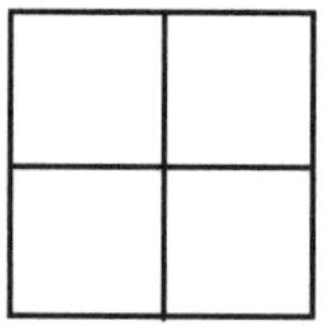

___4___ square centimeters

B.

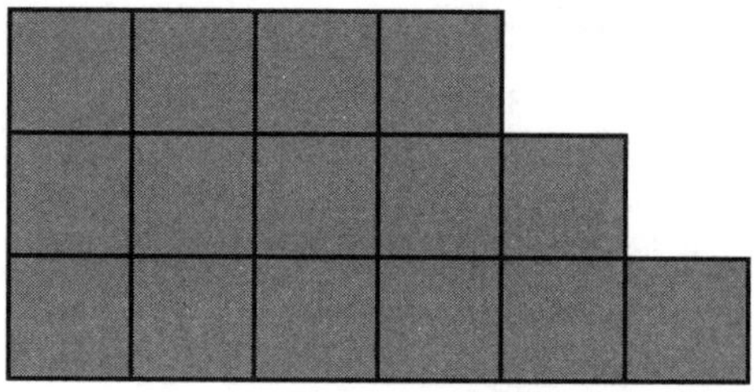

___ ___

C.

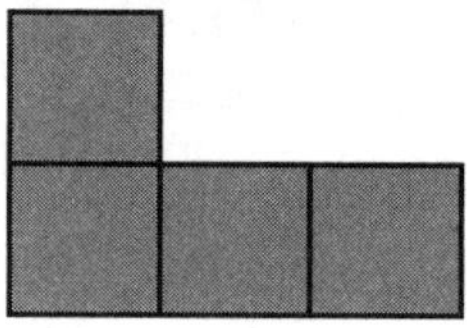

___ ___

D.

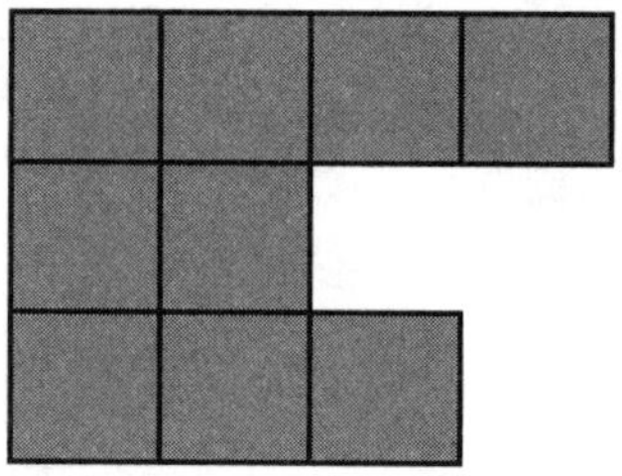

___ ___

E. Shade in an area of 10 square centimeters.

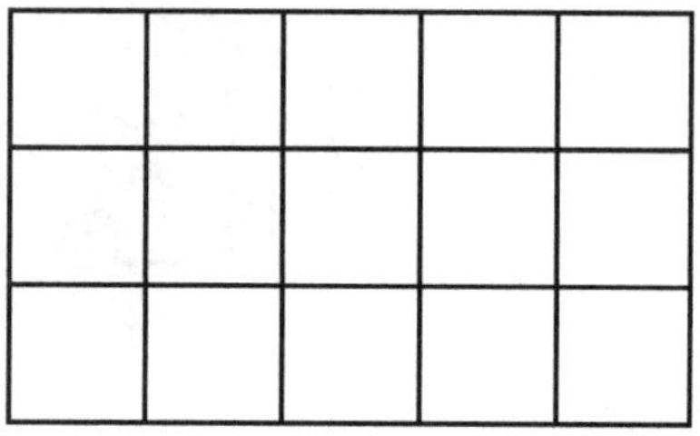

Name _____

Perimeter Picture

Write the perimeter of each shape on the blank line. Then find the answer in the picture and color it. Use the same color for each identical answer.

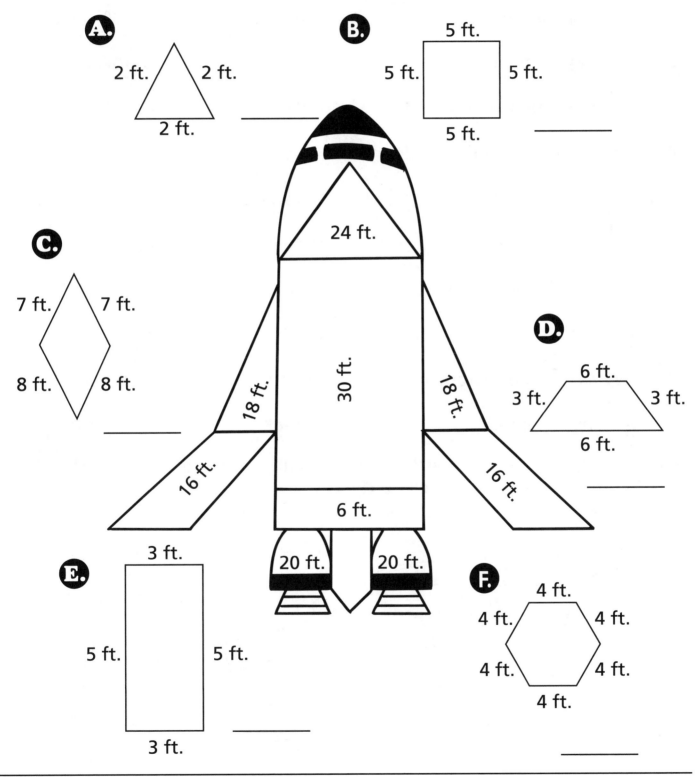

A.
2 ft. 2 ft.
2 ft. _____

B.
5 ft.
5 ft. 5 ft.
5 ft. _____

C.
7 ft. 7 ft.
8 ft. 8 ft.
_____

D.
6 ft.
3 ft. 3 ft.
6 ft.
_____

E.
3 ft.
5 ft. 5 ft.
3 ft. _____

F.
4 ft.
4 ft. 4 ft.
4 ft. 4 ft.
4 ft.
_____

24 ft.

30 ft.

18 ft.

18 ft.

16 ft.

16 ft.

6 ft.

20 ft. 20 ft.

Name _____

Excellent Estimations

Circle the best estimate.

1. How long is a football field?   a. 100 feet   b. 100 yards

2. How long is a pencil?   a. 6 inches   b. 10 inches

3. How far is it between two cities?   a. 100 yards   b. 100 miles

4. How wide is your bedroom door?   a. 3 feet   b. 3 yards

5. How long is a book?   a. 12 inches   b. 2 feet

6. How long is your bed?   a. 15 feet   b. 5 feet

7. How heavy is your backpack?   a. 50 pounds   b. 5 pounds

8. How long is a crayon?   a. 4 inches   b. 10 inches

9. How heavy is the average dog?   a. 25 pounds   b. 25 tons

10. How long is your arm?   a. 1½ feet   b. 1½ yards

Look around your house and estimate the length, width, and weight of various items. Measure to see how close you came.

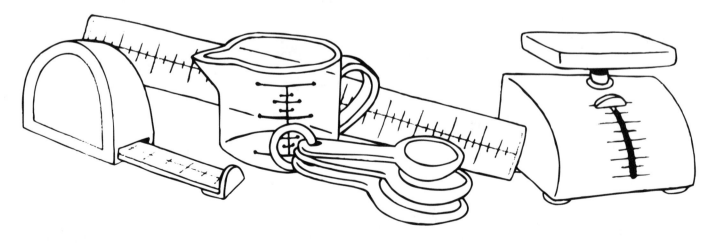

Name_____

At the Circus

The Super Duper Circus has many wonderful performers.
The picture graph below shows the number of performers.

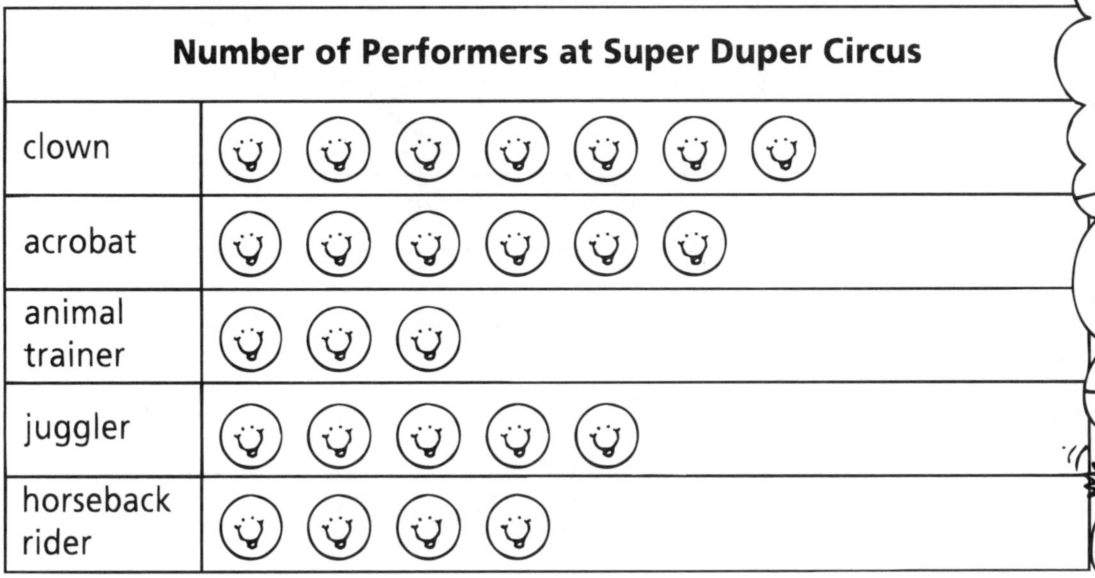

Number of Performers at Super Duper Circus							
clown	☺	☺	☺	☺	☺	☺	☺
acrobat	☺	☺	☺	☺	☺	☺	
animal trainer	☺	☺	☺				
juggler	☺	☺	☺	☺	☺		
horseback rider	☺	☺	☺	☺			

Each ☺ stands for one performer.

Use the picture graph to answer the questions.

A. How many clowns work at the circus? _____

B. Are there more jugglers or acrobats? _____

C. How many animal trainers are there? _____

D. How many more clowns are there than horseback riders? _____

E. Which group has the most performers? _____

F. Which group has the fewest performers? _____

G. What is the total number of performers shown on the graph? _____

Name_____

Changes Over Time

A line graph can show how something changes over time. The dots on the graph at the right show how Grandview School's student population changed over the years.

Number of Students at Grandview School

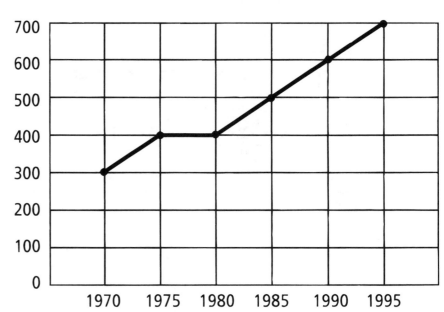

Look at the line graph and answer the questions.

A. How many students attended Grandview School in 1970? _____

B. How many students attended the school in 1980? _____

C. When did the student population stay the same? _____

D. How did the population change between 1985 and 1995?

_____

E. How many more students attended the school in 1995 than in 1970?

_____

F. Do you think the school population will go up or go down by the year 2000? Why? _____

_____

Name_____

Starch to Sugar

Try this experiment.

1. Put a cracker in your mouth.

2. Chew the cracker, but do not swallow it.

3. Hold the cracker in your mouth for at least two minutes.

4. Now, chew again and taste the cracker.

5. How does it taste?_____

_____

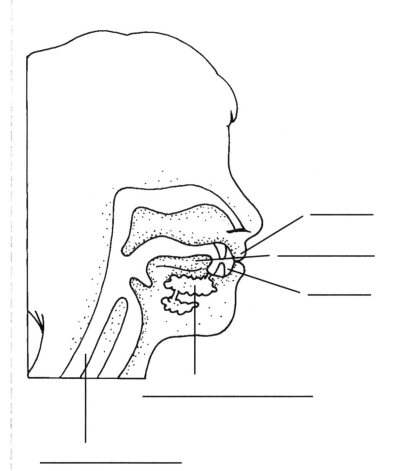

Digestion begins in the mouth. Saliva changes starches (crackers) called *carbohydrates* into a product the body can use–sugar!

This is not the simple sugar found in cookies and candy. This is a complex sugar the body uses for energy.

Label the diagram with the following words:

teeth	salivary gland
lips	esophagus
tongue	

Daily Learning Drills Grade 3

Name_____

The Digestive System

Write the path food takes as it travels through the digestive system.
Use some of the words in the diagram in your sentences.

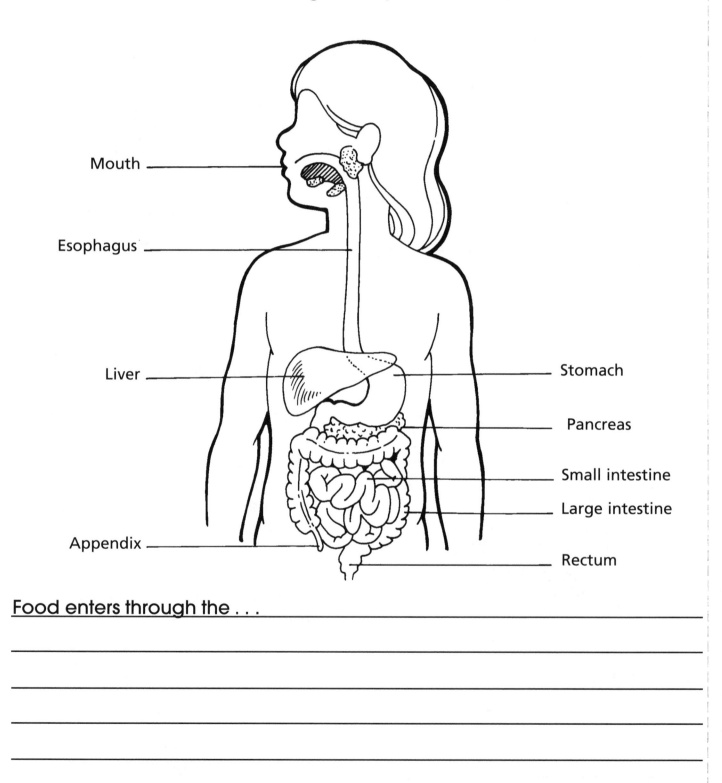

Food enters through the . . ._____

_____

_____

_____

_____

Name_____

A Springtime Surprise!

1. Color the shapes and cut them out.

2. Cut a construction paper strip like an accordion.

3. Paste each end of the paper strip to one of the two pictures, as shown below. Fold down.

Away it flew!

A caterpillar grew and grew, until one day...

Name_____

Birds

Read about birds then color the pictures.

Birds

1

Do you know what makes birds different from all other animals?

2

All birds have feathers. Besides helping them fly, feathers also protect their skin and keep them warm.

3

All birds also have wings. Even birds that don't fly, like penguins and ostriches, have wings. Are birds the only animals with wings?

4

Daily Learning Drills Grade 3

SCIENCE REVIEW

Name_____

Penguins

Penguins have been around for a long time. Though they could fly millions of years ago, over time their wings developed into flippers. Today, penguins are great swimmers. They can spend much of their time in the ocean.

There are 17 species of penguins. The largest is the emperor penguin. These penguins can be about four feet tall and weigh close to 100 pounds. Fairy penguins are the smallest. They only grow about one foot high.

Almost all penguins live far south of the equator, where the water is cold. Many live in Antarctica, where it is very cold. Others can be found near South Africa, Australia, and New ealand where it is warmer.

Although penguins spend most of their time in water, they lay eggs and raise their young on land. After the female emperor penguin lays an egg on ice, the male keeps it warm on his feet until it hatches. The mother penguin then comes back to care for the chick.

Name_____

Write *True* or *False* for each statement below.

1. Penguins fly south in the winter.

_____

2. Emperor penguins are the largest penguins.

_____

3. There are 20 species of penguins.

_____

4. The largest penguins can weigh 100 pounds.

_____

5. Penguins live at the North Pole.

_____

6. Almost all penguins live south of the equator.

_____

7. Penguins are great swimmers.

_____

8. The male emperor penguin keeps the egg warm on his feet.

_____

SCIENCE REVIEW

Name _____

Dear Zookeeper

Many zoos have an adopt-an-animal program. Communities, clubs, or families can "adopt" an animal, which means they send donations to the zoo to help care for that animal. Sometimes you can even pick the animal you would like to help.

Contact your local zoo and find out if it offers such a program. Use the form below to write a letter to the zookeeper telling about the animal you have selected. Remember to check your spelling and punctuation!

_____
(name and title)

_____
(street address)

_____
(city, state, zip)

_____
(date)

Dear _____ ,

_____

_____

_____

_____

_____

Your friend,

_____
(signature)

Name_____

Slimy or Scaly

Circle the names of the reptiles and amphibians. They may go across, down, or diagonally. Circle the pictures of reptiles.

Word Bank
ALLIGATOR
CHAMELEON
CROCODILE
FROG
IGUANA
LIZARD
NEWT
SALAMANDER
SNAKE
TUATARA
TURTLE

```
C A R T U R N R M F R O G E C H A
R D I G U A N A M R G N L K T M L
O S E S A L C R A O S N A W U E L
C H A M E L E O N D N D E K A E I
O O U L N A I C R E A N E W T O G
D G L A M A G Z O I K L E F A N A
I E T U R T L E A D E W L A R C T
L N A U A L I Z E R I T F I A G O
E A R S A L A M A N D E R G T O R
```

SCIENCE REVIEW

Daily Learning Drills Grade 3

Name_____

Chimpanzees

Chimpanzees live in African rain forests. They live in groups. Some groups can include 60 animals. They are sociable, greeting old friends with hugs and kisses. They talk by barking, grunting, and screaming.

Chimpanzees are very intelligent and skillful. They have been known to make "sponges" to soak up water to drink. They can also use simple tools to help get the food they want.

Name_____

Write *True* or *False* for each statement below.

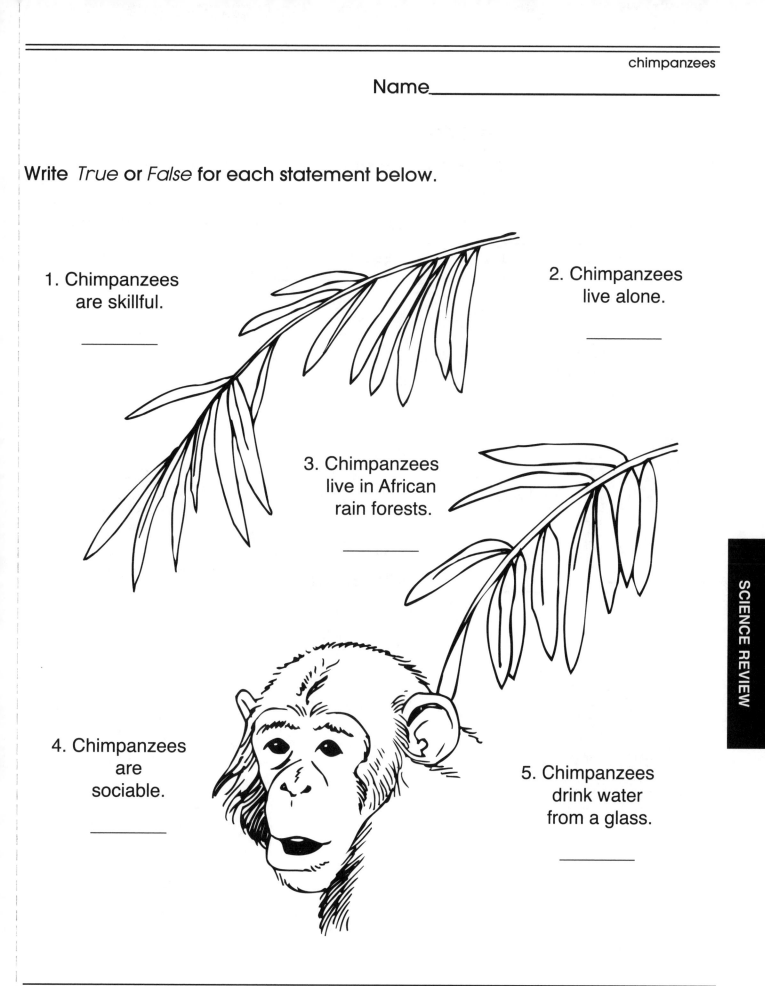

1. Chimpanzees
   are skillful.

   _____

2. Chimpanzees
   live alone.

   _____

3. Chimpanzees
   live in African
   rain forests.

   _____

4. Chimpanzees
   are
   sociable.

   _____

5. Chimpanzees
   drink water
   from a glass.

   _____

SCIENCE REVIEW

Name_____

Life Cycle of a Flowering Plant

Label the stages of the cycle with the words and phrases below.

adult plant	adult plant with fruit	adult plant with flowers
seedling	seed	

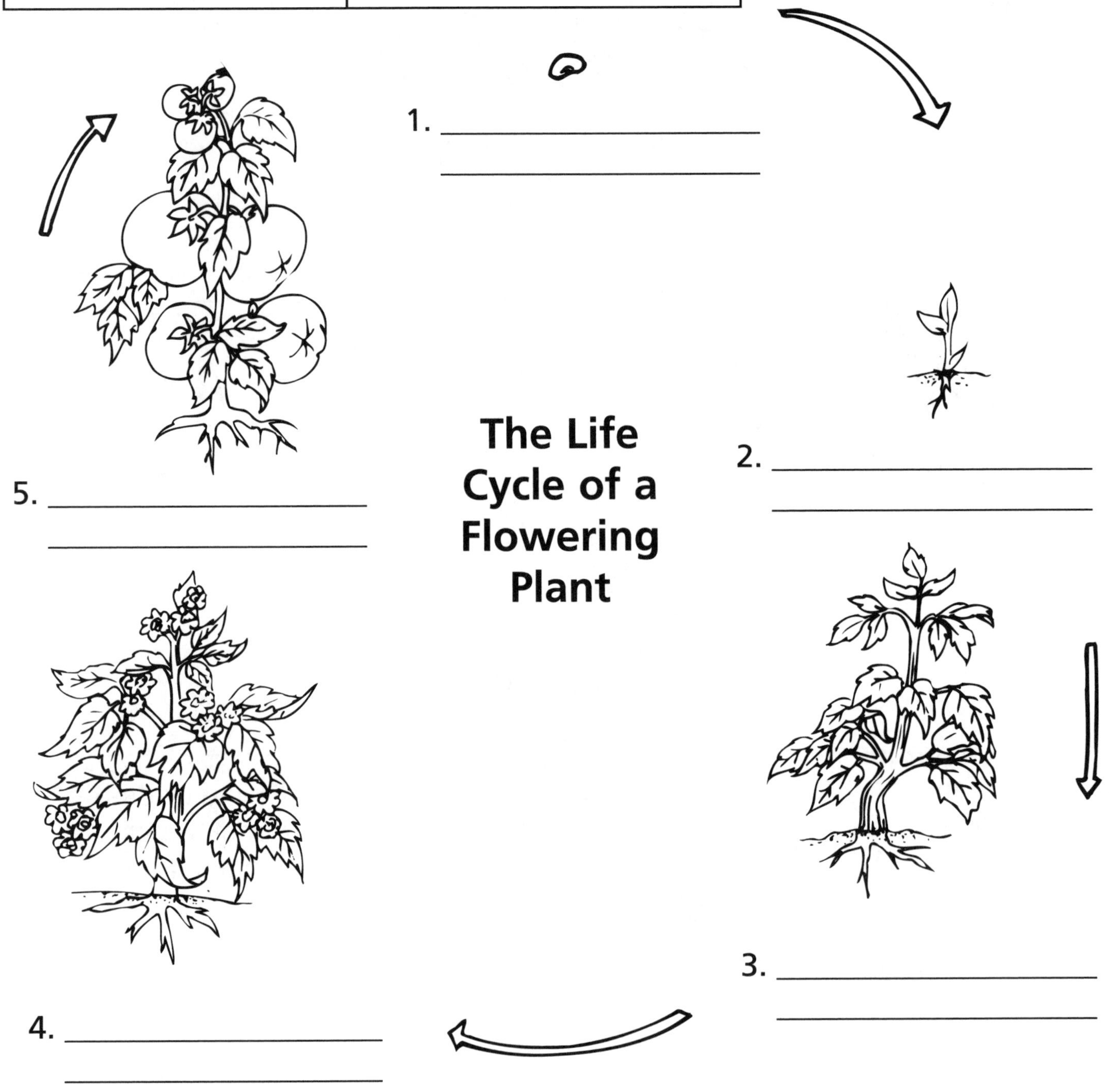

1. _____
   _____

2. _____
   _____

The Life Cycle of a Flowering Plant

3. _____
   _____

4. _____
   _____

5. _____
   _____

Name_____

Super Stem!

What is a stem's job? Try this activity to find out.

Materials: a clear plastic cup or glass • blue or red food coloring • water
scissors • celery stalk

1. Use the scissors to cut off the bottom of the celery.

2. Pour about an inch of water in the glass. Add 8 drops of food coloring.

3. Place the celery in the glass. Leave it in the glass overnight.

4. Answer the first question after you set up the activity.

What do you predict will happen to the celery when it is left in the colored water overnight? _____

_____

What happened when the celery was left in the colored water overnight?

_____

_____

Why did it happen? _____

_____

What is the job of a stem, and why is the stem important to the plant?

_____

_____

SCIENCE REVIEW

Name_____

Layers of the Rain Forest

A rain forest has four layers. They are the forest floor, the understory, the canopy, and the emergent layer.

Only a few plants, such as ferns and mosses, which need very little sunlight, are able to grow on the forest floor among the trunks of the taller trees. Beetles, spiders, and tapirs make the forest floor their home.

The understory layer is directly above the forest floor. This layer gets very little sunlight. Small trees, bushes, and shrubs can be found here. Frogs and cats, such as ocelots and jaguars, live here. Bats fly from tree to tree, helping to spread the seeds of tropical fruits.

The canopy extends above the understory, rising to about 150 feet above the forest floor. The taller trees act like giant umbrellas. This layer is full of beautiful flowering trees and orchids. Monkeys, parrots, and sloths can all be found here.

Giant trees grow to the heights of the emergent layer, towering as much as 200 feet above the forest floor. One type of giant tree is the tualang. Eagles and butterflies can be seen flying around this layer.

Name_____

Fill in the chart using the information from the story.

Layer	Plants	Creatures
Emergent layer		
Canopy		
Understory		
Forest floor		

SCIENCE REVIEW

Name_____

The Oceans

The largest bodies of water on earth are oceans. They cover more than 70 percent of the world's surface. There are five oceans: the Atlantic, the Pacific, the Indian, the Arctic, and the Antarctic. All of these oceans are actually connected together.

Oceans are very important to our lives. For example, they provide us with four major resources: food, energy, minerals, and medicine. Oceans influence our climate. The movements of their waters affect our air temperature. Oceans also account for most of the precipitation that falls to the surface of the earth. For thousands of years, people have sailed ships on the oceans. These are just a few of the ways in which oceans influence our lives. What would happen if the oceans dried up?

Name_____

Notes are phrases or short sentences that help us remember information from a story or book. Write notes below, using facts from the story.

The five oceans

1.

2.

3.

4.

5.

Four major resources that oceans provide

1.

2.

3.

4.

How our climate is influenced by oceans

1. Water movement affects the _____ _____.

2. Most of the _____ that falls to the surface of the earth comes from the oceans.

Name_____

Listen to Nature

Nature is full of sounds. Try to remember a place in nature where you have been. Then fill in the flower with the things you saw there and the noises they made. Look at the example of the ocean to help you.

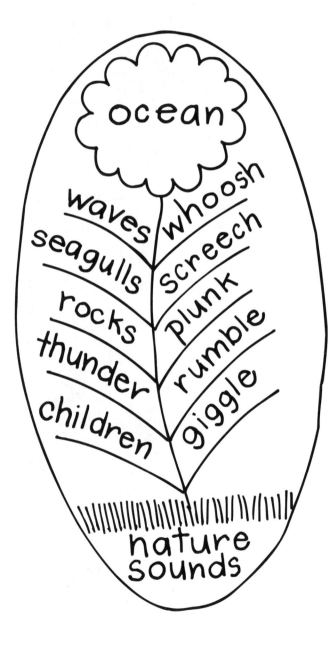

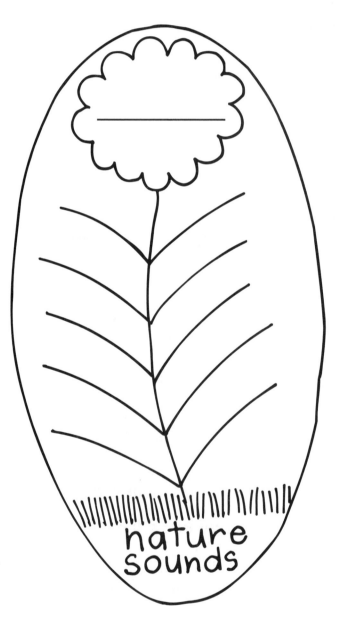

Name_____

Out of This World

Circle the words. They may go across, down, or diagonally.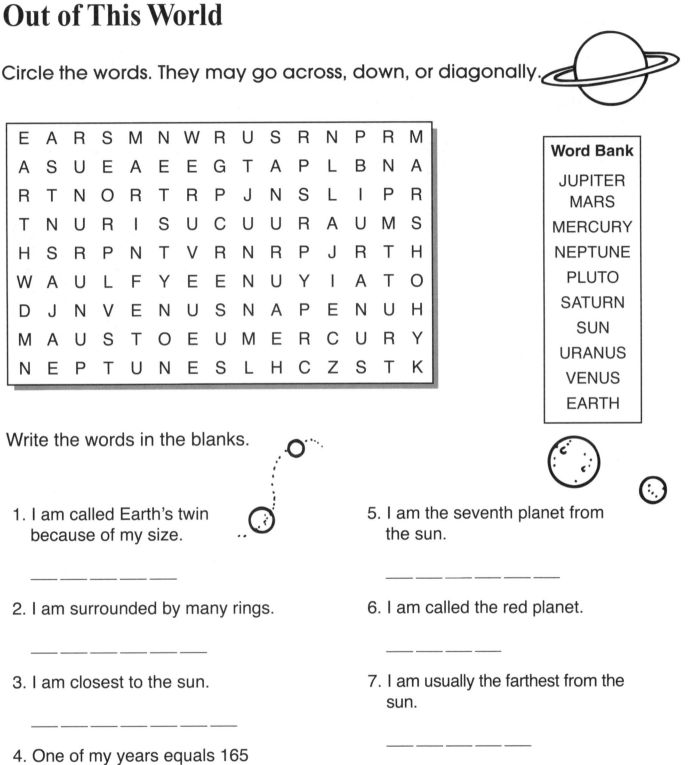

E	A	R	S	M	N	W	R	U	S	R	N	P	R	M
A	S	U	E	A	E	E	G	T	A	P	L	B	N	A
R	T	N	O	R	T	R	P	J	N	S	L	I	P	R
T	N	U	R	I	S	U	C	U	U	R	A	U	M	S
H	S	R	P	N	T	V	R	N	R	P	J	R	T	H
W	A	U	L	F	Y	E	E	N	U	Y	I	A	T	O
D	J	N	V	E	N	U	S	N	A	P	E	N	U	H
M	A	U	S	T	O	E	U	M	E	R	C	U	R	Y
N	E	P	T	U	N	E	S	L	H	C	Z	S	T	K

Word Bank

JUPITER
MARS
MERCURY
NEPTUNE
PLUTO
SATURN
SUN
URANUS
VENUS
EARTH

Write the words in the blanks.

1. I am called Earth's twin because of my size.

___ ___ ___ ___ ___

2. I am surrounded by many rings.

___ ___ ___ ___ ___ ___

3. I am closest to the sun.

___ ___ ___ ___ ___ ___ ___

4. One of my years equals 165 Earth years.

___ ___ ___ ___ ___ ___ ___

5. I am the seventh planet from the sun.

___ ___ ___ ___ ___ ___

6. I am called the red planet.

___ ___ ___ ___

7. I am usually the farthest from the sun.

___ ___ ___ ___ ___

8. I am the largest planet.

___ ___ ___ ___ ___ ___ ___

SCIENCE REVIEW

Name_____

Messages in Braille

Use the Braille alphabet below to write your name or a message. First, on a separate piece of paper, make pencil dots for each letter of each word. Then use glue to make raised dots on top of each pencil dot. You can sprinkle a pinch of sand on the wet glue so that the dots will have more texture. Let the glue dots dry completely. Ask a friend to read your words with her or his fingertips.

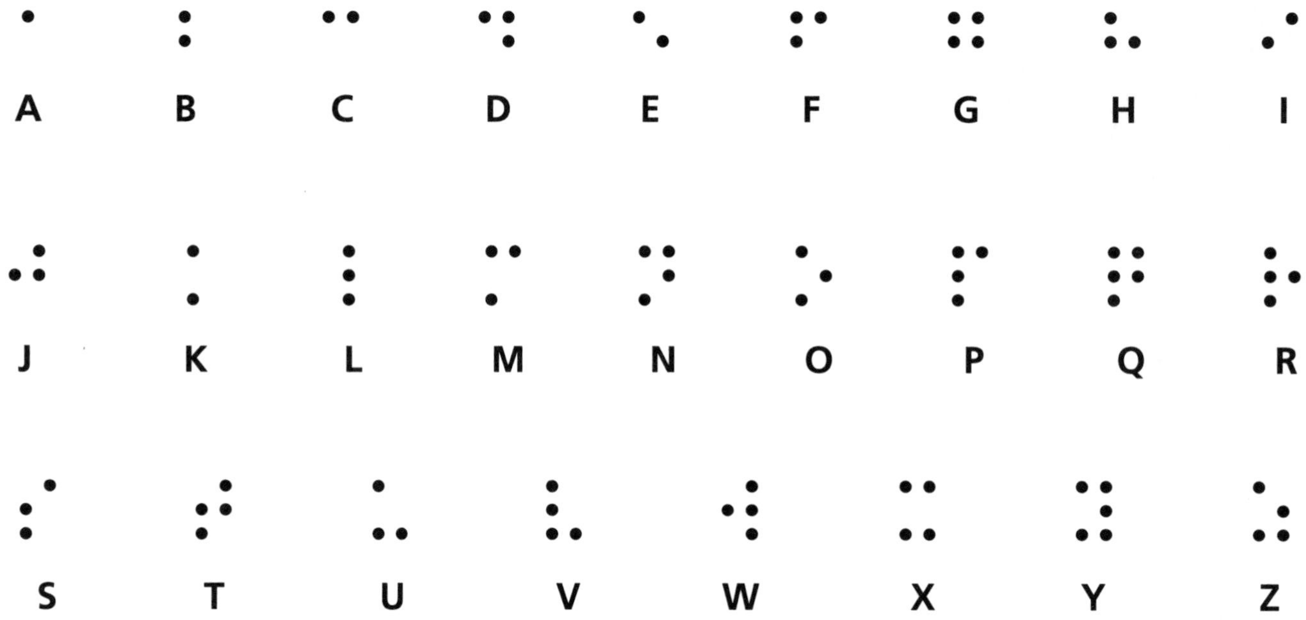

A B C D E F G H I

J K L M N O P Q R

S T U V W X Y Z

Name_____

Read a Map

Circle the words. They may go across, down, diagonally, or backward.

e	a	s	n	w	b	a	n	t	s	a	e
a	p	r	o	e	m	a	r	k	r	a	m
s	t	a	r	s	o	u	t	h	s	n	b
c	m	o	r	t	h	p	a	r	o	o	a
h	a	k	c	k	k	a	t	e	u	r	n
o	r	e	t	s	c	n	w	s	h	t	p
o	p	a	t	n	o	r	a	e	a	h	a
l	m	a	r	k	e	t	a	b	s	w	e

Word Bank
bank
east
market
north
park
school
south
west

Use the words and the map to help you fill in the blanks.

1. The _____ is west of the school.

2. The _____ is north of the post office.

3. The _____ is south of the market.

4. The _____ is directly east of

   the apartments.

5. The market is on the _____ side

   of First Street.

6. The post office is on the _____ side

   of Oak Street.

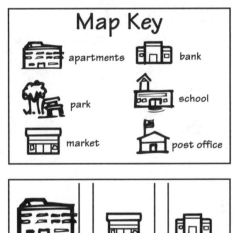

Map Key

apartments   bank

park   school

market   post office

FIRST STREET

ELM STREET   OAK STREET

SOCIAL STUDIES REVIEW

Name_____

Mount Rushmore

The Mount Rushmore National Memorial is located in the Black Hills of South Dakota. It shows the faces of four American presidents: George Washington, Thomas Jefferson, Theodore Roosevelt, and Abraham Lincoln from left to right. These faces are carved on the granite cliff of Mount Rushmore. Washington's head is as tall as a five-story building!

It took about 400 workers almost 14 years to complete this project. They were strapped into special chairs with safety lines. The workers used drills, jackhammers, and dynamite to shape the rock and carve the faces.

Name_____

Answer the questions below with information from the story.

1. What is the Mount Rushmore National Memorial? _____

_____

_____

2. Where is Mount Rushmore located?

_____

_____

3. How long did it take to complete the memorial?

_____

4. What tools did workers use?

_____

_____

_____

5. Why do you think these four presidents were chosen?

_____

_____

_____

_____

SOCIAL STUDIES REVIEW

Name_____

The First and the Fiftieth

Fifty states make up the United States of America. Delaware became the first state on December 7, 1787. Hawaii became the fiftieth state on August 21, 1959.

Delaware is the second smallest state. Its nickname is First State. It is located on the east coast next to the Atlantic Ocean. The capital city of Delaware is Dover. The main industry is manufacturing.

Hawaii, nicknamed the Aloha State, actually consists of over 100 islands in the Pacific Ocean. Only three states are smaller than Hawaii. Honolulu is the capital city, located on the island of Oahu. Tourism is Hawaii's most important industry.

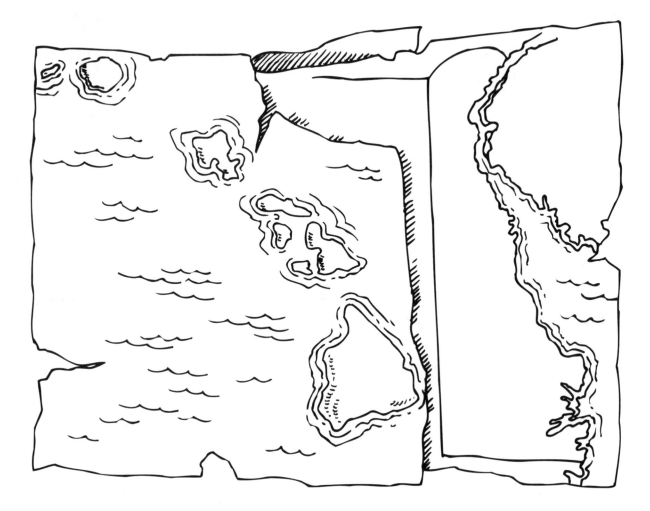

Name_____

Fill in the chart to compare Delaware and Hawaii.

	Delaware	**Hawaii**
Date it became a state		
Nearby ocean		
Main industry		
Capital city		
Size of state		
Nickname		
Would you like to visit?		

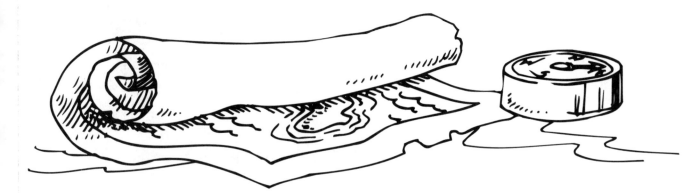

Name_____

Presidential Trivia

Circle the words. They may go across, down, diagonally, or backward.

```
N  R  K  L  E  A  L  R  H  R  I  W
S  O  E  N  O  X  I  G  J  O  N  D
K  C  T  A  G  N  W  V  M  O  M  C
E  H  T  G  L  O  C  O  S  S  V  R
N  R  L  N  N  J  N  R  H  E  S  E
N  O  F  I  O  I  E  C  I  V  R  V
E  O  E  X  N  F  H  F  O  E  Y  O
D  S  V  D  F  C  T  S  F  L  U  A
Y  L  N  E  Y  S  O  P  A  T  N  H
T  E  J  H  R  H  N  L  I  W  E  O
K  N  G  R  E  A  G  A  N  X  C  O
```

Word Bank

JEFFERSON
KENNEDY
LINCOLN
REAGAN
ROOSEVELT
WASHINGTON

Write the correct name from the list in each blank.

1. He was America's first elected
   president.

   _ _ _ _ _ _ _ _ _ _

2. The teddy bear was named for
   this president.

   _ _ _ _ _ _ _ _ _ _

4. This president wrote the
   Declaration of Independence.

   _ _ _ _ _ _ _ _ _ _

5. He was the youngest man to be
   elected President.

   _ _ _ _ _ _ _ _

6. This president led the Union
   through the Civil War.

   _ _ _ _ _ _ _ _

7. This president was a former
   movie star.

   _ _ _ _ _ _ _

Name_____

Abraham Lincoln Collage

Use this silhouette to create a collage about President Abraham Lincoln.
Directions:

1. Cut out this silhouette, then cut another out of black construction paper.

2. Color, cut, and glue the pictures from page 395 in a collage on the front of the silhouette, and glue the fact strips to the back.

3. Title the collage as shown, punch a hole in the top of the profile, and hang.

Daily Learning Drills Grade 3

Name _____

Abraham Lincoln Collage

Color and cut the elements below and glue to the silhouette of Abraham Lincoln.

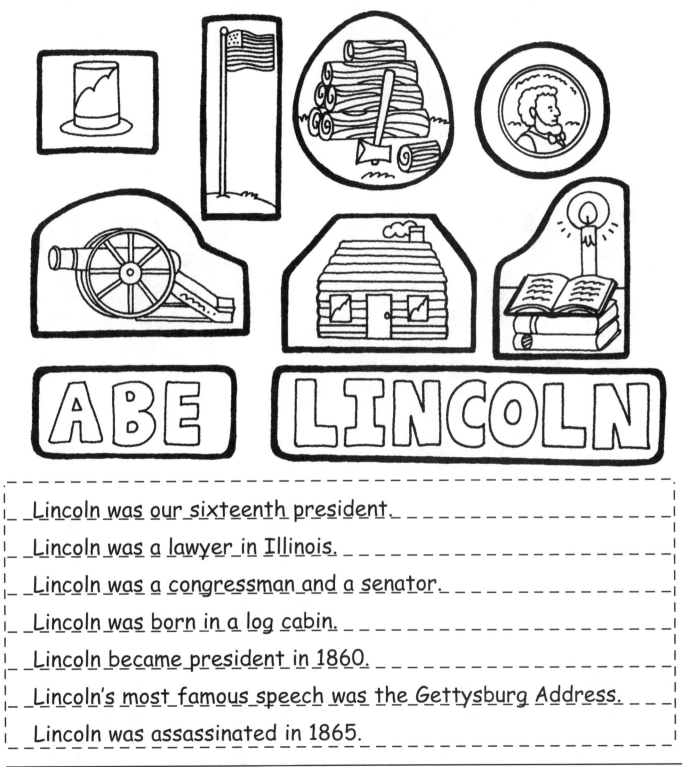

Lincoln was our sixteenth president.

Lincoln was a lawyer in Illinois.

Lincoln was a congressman and a senator.

Lincoln was born in a log cabin.

Lincoln became president in 1860.

Lincoln's most famous speech was the Gettysburg Address.

Lincoln was assassinated in 1865.

SOCIAL STUDIES REVIEW

Name_____

Squanto

A **biography** is a true story about someone's life, written by another person. *Squanto: Young Indian Hunter* is a biography written by Augusta Stevenson.

Squanto was born around 1585. His real name was Tisquantum. Squanto lived in the Indian village of Patuxet in the early 1600s. In 1614, he was taken as a slave to Spain. He later escaped to England, where he learned to speak English. Squanto returned home in 1619.

When the Pilgrims settled in America, Squanto showed them where to hunt and fish. He also showed them how to plant corn. He helped the Pilgrims trade with other Indians. The Pilgrims knew that they would not have survived without him.

SOCIAL STUDIES REVIEW

Name_____

Squanto (continued)

Use the words from the Word Bank to answer the questions.

1. A true story of someone's life written by _____ person is a _____ .

2. _____ was Squanto's real name.

3. The _____ village of _____ is where Squanto lived.

4. In 1614, Squanto was taken as a _____ to _____.

5. He learned to speak English in _____.

6. Squanto taught the _____ many important survival skills.

7. He showed them how to plant _____.

Word Bank
Spain
another
biography
slave
Tisquantum
England
Patuxet
corn
Pilgrims
Indian

Name_____

You're a Grand Old Flag

Learn more about the United States flag and Betsy Ross. Cut off the bottom of this page, cut the facts apart, and glue them on the flag in the correct order.

- cut here -

As a young woman, she became an expert flag maker.

Betsy Ross was born in Philadelphia in 1752.

The new flag was adopted by Congress on June 14, 1777.

Today, we celebrate Flag Day every fourteenth of June.

According to legend, George Washington asked her to make a flag in June, 1776.

Betsy Ross made a flag with thirteen stars.

Name_____

The Netherlands

In the spring, miles of tulip fields bloom in the Netherlands. Farmers grow tulips to be shipped all over the world. The people march in parades that go from town to town. They visit a park that has more than six million flowers! They sing, dance, and eat special foods. Spring is tulip time in the Netherlands.

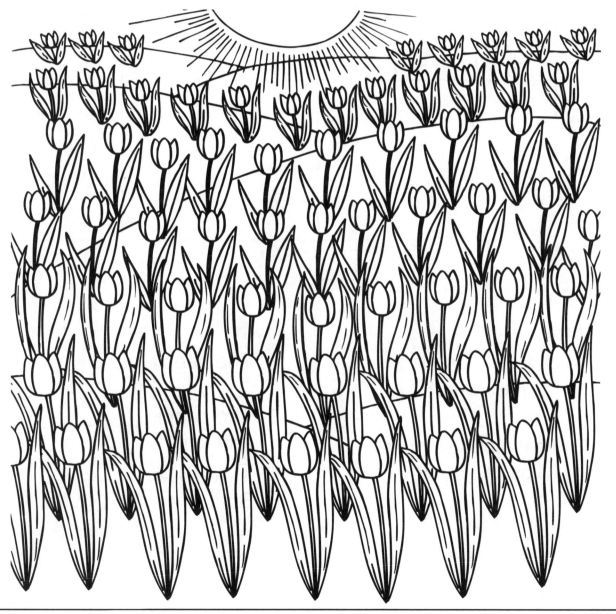

SOCIAL STUDIES REVIEW

Name_____

The Netherlands (continued)

Use facts from the story to fill in the puzzle. The Word Bank will help you.

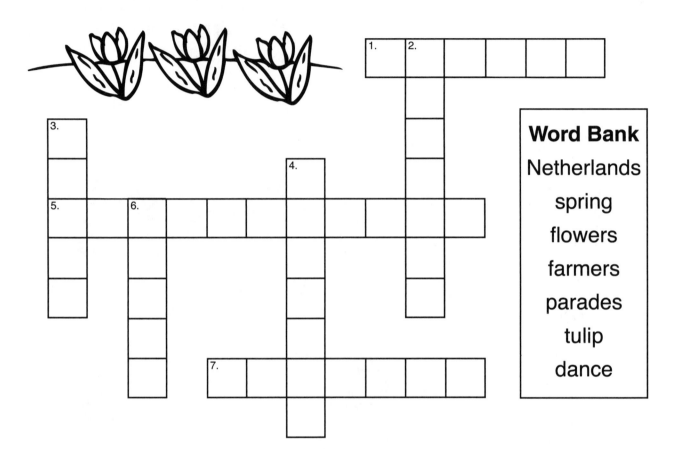

Word Bank

Netherlands

spring

flowers

farmers

parades

tulip

dance

Across

1. Season when tulips grow
5. Country where tulips are grown
7. These people grow tulips.

Down

2. The people march in _____ through town.
3. The people _____ and sing.
4. Tulips are _____.
6. Spring is _____ time.

Name_____

Turkey Hunt

Circle the hidden Thanksgiving words in the puzzle. Check off each word as you find it.

f	l	t	r	i	b	e	x	v
i	h	u	n	t	q	x	h	P
s	x	r	c	o	r	n	a	i
h	w	k	h	a	n	t	r	l
o	c	e	a	n	g	y	v	g
M	a	y	f	l	o	w	e	r
v	g	o	b	b	l	e	s	i
d	i	n	n	e	r	v	t	m
r	d	o	n	a	t	i	v	e

ocean	gobble	corn	fish
Pilgrim	Mayflower	native	tribe
harvest	turkey	hunt	dinner

Daily Learning Drills Grade 3

SOCIAL STUDIES REVIEW

Review Answer Key

321 — You're Invited!

Imagine that you are planning a slumber party. Think of ten friends you would like to invite and write their names on the invitations below. Then color the invitations.

Now, alphabetize the names according to the first or last name.

Answers will vary.

322 — Seed Syllables

Say each word aloud. How many syllables do you hear? Write each word on the seed packet with the correct number.

1
peas
squash
dill
beets

2
carrot
parsley
lettuce
pumpkin
parsnips
pepper

3
tomato
zucchini
cucumber
celery
broccoli

carrot	parsley	lettuce
tomato	pumpkin	peas
zucchini	cucumber	squash
dill	celery	parsnips
beets	pepper	broccoli

323 — Crazy Compounds

Compound words are created by putting two smaller words together. Make compound words by drawing a line from each word in the left-hand columns to a word in the right-hand columns.

Left column 1: black, eye, type, class, milk, bag, north, earth, work, drive, door
Right column 1: shake, pipe, top, writer, quake, mate, brow, way, knob, west, shop

Left column 2: sun, button, grape, corn, sand, stage, zoo, pin, butter, bird, shoe
Right column 2: stalk, shine, keeper, hole, vine, box, coach, lace, cushion, house, fly

324 — Picnic Puzzlers

Fill in each basket by writing the words from the Word Bank with the same vowel sound as the word on the basket. Remember, vowel combinations don't have to look the same to sound the same!

town: brown, sound, around
taught: brought, blonde, straw
new: through, clue, blue
meat: feel, treat, seat
blow: toe, throw, coat

Word Bank

brown	blonde	sound
feel	toe	treat
through	clue	around
brought	blue	throw
straw	coat	seat

325 — Silent Search

Some words contain letters that are silent. These words can be tricky to spell. Watch carefully for the silent letters *e, kn, ght,* and *wr* in this story. Circle the words that have these silent letter combinations.

It was Saturday night. Jamie was having some friends over to spend the night. He had written letters inviting them to come. Everyone said they would be there.

There was a knock on the door! Jamie ran to answer it. All three friends were waiting on the porch. "Come in!" shouted Jamie. Simon, Ahman, and Lei came in carrying their sleeping bags. They put their things in Jamie's room.

Jamie's mother came in with cake and fruit juice. She cut the cake with a knife and served the boys a snack. She wrapped the extra pieces in plastic wrap for later. She knew they would be hungry again.

The boys watched videos and played board games. Then they ate the rest of their snacks. Finally, they turned out the lights and told scary stories to frighten each other. What a fun night!

326 — Name it!

A **proper noun** names a special person, animal, place, or thing. It begins with a capital letter. Read the common noun and proper noun in each brick. Write another proper noun to match.

Answers will vary.

boy / Ramon	girl / Ashley	teacher / Ms. Sorovic
month / February	school / Pima College	street / First Avenue	day / Wednesday
city / Salt Lake City	state / Missouri	country / India
artist / Mary Cassatt	president / George Washington	athlete / Jesse Owens	author / Jane Yolen
book / The King's Equal	song / "This Land Is Your Land"	movie / Bambi
ocean / Arctic	planet / Neptune	store / Toyland	pet / Spice

327 — Mouse-Mice

A **singular noun** names one person, animal, place, or thing.
A **plural noun** names more than one.

Most nouns are made plural by adding *s*.
Examples: house-houses, shark-sharks

Some nouns have irregular, or strange, plural forms. You need to memorize them.
Examples: elf-elves, fish-fish

Read each plural noun. Write the matching singular noun.

1. mouse — mice
2. louse — lice
3. man — men
4. woman — women
5. child — children
6. wolf — wolves
7. half — halves
8. shelf — shelves
9. leaf — leaves
10. tooth — teeth
11. foot — feet
12. goose — geese
13. octopus — octopi
14. cactus — cacti
15. fungus — fungi
16. potato — potatoes
17. tomato — tomatoes
18. hero — heroes
19. echo — echoes
20. die — dice
21. ox — oxen
22. deer — deer
23. moose — moose
24. sheep — sheep

328 — Find the Verbs

A **verb** is an action word. *Sing, race,* and *understand* are verbs.

Read these sentences. Underline the verbs. Some sentences have more than one. Then make the verbs fit in the puzzle.
Note: There will be one extra word space in the puzzle. Write your own verb in it.

1. My mom and I drive to the toy store to buy a bike.
2. We look at all the mountain bikes.
3. I find one that I like.
4. My mom tells me to try it.
5. I worry about the narrow store aisles.
6. I start to ride slowly.
7. My bike wobbles.
8. Suddenly I crash into some toys.
9. We both laugh.
10. My mom helps me clean up the toys.
11. Then we take my new bike home.

329 — Pronoun Match-up

A **pronoun** is a word that takes the place of a noun.

Draw lines to match each noun to the pronoun that can take its place. On the blank lines, write your name.

A **subject pronoun** takes the place of a noun in the subject part of a sentence.

Tamara can ride a unicycle.
She can ride a unicycle.

Noun	Subject Pronoun
Greg and Sarah	He
Melinda	They
My cousin and I	I
Mr. Weisberg	She
The towering pine tree	We
Answers will vary.	It

An **object pronoun** takes the place of a noun that follows a verb or a word such as *to, from, of,* or *by.*

Please give this note to Mike.
Please give this note to him.

Noun	Object Pronoun
my family and I	it
the bus	her
Valerie	us
the flowers	me
Peter	them
Answers will vary.	him

A **possessive pronoun** takes the place of a possessive noun.

Dan and Claire's grandpa is visiting.
Their grandpa is visiting.

Possessive Noun	Possessive Pronoun
the dinosaur's	her
John's	his
Aunt Nancy's	its
the students'	our
my friends and my	their

Describe it!
An **adjective** is a word that describes a noun (person, animal, place, or thing). *Blue*, *delicious*, *fuzzy*, and *smart* are adjectives.

Look at these nouns. Write an adjective to describe each. Finish drawing the picture and color it. You may use the cartoon faces as a guide.

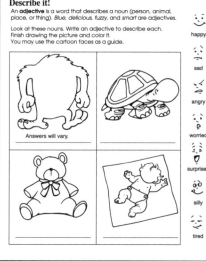

Answers will vary.

happy
sad
angry
worried
surprised
silly
tired

330

Punctuation Puzzler
Punctuation and capitalization are important to understanding what you read. Rewrite these sentences, putting in the correct capitalization and punctuation.

1. hurry and deliver this pizza
   Hurry and deliver this pizza!
2. i have collected 1324 stamps
   I have collected 1,324 stamps.
3. how long should i walk your dog mr. hill
   How long should I walk your dog, Mr. Hill?
4. you are doing a great job he said
   You are doing a great job, he said.
5. watch out don't crash your model plane she cried
   Watch out! Don't crash your model plane! she cried.
6. i went to the store to buy some comics
   I went to the store to buy some comics.
7. boating is julies favorite hobby
   Boating is Julie's favorite hobby.
8. where can you buy the newest copy of zoo magazine
   Where can you buy the newest copy of *Zoo Magazine*?
9. how many stitches should i knit to complete that row
   How many stitches should I knit to complete that row?
10. i need to weed the tulips today said mother
    I need to weed the tulips today, said mother.

331

Science Fair
Proofread this story Sean wrote. Check off each step as you do it.
☐ Underline three times the 6 letters that should be capitalized. (e̱)
☐ Write the 4 missing periods. (.)
☐ Write the 2 missing question marks. (?)
☐ Write the 2 missing sets of quotation marks. (" ")

"Hey, Mom!" I called out." Guess what I am going to do for the Science Fair."

"You re not doing a vinegar and baking soda experiment, are you?" she asked.

I go to Thomas edison Elementary School. Every January my school holds Its Science Fair. And every January I do a vinegar and baking soda experiment.

I used to find my experiments in science books. In first grade, I made a balloon inflate. In second grade, I created an erupting volcano!

this year I tried my own experiment. I read that when vinegar and baking soda react, they produce heat along with carbon dioxide. So I poured vinegar in a jar and measured its temperature. I predicted that when I added the baking soda, the new liquid mixture would be hotter. Can you guess what happened? The temperature was about 15¡ cooler!

"that not right!" I yelled. "It supposed to be hotter."

Then I thought about it. The vinegar and baking soda must give off their own heat to make heat. maybe that is why they ended up colder.

332

American Tall Tales
A **comma** (,) tells the reader to pause.

Use a comma to separate words in a series of three or more items.
Paul Bunyan, John Henry, and Slue-Foot Sue are tall-tale characters.
Tall-tale characters are larger, mightier, smarter, or bolder than regular folks.

Read these sentences. Write the missing commas.
1. Paul Bunyan was the biggest, strongest, and friendliest lumberjack ever.
2. Babe the Blue Ox was shaking, shivering, and shuddering when Paul Bunyan found him in a blue snowstorm.
3. Johnny Appleseed wore a tin pot on his head, a sack for a shirt, and no shoes on his feet.
4. Pennsylvania, Ohio, and Indiana are filled with the apple trees he planted.
5. John Henry was a strong, brawny, and muscular baby who was born with a hammer in his hand.
6. Stormalong could steer his boat through the wind, rain, or waves of any storm.
7. Bears, cougars, and wolves lived in the Tennessee woods with Davy Crockett.
8. Sally Ann Whirlwind could out-run, out-swim, and out-wrestle any critter when she was just a little girl.
9. Pecos Bill, his wife Slue-Foot Sue, and his horse Widow-Maker lived in the Southwest.
10. Pecos Bill picked up a rattlesnake, tied it in a loop, and used it for a lasso.
11. Mike Fink was the best keelboatman on the Ohio, the Mississippi, the Missouri, or any other river.

333

What Big Teeth You Have!
Use **quotation marks** (" ") to show the exact words a speaker says.
Tina, called Brandon, guess which animal uses its teeth to hold onto its mom.
A bird? guessed Tina.

Read this conversation.
Write quotation marks around the exact words being said.

1. Jose chimed in, "Birds don t have teeth."
2. "Oh, yeah," said Tina." I forgot."
3. "What book are you reading?" asked Michelle.
4. "*What Big Teeth You Have!*" answered Brandon.
5. Michelle scowled. "I don t have big teeth!"
6. "No," laughed Brandon. "That s the title of the book."
7. "Oh!" said Michelle. "I was afraid you were being rude."
8. "So," asked Tina, "which animal uses its teeth to hold onto its mom?"
9. "A flying fox," replied Brandon.
10. "Birds don t have teeth and foxes don t fly," said Jose.
11. Brandon responded, "A flying fox is a type of bat."
12. "Hmm," said Jose, "I never knew that."
13. "Which animal has the most teeth?" asked Tina.
14. "I m not sure," answered Brandon. "It says a tiger shark may use up 12,000 teeth in five years."
15. "Wow!" exclaimed Tina, Jose, and Michelle in unison.

334

Up, Up, and Away!
Look at the words on the kite tails. Choose a synonym for each word from the Word Bank and write it on the correct tail piece. Can you think of others?

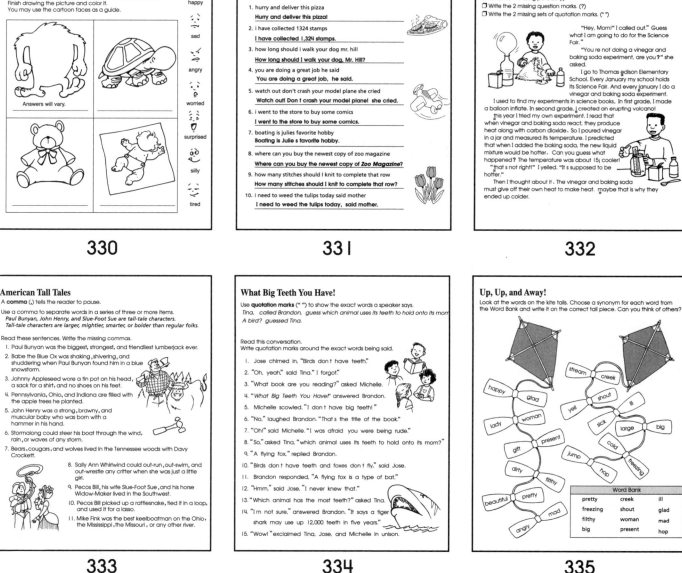

happy — glad
lady — woman
gift — present
dirty — filthy
beautiful — pretty
angry — mad

stream — creek
yell — shout
sick — ill
large — big
cold — freezing
jump — hop

Word Bank		
pretty	creek	ill
freezing	shout	glad
filthy	woman	mad
big	present	hop

335

Here Come the "Ant"onyms!
Antonyms are words with opposite meanings, for example, *hot* and *cold*. Write each word from the Word Bank on the correct antonym ant.

Word Bank					
careful	save	sour	fat	dirty	pretty
cry	far	poor	under	winter	low

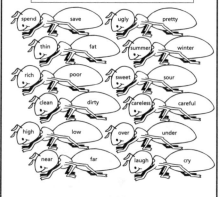

spend — save
thin — fat
rich — poor
clean — dirty
high — low
near — far

ugly — pretty
summer — winter
sweet — sour
careless — careful
over — under
laugh — cry

336

Homophone Match–up
Homophones are words that sound alike but have different spellings and meanings. They are also called **homonyms**.

Draw lines to match each word to its correct meaning.

ate — the past tense of eat
eight — the number after 7

blue — the color of the sky
blew — the past tense of blow

new — the opposite of old
knew — the past tense of know

hole — an empty or missing part
whole — the entire amount; all

you're — a contraction for you are
your — belonging to you

weight — how heavy something is
wait — to pause or stay

our — belonging to us
hour — 60 minutes

one — the number before 2
won — the past tense of win

right — correct or the opposite of left
write — to put words on paper

its — belonging to it
it's — a contraction for it is

Think of another homophone pair. Write each word and its meaning.
Answers will vary.

337

Caterpillar Crawl
While camping you might see some interesting insects! Add prefixes and suffixes to the words below to make new words. Write each new word in a section of the caterpillar. The first one is started for you.

Possible answers include:

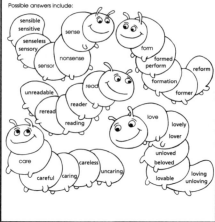

sensible
sensitive
senseless
sensory
sensor
nonsense
sense

form
formed
perform
reform
formation
former

unreadable
reread
read
reader
reading

love
lovely
lover
unloved
beloved
lovable
loving
unloving

care
careless
uncaring
careful
caring

338

Daily Learning Drills Grade 3

What's the Answer?

A **contraction** is a shortened form of two or more words.
An **apostrophe** ( ) takes the place of the missing letters.

Examples: It is → it s   of the clock → o clock   he would → he d

Read these riddles and answers. Underline the contraction in each line.
Write its missing apostrophe where it belongs.
Then write the two words that make up the contraction.

Riddles

1. What's the difference between a dog and a flea? __What is__

2. Why won't anyone play cards with this cat? __will not__

3. Why isn't the mayonnaise ever ready? __is not__

4. Why don't sea gulls fly over bays? __do not__

5. Who's smarter —a reptile or a fish? __Who is__

6. Why doesn't a pro hockey player ever tell jokes? __does not__

Answers

1. A dog can have fleas, but a flea can't have dogs! __cannot__
2. Because she's a cheetah! __she is__
3. Because it's always dressing! __it is__
4. Because then they'd be bagels! __they would__
5. Fish, because they're always in schools! __they are__
6. He's worried the ice might crack up. __He is__

Write a riddle you know. Make it have a contraction in the question or the answer.

__Answers will vary.__

_____

A Sparkler Story

Read the story and then answer the questions below.

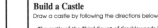

Carl was so excited! His cousins were coming to the annual Fourth of July barbeque. He hadn't seen them in over a year!

Carl's father bought ten boxes of sparklers. Each box cost $1.15. Then he went to the market and bought hot dogs, buns, chips, watermelon, and corn on the cob.

Pretty soon Carl's cousins arrived, and they all ran outside to play. Everyone had a wonderful time. But Carl couldn't wait for the fireworks. He sneaked around the side of the house and opened a box of sparklers. He lit one and it sparkled and crackled in his hand. As he waved it in the air, he noticed a tiny being sitting on the bush. Carl couldn't believe his eyes, so he blew out the sparkler to get a better look. But the being disappeared! Carl decided it must have been his imagination, so he lit another sparkler. As soon as the sparkler crackled to life, the being appeared again—this time on Carl's shoulder!

1. How long had it been since Carl had seen his cousins?
__Over a year__

2. How much did Carl's father spend on sparklers? __$11.50__

3. What food did Carl's father buy for the barbeque?
__hot dogs, buns, chips, watermelon, and corn on the cob__

4. Why did Carl go around the side of the house?
__Because Carl wanted to light a sparkler.__

On another sheet of paper, write about what happened next. Who was this tiny being? Did Carl tell his cousins about it? Finish the story.

Build a Castle

Draw a castle by following the directions below.

The castle of the Third Count of Cracklewoods is located in the center of an oval island. The main part of the castle is a cube-shaped building with an arched door in the front. On either side of the door is a pentagon-shaped window. A rectangular drawbridge is lowered out from the door to let in visitors. On the left of the main building is the Tower of Joy. It is a tall cylinder topped with a cone. There are four triangle windows on the tower, facing out. On the right of the main building is the Tower of Triumph. This tower is shaped like a rectangular solid topped with a pyramid. It is the Knight's room, the Count's son. This tower has three round windows facing out. Two triangular flags fly from the top of this tower whenever the knight is home. That's when the castle is filled with happiness, and everyone dances and sings!

A Goat Dairy Farm

A **sentence** is a group of words that tells a complete thought. The words in a sentence are in an order that makes sense. A sentence begins with a capital letter and ends with a period (.), question mark (?), or exclamation mark (!).

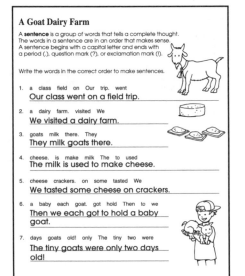

Write the words in the correct order to make sentences.

1. a class field on Our trip. went
__Our class went on a field trip.__

2. a dairy farm. visited We
__We visited a dairy farm.__

3. goats milk there. They
__They milk goats there.__

4. cheese. is make milk The to used
__The milk is used to make cheese.__

5. cheese crackers. on some tasted We
__We tasted some cheese on crackers.__

6. a baby each goat. got hold Then to we
__Then we each got to hold a baby goat.__

7. days goats old! only The two were tiny
__The tiny goats were only two days old!__

Who? What? Where? When?

Write A before the phrase if it tells *who*.
Write B before the phrase if it tells *what*.
Write C before the phrase if it tells *where*.
Write D before the phrase if it tells *when*.

1. __C__ in the garden
2. __D__ before the sun came up
3. __A__ the farmer in his overalls
4. __B__ the rain came down hard
5. __B__ weeds sprouted
6. __D__ early in the summer
7. __A__ a hard-working gardener
8. __B__ seven rows of peas
9. __C__ near the cornfield
10. __B__ a scraggly scarecrow
11. __D__ after the snow arrived
12. __B__ tall rows of beautiful flowers
13. __C__ out in the backyard
14. __A__ the boys and girls
15. __B__ the carrots
16. __D__ in the afternoon
17. __A__ the hungry bunny
18. __C__ over the fence
19. __B__ the broken fence
20. __B__ the rusted hoe
21. __D__ before the frost
22. __C__ among the carrots

Missing Object

What does the magician need? To find out, color the squares with answers that are products of 5. Write the name of the picture you color in the blank.

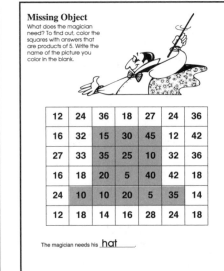

12	24	36	18	27	24	36
16	32	15	30	45	12	42
27	33	35	25	10	32	36
16	18	20	5	40	42	18
24	10	10	20	5	35	14
12	18	14	16	28	24	18

The magician needs his __hat__

Wall of Numbers

Write the numeral that matches the number words on each brick. Then color the bricks following the Color Key.

Color Key
2-digit number = blue
3-digit number = red
4-digit number = yellow

7,900 seven thousand nine hundred	276 two hundred seventy-six	1,001 one thousand one
340 three hundred forty	647 six hundred forty-seven	74 seventy-four
611 six hundred eleven	989 nine hundred eighty-nine	83 eighty-three
890 eight hundred ninety	403 four hundred three	39 thirty-nine
672 six hundred seventy-two	9,600 nine thousand six hundred	210 two hundred ten
4,061 four thousand sixty-one	875 eight hundred seventy-five	23 twenty-three
102 one hundred two	9,022 nine thousand twenty-two	3,062 three thousand sixty-two
7,010 seven thousand ten	5,600 five thousand six hundred	99 ninety-nine

---

Missing Numbers

Find the missing number for each problem.

1. $3 + \boxed{7} = 10$ 2. $9 + \boxed{2} = 11$

3. $11 - \boxed{3} = 8$ 4. $\boxed{9} - 6 = 3$ 5. $\boxed{18} - 9 = 9$

6. $\boxed{12} - 6 = 6$ 7. $\boxed{13} - 5 = 8$ 8. $4 - \boxed{2} = 2$

9. $9 + \boxed{7} = 16$ 10. $15 - \boxed{7} = 8$ 11. $5 + \boxed{6} = 11$

12. $13 - \boxed{4} = 9$ 13. $9 + \boxed{2} = 11$ 14. $12 - \boxed{8} = 4$

15. $17 - \boxed{9} = 8$ 16. $8 + \boxed{3} = 11$ 17. $5 + \boxed{5} = 10$

18. $20 - \boxed{10} = 10$ 19. $18 - \boxed{9} = 9$ 20. $\boxed{14} - 7 = 7$

Math Parade

Add the numbers to solve each problem.

1.
```
  679
  816
+  11
 1506
```

2.
```
  784
   43
+ 123
  950
```

3.
```
  634
  122
+ 441
 1197
```

4.
```
  249
  617
+  73
  939
```

5.
```
  538
   72
+  34
  644
```

6.
```
  321
  111
+ 203
  635
```

7.
```
   43
  876
+ 311
 1230
```

8.
```
  765
    7
+ 276
 1048
```

9.
```
 $2.99
  1.34
+ 3.55
 $7.88
```

10.
```
 $1.27
  6.76
+ $ .33
 $8.36
```

11.
```
  $.89
  1.66
+ 8.99
$11.54
```

12.
```
 $3.45
  2.77
+ 1.76
 $7.98
```

Daily Learning Drills Grade 3   406

348 — Zany Zeros!

Subtract to solve each problem. Check your work by adding. Make sure to watch for the zeros! The first one is done for you.

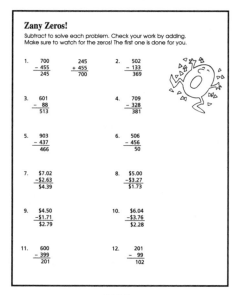

1.
$$700 - 455 = 245$$
$$245 + 455 = 700$$

2.
$$502 - 133 = 369$$

3.
$$601 - 88 = 513$$

4.
$$709 - 328 = 381$$

5.
$$903 - 437 = 466$$

6.
$$506 - 456 = 50$$

7.
$$\$7.02 - \$2.63 = \$4.39$$

8.
$$\$5.00 - \$3.27 = \$1.73$$

9.
$$\$4.50 - \$1.71 = \$2.79$$

10.
$$\$6.04 - \$3.76 = \$2.28$$

11.
$$600 - 399 = 201$$

12.
$$201 - 99 = 102$$

349 — Fact Toss

Practice your math facts by writing the answers to the problems below. Time yourself to see how fast you can finish!

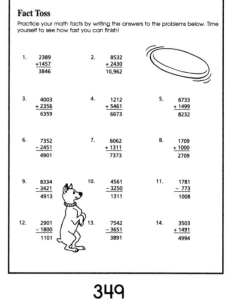

1. $2389 + 1457 = 3846$
2. $8532 + 2430 = 10{,}962$
3. $4003 + 2356 = 6359$
4. $1212 + 5461 = 6673$
5. $6733 + 1499 = 8232$
6. $7352 - 2451 = 4901$
7. $6062 + 1311 = 7373$
8. $1709 + 1000 = 2709$
9. $8334 - 3421 = 4913$
10. $4561 - 3250 = 1311$
11. $1781 - 773 = 1008$
12. $2901 - 1800 = 1101$
13. $7542 - 3651 = 3891$
14. $3503 + 1491 = 4994$

350 — Circus Dogs

Fill in the missing factors.

A. $7 \times \underline{7} = 49$ $5 \times \underline{7} = 35$ $4 \times \underline{6} = 24$

B. $6 \times \underline{9} = 54$ $6 \times \underline{0} = 0$ $4 \times \underline{3} = 12$

C. $3 \times \underline{7} = 21$ $5 \times \underline{5} = 25$ $3 \times \underline{3} = 9$

D. $4 \times \underline{7} = 28$ $5 \times \underline{3} = 15$ $5 \times \underline{9} = 45$

E. $5 \times \underline{6} = 30$ $6 \times \underline{3} = 18$ $7 \times \underline{9} = 63$

F. $6 \times \underline{8} = 48$ $5 \times \underline{6} = 30$ $6 \times \underline{9} = 54$

G. $5 \times \underline{7} = 35$ $7 \times \underline{8} = 56$ $5 \times \underline{8} = 40$

H. $7 \times \underline{4} = 28$ $7 \times \underline{1} = 7$ $6 \times \underline{1} = 6$

I. $6 \times \underline{6} = 36$ $7 \times \underline{2} = 14$ $5 \times \underline{1} = 5$

J. $5 \times \underline{4} = 20$ $5 \times \underline{2} = 10$ $4 \times \underline{8} = 32$

351 — Keeping on Target

Multiply to find the answers. Write the answers in the darts.

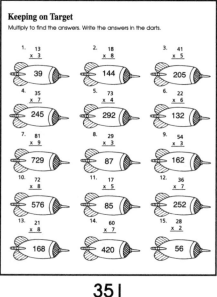

1. $13 \times 3 = 39$
2. $18 \times 8 = 144$
3. $41 \times 5 = 205$
4. $35 \times 7 = 245$
5. $73 \times 4 = 292$
6. $22 \times 6 = 132$
7. $81 \times 9 = 729$
8. $29 \times 3 = 87$
9. $54 \times 3 = 162$
10. $72 \times 8 = 576$
11. $17 \times 5 = 85$
12. $36 \times 7 = 252$
13. $21 \times 8 = 168$
14. $60 \times 7 = 420$
15. $28 \times 2 = 56$

352 — Roar with Pride!

Here's another way to think about division problems! Rewrite each question as a number sentence and solve the problem.

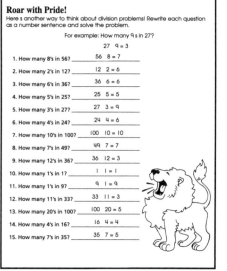

For example: How many 9's in 27?
$$27 \div 9 = 3$$

1. How many 8's in 56? $56 \div 8 = 7$
2. How many 2's in 12? $12 \div 2 = 6$
3. How many 6's in 36? $36 \div 6 = 6$
4. How many 5's in 25? $25 \div 5 = 5$
5. How many 3's in 27? $27 \div 3 = 9$
6. How many 4's in 24? $24 \div 4 = 6$
7. How many 10's in 100? $100 \div 10 = 10$
8. How many 7's in 49? $49 \div 7 = 7$
9. How many 12's in 36? $36 \div 12 = 3$
10. How many 1's in 1? $1 \div 1 = 1$
11. How many 1's in 9? $9 \div 1 = 9$
12. How many 11's in 33? $33 \div 11 = 3$
13. How many 20's in 100? $100 \div 20 = 5$
14. How many 4's in 16? $16 \div 4 = 4$
15. How many 7's in 35? $35 \div 7 = 5$

353 — Rising Remainders

Solve each problem. Write the remainder on the balloon.

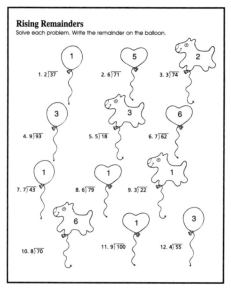

1. $2 \overline{)37}$ — 1
2. $6 \overline{)71}$ — 5
3. $3 \overline{)74}$ — 2
4. $9 \overline{)93}$ — 3
5. $5 \overline{)18}$ — 3
6. $7 \overline{)62}$ — 6
7. $7 \overline{)43}$ — 1
8. $6 \overline{)79}$ — 1
9. $3 \overline{)22}$ — 1
10. $8 \overline{)70}$ — 6
11. $9 \overline{)100}$ — 1
12. $4 \overline{)55}$ — 3

354 — Money Matters

There's so many things to buy at the fair! Do you have enough money? Circle Yes or No.

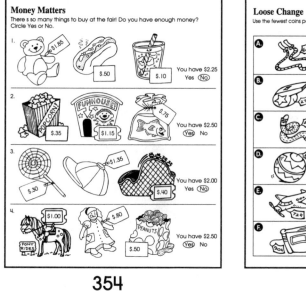

1. Bear $1.85, Hot dog $.50, Drink $.10 — You have $2.25 — Yes / **No**
2. Popcorn $.35, Funhouse $1.15, Fish $.75 — You have $2.50 — **Yes** / No
3. Lollipop $.30, Net $1.35, Peanuts $.40 — You have $2.00 — Yes / **No**
4. Pony rides $1.00, Doll $.80, Peanuts $.50 — You have $2.50 — **Yes** / No

355 — Loose Change

Use the fewest coins possible. Draw coins to show each amount.

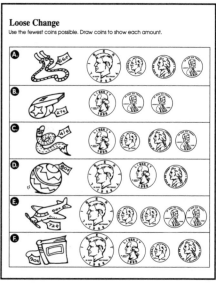

A. $.66
B. $.74
C. $.84
D. $.44
E. $.74
F. $.90

356 — At the Carnival

Read each problem carefully. Then solve the problem, showing your work.

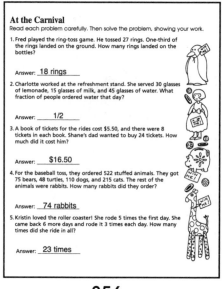

1. Fred played the ring-toss game. He tossed 27 rings. One-third of the rings landed on the ground. How many rings landed on the bottles?

Answer: __18 rings__

2. Charlotte worked at the refreshment stand. She served 30 glasses of lemonade, 15 glasses of milk, and 45 glasses of water. What fraction of people ordered water that day?

Answer: __1/2__

3. A book of tickets for the rides cost $5.50, and there were 8 tickets in each book. Shane's dad wanted to buy 24 tickets. How much did it cost him?

Answer: __$16.50__

4. For the baseball toss, they ordered 522 stuffed animals. They got 75 bears, 48 turtles, 110 dogs, and 215 cats. The rest of the animals were rabbits. How many rabbits did they order?

Answer: __74 rabbits__

5. Kristin loved the roller coaster! She rode 5 times the first day. She came back 6 more days and rode it 3 times each day. How many times did she ride in all?

Answer: __23 times__

357

Math Trails

Calculate how far each person hiked at Golden Canyon. Use the trail sign to help you.

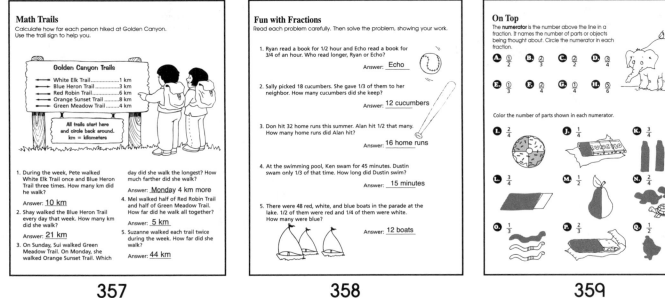

Golden Canyon Trails
- White Elk Trail ....1 km
- Blue Heron Trail ....3 km
- Red Robin Trail ....6 km
- Orange Sunset Trail ....8 km
- Green Meadow Trail ....4 km

All trails start here and circle back around.
km = kilometers

1. During the week, Pete walked White Elk Trail once and Blue Heron Trail three times. How many km did he walk?

Answer: __10 km__

2. Shay walked the Blue Heron Trail every day that week. How many km did she walk?

Answer: __21 km__

3. On Sunday, Sui walked Green Meadow Trail. On Monday, she walked Orange Sunset Trail. Which day did she walk the longest? How much farther did she walk?

Answer: __Monday 4 km more__

4. Mel walked half of Red Robin Trail and half of Green Meadow Trail. How far did he walk all together?

Answer: __5 km__

5. Suzanne walked each trail twice during the week. How far did she walk?

Answer: __44 km__

358

Fun with Fractions

Read each problem carefully. Then solve the problem, showing your work.

1. Ryan read a book for 1/2 hour and Echo read a book for 3/4 of an hour. Who read longer, Ryan or Echo?

Answer: __Echo__

2. Sally picked 18 cucumbers. She gave 1/3 of them to her neighbor. How many cucumbers did she keep?

Answer: __12 cucumbers__

3. Don hit 32 home runs this summer. Alan hit 1/2 that many. How many home runs did Alan hit?

Answer: __16 home runs__

4. At the swimming pool, Ken swam for 45 minutes. Dustin swam only 1/3 of that time. How long did Dustin swim?

Answer: __15 minutes__

5. There were 48 red, white, and blue boats in the parade at the lake. 1/2 of them were red and 1/4 of them were white. How many were blue?

Answer: __12 boats__

359

On Top

The **numerator** is the number above the line in a fraction. It names the number of parts or objects being thought about. Circle the numerator in each fraction.

A. $\frac{1}{2}$ B. $\frac{2}{3}$ C. $\frac{2}{2}$ D. $\frac{3}{4}$

E. $\frac{1}{3}$ F. $\frac{2}{2}$ G. $\frac{1}{2}$ H. $\frac{5}{6}$

Color the number of parts shown in each numerator.

I. $\frac{2}{4}$ J. $\frac{1}{4}$ K. $\frac{3}{4}$

L. $\frac{3}{4}$ M. $\frac{1}{2}$ N. $\frac{3}{4}$

O. $\frac{1}{3}$ P. $\frac{2}{3}$ Q. $\frac{1}{2}$

360

The Shape of Things

Divide and shade in each shape for the fraction shown.

A. $\frac{4}{8}$

B. $\frac{3}{4}$

C. $\frac{1}{2}$

D. $\frac{1}{3}$

E. $\frac{2}{6}$

F. $\frac{1}{4}$

G. $\frac{7}{10}$

H. $\frac{4}{4}$

361

Time Out

Look carefully at each clock. Then write the exact time on the line.

1. __8:05__   2. **6:15**   3. **7:20**

4. **10:35**   5. **2:10**   6. **8:25**

7. **11:55**   8. **12:50**   9. **10:40**

362

In the Area

1 centimeter ___   1 square centimeter □

The **area** of a shape tells how many square centimeters will cover it. The square centimeter is used to measure area.

Write the area of each shape on the blank line. The first one is done for you.

A. __4__ square centimeters

B. __15__ square centimeters

C. __4__ square centimeters

D. __9__ square centimeters

E. Shade in an area of 10 square centimeters.

Example
Answers may vary.

363

Perimeter Picture

Write the perimeter of each shape on the blank line. Then find the answer in the picture and color it. Use the same color for each identical answer.

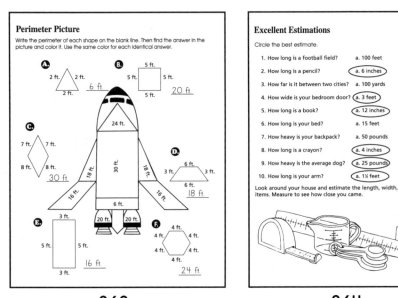

A. 2 ft. 2 ft. 2 ft. — __6 ft__

B. 5 ft. 5 ft. 5 ft. 5 ft. — __20 ft__

C. 7 ft. 7 ft. 8 ft. 8 ft. — __30 ft__

D. 3 ft. 3 ft. 6 ft. 6 ft. — __18 ft__

E. 3 ft. 5 ft. 5 ft. 3 ft. — __16 ft__

F. 4 ft. 4 ft. 4 ft. 4 ft. 4 ft. 4 ft. — __24 ft__

364

Excellent Estimations

Circle the best estimate.

1. How long is a football field?   a. 100 feet   **b. 100 yards**
2. How long is a pencil?   **a. 6 inches**   b. 10 inches
3. How far is it between two cities?   a. 100 yards   **b. 100 miles**
4. How wide is your bedroom door?   **a. 3 feet**   b. 3 yards
5. How long is a book?   **a. 12 inches**   b. 2 feet
6. How long is your bed?   a. 15 feet   **b. 5 feet**
7. How heavy is your backpack?   a. 50 pounds   **b. 5 pounds**
8. How long is a crayon?   **a. 4 inches**   b. 10 inches
9. How heavy is the average dog?   **a. 25 pounds**   b. 25 tons
10. How long is your arm?   **a. 1½ feet**   b. 1½ yards

Look around your house and estimate the length, width, and weight of various items. Measure to see how close you came.

365

At the Circus

The Super Duper Circus has many wonderful performers. The picture graph below shows the number of performers.

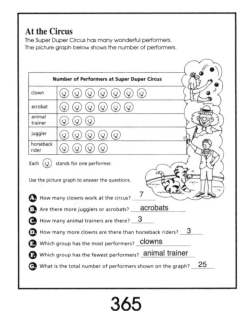

Number of Performers at Super Duper Circus	
clown	ⓥ ⓥ ⓥ ⓥ ⓥ ⓥ ⓥ
acrobat	ⓥ ⓥ ⓥ ⓥ ⓥ ⓥ
animal trainer	ⓥ ⓥ ⓥ
juggler	ⓥ ⓥ ⓥ ⓥ ⓥ
horseback rider	ⓥ ⓥ ⓥ ⓥ

Each ⓥ stands for one performer.

Use the picture graph to answer the questions.

A. How many clowns work at the circus? __7__

B. Are there more jugglers or acrobats? __acrobats__

C. How many animal trainers are there? __3__

D. How many more clowns are there than horseback riders? __3__

E. Which group has the most performers? __clowns__

F. Which group has the fewest performers? __animal trainer__

G. What is the total number of performers shown on the graph? __25__

Changes Over Time

A line graph can show how something changes over time. The dots on the graph at the right show how Grandview School's student population changed over the years.

Number of Students at Grandview School

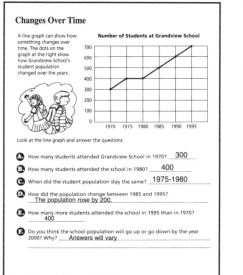

Look at the line graph and answer the questions.

A How many students attended Grandview School in 1970? __300__

B How many students attended the school in 1980? __400__

C When did the student population stay the same? __1975-1980__

D How did the population change between 1985 and 1995?
__The population rose by 200.__

E How many more students attended the school in 1995 than in 1970? __400__

F Do you think the school population will go up or go down by the year 2000? Why? __Answers will vary__

366

Starch to Sugar

Try this experiment.

1. Put a cracker in your mouth.

2. Chew the cracker, but do not swallow it.

3. Hold the cracker in your mouth for at least two minutes.

4. Now, chew again and taste the cracker.

5. How does it taste? __The cracker tastes sweet.__

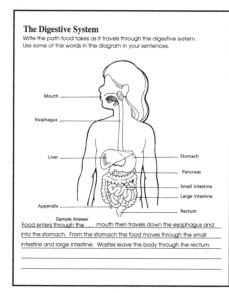

Digestion begins in the mouth. Saliva changes starches (crackers) called *carbohydrates* into a product the body can use—sugar!

This is not the simple sugar found in cookies and candy. This is a complex sugar the body uses for energy.

Label the diagram with the following words:

teeth   salivary gland
lips   esophagus
tongue

lips
tongue
teeth
salivary gland
esophagus

367

The Digestive System

Write the path food takes as it travels through the digestive system. Use some of the words in the diagram in your sentences.

Mouth
Esophagus
Liver
Appendix
Stomach
Pancreas
Small intestine
Large intestine
Rectum

Sample Answer
Food enters through the . . . mouth then travels down the esophagus and into the stomach. From the stomach the food moves through the small intestine and large intestine. Wastes leave the body through the rectum.

368

Birds

Read about birds then color the pictures.

Birds

Do you know what makes birds different from all other animals?

1

All birds have feathers. Besides helping them fly, feathers also protect their skin and keep them warm.

3

All birds also have wings. Even birds that don't fly, like penguins and ostriches, have wings. Are birds the only animals with wings?

4

Answer: No, bats and insects also have wings.

371

Write *True* or *False* for each statement below.

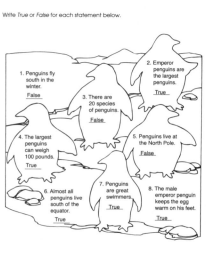

1. Penguins fly south in the winter. __False__

2. Emperor penguins are the largest penguins. __True__

3. There are 20 species of penguins. __False__

4. The largest penguins can weigh 100 pounds. __True__

5. Penguins live at the North Pole. __False__

6. Almost all penguins live south of the equator. __True__

7. Penguins are great swimmers. __True__

8. The male emperor penguin keeps the egg warm on his feet. __True__

373

Dear Zookeeper

Many zoos have an adopt-an-animal program. Communities, clubs, or families can adopt an animal, which means they send donations to the zoo to help care for that animal. Sometimes you can even pick the animal you would like to help.

Contact your local zoo and find out if it offers such a program. Use the form below to write a letter to the zookeeper telling about the animal you have selected. Remember to check your spelling and punctuation!

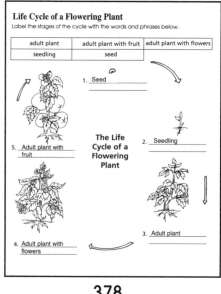

(name and title)

(street address)

(city, state, zip)

(date)

Dear_____

Answers will vary

Your friend,

_____
(signature)

374

Slimy or Scaly

Circle the names of the reptiles and amphibians. They may go across, down, or diagonally. Circle the pictures of reptiles.

Word Bank
ALLIGATOR
CHAMELEON
CROCODILE
FROG
IGUANA
LIZARD
NEWT
SALAMANDER
SNAKE
TUATARA
TURTLE

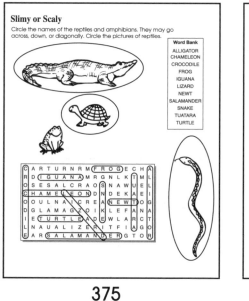

```
C A R T U R N R M F R O G E C H A
R D I G U A N A M R G N L K T M L
O S E S A L C R A O S N A W U E I
C H A M E L E O N D N D E K A E N
O U L N A I C R E A N E W T O G O
D G L A M A Z O I K L E F A N A
I E T U R T L E A D E W L A R C T
L N A U A L I Z E R I T F I A G O
E A R S A L A M A N D E R G T O R
```

375

Write *True* or *False* for each statement below.

1. Chimpanzees are skillful. __True__

2. Chimpanzees live alone. __False__

3. Chimpanzees live in African rain forests. __True__

4. Chimpanzees are sociable. __True__

5. Chimpanzees drink water from a glass. __False__

377

Life Cycle of a Flowering Plant

Label the stages of the cycle with the words and phrases below.

adult plant	adult plant with fruit	adult plant with flowers
seedling	seed	

1. Seed

The Life Cycle of a Flowering Plant

2. Seedling

3. Adult plant

4. Adult plant with flowers

5. Adult plant with fruit

378

Super Stem!

What is a stem's job? Try this activity to find out.

Materials: a clear plastic cup or glass ✶ blue or red food coloring ✶ water scissors ✶ celery stalk

1. Use the scissors to cut off the bottom of the celery.

2. Pour about an inch of water in the glass. Add 8 drops of food coloring.

3. Place the celery in the glass. Leave it in the glass overnight.

4. Answer the first question after you set up the activity.

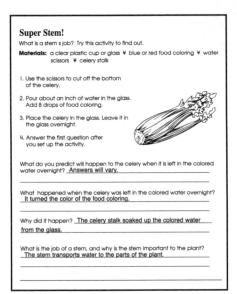

What do you predict will happen to the celery when it is left in the colored water overnight? _Answers will vary._

What happened when the celery was left in the colored water overnight? _It turned the color of the food coloring._

Why did it happen? _The celery stalk soaked up the colored water from the glass._

What is the job of a stem, and why is the stem important to the plant? _The stem transports water to the parts of the plant._

379

Fill in the chart using the information from the story.

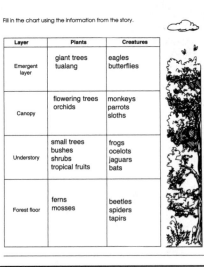

Layer	Plants	Creatures
Emergent layer	giant trees tualang	eagles butterflies
Canopy	flowering trees orchids	monkeys parrots sloths
Understory	small trees bushes shrubs tropical fruits	frogs ocelots jaguars bats
Forest floor	ferns mosses	beetles spiders tapirs

381

Notes are phrases or short sentences that help us remember information from a story or book. Write notes below, using facts from the story.

The five oceans
1. Atlantic
2. Pacific
3. Indian
4. Arctic
5. Antarctic

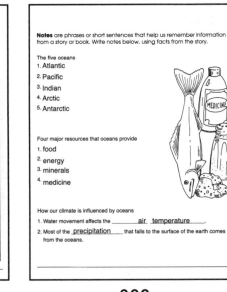

Four major resources that oceans provide
1. food
2. energy
3. minerals
4. medicine

How our climate is influenced by oceans
1. Water movement affects the _____ air temperature _____.
2. Most of the _precipitation_ that falls to the surface of the earth comes from the oceans.

383

Listen to Nature

Nature is full of sounds. Try to remember a place in nature where you have been. Then fill in the flower with the things you saw there and the noises they made. Look at the example of the ocean to help you.

Answers will vary.

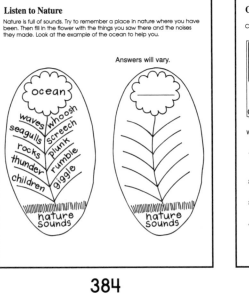

ocean — waves, whoosh, seagulls, screech, rocks, plunk, thunder, rumble, children, giggle — nature sounds

nature sounds

384

Out of This World

Circle the words. They may go across, down, or diagonally.

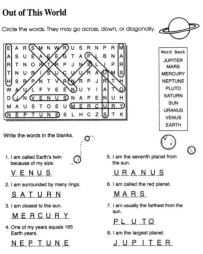

Word Bank
JUPITER
MARS
MERCURY
NEPTUNE
PLUTO
SATURN
SUN
URANUS
VENUS
EARTH

Write the words in the blanks.

1. I am called Earth's twin because of my size.
V E N U S

2. I am surrounded by many rings.
S A T U R N

3. I am closest to the sun.
M E R C U R Y

4. One of my years equals 165 Earth years.
N E P T U N E

5. I am the seventh planet from the sun.
U R A N U S

6. I am called the red planet.
M A R S

7. I am usually the farthest from the sun.
P L U T O

8. I am the largest planet.
J U P I T E R

385

Messages in Braille

Use the Braille alphabet below to write your name or a message. First, on a separate piece of paper, make pencil dots for each letter of each word. Then use glue to make raised dots on top of each pencil dot. You can sprinkle a pinch of sand on the wet glue so that the dots will have more texture. Let the glue dots dry completely. Ask a friend to read your words with her or his fingertips.

A B C D E F G H I

J K L M N O P Q R

S T U V W X Y Z

Messages will vary.

386

Read a Map

Circle the words. They may go across, down, diagonally, or backward.

Word Bank
bank
east
market
north
park
school
south
west

Use the words and the map to help you fill in the blanks.

1. The _park_ is west of the school.

2. The _bank_ is north of the post office.

3. The _school_ is south of the market.

4. The _market_ is directly east of the apartments.

5. The market is on the _north_ side of First Street.

6. The post office is on the _east_ side of Oak Street.

Map Key

387

Answer the questions below with information from the story.

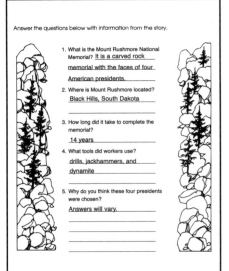

1. What is the Mount Rushmore National Memorial? _It is a carved rock memorial with the faces of four American presidents._

2. Where is Mount Rushmore located? _Black Hills, South Dakota_

3. How long did it take to complete the memorial? _14 years_

4. What tools did workers use? _drills, jackhammers, and dynamite_

5. Why do you think these four presidents were chosen? _Answers will vary._

389

Fill in the chart to compare Delaware and Hawaii.

	Delaware	Hawaii
Date it became a state	December 7, 1787	August 21, 1959
Nearby ocean	Atlantic	Pacific
Main industry	manufacturing	tourism
Capital city	Dover	Honolulu
Size of state	second smallest	over 100 islands/ fourth smallest
Nickname	first state	Aloha state
Would you like to visit?	Answers will vary.	

391

Presidential Trivia

Circle the words. They may go across, down, diagonally, or backward.

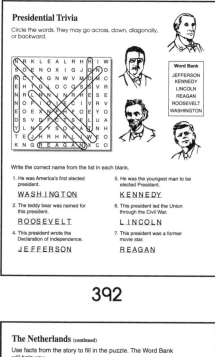

Word Bank
JEFFERSON
KENNEDY
LINCOLN
REAGAN
ROOSEVELT
WASHINGTON

Write the correct name from the list in each blank.

1. He was America's first elected president.
   WASHINGTON

2. The teddy bear was named for this president.
   ROOSEVELT

4. This president wrote the Declaration of Independence.
   JEFFERSON

5. He was the youngest man to be elected President.
   KENNEDY

6. This president led the Union through the Civil War.
   LINCOLN

7. This president was a former movie star.
   REAGAN

392

Squanto (continued)

Use the words from the Word Bank to answer the questions.

1. A true story of someone's life written by _another_ person is a _biography_ .

2. _Tisquantum_ was Squanto's real name.

3. The _Indian_ village of _Patuxet_ is where Squanto lived.

4. In 1614, Squanto was taken as a _slave_ to _Spain_ .

5. He learned to speak English in _England_ .

6. Squanto taught the _Pilgrims_ many important survival skills.

7. He showed them how to plant _corn_ .

Word Bank
Spain
another
biography
slave
Tisquantum
England
Patuxet
corn
Pilgrims
Indian

398

You're a Grand Old Flag

Learn more about the United States flag and Betsy Ross. Cut off the bottom of this page, cut the facts apart, and glue them on the flag in the correct order.

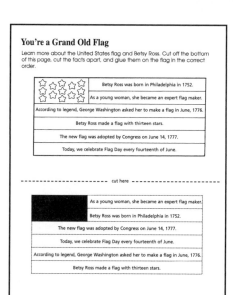

Betsy Ross was born in Philadelphia in 1752.

As a young woman, she became an expert flag maker.

According to legend, George Washington asked her to make a flag in June, 1776.

Betsy Ross made a flag with thirteen stars.

The new flag was adopted by Congress on June 14, 1777.

Today, we celebrate Flag Day every fourteenth of June.

-------------------- cut here --------------------

As a young woman, she became an expert flag maker.

Betsy Ross was born in Philadelphia in 1752.

The new flag was adopted by Congress on June 14, 1777.

Today, we celebrate Flag Day every fourteenth of June.

According to legend, George Washington asked her to make a flag in June, 1776.

Betsy Ross made a flag with thirteen stars.

399

The Netherlands (continued)

Use facts from the story to fill in the puzzle. The Word Bank will help you.

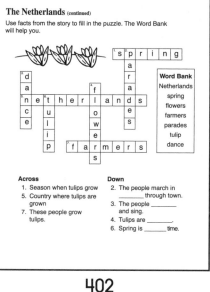

Word Bank
Netherlands
spring
flowers
farmers
parades
tulip
dance

Across
1. Season when tulips grow
5. Country where tulips are grown
7. These people grow tulips.

Down
2. The people march in _____ through town.
3. The people _____ and sing.
4. Tulips are _____.
6. Spring is _____ time.

402

Turkey Hunt

Circle the hidden Thanksgiving words in the puzzle. Check off each word as you find it.

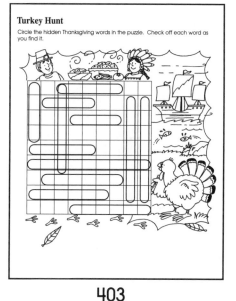

403

Daily Learning Drills Grade 3